In Flagrante Collecto

In Flagrante Collecto

(caught in the act of collecting)

Marilynn Gelfman Karp

Abrams, New York

for A, E, I, and oh, you J

Table of Contents

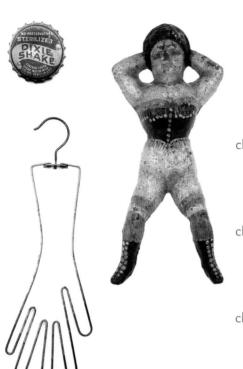

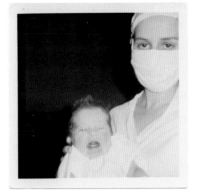

The Act of Collecting

chapter 1

3725. STAND ROCK, DELLS OF THE WISCONSIN RIVER.

ON A SUNNY day in April, brimming with anticipation, I entered a shop, a grotto of previously owned goods, terra incognita of things, a store filled with possibilities. My vision adjusting to the comparative lack of light, I gravitated toward a gaggle of objects casually arrayed (spilled?) upon a not-noteworthy table. A disembodied voice from an indeterminate location asked, "Can I help you?"

"Thanks, I'd just like to look around," I responded. Having scanned the miscellany on the table, I glanced at the crippled tricycle below and an open toolbox with a cast-iron level. I was moving toward the shelves with china oddments when the voice became a shadowy outline toward the back of the shop asking, "Are you looking for anything in particular?"

"Not really," as my eyes lit on a box of picture postcards that I casually (be still my heart) began investigating. They were mostly of conventional locations, having been sent home by the "wish you were here" set in the 1950s. I am ever hopeful of finding one that qualifies for one of my esoteric postcard categories such as SAND SCULPTURES, HOLD-TO-LIGHTS, WAITING ROOMS, BEFORE AND AFTER, or GORGEOUS SCENES. Sorting through a handful I found myself staring at a man frozen mid-air in Wisconsin, who had leapt from one three-story rock pile toward another. Two bystanders wearing 1910 garb, with low self-esteem posture, regard him from the rear. They are too small and distant for me to read their facial expressions. From my viewpoint, the leaper's angle of trajectory doesn't seem too hopeful. Eureka! In an instant a new collection was born: LEAPS OF FAITH. For a nanosecond I contemplated that it might be a leap of faith on my part to believe that I could locate other tangible examples of this idiom.

"Find something?" asked the undaunted proprietor who materialized beside an oak cupboard.

"Does a postcard count?" I handed it over.

"I'll give you a good price," he replied, "if you take all of them." Acuity elevated by my discovery, my eye lit on a cigar box filled with buttons. I said that I'd probably find some other stuff, but didn't need more postcards.

Posthumously revealed old ladies' button boxes are rife with potential. My right index finger coaxing layers aside, I exposed ex-campaign buttons, a Cracker Jack charm, and a couple of blood-donor lapel pins.

"You can have the box for five bucks."

"If you said four, I'd say yes." Prolonging the thrill of the hunt, musing upon my rendezvous with minutiae, I was savoring the thought of fingering Ur-trinkets and fondling booty in the confines of my cave. A flexible dealer lubricates the hunter-gatherer process.

"Four dollars is just dandy."

"Okay," came my acceptance of the deal as I moved on to a glass case with sundry remnants of dismal lives and spotted a homely, pathetically taped, gilt-flaking, palpably prayerful attempt to construct an item to gain Christ's attention and ease someone's life. This third-class relic screamed at me, "Take me home! I am the second piece in your LEAPS OF FAITH collection."

"May I see those?" I said, pointing to a lithographed tin pin-up ashtray and my relic.

Handing them across the counter, the shopkeeper asked, "What are you really looking for?"

"The Holy Grail," was my reply. This is my constant and much-used retort when pressed in this vexatious way. It's an instant conversation stopper. Collecting is an intimate act, not to be shared offhandedly.

I've had many a triumphal return from uncharted terrain and I've charted a bit of it too. I have junking

buddies with whom it's a pleasure to bag bounty and collector friends with whom trophies are jubilantly compared. The dieter's ecstasy of denial is not in the collector's lexicon. Collecting is an act of very personal commitment. It's about erecting a bond between yourself and an object; it's all about what you choose to be responsible for. Whoever collects understands this. Humanity can be divided into two parts: those who collect and the others.

THE RELATIVE VALUES OF COLLECTIONS

Collecting is not about what you collect as much as it is about who you are. Possession somehow connotes transference of the object's virtues to its owner. Collections are about recollection. Collections exclude the world and are symbolic of it. Writing about why one collects what one collects is a bit like self-psychoanalysis; it's hard to be objective. Taking the longest view, I have observed and deduced that the Collector Pie may be divided into three wedges: those with full pockets, deep pockets, or big pockets; and each is epitomized by a literary or historical character.

Full Pockets: Silas Marner

Silas Marner is Western literature's most famous collector. He is George Eliot's weaver in rural England who was utterly consumed by his amassed coins. They were a necessary supplement to his persona, and their physical proximity provided Marner with his motivation to live.

But at night came his revelry: at night he closed his shutters, and made fast his doors, and drew out his gold. Long ago the heap of coins had become too large for the iron pot to hold them, and he had made for them two thick leather bags, which wasted no room in their resting place, but lent themselves flexibly to every corner. How the guineas shone as they came pouring out of the dark leather mouths.... He spread them out in heaps and bathed his hands in them; then he counted them and set them up in regular piles, and felt their rounded outline between his thumb and fingers.... He handled them, he counted them, till their form and colour were like the satisfaction of a thirst to him; but it was only in the night, when his work was done, that he drew them out to enjoy their companionship.

George Eliot, *Silas Marner* (New York: Penguin, 1981), 21–23.

3

As the narrative progresses, Marner is monumentally afflicted by the theft of his coins; halfway through the story he awakens from slumber and sees his missing gold in front of the hearth:

Gold, his own gold—brought back to him as mysteriously as it had been taken away! He felt his heart begin to beat violently, and for a few moments he was unable to stretch out his hand and grasp the restored treasure. The heap of gold seemed to glow and get larger beneath his agitated gaze. He leaned forward at last, and stretched forth his hand; but instead of the hard coin with the familiar resisting outline, his fingers encountered soft, warm curls.

Eliot, *Silas Marner*, 115.

4

Through his new golden treasure, young Effie, he finds his humanity. Eliot's story is brilliant fiction depicting a collector who loved a universally coveted tool. Silas Marner loved the universally beloved. Gold has *intrinsic* value. Its economic status resides in the metal itself, and it is highly desirable to everyone regardless of its shape or form. Intrinsically valuable things are rare commodities. Their value increases because there is an increasing population in the world and valuable things do not increase at the same rate. There is security in their ownership; they are convertible to anything that is needed. Wars have been fought for them. A diamond may be recut or reset but it will never be discarded or reduced to cinder because its owner tires of it. Barring an utter and complete apocalypse, its rarity guarantees its increasing value.

Deep Pockets: Lorenzo de' Medici

Lorenzo de' Medici, also known as Lorenzo the Magnificent, made Florence the most powerful state in Italy during his lifetime. The Medici family had great wealth and influence as bankers, and their cultural interests led them to become patrons of the arts. Michelangelo and Raphael were among the great artists who benefited from Medici patronage.

5

6

7

8

9

6
Hans Holbein, *The Rich Man*, 1523–25. Woodcut

7
Marinus van Reymerswaele, *The Money Changer and His Wife*, 1539. Oil on panel, 32³/₅ x 38¹/₅"

8
Hans Holbein, detail of *Death Takes the Miser's Gold*. From the "Dance of Death" series, c. 1526

9
Georgio Vasari, *Lorenzo de' Medici*, 16th century

10

Florence became an art vortex under their rule. Lorenzo accumulated paintings, sculptures, and buildings, as well as jewelry and objects crafted by the greatest artists of Italy. The Medici Chapel, designed by Michelangelo, houses Lorenzo de' Medici's tomb, which was created by Michelangelo along with allegorical sculptures of Twilight and Dawn. Unlike Silas Marner's gold, Lorenzo de' Medici's art did not have *intrinsic* value. Canvas, paint, wood, and marble have no universal value. However, the objects into which they were fashioned by the artists and artisans were imbued with great value by a competitive collectorship. This is extrinsic value. Gold has intrinsic value; art has extrinsic value—value acquired or developed, value originating from without, value from a competitive marketplace that wishes to acquire the limited artworks that a few highly prized artists create.

Art has never been as universally coveted as gold, but it takes only a few collectors desirous of the same object (and willing to convert gold for it) to establish extrinsic value. The incidence of the artist's production and the number of ready collectors who desire the object determines its value.

The baseball-card collector and the stamp collector are contemporary variants of the extrinsic-value version of collecting. In practice, these collectors are no different from Lorenzo the Magnificent, J. Pierpont Morgan, Henry Clay Frick, William Randolph Hearst, or other great art collectors. There is a distinctly circumscribed body of material from which to collect and formalized "rules" of desirability (for example, centering the card or stamp image evenly within its borders). The year and place of origin and the number of objects produced in direct relationship to the number of desirous collectors are what determine extrinsic value. It's a formula, and little imagination is required. Although there are comfortingly limited choices (organizing and upgrading are the extent of what is demanded of the collector) there are, nonetheless, collecting criteria. Baseball cards have imagery and text that record and relate directly to a romantic and lively sport, filled with heroes and villains, which further engage collectors based on each player's seasonal performance, personality, and lifetime history. Some cards are more desirable and valuable than others.

It is my nature to collect, he once told his wife. "Picture-mad," a friend from his youth called him—one person's nature being another's idea of madness; of immoderate desire.

As a child he collected coins, then automata, then musical instruments. Collecting expresses a free-floating desire that attaches and re-attaches itself—it is a succession of desires. The true collector is in the grip of not what is collected but of collecting. By his early twenties the Cavaliere had already formed and been forced to sell, in order to pay debts, several small collections of paintings.

   Susan Sontag, *The Volcano Collector* (New York: Farrar, Straus, & Giroux, 1992), 24.

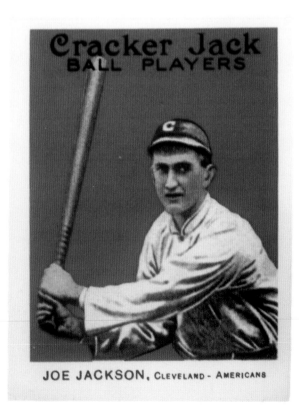

12

13

14

15

16

17

18

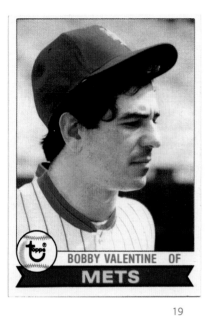

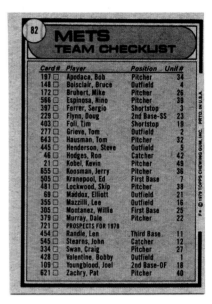

19

19
Baseball card, 1979.
Bobby Valentine of Mets
(front and back), #428,
3½" high. Topps Chewing
Gum, Inc.

20
Baseball card, 1979.
Joe Torre Manager Mets,
manager (front and back),
#82, 2½" high. Topps
Chewing Gum, Inc.

21
Baseball card, 1990. Mets
Darryl Strawberry RF
(front and back), #200,
3½" high. Score, Inc.

22
Baseball card, 1988. Mets
Jerry Koosman Pitcher,
#66, 3½" high. Pacific
Trading Cards, Inc.

20

21

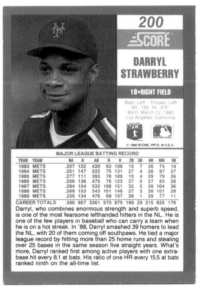

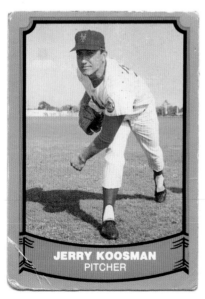

22

Comic books are another flavor of this kind of collecting. The desirability of specific issues based on their heroes and villains, story-line events, and creative teams makes them extremely valuable to a collectorship that exceeds the number of comic books printed. Their rarity may be increased by parental trashing or destruction based on periodic reassessment of one's literary interests, but the same ardent collectorship for limited "treasures" that drove Lorenzo de' Medici's acquisitions drives my brother Bill's baseball-card collecting and my son Jesse's comic-book collecting.

23

25

26

23
Comic book, 1962.
*Amazing Fantasy
(introducing Spider-Man)*,
#15, 10¼" high

24
Comic book, 1963. *The
Amazing Spider-Man*, #1,
10¼" high

25
Comic book, 1967.
Captain America, #100,
10¼" high

26
Comic book, 1947.
World's Finest Comics,
#29, 10¼" high

Big Pockets: Tom Sawyer

Having dispatched the first two slices of the Collector Pie, we've moved down the ranks of material culture from its most universally valued loot to its attractive bounty with less of a covetous following. We have all the while been considering loving the beloved. Let's move along to material culture's most devalued objects—objects without intrinsic value and without a competitive collectorship to give them extrinsic value.

While painting his Aunt Polly's fence, Tom Sawyer is asked by his friend Ben whether Ben may paint some of it.

27
True W. Williams illustration for *The Adventures of Tom Sawyer* by Mark Twain. American Publishing Company, Hartford, Connecticut, 1875.

28
Worth Brehm, cover illustration for *The Adventures of Tom Sawyer* by Samuel L. Clemens. New York and London: Harper & Brothers, 1910

29
Adventures of Tom Sawyer by Mark Twain. Illustrated with scenes from the David O. Selznick photoplay, 8" high. New York: Grosset & Dunlap, 1922, page 53

30
Wrecked toy pick-up truck, c. 1958. Hubley Kiddie Toy, #402, 2¾" high. Lancaster, Pennsylvania

"Ben, I'd like to, honest injin; but Aunt Polly—well Jim wanted to do it, but she wouldn't let him. Sid wanted to do it, and she wouldn't let Sid. Now don't you see how I'm fixed? If you was to tackle this fence and anything was to happen to it—" "Oh, shucks, I'll be just as careful. Now lemme try. Say—I'll give you the core of my apple." "Well, here—No, Ben, now don't; I'm afeard—." "I'll give you *all* of it!"

Tom gave up the brush with reluctance on his face but alacrity in his heart. And while Ben worked and sweated in the sun, the retired artist sat on a barrel in the shade close by, dangled his legs, munched his apple, and planned the slaughter of more innocents. There was no lack of material; boys happened along every little while; they came to jeer, but remained to whitewash. By the time Ben was fagged out, Tom had traded the next chance to Billy Fisher for a kite, in good repair; and when *he* played out Johnny Miller bought in for a dead rat and a string to swing it with; and so on, and so on, hour after hour. . . . He had, beside the things before mentioned, twelve marbles, part of a jewsharp, a piece of blue bottle glass to look through, a spool cannon, a key that wouldn't unlock anything, a fragment of chalk, a glass stopper of a decanter, a tin soldier, a couple of tadpoles, six firecrackers, a kitten with only one eye, a brass doorknob, a dog collar—but no dog,—the handle of a knife, four pieces of orange peel, and a dilapidated old window sash.

Mark Twain, *The Adventures of Tom Sawyer* in *Treasures from the Prose Word* (Chicago: Elliott & Beezley, 1884), 38–39.

We find ourselves smiling inwardly at Tom's naiveté or in sympathy with his affection for "stuff." Rolling in riches of your own decree has its own special satisfaction. One of my collections is of literary insights about collecting; employing them in this book has implicit appeal. There are collectors who take license and run with the possession of humble or "unlovable" objects that most other people consider the jetsam of the past and flotsam of the present. There is a community of these collectors who find worth, even nobility in these objects, as well as a compelling dynamic inherent in common, overlooked, material goods that the majority of the population regards with disregard, if they even take notice of them at all beyond their short-lived functionality. The objects have no competing collectors to speak of and no intrinsic value. Each collector partly defines him/herself by what is collected.

"AIN'T THAT WORK?"

27

28

29

30

chapter 2

1

DIFFERENT THINGS call out to each of us for different reasons. Each collectible object has a different level of complexity for each of us and may be perceived singularly as revelatory or captivating. As the saying goes, "One man's meat is another man's poison."

I have about two hundred collections that could be classified among the "unlovable" or the "unloved." These objects were never precious. What is valueless beyond its functional use is usually not kept (unless you're a Collyer brother). Once its service has been spent, it's likely discarded, transformed to cinder, dumped. These "diamonds in the rough" are not reset, reframed, or even recycled.

The Object's Voice

2

1
Group of soda-bottle caps,
c. 1943. Printed crimped
steel, each 1¼" diameter

2
Soda-bottle cap, 1946.
Wax-filled shooter, 1¼"
diameter

3
Group of marbles, 20th
century. Glass, cat's eyes,
nines, micas, corkscrews,
aggies, slags, and mibs,
¾–1" diameter. USA

EARLY COLLECTIONS

My earliest collecting memory is of "saving" soda-bottle caps from the broom closet and dustbin of the corner candy store floor in the early 1940s, from my third to eighth years. I collected for quantity but was exhilarated by an unfamiliar find. One Birch Beer cap among thirty-five Mission Orange Soda tops had the power to inspire rapture. My brother Bill used his bottle caps to wager with the boys on our block. Their game board was a cement sidewalk square with chalked quadrants and corners, and the *skelly* rules were not unlike shuffleboard. The players were four kids, usually boys. The game pieces were bottle caps on their backs, sometimes wax-filled for weight. They were finger-flicked toward a chalked territory. I would never subject my caps to the mutilating scraping necessitated by this form of gaming. However, I regularly risked my duplicate marbles and won fortune every spring when "marble season" happened in the Bronx. As my husband, Ivan, knows, I still have all my marbles.

"THE MAN FROM CHEYENNE"
Playing in · A Republic Picture
ROY ROGERS
4

"THE LADY FROM SHANGHAI"
Playing in · A Columbia Picture
RITA HAYWORTH
5

Save Any 12 Dixie Picture Lids For A Large Picture Of Us · See Your Dealer For Instructions
LUCILLE BALL AND DESI ARNAZ
Stars of the Fabulous Philip Morris
"I Love Lucy" Show
CBS-TV TELEVISION STARS
6

PACKAGE MADE BY DIXIE CUP COMPANY, CHICAGO, ILL. & EASTON, PA., U.S.A. FILLED AND FROZEN AT THE ICE CREAM PLANT
Dixie
NELSON'S
Cloverland
ICE CREAM
3 FL. OZ.
PATENTS 1850493-4 OTHERS PENDING
7

Save Any 12 Dixie Picture Lids For A Colored Picture Of Me · See Your Dealer For Instructions
JOHN WAYNE
Co-Star of
★ John Ford's "The Quiet Man" ★
(Technicolor)
A REPUBLIC PICTURE

Save Any 12 Dixie Picture Lids For A Colored Picture Of Me · See Your Dealer For Instructions
JOHN WAYNE
Co-Star of
★ John Ford's "The Quiet Man" ★
(Technicolor)
A REPUBLIC PICTURE

4
Dixie lid, 1942. *Roy Rogers,*
2¼" diameter

5
Dixie lid, 1948. *Rita
Hayworth,* 2¼" diameter

6
Dixie lid, 1953. *Lucille
Ball and Desi Arnaz,* 2¾"
diameter

7
John Wayne Dixie lids,
1952. Three views: back,
wax-papered front, and
revealed front with
instructions for receiving
colored-picture premium,
each 2¾" diameter

8
Dixie lid, 1953. *Monte Irvin,*
2¾" diameter

9
Dixie lid, 1953. *Milton
Berle,* 2¾" diameter

Save Any 12 Dixie Picture Lids For A Large Picture Of Me · See Your Dealer For Instructions
MONTE IRVIN
NEW YORK GIANTS
8

Save Any 12 Dixie Picture Lids For A Large Picture Of Me · See Your Dealer For Instructions
MILTON BERLE
Star of
"The Texaco Star Theatre"
APPEARING ON NBC-TV
9

DIXIE LIDS, which covered ice cream cups from 1930
to 1954, the last year they put personalities on lids,
were another childhood collection obtainable from
the local candy store. At a nickel apiece, they were
not as available as the bottle caps but were very
deeply fulfilling. The lid was removed from the cup
by lifting a tab that protruded from the magic circle.
An opaque sheen of ice cream, deftly licked, revealed
a photograph of an actor or actress, perhaps a baseball
player, hopefully a cowboy, through a layer of waxed
paper. Heart racing with anticipation, I lifted the
waxed paper to reveal the treasure of a fresh image
or a tradable duplicate. The ice cream was good but
beside the point. Bounty multiplied if victims of
collectile dysfunction discarded their lids at the curb.

I had about twelve hundred lids in three columns
in a shoebox when I was told by my mother that my
Dixie lids and my stash of Log Cabin syrup bottles
had been discarded because anything that had contained food could attract vermin. How did the bottle
caps escape? My mother was exceeded in deed by the
mother of my physician friend Howard, a sheet music collector. He returned from the U.S. Army to find
two stacks of sheet music in his closet instead of the
three he'd left behind. His mother had discarded the
"loose" middle pages of each piece of music to make
more room in the closet. These acts did not improve
parent-child relations. Nor did my Dixie lid tragedy
deter me. To paraphrase Nietzsche, "What doesn't
kill you makes you stronger."

10

By this time I had significant collections of the unloved: my father's cigar rings and cigar boxes filled with sugar packets with U.S. President and state flower graphics; Indian bubble-gum cards; actor and actress decals; milk bottle lids; campaign buttons; skate keys; blotters with advertising graphics; figural matches; radio premium rings and product premium spoons; cocktail mixers; figural soaps; greeting cards from anyone to anyone on any occasion; playbills; advertising giveaways; postcards depicting colossal foods; Disabled Veterans key-chain miniature license plates; papier mâché Jack O' Lanterns; card deck Jokers; disused soda fountain cutouts; fruit crate labels; wooden cheese boxes; pipe tobacco tins; ball-in-hole games; bathroom decals; pictorial needle books; cockamamies; and foreign coins that my mother's several brothers brought back for me from their places of service in World War II.

10
Indian Gum bubble gum card (front and back), 1940. Printed card stock, 2¾" high. Goudey Gum Company, Boston, Massachusetts

11
Decals of movie stars Ann Blyth and Glenn Ford, 1950. Each 5" high. Meyercord Company

12
Skate key (back), 1949. 2½" high. Chicago Skate Company

13
Birthday cards for specific birthday recipients, c. 1935. Silk-screened paper and ribbon, 3–3½" high

14
Jack O' Lantern, 1948. Papier mâché with wire handle, 4½" high. Woolworth's

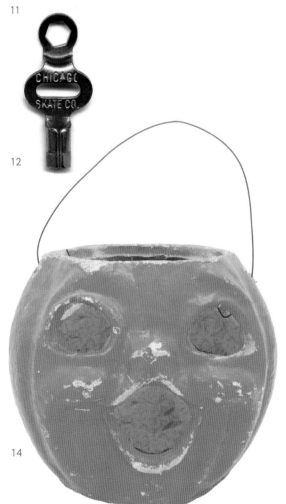

11

12

14

13

15
Lee Lorenz, *The New Yorker*, 4" high. © The New Yorker Collection 2004 Lee Lorenz from cartoonbank.com. All Rights Reserved

15

THE PUREST COLLECTING

Loving the unloved is the undefiled state of collecting from which the motives of all collectors may be deduced. Of all the faces of collecting, this is the purest: collector and object, no intervening issues of value or competition, wholly unselfconscious choices. Children who collect, collect in this way.

In 1979 I exhibited "Children's Collections" at New York University's 80 Washington Square East Galleries, which *The New York Times* covered. Figuring among the collections were YOGURT-LID INSERTS; BROKEN RUBBER BANDS; AIRLINE SAFETY INSTRUCTIONS; CIGARETTE BUTTS (filtered and unfiltered subsets); MISSHAPEN PRETZELS; FLAT TENNIS BALLS; FEATHERS; PENCIL SHAVINGS; USED SODA STRAWS; SINGLE GLOVES; and EMPTY CHAPSTICK TUBES.

What moved these children to value and save what others regularly ignore, kick aside, or throw away is that sublimely logical designation that separates the world's population into collectors and others. The former must be in the minority or they wouldn't be so interesting. Are they collectors because of fastidious or unsympathetic parents? No. Some kids just need to collect, others don't.

NEEDING TO COLLECT

What then, are the shared traits, the commonalities among these, the least biased of collectors, lovers of the unloved, that can be ascribed to all collectors?

1. Unquestionable Dominion

Collecting gives a province of absolute control, a domain. The collector is pharaohonic, the godly king and absolute monarch of a singular and self-defined territory, master of all he or she surveys.

2. Hands-On Gratification

There is deep satisfaction in organizing, inventorying, embracing, handling, and communing with the booty. Touching material objects connects us with the time and place in which they were made. Fondling the objects within one's own realm and arranging discrete and fluid categories is a gleeful exercise, a personal potlatch.

3. Empowerment by Delimitation

The choices within one's collecting sphere are limited only by one's imagination. Answers to one's own questions of what to seek are self-imposed. Should the quest be directed toward variety or quality? Quality or quantity? Quantity or one of a kind, each perfect? Should one upgrade? Should one trade? The boundaries, criteria, and standards are one's own. Limitations of budget are personal and may be built into one's criteria, a fungible scale of allowable desire.

16
Georgia Dullea, "Collections Harking Back to the Trash Can School," *The New York Times*, May 11, 1979, page B-6. David Owens collects yogurt tops

17
Georgia Dullea, "Collections Harking Back to the Trash Can School," *The New York Times*, May 11, 1979, page B-6. Jesse Karp with his collection of emergency instructions from airplanes

18
Patricia Leigh Brown, "When Child's Play Is Collecting," *The New York Times*, December 14, 1989, page C-1. Amy Karp with her dice collection

16

17

4. Hunting and Gathering

Exhilaration in the quest and the satisfaction attendant to acquisition encourage a refined sense of strategic reconnaissance and a fulfilling sense of personal acuteness, judgment, attainment, and achievement. Regarding one's own collection, choices that were individually made hone self-respect and invite responses from others ranging from curiosity, consternation, admiration, and astonishment to envy.

5. Possession

Ownership is an act of self-affirming intimacy and self-committing responsibility. Acquisitions require maintenance and other kinds of attention. A collector's singular voice is witnessed in a collection. A collection is a constructed self-redefinition of the collector who amassed it. An era may be possessed through ownership of its artifacts. A collector owns history by osmosis.

6. Husbanding and Transference of Characteristics

Husbanding grants protective custody over or of the object, in some cases granting asylum, resurrecting, or gripping the object back from the maw of oblivion. A collection is a charm against chaos, the ordered bit, the finger in the dike. Husbanding confers transference of the characteristics that define what is collected (beauty, wisdom, strength, poise, dignity, quirkiness). The salient attributes of the collection accrue to the collector. Since the source of these characteristics is the material object, they consequently transfer to successive owners (each owner adding patina to that object).

18

I hurried my way down the basement steps to the sewing machine, where Mother kept an ashtray filled with old buttons of varied colors and sizes. Fingering through these ... victims of loose threads, I listened to their crisp clicks and decided they deserved a better home than this musty basement. I padded upstairs with the ashtray and set it on a shelf beside my model airplanes.

The thought of those buttons—a little pool of circular waves—distracted me all through my day at school until finally, during social studies, I abandoned my textbook in exasperation and chewed a little arc of nail from my thumb. It peeled off smoothly and I stopped to examine it: one edge curved and stiff, the other ragged and surprisingly soft. I worried the rest of my nails until I had a tiny pile of crescents on my desk that could have been miniature white eyebrows, boomerangs, disembodied smiles or frowns. Why not collect these too? I thought, and slipped them in my pocket.

Back home I took a shot glass from the pantry cabinet and this soon sat brimming with nail clippings, right beside the ashtray of buttons on my shelf. Over the next few days I collected chicken and fish bones from dinner plates and crammed them into a Flintstones jelly jar: a potential dinosaur skeleton, they were the perfect background for Fred's stenciled face smiling from the curved glass. I liked to imagine that if I fit them together the most extraordinary creature would be revealed.

My collection grew in the following weeks: a sandwich bag of stray feathers, gathered from the park; a long-stemmed glass half filled with paper clips; and an old bowling bag so stuffed with Styrofoam peanuts that it seemed a real bowling ball nestled inside the cracked imitation leather.

When summer recess began I had to forgo gathering leftover chalk scrap from the classroom blackboard, but this was a minor setback. Already I had plans to scour back lots for stray bottle caps.... It was true that I had to place each container just right on the shelves, its own little pocket of order. Alone in my room I could settle so easily into the solace of things and stare at them for hours.

Philip Graham, *How to Read an Unwritten Language* (New York: Warner Books, 1997), 41–42.

19
Johann Phillipp Ferdinand
Preiss, *Flapper,* c. 1926.
Cold painted bronze on
marble base, 6¼" high

20
Johann Phillipp Ferdinand
Preiss, *Show Girl,* c. 1928.
Cold painted bronze on
black veined marble base,
12½" high

21
Wheat pattern ironstone
gravy boat, 1859. 5½"
high. Elsmore & Forster

22
Corkscrew (closed), 19th
century. German, celluloid
and steel, 2½" high

23
Mechanical bank,
1886. Uncle Sam as
carpetbagger, 11½" high

19

20

21

22

23

Once again: loving the unloved is the purest state
of collecting from which all collectors' motives may
be deduced.

Only now may I confess to also collecting objects
of value. My husband, Ivan, art dealer and founder
and director of OK Harris Works of Art, and I together
collect Dark Ages jewelry; Art Deco figures; wheat
pattern ironstone china; cast-iron mechanical banks;
figural glass bottles; Oriental carpets; corkscrews;
Bennington dishes; American Sweetheart Monax
Depression glass; English mourning jewelry; slip-
ware dishes; South Arabian antiquities; Staffordshire plates; salt-glazed stoneware; Hupa baskets;
patchwork quilts; cufflinks; ancient coins; paintings;
and sculpture. All of these have hearty, established,
and wide collectorships, endowing them with extrinsic value. However, they are not more precious or
more venerable to me than my "valueless" objects of
virtue.

An object of material culture is any object that a
person deems worthy of collecting. Who finds what
specimens worthy of collecting is an abiding fascination. My own collections lie somewhere between
Tom Sawyer's pockets and the Smithsonian Institution's storage shelves.

24

25

26

27

24
Bennington creamer,
c. 1870. 4" high

25
Penny candy, 1949. *Indian
Brand Salted Pistachio
Nuts* (back), two cents,
1½" high. Agress Nut and
Seed Company, Brooklyn,
New York

26
Penny candy, 1951.
Good and Plenty, 1 cent,
1¼" high. Quaker City
Confectionery Company,
Philadelphia, Pennsylvania

27
Baseball player still bank,
c. 1890. Painted cast iron,
5½" high

28
Ironstone soup bowl,
1820. Glazed, hand-
painted (front and back),
10" diameter. Mason,
England

28

WHY ARE DIXIE LIDS SCARCE?

The real question is, why are there any left? They were fostered during their useful lifetimes for their function, and most people don't have the visual dexterity to locate beauty in ordinariness. For the collector, there is a disjunction between the "wrappers" and the commodity. Ephemera are and have always been just that: ephemeral, a dwindling phenomenon.

Jefferson R. Burdick (1900–1963) is one of my great heroes. I found him by chance only seven years ago while speaking with Ellen H., a curator of photography, about my DIXIE LID collection. The Burdick collection of paper Americana resides in the Department of Drawings and Prints at the Metropolitan Museum of Art. Frail from childhood and increasingly debilitated by lifelong arthritis, Burdick, beginning in early youth in Syracuse, New York, spent a lifetime collecting and organizing a massive assembly of ephemera including postcards, trade cards, product labels, social and business cards, calling cards, acquaintance cards, greeting cards and souvenir cards, banners, product booklets, scrapbook materials, manufacturers' illustrated catalogues, cigarette and cigar papers. In 1947 he offered them to the Metropolitan Museum through the sympathetic offices of A. Hyatt Mayor, then curator of the Department of Drawings and Prints. James Rorimer, director of the Museum from 1955 through 1966, ratified the residence of Burdick's collection.

Between 1948 and 1959, Burdick regularly shipped cartons of his paper ephemera to the Met. Soon after, he moved to New York City and, at a desk in a corner of the department, began pasting his treasures into 394 numbered 12½-by-15-inch scrapbook binders and boxes. There are 306,353 items arranged by category, subject, and by instinct that reveal a great deal of Jefferson Burdick's personality as well as his love for these specimens. In the winter of 1963, shortly after he gave safe haven to the last card, his legacy to us, he died.

I spent Thursdays of my sabbatical year from New York University in 2002 at a long study table in the Department of Drawings and Prints at the Metropolitan Museum with Dorothy G., communing with Jefferson Burdick through his scrapbooks. Dorothy had been Cooper Hewitt's curator of exhibitions for twenty years. One needs someone who understands, to exclaim to when visiting ancient cities and while examining a great collection. Every Thursday there was a serious academic scholar studying a wood engraving or fourteenth-century German etchings, centimeter by molecule, for the duration of our visit. We were likely having a much better time than they were. Burdick had the most profound conviction that there was something singular about the transient attendants to the functional commodities produced during his lifetime.

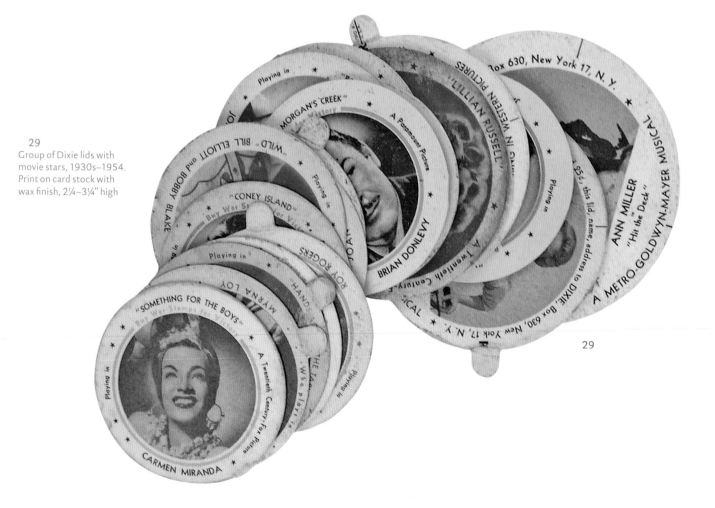

29
Group of Dixie lids with movie stars, 1930s–1954. Print on card stock with wax finish, 2¼–3¼" high

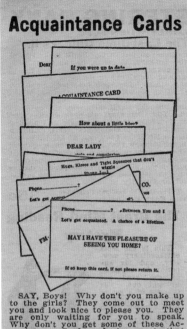

Acquaintance Cards

SAY, Boys! Why don't you make up to the girls? They come out to meet you and look nice to please you. They are only waiting for you to speak. Why don't you get some of these Acquaintance Cards and give one to that jolly girl? She will love you for it. Even with nice girls with whom you are already acquainted it sometimes happens to be difficult, from diffidence or shyness, to get on to friendly terms; these cards provide subjects for pleasant jokes and amusing conversation, and thus smooth the way to a more familiar acquaintance and cordial friendship.

Please remember there is nothing about them to offend anyone. They are very wittily worded and quite unobjectionable. Here are some specimens of the stimulative gentle hints:

"May I have the pleasure of escorting you home? If not, can I sit on the fence and watch you go by?"

"I'd like to make a date with you. If your answer is YES just keep this card and if it is NO, just hand it back."

"I'm somewhat of a liar myself, but go on with your story. I'm listening."

"How about a little kiss? For both it'll be bliss. Just one you'll never miss, and I won't make you do that or this."

"If you were up to date you'd go riding with my Straight 8. You know it's never too late. Jump in—don't hesitate."

"Dear Miss, I feel lonesome and dejected. I fear my heart you have affected, and if I don't get rejected, I'll take you home and you'll get everything you expected."

and so on. There are 10 cards to the set, all different. The cards are neatly printed, measuring about 3¼ x2 inches.
No. 2072. Price Per Set.........10c
3 sets for 25c., or 1 doz sets for 75c.

320   *JOHNSON SMITH & CO.*

30

31

32

33

34

30
Acquaintance card ad, 1929. 7½" high. Johnson Smith & Company catalog, Detroit, Michigan, page 320

31
Acquaintance card, 1900. Social intercourse by means of a card, print on card stock, ¾" high

32
Novelty acquaintance card, c. 1910. Social intercourse by means of a clever card, print on card stock, 2" high

33
Hidden-name calling card, c. 1880. Printed embossed paper affixed over name on edge-painted card stock, 2½" high

34
Rebus acquaintance card, c. 1890. Social intercourse by means of a card, print on card stock, 1¾" high

He believed that they were worth saving and that someone had to do it. Now we have them. Describing his dominion of cards in 1962, he said: "In older material, the problem has been to find cards. It is impossible to over-emphasize the extreme scarcity of many old cards. Many whole sets are known by a single specimen and even where a considerable quantity survive, they are often found as a single lot and never appear again. The fortunate finder of the lot has all there is."

35
Dixie lid, 1938. *Bronko Nagurski,* 2¾" diameter

36
Dixie lid, 1947. *June Allyson,* 2¾" diameter

37
Dixie lids, 1934. Ronald Colman *"Bulldog Drummond Strikes Back"* (back and front of mystery card and front of portrait card), each 2¼" diameter

LOVING THE UNLOVED

Hats off to Burdick. My eBay tag is *thankyouburdick.* It pleases me to think that for a few years our collecting impulses overlapped. My collecting began in 1942 with bottle caps and Dixie lids. Jefferson Burdick traded his lids back to the Dixie Cup Company for "premiums," which were 8-by-10-inch actor or actress portrait pages in lurid color with loose-leaf perforations at the left and related film information and fodder for the fans on the back. These premiums cost their owner twelve lids each. There are many premiums in the J. R. Burdick Collection; there are no Dixie lids.

    I sent twelve duplicate lids for one premium of John Wayne. I still have it, and it reminds me that one has to make the collecting choices in life that feel right. I liked my lids better than the premiums and I still do.

    At any rate, it's a miracle that the lids and the premiums still exist. There are twenty-one announced Dixie lid collectors across the United States. For a sliver of time by the collector clock there was a Dixie lid newsletter. I have all fifteen issues. How much can you say about Dixie lids? They are what they are. Besides, collectors tend to be loners about what they amass, and a group project or sharing hits too close to a nerve. There are probably many more who remember having encountered Dixie lids as the means to getting to the ice cream, one of the great treats of childhood. So, one way these treasures become rare is that they are simply the disposable means to a goal.

35

36

37

38

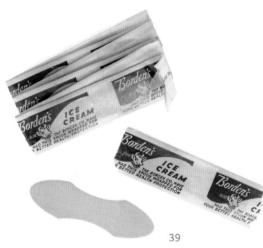

39

40

41

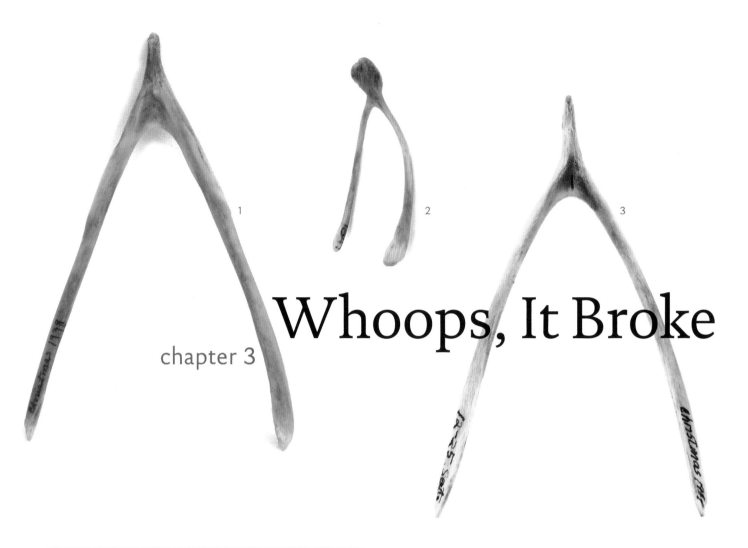

Whoops, It Broke

chapter 3

WISHBONES ARE destined to be broken. Yet, someone cleaned and saved a bouquet's worth, a reunion of them apparently commemorating specific meals. In ink, on the wider portion of each bone, a date ranging from December 25, 1938, through April 20, 1956, has been inscribed. Why did someone do this? Was there such a paucity of celebration in this person's life that a wishbone monument had to become a marker for each? If this was the case, why weren't the wishbones used to wish for a better lot in life?

Why is this group of bones so evocative for me? It touches me and binds me to some time in a not-too-distant past in a general way. This group of artifacts, these inscribed bones, are a pilgrimage to a shared common memory, the tangible residence of the intangible memories, visions, and incidents of personal history.

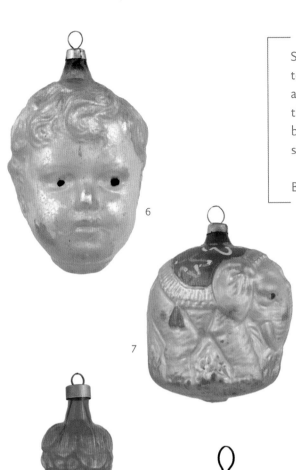

THE MORE perfect and intact the object, the greater its power to intoxicate and pass on its package of dynamic energy. My architectural historian friend Carlo L.'s collection of glass Christmas tree ornaments is a prime example of the perfection-to-energy ratio, and there are fewer of these left every year. Like wishbones, but for different reasons, these ornaments were destined to be broken.

Glass Christmas tree ornaments are synonyms for brittle brilliant prizes, frail reflective treasures, shatterable shimmering fantasies. They are connected to a season laden with sentiment and memories of childhood. These blown or blown-molded orbs and figural shapes with metallic insides and painted or lacquered details are the most direct stimuli for releasing murmurs, sparks, explosions of associative connection in each sense for the susceptible viewer. They also have a separate life as cultural artifacts.

1
Wishbone (turkey), 1938. Inscribed *Christmas 1938*, 4½" high

2
Wishbone (chicken), 1947. Inscribed *Xmas 1947*, 2¼" high ·

3
Wishbone (turkey), 1954. Inscribed *Xmas 1954*, 4½" high

4
Valentine postcard with wishbone, 1907. 3½" high

5
Thanksgiving postcard with wishbone, 1904. 3½" high

6
Head of a blond boy Christmas tree ornament, 1890. Painted glass, 3½" high. Germany

7
Elephant Christmas tree ornament, 1880. Painted glass, 3" high. Germany

8
Grapes Christmas tree ornament, 1890. Painted glass, 2½" high. Czechoslovakia

9
Snow-baby Christmas tree ornament, 1870. Painted glass, 3¼" high. Germany

10
Snowflake Christmas tree ornament, 1850. Painted glass, 3½" high. Germany

11
St. Nicholas Christmas tree ornament, 1920. Painted mercury glass with sand, 3½" high. Germany

12
Indian-chief Christmas tree ornament, c. 1925. Painted glass, 4½" high. Czechoslovakia

13
Santa Christmas
tree ornament on
candleholder clip, 1949.
Painted mercury glass,
4¼" high. Russia

14
Standing Santa with sack
Christmas tree light bulb,
c. 1945. Painted glass, 3"
high. Japan

15
Clown Christmas
tree ornament, 1920.
Painted glass with
sand texture, 4¾" high.
Czechoslovakia

16
Young boy Christmas
tree light bulb, c. 1945.
Painted glass, 3¼" high.
Japan

17
Santa head (face on each
side) Christmas tree light
bulb, c. 1945. Painted
glass, 2½" high. Japan

18
Fish Christmas tree light
bulb, c. 1945. Painted
glass, 3" high. Japan

For each of us, a cultural artifact is replete with
an amalgam of unique personal experiences, books,
movies, poetry, stories, conversations, theater, works
of art, cartoons, photographs, and TV enactments
about the period and place that grew the objects. An
object of material culture evokes, articulates, and
crystallizes the culture in which it was created.

Some vibrant and easily fragmented Christmas
tree jewels were made in Germany beginning in the
eighteenth century and, shortly after, in Czechoslovakia and Poland. By the mid-1800s they were made
in New York and New Jersey by immigrants. Many
of Carlo's ornaments date from 1840 to 1940, and the
style of each crystallizes the place and time of its
origin. Carlo is very specific about the material
foundations from which the voice of each ornament
emerges.

19

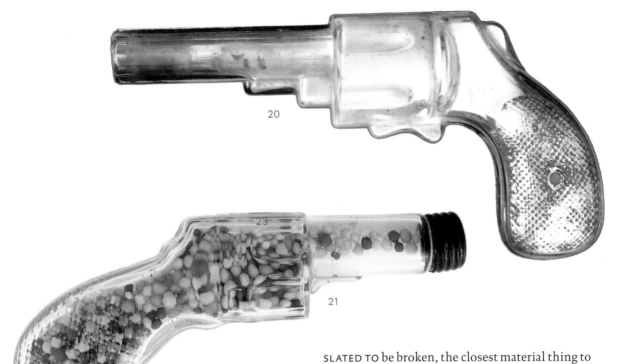

20

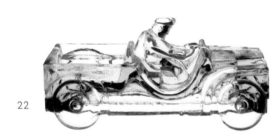

21

22

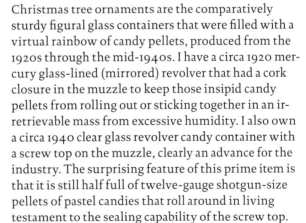

23

19
Locomotive candy
container, 1944. Glass
and candy pellets, 2¼"
high. Victory Glass
Company, Jeanette,
Pennsylvania

20
Revolver candy container,
c. 1910. Mercury glass,
8" long

21
Revolver with screw-top
candy container, c. 1938.
Glass, tin cap, and candy
pellets, 7¼" long. Stough
Company, Jeanette,
Pennsylvania

22
Jeep with driver candy
container, 1944. Glass,
2" high. Victory Glass
Company, Jeanette,
Pennsylvania

23
Tank with driver candy
container, 1945. Glass,
1¾" high. Victory Glass
Company, Jeanette,
Pennsylvania

SLATED TO be broken, the closest material thing to Christmas tree ornaments are the comparatively sturdy figural glass containers that were filled with a virtual rainbow of candy pellets, produced from the 1920s through the mid-1940s. I have a circa 1920 mercury glass-lined (mirrored) revolver that had a cork closure in the muzzle to keep those insipid candy pellets from rolling out or sticking together in an irretrievable mass from excessive humidity. I also own a circa 1940 clear glass revolver candy container with a screw top on the muzzle, clearly an advance for the industry. The surprising feature of this prime item is that it is still half full of twelve-gauge shotgun-size pellets of pastel candies that roll around in living testament to the sealing capability of the screw top.

These are but addenda to my real fascination with the products of the Victory Glass Company of Jeanette, Pennsylvania, which, during the 1940s, in the midst of World War II, produced clear glass candy containers of Jeeps, Willys Jeeps, U.S. Army tanks with two cannon and a star on the front, Army

24

25

26

27

28

29

30

bombers with P-15-7 on one wing and a star on the other, battleships and cabin cruisers, woody station wagons, lanterns, and baby bottles. I have one of these baby bottles filled with nonpareil-size candy pellets and a still-flexible rubber nipple with which to nourish one's baby doll. This item remains unopened and retains its original label revealing the simple ingredients of the candy pellet as sugar, starch, corn syrup, and artificial coloring. This charming piece was confection-filled by the Stough Company, also of Jeanette, Pennsylvania. What a revelation. During the war years, when everything about the survival of your mother's three brothers (and your future husband) was up in the air, a kid in the Bronx, learning to blow bubbles on Yanks bubble gum, could go to the French Bakery and purchase a Charlotte Russe and a tank filled with candy from Jeanette, Pennsylvania, in solidarity with our guys overseas.

Victory Glass Company products of this vintage had white cardboard closures sealed with wax. The ingredients and manufacturer were printed on the cardboard, which was difficult to remove. They were the means to an end sought by an impatient kid, so those labeled closures survive only in my memory. The vehicles were played with and were more vulnerable than their metal or wood counterparts, so they readily lost parts such as wheels and wings because they were subjected to crashes and friction.

When asked in a *New York* magazine interview, "What was the one that got away?" I answered that it was my collection of figural glass candy containers that I sold to the late Werner Leroy in the 1960s. He was smitten with them, and I thought that I could live without them. My brother, Bill, who is an oral surgeon and the aforementioned collector of baseball cards and American coins, read the article and sent me his glass candy containers, individually bubble wrapped. It was an act of the highest magnanimity. He said that I had given him most of them anyway, though we had both gone to the French Bakery together to buy these gems. I accepted them in the spirit in which they were given. The Victory Glass Company of Jeanette, Pennyslvania, no longer exists. There is a Victory Glass Company in Waukee, Iowa, that offers replacement parts for vintage jukeboxes . . . no connection.

Material culture is a voice through which collective history speaks. Replicas, reproductions, facsimiles, and simulacra just don't do the job. Singular objects have their meanings and their auras. The filament of their continuity is retained in the community comprised of a collection of their kind.

TAKE, FOR example, my collection of POIGNANT REPAIRS. It is a crossover collection in that it isn't a straightforward vertical collection of genera such as corkscrews or birds' nests or seed packets. It crosses all categories. It is comprised of common objects, through the ages, that broke and were repaired, not discarded. To qualify for this collection, these objects need to have been transmuted by their repair. A repair of some transfiguring artistry uniquely distinguishes each object from the run of common goods.

24
Telephone candy container, 1938. Glass, wood, steel wire, and string, 5" high. Victory Glass Company, Jeanette, Pennsylvania

25
Woody station wagon candy container, 1948. Glass, 2" high

26
P-15-7 Army bomber candy container, 1944. Glass, 1¼" high. Victory Glass Company, Jeanette, Pennsylvania

27
Locomotive 1028 candy container, 1930. Glass, 1½" high

28
Sedan candy container, 1944. Glass, 1½" high. Victory Glass Company, Jeanette, Pennsylvania

29
Doll's bottle candy container, 1925. Glass, rubber, and candy pellets, 3" high. Stough Company, Jeanette, Pennsylvania

30
Pistol candy container, 1947. Glass with metal screw cap and paper whistle insert, 4¾" long. Stough Glass Company, Jeanette, Pennsylvania

31
Ironstone sauce tureen and lid with wood and mother-of-pearl replacement knob, c. 1875. 6½" high

32
Pressed-glass candlestick with replaced Vermont marble foot, c. 1870. 5½" high

33
Lusterware cream pitcher with bolted brass replacement handle, c. 1840. 3½" high

A Colonial American lusterware teapot had a broken handle. It was rendered nonfunctional, a hot teapot with no way to hold it. Someone constructed a plain metal corset of subtle delicacy, considered ingenuity, and refined taste, transforming this beloved companion into a work of art. There is tangible evidence that someone loved this piece before I did.

A pressed glass stemmed wine goblet of no rarity had its foot broken and discarded in the nineteenth century. This is a common glass. Seen unbroken, it is without particular distinction even in the twenty-first century. With plain no-nonsense workingman sense and trade-level skill, someone cared enough to construct a prosthetic foot for its stem and bowl. The etched Flip glass from eighteenth-century New England was probably and understandably dropped between gulps of frothy Flip, a Colonial drink of heated beer and liquor. The fineness of the etching

34
Glazed porcelain teapot and lid with soldered tin corset replacing handle, c. 1760. 5½" high

35
Jeweler's saw (side view) with handle replaced by deer antler, 1964. 11" long

36
Etched Flip glass repaired with three double metal staples, c. 1790. 6½" high

37
Stemmed, paneled, pressed glass wine goblet with soldered tin replacement foot, c. 1870. 6¾" high

of hound chasing stag through the forest surrounding the glass probably saved it from being hurled into the fireplace. Instead, someone patiently drilled six holes into the bottom of the glass and its contiguous sides and inserted three metal pins, foreshadowing the staple. These pins hold bottom to top, rendering the glass functional and much better than it was in its earlier life. It was the first object in my POIGNANT REPAIRS collection.

Consider the coping saw with the striking addition of a deer-antler handle that perfectly fits a user's palm; the original could not have been more satisfactory. Where was Mr. Fixit when the handle broke? What necessity drove him to try the deer antler? The carved tortoiseshell comb for a Spanish mantilla broke at its two weakest places, probably in the course of fastening a shawl to a thickly coiled mass of dark hair. Someone repaired it with two tiny silver findings, finely engraved in a floral design on both sides; now it's a masterpiece. The simplest piece in this collection is a file that required a functional handle. Someone took a piece of a branch and set the file handle into it. It's the polar opposite of the tortoiseshell comb repair because it is so stunningly simple. Handles are the most vulnerable parts of pitchers, cups, and creamers. *W. Liebensbiger* was so proud of his fine tin handle replacement on a Bennington pitcher that he made a brass plate for his name that is about as big as the handle. The neck of a horn or shell

38
Tortoiseshell comb with two engraved sterling silver reinforcements, c. 1900. 6½" high

39
File with branch section replacing missing handle, 1956. 10" long

40
Glazed porcelain China export mug with wrought-iron replaced handle, c. 1830. 5¼" high

41
Bennington pitcher with galvanized tin and brass handle replacement, stamped *W. Liebensbiger,* c. 1910. Wood screws and bolt, 8" high

38

39

40

41

42
Horn spoon (front and back) with tin reinforced neck, c. 1860. 7" long

43
Horn snuff box with hinged lid, incised designs, and copper staple repair, c. 1790. 3¼" across

44
Pin cushion made from the broken base of a pressed-glass candlestick, 1870. Velvet, seeds, beads, pinecones, and nuts, 7" high

45
Carved wood laundry stick initialed *FS* with glass inlays and wire repairs, c. 1825. 15" high

46
Dead Sea pot, 1900–1550 B.C. Unglazed clay, 5" high. Tel-al-Sultan, Jericho

spoon is clearly its weak spot since the contents are levered by the handle. The weight of the contents in the bowl of the spoon causes the neck to flex, and homemade spoons often snapped. If someone was skillful and cared, the neck was repaired and fortified against future breakage.

As collections go, POIGNANT REPAIRS are the rarest of the rare. Each object in the collection requires the uncommon complicity of the intention to save it, the artistry to conserve it, safe haven thereafter, and someone who will buy and cherish "damaged goods."

The reason that there are very few Dead Sea pots or twentieth-century Moxie glasses or eighteenth-century jelly glasses on the market is that they broke in the normal course of use. They were replaced by a different or "better" model. Time marches on. This brings us to another reason that a bevy of things are scarce.

47
Moxie glasses, c. 1925. Pressed glass, 4" high

48
Jelly glasses, 1780–1860. Blown glass with turned lip, 3¾–4" high. USA

49
Dead Sea pot, 1900–1550 B.C. Unglazed clay, 6" high. Tel-al-Sultan, Jericho

47

There are some qualities—some incorporate things,
That have a double life—life aptly made
A type of that twin entity which springs
From matter and light—evinced in solid and shade.

Edgar Allan Poe, "Silence—A Sonnet" in letter from Poe to Boyd, December 25, 1839, E. A. Poe Society of Baltimore.

48

49

chapter 4

Obsolescence &
the Better Mousetrap

I NEVER IMAGINED and was delighted to discover that *approximately 40 sheets* of waxed paper of *Extra Good Quality* in an assortment of *Dainty Chintz Prints, Colorful Modernistic Designs,* were a means to making my *picnics different* and my *parties distinctive.* This packet of food-related magic was made by the Kalamazoo Vegetable Parchment Company in the 1930s. KVP packaging for *Fancy Waxed Paper* lists among its uses: place doilies; brightening sick-room trays; wrapping jellies and confections; and wrapping children's lunches.

1
Package of *Kalamazoo Vegetable Parchment Company Fancy Waxed Paper* (outside), 1931. 13¾" high. Parchment, Michigan

2
Packages of *Kalamazoo Vegetable Parchment Company Fancy Waxed Paper* (outside and inside), 1934–38. 13¾" high. Parchment, Michigan

1

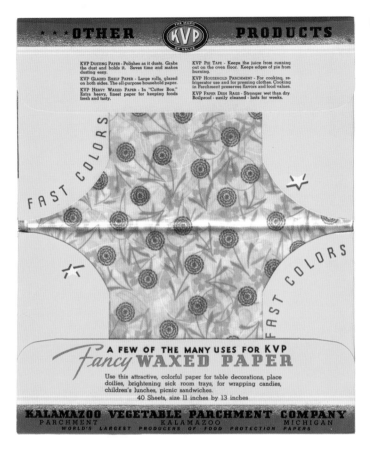

The Kalamazoo Vegetable Parchment Company must have been the biggest game in town: it was located in Parchment, Michigan. Other products include the KVP Paper Dishrag, a *boilproof paper, good for several weeks' use.* I live in anticipation of finding one of those. The waxed-paper packet boasts *fast colors.* I bet not in a microwave. I'm tempted to try microwaving potatoes, serving them tattooed with blue-and-green silhouettes of the cow jumping over the moon. I won't, because I don't feel that I can sacrifice even one sheet of this precious material to my curiosity. Besides, I'm sure that the wax transfer would be carcinogenic. It amazes me to think that this product is so guilelessly presented as the route to homely sophistication. This extraordinary product was the up-market precursor of the less exciting but more efficient Saran Wrap, predecessor of Ziploc bags and aluminum foil. Do I have the last package of this stuff?

3

4

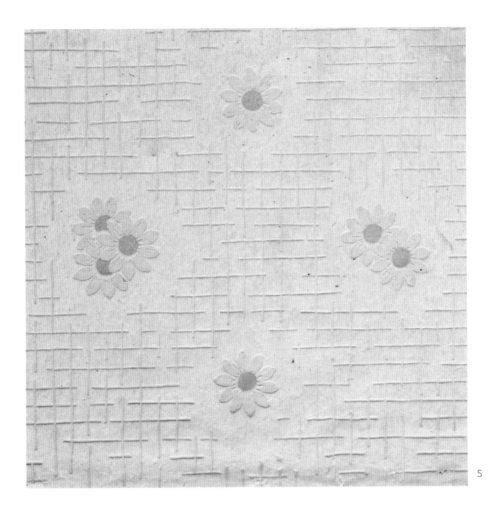

5

6

3
Nursery rhyme
pattern, *Kalamazoo
Vegetable Parchment
Company Fancy Waxed
Paper*, 1938. 13" x 12".
Parchment, Michigan

4
Yellow, red, and green
fruit pattern, *Kalamazoo
Vegetable Parchment
Company Fancy Waxed
Paper*, 1938. 13" x 12".
Parchment, Michigan

5
Yellow daisy and
crosshatch pattern,
*Kalamazoo Vegetable
Parchment Company
Fancy Waxed Paper*,
1938. 13" x 12".
Parchment, Michigan

6
Abstract Indian
pattern, *Kalamazoo
Vegetable Parchment
Company Fancy Waxed
Paper*, 1938. 13" x 12".
Parchment, Michigan

7
Group of figural pencil sharpeners, 1940–42. Bakelite, pot metal, steel, paint, decals, and printed paper, ¾–2" high

8
Keep 'em Flying airplane pencil sharpener (front and back), 1940. Bakelite, decals, and steel, 2¼" long

9
Pistol pencil sharpener (front and back), 1940. Red Bakelite and steel, 1½" long

10
Group of figural pencil sharpeners (fronts and backs), 1920–40. Painted pot metal and steel, ½–1¾" high

11
Luger pencil sharpener (back, open), 1925. Painted lead and steel, 1½" high

12
Pistol Deluxe pencil sharpener with swivel lid to contain shavings (open), 1920. Painted lead and steel, 2" high

13
Trombone pencil sharpener with pencil, 1920. Painted lead and steel, 2¼" high

14
Uncle Sambo in top hat and bow tie (front and back) pencil sharpener, 1946. Painted lead and steel, 1¾" high. Made in Occupied Japan

15
Cowboy pencil sharpener (front and back), c. 1930. Painted lead and steel, 1½" high

16
Touring car pencil sharpener (side and top views), c. 1925. Lead and steel, ¾" high

17
Group of figural pencil sharpeners (fronts and backs), 1930–40. Bakelite and steel, 1–1½" high

HOW MANY pencils can a kid sharpen before the *Keep 'em Flying* wears off the wings of the Bakelite World War II airplane pencil sharpener or the G-Men decal rubs off the pistol sharpener? How many angels can dance on the head of a pin? Did a figural pencil sharpener in one's pencil box actually brighten the succession of mundane school days? They certainly were manufactured in a variety of forms, materials, and places. But all had the same (some rusted) now-dull blade. A small proportion of the painted pot-metal sharpeners were deluxe models, produced with an eraser or a cap that formed a shavings catcher so that every honing of the point didn't necessitate a trip to the wastebasket. The Bakelite models were virtually without detail save the outline and decal and were produced primarily in the 1930s and 1940s in the United States. They seem to recur in an endless procession of Scotty dogs, pistols, clocks, tanks, and airplanes. Each shows varying traces of previous ownership. Metal versions reveal themselves in a profuse variety of detailed cast objects from alarm clocks to automobiles to Eiffel towers and trumpets (the pencil is the straight mute). They were manufactured in the United States, Germany, France, England, and Japan. Each has a screw to secure the blade and to change it; if anyone ever purchased replacement blades, it's unlikely that they could be found decades later when the blade needed replacement. The figural sharpeners were inexpensive (but useful) souvenirs of destinations and of a time in which pencils were important and ubiquitous. These small useful items that were halfway between a toy and a reminder to do your homework coexisted with the mechanical pencil sharpener, usually affixed to the schoolroom window ledge. The model that is best known is a side-churn device, commonly sporting multiple graduated apertures for pencils of different diameters, which evolved into the electric pencil sharpener. Today, aside from crossword aficionados, editors, and certain artists, who requires a pencil?

8

9

10

11   12

13

14   15   16   17

18

19

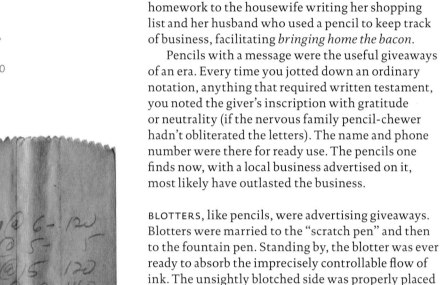

20

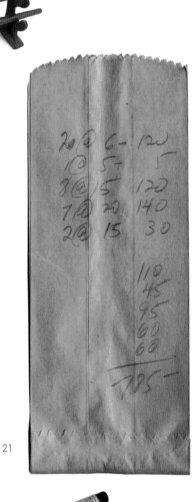

18
Lead pencils, 1946.
Eberhard-Faber, 7" long

19
Lead pencil, 1944.
2¼" long

20
Cast-iron pen stand,
c. 1875, 3" high

Pens, wood holders,
brass, and slit steel nibs,
1850–1915. 5–8" long

21
Brown bag with pencil
figures, 1946. 8½" high

22
Group of pencils with
printed advertising,
1948–56. 7–7½" long

21

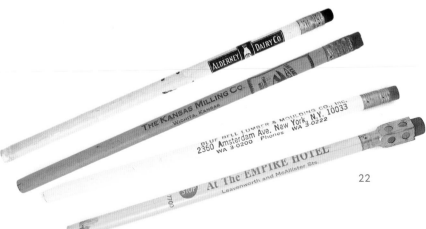

22

LEAD PENCILS, then graphite, were the greatest advance in writing since the crow quill pen. Graphite is the solid lubricant form of crystalline allotropic carbon used in pencils. The graphic arts no doubt take their name from this mineral. The study of the Earth's physical features, geography, includes this mineral as does every other "-graphy." Then came the fountain pen and typewriter, the ballpoint pen, the gel pen, and word-processing programs. That leaves as the pencil's primary functions sketching and advertising. The pencil once was a necessity for everyone, from the greengrocer adding up purchases on the side of the brown bag to the schoolchild doing homework to the housewife writing her shopping list and her husband who used a pencil to keep track of business, facilitating *bringing home the bacon*.

Pencils with a message were the useful giveaways of an era. Every time you jotted down an ordinary notation, anything that required written testament, you noted the giver's inscription with gratitude or neutrality (if the nervous family pencil-chewer hadn't obliterated the letters). The name and phone number were there for ready use. The pencils one finds now, with a local business advertised on it, most likely have outlasted the business.

BLOTTERS, like pencils, were advertising giveaways. Blotters were married to the "scratch pen" and then to the fountain pen. Standing by, the blotter was ever ready to absorb the imprecisely controllable flow of ink. The unsightly blotched side was properly placed face down. The face-up side was a ready reminder of whom to vote for; what tires, shoes, or coal to purchase; which paint, bank, garage, or milk delivery company to patronize; and what cereal or soft drink to consume.

When compared to the pencil's cramped text facet, blotters had ample space for imagery to reinforce the message. Blotters foreshadowed TV with seductive visual snippets coupled with beckoning text. Some enterprises paired their advertising messages with lessons in natural history—birds of the northeast, flags of the world—pitched to children doing their penmanship homework. Other businesses proffered pinups that migrated toward Dad's shop or the garage to be located beside the pinup calendar. Blotters were a necessary attendant to the inked word and legibility. Their advertisements hung around by the phone or on the desk, and unlike the radio, you couldn't turn them off. If placed face down, one faced the blue-black inkblot ghosts of what had been written. Detective stories of the 1940s gave equal time to the hard-boiled private eye solving a mystery based on the revelation of the blotter's mirror image and the pencil's indentation on the page beneath the one that had been inscribed. The gel pen and the word processor are more efficient, but not half as exciting.

23

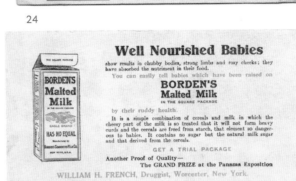

24

QUALITY COAL...
as near as your phone
OLD COMPANY'S LEHIGH PREMIUM HARD COAL
It lasts longer !

E. B. SALISBURY & SONS INC.

ALBANY
Stop 41, Central Ave.
PHONE: 8-3317

SCHENECTADY
164 Erie Blvd.
PHONE: FR 4-9166

Printed in U.S.A.   #785

25

Well Nourished Babies

show results in chubby bodies, strong limbs and rosy cheeks; they have absorbed the nutriment in their food.

You can easily tell babies which have been raised on

BORDEN'S
Malted Milk
IN THE SQUARE PACKAGE

by their ruddy health.

It is a simple combination of cereals and milk in which the cheesy part of the milk is so treated that it will not form heavy curds and the cereals are freed from starch, that element so dangerous to babies. It contains no sugar but the natural milk sugar and that derived from the cereals.

GET A TRIAL PACKAGE

Another Proof of Quality—
The GRAND PRIZE at the Panama Exposition

WILLIAM H. FRENCH, Druggist, Worcester, New York.

26

27

28

29

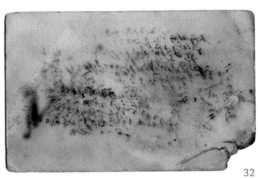

30

31

(illegible blotter image)

32

23
Blotter, 1928. *Illinois Bell Telephone Company*, 3¼" high

24
Blotter, c. 1955. Giveaway with the purchase of Bond Bread, 3¾" high

25
Blotter, c. 1935. *Lehigh Premium Hard Coal*, 3½" high

26
Blotter, 1922. *Borden's Malted Milk*, 3" high

27
Blotter, 1938. *Kellogg's Rice Krispies*, 3" high

28
Blotter, 1947. *Wampole's Preparation Stimulant Tonic*, 3½" high

29
Blotter, 1947. *Service Welders Inc.*, 4" high

30
Blotter, c. 1935. Giveaway with the purchase of Ward's Bread, 3" high

31
Blotter, 1951. *Atlanta Aggregate Co., Inc.*, 4" high

32
Blotter, 1927. *Sun-Maid Nectars* (used back side), 3½" high

ANIMAL CAN openers are most commonly found in the form of a bull's head and tail. They look medieval, but all can openers are contemporaneous with metal cans. I imagine that metal cans were easier for cowboys to carry out on the range than a Mason jar, and offered greater culinary variety than Jerky tasting of saddlebag. The image I have in my mind's eye is of cowboys sitting down to dinner around the campfire after a day of roping, branding, preempting stampedes, and whatever else cowboys do. There must be nothing more satisfying after a day with the dumb unruly beasts than whacking a cast-iron effigy of a bull's head with a sharp horn to puncture the lid of a can of beans. Once punctured, it was cut around the rim with staccato wrist motions utilizing the blade beneath the bull's neck, perpendicular to the horn. All this was managed by holding the bull's tail. Other animal can openers come in the form of fish and fantasy animals that cowboys might have dreamed of. Housewives had to use these openers too, which is probably why mechanical and electrical can openers were invented.

33
Bull can opener, c. 1870. Cast iron, paint, and steel blade, 6½" long

34
Bull can opener, c. 1870. Cast iron, paint, and steel blade, 6½" long

35
Bull can opener, c. 1870. Cast iron, paint, and steel blade, 7" long

36
Bull can opener, c. 1870. Cast iron, paint, and steel blade, 6" long

37
Bull can opener, c. 1870. Cast iron, paint, and steel blade, 7" long

38
Bull can opener, c. 1870. Cast iron, paint, and steel blade, 7" long

39
Sea serpent can opener, c. 1880. Cast iron, paint, and steel blade, 5¾" long

40
Sea serpent can opener, c. 1880. Cast iron, paint, and steel blade, 5¼" long

33

34

35

36

37

38

39

40

INSULATORS were devised in the 1840s and were used throughout the twentieth century to support and separate telegraph and telephone wires stretched from pole to pole across the country. Most often they were made of glass (sometimes porcelain), and exposure to the sun refined their remarkable glassy colors. There are 185 styles documented to date, and 14 U.S. manufacturers of glass insulators coincidentally made canning jars as well. Kerr, Corning-Pyrex, Hemingray, and Whitall-Tatum are a few names.

Insulators prevented contact between electrical conductors and were affixed to the cross members of poles. Their undersides were hollow and threaded. Their domes were rounded to facilitate rain run-off. They were molded with ridges, grooves and a skirt so that their charges, the wires, wouldn't slip toward each other. They made possible the replacement of the Pony Express, as today e-mail has replaced the telegraph and many of the telephone's functions. Most telephone poles have been removed, replaced by fiber-optic cables that have been buried in rural areas thanks to easements purchased throughout farmland and range. I had insulators on the windowsills of our country home for years; sunshine illuminated them brilliantly. Recently glass inkwells have replaced them and sunshine treats them kindly as well.

There are myriad collectors of these intriguing glass artifacts throughout the land. If you don't believe me, check out www.insulators.com, which takes insulators very seriously. In rural areas when the phone company takes a creosote-saturated log down in the name of progress, it often asks the landowner if it can put the pole somewhere on the property before resorting to carting it off. Every so often, walking in the woods or on land off the beaten path, one may be lucky enough to find a downed pole with its insulators still screwed on. There are thousands more collectors of insulators than there are of Dixie lids and www.insulators.com can put you in touch with almost all of them.

41
7-Up Green Hemingray insulator No. 43 (CD #214), c. 1925. Glass, 4½" high

42
Red amber F. M. Locke & Co. insulator (CD #287.1), c. 1910. Glass, 3¾" high

43
Carnival Hemingray Co. insulator No. 19 (CD #162), c. 1934. Glass, 4" high

44
Peacock blue H. G. Company insulator (CD #164), c. 1900. Glass, 4" high

45
Golden amber Hemingray No. 8 insulator (CD #112.4), c. 1895. Glass, 3½" high

46
Electric blue Hemingray insulator (CD #257), c. 1910. Glass, 5¼" high

41

42

43

44

45

46

47
Flashed amber
Hemingray insulator No.
600 (CD #216), c. 1941.
4" high

48
Yellow H. G. Company
insulator (CD #162),
c. 1900. 4" high

49
Electric blue H. G.
Company insulator (CD
#162), c. 1905. 4" high

50
Inky cobalt H. G.
Company insulator No.
19 (CD #162), c. 1925.
4" high

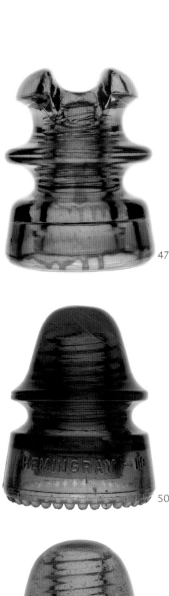

51
Olive green patent
December 19, 1871,
insulator (CD #134),
c. 1880. 4" high

52
Purple patent December
19, 1871, No. 2 insulator
(CD #132), c. 1875.
4¼" high

53
Yellow amber H. G.
Company insulator (CD
#145), c. 1885. 4¼" high

54
Peacock blue H. G.
Company insulator (CD
#151), c. 1895. 4¼" high

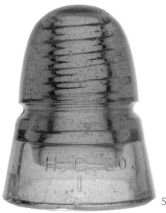
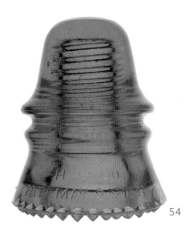

55
Green with amber swirls
Hemingray insulator No.
4 (CD #124), c. 1905.
4" high

56
Cornflower blue patent
December 19, 1871,
insulator (CD #126.4),
c. 1885. 4½" high

57
Dark purple patent
December 19, 1871,
insulator No. 1 (CD
#131–34), c. 1871.
4" high

58
Orange amber H. G.
Company insulator (CD
#133), c. 1890. 4" high

HOME MADE
BEEF SAUSAGES

SHEEPS LIVER

YUGOSLAVIAN

59
Group of butcher display
tags for a variety of
meats, c. 1945. Printed
plastic with steel pin,
each 2¼" high

JELLIED VEAL

CASSEROLE
STEAK

CHOICE MUTTON

BUTCHER DISPLAY tags for meat cuts went out with the neighborhood butcher. Meats that come from today's markets are packaged on Styrofoam trays, clinically wrapped and pre-cut into industrially conceived serving portions. In a large supermarket, the selection of meat cuts that are made available is determined at corporate headquarters. In Manhattan, everything may be obtained at a price, and I have bonded with my neighborhood butchers over the years. They have been like members of the family to me and mine. They are a lifeline to the past as well as the surest way to have your meat cut and prepped any way you want it.

> As transhumance gives way to trance
> And shaman gives way to Santa
> And butcher's string gives way to vacuum pack
> And the ineffable gives way to the unsaid . . . .
> I give way to you.
>   Paul Muldoon, *Moy Sand and Gravel*
> (New York: Farrar, Straus & Giroux, 2002), 37.

"I'll take five pounds of that rib roast. Please cut it off the bone and tie it back on for roasting, but wrap the short ribs separately and grind the deckle." There's mutual respect exchanged when you and your butcher engage. When I am living in my rural home in upstate New York, however, I have only one choice to make about meat, and that is to which supermarket I will go. Each has a "prime" meat section where someone in a white jacket stands behind the showcase and hands you pre-cut ¾-inch pork chops.

"Could you please cut five 1½ -inch loin pork chops for me?" "Do you have skirt steak today?" "May I please have six chicken breasts split, bone out, skin on?" The answer to all these questions is "No." Chicken breasts without bones are chicken cutlets, and they only come without skin. Fajitas and Roumanian steak can have the flavor and texture that is authentically theirs only if they are made from skirt steak. But no dice with these corporate ciphers in white jackets. Pork chops are cut into ¾-inch chops. I have tried charm and humor to find out when the motherlode of meat arrives so that I might have something "custom"cut. I have never been able to ascertain if the meat is delivered prepacked or if guidelines permit no deviation from the norm. The printed meat tag on a steel spike thrust into a saddle of lamb, awaiting its destiny as single- or double-cut lamb chops or a crown or rack of lamb is a thing of the past. As standard rules are imposed, our choices dwindle. The straightforward proclamation of variety that these tags announce is a remnant of times gone by. Some are still around because they are more durable than waxed paper.

> One day last spring the fire in the kitchen woodstove went out and was never relit. I didn't record the date, because some endings are lost in a crowd of beginnings, passing unnoticed until months later, when the oversight seems almost melancholy.
>   Verlyn Klinkenborg, *The Rural Life*
> (New York: Little, Brown & Co., 2002), 111.

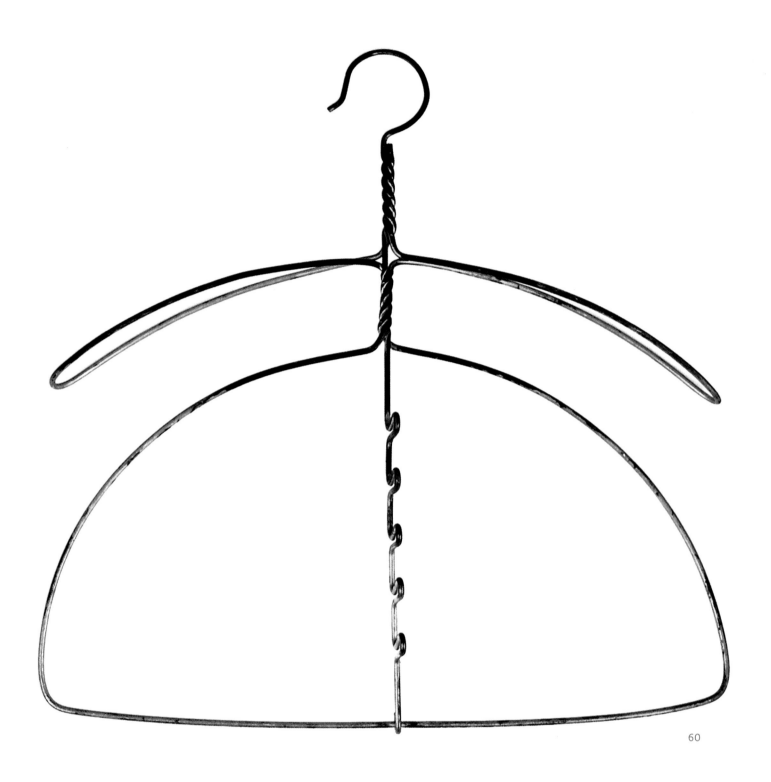

60

HANGERS CAME in with the closet. In old homes there were no built-in closets. Clothing was placed on hooks or doorknobs or folded and put into drawers or thrown over furniture until it was needed again. Closets were a Victorian idea, consistent with the spirit of putting personal items and most of one's anatomy out of sight. The idea of a "skeleton in the closet" grew up with the development of the hanger. I have seen as many inventive hanger styles as varieties of mousetrap. These days there are a few standard hangers: some are general purpose; others are specifically molded for shirts, jackets, or suits; and others have clamps for pants or skirts.

61

62

60
Wire hanger for lady's jacket and skirt with five hooks for other garments, 1922. 14½" high

61
Child's hanger, c. 1920. Screen-printed wood and steel, 7" high

62
Clamp-type hanger for man's trousers, c. 1920. Wood (imprinted with advertising) and steel, 8" high

63
Wing advertising hanger,
c. 1930. Printed steel
and steel wire, 9½" high

64
Extendable clamp
hanger (closed and
open positions), 1949.
Printed steel, 6¾–11"
long. Grim's Pres-gard
Company, USA

65
Dress hanger with
crocheted cover, c. 1940.
Wood and steel, 5" high

66
Shirt hanger (back),
c. 1925. Wood
(imprinted with
advertising) and
steel, 8" high

67
Glove hanger, c. 1950.
Aluminum and steel,
13" high

63

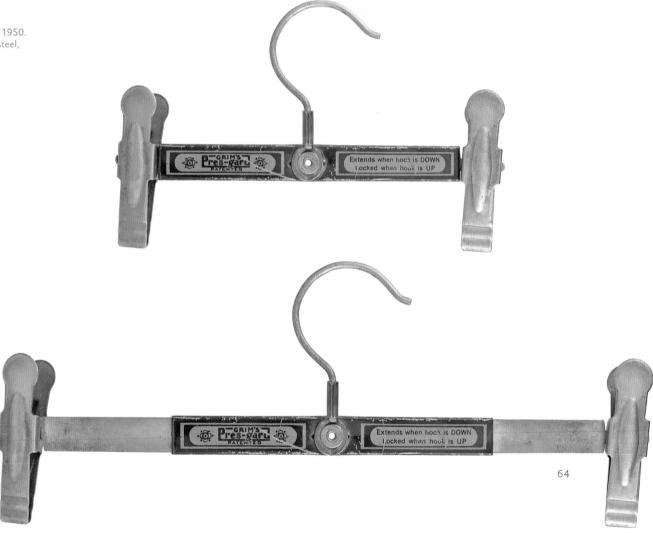

64

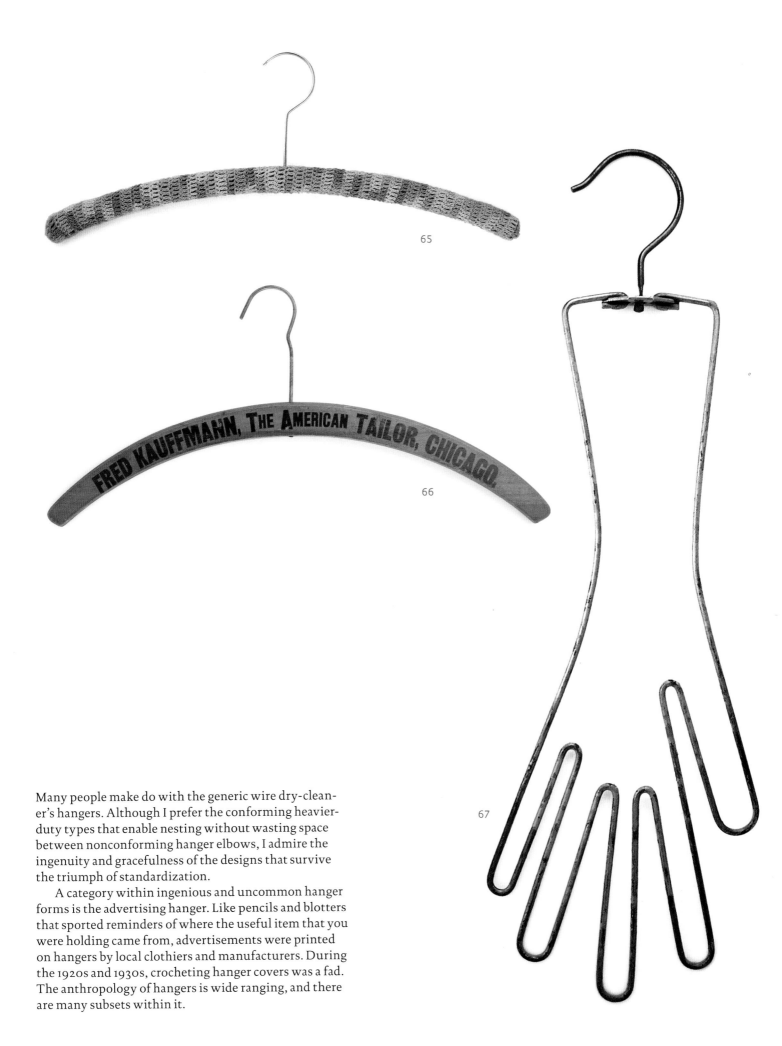

Many people make do with the generic wire dry-cleaner's hangers. Although I prefer the conforming heavier-duty types that enable nesting without wasting space between nonconforming hanger elbows, I admire the ingenuity and gracefulness of the designs that survive the triumph of standardization.

A category within ingenious and uncommon hanger forms is the advertising hanger. Like pencils and blotters that sported reminders of where the useful item that you were holding came from, advertisements were printed on hangers by local clothiers and manufacturers. During the 1920s and 1930s, crocheting hanger covers was a fad. The anthropology of hangers is wide ranging, and there are many subsets within it.

68
Clothespin, c. 1990.
Machine-cut wood and
spring-loaded steel wire,
2¾" high

69
Clothespin, c. 1910.
Hand-cut and lathe-
turned wood, 5¼" high

70
Clothespin, c. 1900.
Hand-cut wood,
reinforced with steel
band, 5½" high

71
Clothespin, c. 1910.
Hand-cut and drilled
wood, 4" high

72
Clothespin, c. 1900.
Hand-cut wood, 6" high

73
Clothespin, c. 1890.
Made and sold by
Gypsies. Hand-cut wood,
reinforced with steel
band, 5" high

74
Clothespin, c. 1900.
Steel spring-loaded and
reinforced chestnut,
3" high

75
Group of clothespins,
1880–1950. Hand- and
machine-made, 3–9"
high

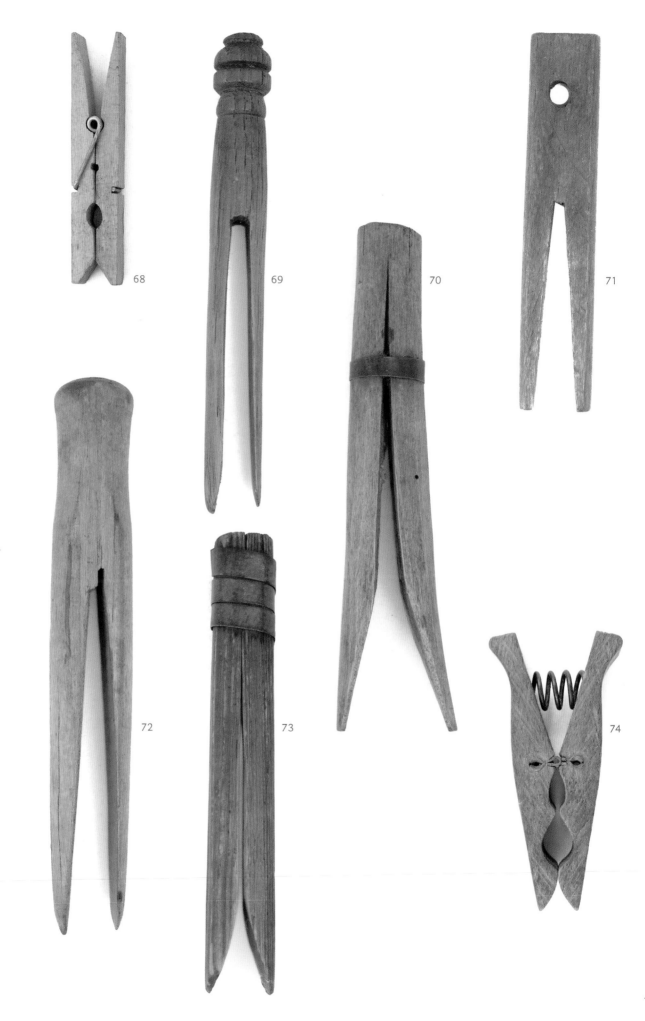

A CLOTHESPIN is a forked device for compelling an article of wet clothing into a temporary liaison with a length of rope, usually out of doors. The object was to dry the laundry. In rural areas this occurred in the fresh air. In urban areas evaporation transpired in the available breeze and ambient soot. Rain was a setback in both geographic locations. The washing machine and dryer replaced the clothesline, and the clothespin had nothing to do anymore.

When I was a child my maternal grandmother lived in a "railroad flat" in a tenement building at 251 East Broadway. Beside her washtub/bathtub/kitchen sink, a pulley device with a clothesline was affixed to the kitchen window frame. The other end of the pulley and clothesline device was anchored to somebody else's window frame in the tenement building next door. You didn't pick your neighbors. This side-by-side exterior space was threaded with a network of clotheslines on pulleys. There was unspoken reciprocity; everyone left everyone else's drying workpants and undershirts alone. The homely necessity of drying laundry crossed all ethnic boundaries as well as self-consciousness about the size and quality of one's underwear.

Clothesline culture was the great equalizer in a raucous immigrant neighborhood in which no two people agreed about much. There was neighborly conversation and copious gossip through this most social of windows. A fraying clothesline became a jump rope, and reliable clothespins were essential because of limited access to the trash-laden courtyard below. It was unpleasant to retrieve a fallen garment through the dank and dismal basement, if indeed it was still there when you noticed that it was no longer where you had put it. I remember a great variety of clothespin styles, ranging from forked pegs to clip devices with springs. I noticed a spectrum of hanging methods as well. Some women hung clothes in a back bend (securely clipped but longer in drying since fabric was doubled back against itself over the line) while others took the chance of pinching the garment over the rope at the top, then clipping (thus drying faster). Those who had fewer clothespins overlapped articles at the edges in a two-for-one spirit. Hauteur is fragile when your bloomers are hanging in plain sight.

75

1

chapter 5

Plumb Wore Out

AN ERASER comes to mind as the most graphic example of a tool that becomes a little smaller, a bit less of itself as it is used. In my youthful pencil-pushing years, I cannot remember one instance of my eraser outlasting its pencil. Never a pencil biter, I did not hesitate to give the brass rim around the eraser a toothy squeeze to propel the last millimeter of eraser forth for that final correction before the pencil was declared unfit. There are other objects that wear themselves out, performing less vivid disappearing acts while engaged in their intended function. Washboards and the clothing they abraded fall into this category.

The 1940s and 1950s were decades in which there were washing machines in laundromats; but that was a biweekly excursion and many things had to be done by hand. Who had enough handkerchiefs, socks, and underwear to last that long? Washboards did the dirty work in the pre–T-shirt, pre-polyester era when wash-day required mother's full attention. On Monday, laundry was separated into a portion that was sturdy enough for the washing machine, mangle, or extractor;

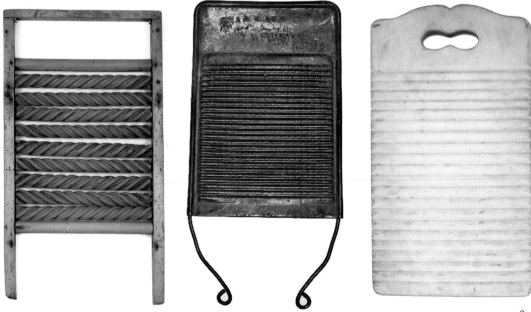

then further segregated into white and colored articles; and then separated into what could be put into the dryer (very little) and what had to be ironed or starched in the bathtub before ironing. My father's and brother's shirts, like my mother's and my blouses, certainly required starch, which came in a navy blue box with crisp white letters: LINIT. The box was filled with white pebbles of potato starch that, when diluted into a suspension, made milky white water into which the clothes were submerged, then wrung out by hand and dried. By Tuesday the still-damp or sprinkled clothes were ready to be ironed. When I came home from school, I ironed the handkerchiefs and shirts. The development of synthetic fabrics, which do not require ironing, as well as less formal apparel codes and washing machines and dryers with various settings made laundry less tedious and demanding. For purely nostalgic reasons I'd like to find a box of LINIT.

My mother kept a washboard in the cabinet beneath the kitchen sink. It was of the wood-frame, mass-produced variety; and the rectangle that saw frictive action was made of rippled and blue-green textured glass. In hardware stores, rows of mass-produced washboards were stacked against each other in a couple of sizes and styles, either wood frame with metal or glass undulations or corrugated metal and frame all-in-one. The ripples simulated and complemented the clenched fingers of the maternal fist that scrubbed the soiled clothing. Primitive by today's standards, the washboard and basin made possible the relocation of the washing process from the stones-at-the-riverbank model as the washing site to one's own kitchen. Social interaction moved from the shoreline to the clothesline.

During the eighteenth through the early twentieth centuries, families settled in rural areas where hardware came only infrequently either by purposeful import or peddler's wagon. As a result, the

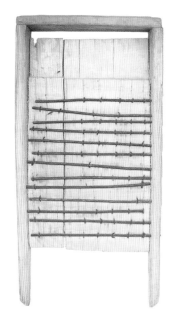

1
Pencils with spent erasers, 1949–61. 3½–4¾" long

2
Group of three washboards, 1900–1935. Hand-carved wood, marble, and manufactured galvanized steel, 21–24½" high

3
Group of six washboards, 1840–1917. Hand-carved wood, glazed ceramic, cast iron, and manufactured galvanized steel, 17½–24½" high

washboard was often unique and handcrafted of whatever was at hand. The unconventional materials that make up the washboards in my collection include cast iron, stoneware, exotic woods, and gravestone marble. They occur in some nifty and ingenious styles in which the action ribs rotate freely or are carved or cast into efficient soil-assaulting textures; "washboard roads" are named for the surface of this tool. Owing to the inevitable wearing down of the parts as they were functionally employed and the caustic action of lye-based soaps, it is surprising that any remain in their washboard form. Some were reframed as their supporting elements gave way and their remaining parts were recycled into other uses.

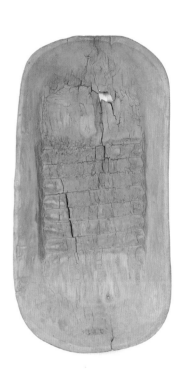

4

4
Group of three washboards, 1840–1900. Hand-carved wood, 17½–24½" high

5
Caustic laundry soap typically used with washboards, c. 1900. 2¼" high

5

ON A FEW occasions I have found a piece of companion soap to a washboard. Each time it has been a yellow caustic soap that retained its straight-sided cubic quality because it grated the fabric against the rippled washboard surface. Laundry soap was a tough gritty tool without emollients, and it left the scrubber's hands bleached, rough, and raw. Its only other recommended uses were cleaning grease off auto mechanics' hands and removing the irritating sap that caused poison ivy to blister skin. As the washboard was replaced by the washing machine, soap evolution seems to have headed in two directions: detergents

that dissolved easily while mechanically cleansing clothes and soaps meant for gentler contact with the human body.

Robert G. is an artist, a painter fascinated by the way objects age and wear down. He collects nubbins of soap that are too small to be comfortably functional. Unlike the yellow laundry soap of yesteryear, these soap shards are softly curved and as polished as beach pebbles. Many of these soap bars started out with curved edges but all were molded from creamy skin-anointing unguents that yield to the human hand. Robert arranges his soap ostraca in much the same

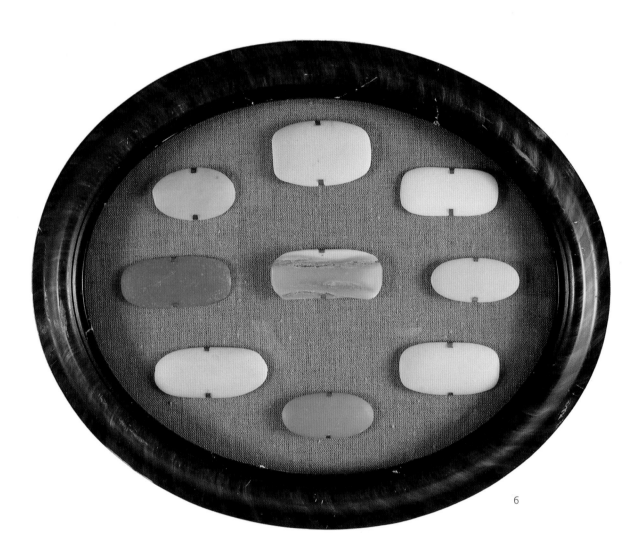

6

6
Framed soap shards,
1995–2004. 16" high

7
Group of soap shards,
1995–99. 2½–3¾" high

7

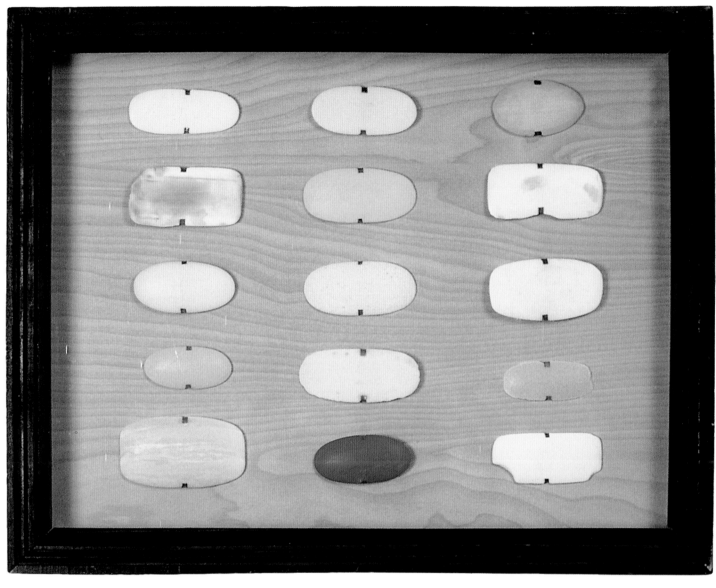

way that Victorians displayed geological specimens
or fossils or seashell collections. They are framed
in poetic passages that are evocative of the curiosity cabinets of an earlier time. Before I knew Robert,
each sliver of my last soap bar was merged with the
next as a smaller Siamese twin. Now there is symme-
try to my lathering, and something that would have
inevitably disappeared with use has instead become a
lasting and artful artifact of our time.

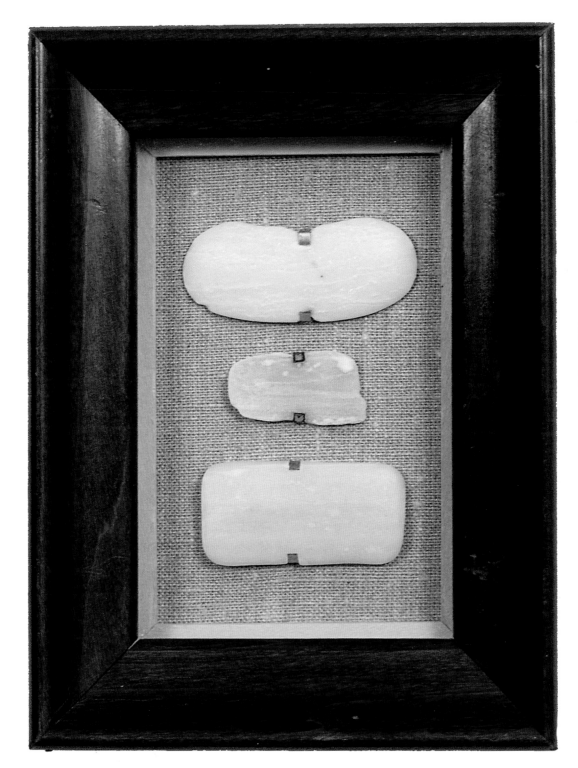

8
Framed soap shards,
1997–99. 13¾" high

9
Framed soap shards,
1995–98. 8" high

9

10
Group of choppers with
hand-carved handles and
wrought iron blades,
c. 1820–70. 3¾–8¼"
high

FOOD CHOPPERS are related to washboards. Each is a singular interpretation of a tool that comes to us trailing visual tales of invention, created by a maker for a specific situation or person or bowl with materials at hand. A chopper, like a washboard, wore down a bit every time it was employed to chop food, as did its partner, the bowl. Every time the dulled blade was resharpened, its substance was reduced. All of my choppers show careful intention in forging and a variety of handle constructions. Many have initials or a date engraved, stamped, or gouged with pride by the maker, and all show traces of multiple sharpenings in the diminishment of its business end. The handles show signs of use and wear, but contact with the rough working hand isn't as punishing as repetitive impact against a honed edge.

> The collection does not displace attention to the past; rather, the past is at the service of the collection… the past lends authenticity to the collection.
>
> Susan Stewart, *On Longing* (Durham, N. C. and London: Duke University Press, 1993), 151.

THERE ARE far fewer old wood bowls than choppers, which speaks to the consequences of repeated impact and minute wood fibers in your chopped liver. Those that remain are generally made of burl, a rounded hard wood excrescence that grows on certain trees. These tree burls, often found on maples, are random occurrences and have a distinctive texture that is prized and often very thinly sliced to be used as veneer on wood furniture. They also have a resinous hardness that is particularly suited to standing up to the steely concussive blows of a chopper. As a matter of practicality, in rural kitchens in eighteenth- and nineteenth-century America, chopping bowls made of other materials did not outlive their choppers. The chopper and its bowl were engaged in the same reciprocal reductive dynamic as the washboard and its soap.

11

13

14

11
Burl bowl (side), c. 1870.
8" high

12
Burl on gingko tree in situ, 2004. 22" diameter

13
Burl bowl, c. 1885.
12" diameter

14
Burl bowl, c. 1870.
Maple, 15" diameter

15

16

17

RICHARD F., WHO is a sculptor, has an impressive collection of lawn sprinklers. Nowadays, when we observe lawns being mechanically showered, we focus on the water, not the device from which it emanates. This was not always so. Traditional Old World landscaping was usually contained within hedgerows, stone walls, or fences. Excepting Versailles and palatial gardens, European lawns are not sprawling. As the concept of American neighborhoods evolved, Richard explains, the birth of the lawn sprinkler became a necessity for lawn maintenance "because the lawn was an extension of the house into the neighborhood." His earliest sprinkler dates from 1894 and is made of cast iron with few moving parts.

As American lawn culture came of age, sprinkler technology became more sophisticated, with rotating parts that spun, spouted, oscillated, gyrated, and sprayed. In the 1920s, figural sprinklers were developed in the forms of turtles, frogs, alligators, peacocks and ducks. In the 1930s, a duck sprinkler with a 360-degree revolving head was only to be outdone by the painted Deco blond mermaid on a red seashell base holding a trident handle fount. In the 1940s and 1950s, the cowboy (a great rarity) was produced at the same time as a variety of tractors that showered while locomoting across the lawn enabled by complicated gear mechanisms and many moving parts. These models were expensive to manufacture, requiring labor-intensive assembly, and were produced and sold across the United States from the East Coast to Lincoln, Nebraska, to Bellingham, Washington, speaking to the house pride of an era in a nation of lawns.

America didn't outgrow lawns, but simpler, less expensive, more efficient systems surfaced to keep our lawns green. None of them included paint that flaked, or cast iron or other metals as connectors that oxidized and accumulated mineral deposits hampering or styming the essential spritz. Fittings and moving parts plumb wore out or broke down. Corroded nozzles and swiveling duck necks were not easily replaced. Changes in temperature caused leakage and seepage. The whale sprinkler and the walking lawn sprinkler were victims of the greening of American lawn culture. Those beauties gave way to low-maintenance systems that delivered water expeditiously and effectively to a cheaper production standard.

15
Group of figural lawn sprinklers, 1925–50. Painted cast iron and brass with brass sprinkler heads, 4¼–9" high

16
Duck lawn sprinkler with swiveling head, c. 1938. Painted cast aluminum, 9" high

17
Mermaid lawn sprinkler, c. 1930. Painted cast iron, 14" high

18
Tractor "walking" lawn sprinkler, c. 1950. Painted cast iron and aluminum with revolving brass sprinkler head, 11" high

19
Tractor *Whale Sprinkler*, c. 1950. Painted cast iron, aluminum, and brass moving sprinkler head, 10" high

18

19

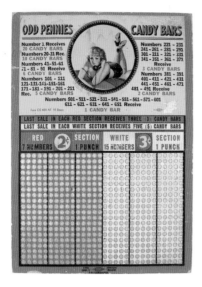

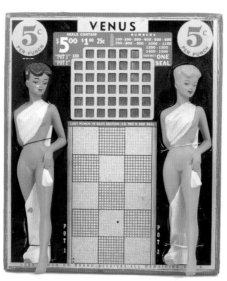

THE EVOLUTION of the punchboard is the story of another aspect of American culture: taking a chance, gaming for pennies with your grocery, bar, or gasoline change. Wager five cents on a chance to win ten gallons of gasoline, Planter's Cocktail Peanuts, a Zippo lighter, or Apollo Chocolates. A 1939 Paramount Grand Prize punchboard offers a five-cent chance to win a fifty-cent grand prize or a one-dollar jackpot. This punchboard, constructed of cardboard with a veneer of attention-nabbing primary color lithography, is typical of its genre. It is 12 inches high by 4½ inches across by 1 inch deep, with hundreds of tissue-covered holes in which nestle tightly accordion-folded fortune-cookie-sized papers with a number printed on each. The pleated paper was eased out of its cylindrical cell by means of a metal punch that resembles a steel wire key with a squared-off nail-like shaft. Each punchboard came with a punch that resided in its own paper-sealed cubbyhole on the rear beside the hanger hardware. Once the punch was bared for use, the punch and board crossed hands with the wager money and small change was in big-chance territory. The winning numbers were printed on the face of the punchboard itself, so gratification or disappointment was immediate and the lucky winner could claim the prize on the spot from the person behind the counter.

Wood-plank punchboards with a series of drilled holes in which nested rolled papers describing the outcomes of as many wagers originated in the Colonial American tavern, which says something about our entrepreneurial spirit. Hanky-panky abounded with the homemade versions. A punchboard renaissance occurred in 1905, when technology was developed to make tampering apparent by broken tissue seals. Machine-made punchboards put the chance back in the game. Merchandise prizes were offered increasingly in lieu of cash during the 1930s and 1940s. Punchboards were pretty much outlawed in most states by the early 1950s, which speaks to finely tuned attitudes toward sin and propriety, politics, and collecting taxes on gaming activities. Pull-tabs in casinos are the last remnant of dead-center punchboard culture. In their time, punchboards, like advertising pencils and blotters, were quiet but insistent venues for product sales pitches and brand-name recognition. A few virgin punchboards are still around. Wasted, perforated cardboard tablets were discarded; spent punchboards inadvertently set aside from trashing were virtually finished off by dampness.

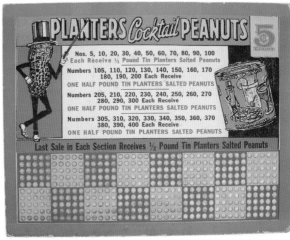

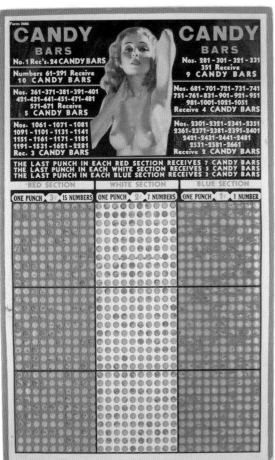

21

22

23

24

20
Group of four punchboards and page of punchboard ads, 1915–50. Printed paper and cardboard, 8½–15¼" high

21
Paramount punchboard, 1942. Printed paper and cardboard, 12½" high

22
Planters Peanuts punchboard (front and back), 1925. Printed paper and cardboard, 6¾" high. Globe Manufacturing Company, USA

23
Candy Bars punchboard, c. 1929. Printed paper and cardboard, 11" high. Charles A. Brewer & Sons, Chicago, Illinois

24
Bar Reaper punchboard, 1945. Printed paper and cardboard, 8¼" high. Union Made

MY FIRST encounter with rubber stamps was in 1944 in my maternal grandmother's railroad flat on East Broadway when my mother's younger brothers were in the U.S. armed forces. Having tired of watching street action from a windowsill perch, I was directed to a baseboard drawer in an old paint-caked cupboard. Behind the shoe polish was a box that contained rubber letters, numbers, symbols and phrases, in reverse on wooden squares, each with a handle. They smelled of dried rubber, and I was told that I could "write" with them. They were my Uncle Harry's aid in vending small sundries, and there were voluted stamps that said *per* and *for* and *as is*. I didn't figure out until later in life that this particular set of rubber stamps was created for salesmen with illegible handwriting or those who wished to appear distanced from the handmade sign. Panache and sophistication could be acquired by stamping.

I've never lost my fascination for the rubber stamp and its vocabulary of graceful outlines. Only recently did I realize that the reason one rubber-stamp set lacked the stamps between one, two, five, ten, twenty, fifty, and one hundred was that it was a bank set for marking packages of bills and that the numbers in between weren't really "missing" at all. There are no thirty-dollar bills. Rubber stamps for peddlers, vendors, and shopkeepers were an adaptable offshoot of the stencil. Generally, packaged raw materials and component parts that were shipped to wholesalers and manufacturers did not require elaborate or seductive labeling. Most barrels, crates, and boxes were stenciled with the purveyor's name and address. Sometimes this data was stamped with a wood block or metal stamp that left a tolerably legible impression. Beginning with Charles Goodyear's 1844 patent for "vulcanizing" rubber, a number of successive technological innovations enabled the development of customized rubber stamps to repetitively deposit a detailed text or pictorial impression upon most surfaces. By the time of my first rubber-stamp encounter, there was a growing market in "educational" rubber-stamp sets for children.

Although processing strides made rubber more manageable than it had been, as rubber products of that era aged, they usually dried out, hardened, and disintegrated. The inks that made their impressions possible contained damaging solvents, and thickeners used to make opaque ink impressions tended to clog the negative spaces around the stamp's image and render the message uncommunicative. When left to harden, these inks destroyed the clarity of the stamp as did mechanical cleaning and aggressive solvents. Consequently, old rubber stamps are rare and valuable treasures.

25

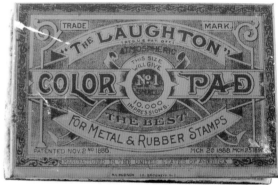

26

27

28

29

WASHINGTON

LINCOLN

30

31

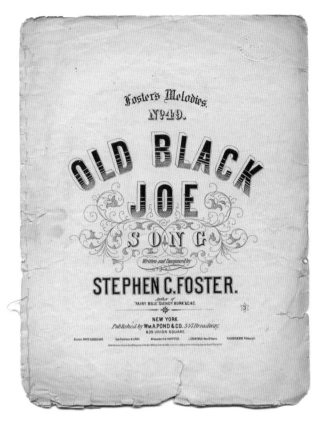

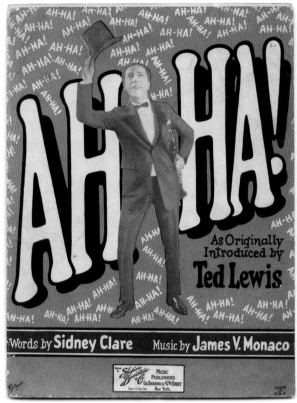

32
Group of sheet music, 1860–1939. Printed paper, 12¼–13⅓" high. New York City

33
Group of Dennison's tape, paper, and cloth for mending sheet music, 20th century. ½–2" high

34
Group of sheet music, 1903–17. Printed paper, 13½–13¾" high. New York City

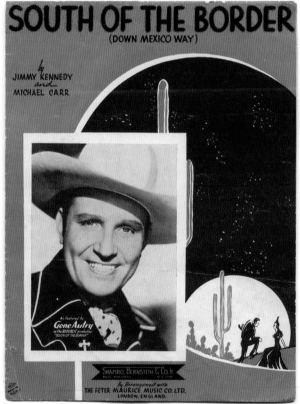

SHEET MUSIC is a paper phenomenon that was meant to be used, and it was. Sheet music reached its zenith during the 1850s through the 1940s when musical evenings in the parlor were part of ordinary life. The radio and phonograph gradually came into parlor play, but the paper on which the accompanying music to the sing-along was printed wasn't acid free. Wood pulp paper, on which most late-nineteenth- and twentieth-century sheet music was printed, was ephemeral in nature; it became yellowed and brittle. Use produced stains, folds, rents, and creases, and took a certain toll on the spine and edges. I have Stephen Foster songs on sheet music from 1860 that have been sewn repeatedly along their spines. Later, taping the torn sheet was a quicker mend, but adhesives inevitably destroyed the paper to which they adhered.

Within about one hundred years, sheet music evolved from comparatively austere black ink engravings on white rag paper to colorful lithographed wood-pulp folios. Sheet music matured from simple to elaborate title pages announcing song title, publisher, composer, arranger, and copyright date (required by the U.S. copyright law of 1871). Beyond the credits and the musical message, sheet music became pictorially complex. Hindsight grants the perspective to observe how completely the title pages synthesized the sentiments, fashions, politics, and attitudes of place and time. Graphically, they crystallized and conveyed volumes of layered information through typeface, costume, caricature, photographs, referents in the background, slogans, and product advertisement.

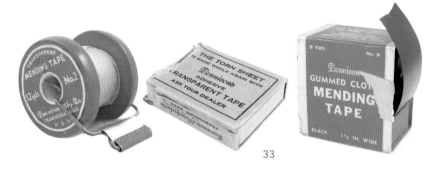

33

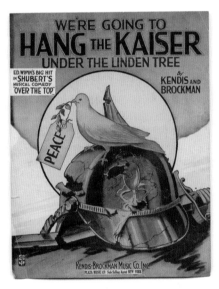

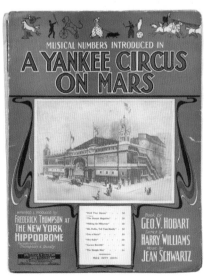

34

Group of soda fountain
show cards, 1949–52.
Lithographed heavy die-
cut cardboard, 4¼–9½"
high

SODA FOUNTAIN show cards used die-cut images and lush chromatic lithography to lure the susceptible toward self-indulgence. I remember Riccardi's Ice Cream Company show cards in my Bronx neighborhood candy store hanging over the grill so that while sitting at the counter awaiting the delivery of a BLT or grilled cheese sandwich, I could visually anticipate the heavenly possibility of a hot fudge sundae. Over the years, the allure of the frappé and ice cream soda show cards were compromised by the card's opportunistic positioning. The accumulation of grease-bound fuzz enhanced by grill vapors rising from America's lunch counters did little for the luster of the image of chocolate ice cream soda froth. Wiping down, albeit infrequently, didn't improve the integrity of the cardboard that conveyed the image. If those beckoning confections were safely placed behind the diner, they lost their power to tempt and thus their raison d'être. Only those cards that were stored undisplayed remain intact; and since there are fewer and fewer unplumbed candy store basements and commercial printer warehouses, soda fountain show cards are a diminishing species. The Woolworth Company lunch counter in my neighborhood put its show cards in metal frames under glass. In the short run, they showed some resistance to the assaults of the grill, but later they hosted fungal nurseries beneath the glass.

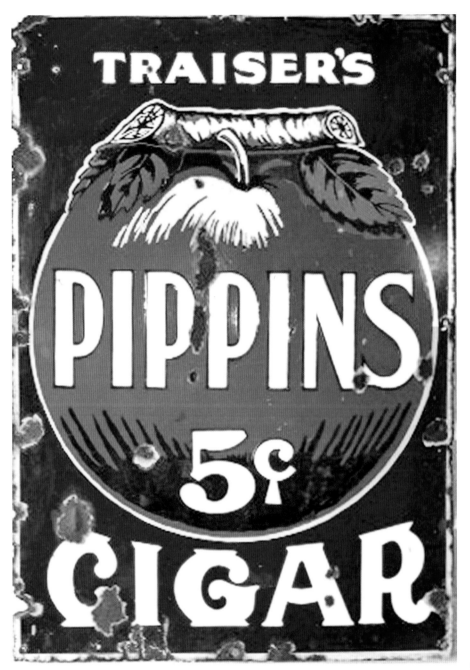

36
Traiser's cigar sign, 1900.
Enamel on steel, 33"
high

MY HOME is safe haven to a broadly ranging collection
of PICTORIAL SIGNS. Like sheet music, these signs
convey a great deal more about the culture from
which they came than do their literal messages. These
signs are now used on my interior walls as paintings
and are displayed everywhere. Most of them have
seen hard lives in the exterior world. Acid rain
notwithstanding, their images are in various states of
material imperfection and disrepair owing to rust,
peeling paint, abrasion, graffiti, and having been
used for target practice.

37
Horn paint sign, 1940.
Die-cut printed steel,
14" high

38
Tydol automotive oil sign,
1931. Embossed die-cut
printed steel, 5¼" high

39
Cook's paint and varnish
sign, 1925. Enamel on
steel, 13¾" diameter

40
Philip Morris cigarette
sign (Johnny the
Bellboy), 1948.
Die-cut painted steel,
44" high

37

38

Each has discrete visual punch and a cultural story to convey. We have a Coca-Cola sign on our barn that seems to have been in an arrested poetic moment that has lasted for twenty-five years. The aesthetics of disintegration seems to be the language through which these signs speak. Aside from their march toward material dissolution, they are endangered as the technology of signage moves toward the immateriality of cyber ads.

39

40

41

42

THE RESIDUAL benefits of Victorian energy, experimentation, and invention are with us today, in unbroken connection, in our transportation systems and educational formats, our consumerism and our housing. Our homes, and their styles, forms, fixtures, and appliances, emerged between the 1870s and early 1900s; and how we live today is in many ways an evolution of Victorian ideas and ideals. In this march of progress toward today, certain artifactual inventions did not survive their era of conception.

Flash-in-the-pan fossils of eight-toed wannabes that didn't work out are epitomized by hummingbird love tokens. The fashion conceits of the Victorians commanded the attention of the world when the young queen took the throne. The British people followed the royal family in both narrative and action to the best of their means. If Queen Victoria wore jewelry made of stuffed hummingbirds, some of her attentive following did the expected. Consequently, I am the awestruck owner of a ruby-throated hummingbird head with inlaid ruby eyes and a silver-sheathed beak that emerges from a silver wire nest to which a silver-brooch back has been affixed. The shimmering ruby and copper throat feathers are nicely offset by the gleaming ruby eyes and the silver surround. The whole object is the size of a quarter. The Queen's hummingbird hat ornaments sometimes took the form of whole birds with wings outspread, as if alighting on her bonnet. The convention of actual hummingbird love tokens took off among those so inclined. Others made do with faux birds of false feathers and facsimiles of the materials of conventional jewelry. Although they were given as a token of affection, the actual wearing of the love token must have posed unique apparel problems as damaging overclothes and unexpected hugs had to be avoided. I've seen the jewelry depicted in fashion prints of the period. The model is always facing the viewer wearing the brooch on the front of a dress or as an adornment on a hat.

I have seen only three of these extraordinary babies in the flesh over a span of nineteen years and felt inexplicably compelled to own each of them. The Victoria and Albert Museum in London probably has storage cases filled with hummingbird love tokens that they don't want anti-vivisectionists to get wind of. My third tiny trophy came in a custom leather-and-velvet clamshell case with a spring catch. Nevertheless, the prize has suffered the vicissitudes of wear and its feathers are ruffled. It is about the size of a nickel with ruby eyes and a gold-sheathed beak, a ruby head, and a copper breast; a gold branch and leaf provide its mount and the support for the brooch back.

This fragile and scarce jewelry form is replete with information about the time in which it was conceived. It simultaneously informs, supports, and dispels cultural assumptions that we might have made without knowing about it. The distinctive singular evidence, to eye and mind, in the bearing of this love token—as in the grace and wear of a washboard and in the codified pedagogy of sheet music—broadcasts material testimony of the past. There aren't many of these things left.

41
Hummingbird head brooch, c. 1875. Set with ruby eyes and silver beak sheath on silver nest mount, 2" diameter. England

42
Hummingbird head brooch (two views), c. 1875. Set with ruby eyes on a gold crossed arrow mount, 1¼" high. England

43
Hummingbird head brooch (two views), c. 1875. Set with ruby eyes and gold beak sheath on gold twig mount, 1½" high. England

43

Taste Changed

IF YOU'VE ever been doubled over trying to budge a tight boot from the wrong angle, you understand that we are just not anatomically constructed to remove our own boots. To say "he died with his boots on" is not so far-fetched. My preferred means of boot removal is a family member purposefully tugging at my heel and gently sliding my boot off with a heel-cupping motion. But what if there is no one in the bunkhouse upon your return from two weeks on the range, having slept in your boots after branding steers and kicking cowpies?

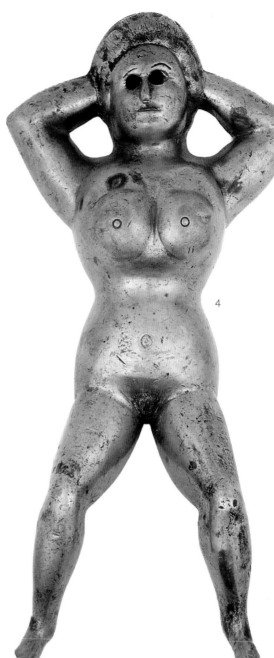

Your handiest and most expeditious resource would be a Naughty Nellie bootjack. Made of cast iron (infrequently of cast bronze), she was often over-painted wearing lace-up boots in the scant garb of a showgirl, bather, circus performer, or loose woman. She invariably reclines with her arms behind her head and a "come hither" look in her eye. Her legs are upraised, spread, and at your service. The heel-yanking action was facilitated by stepping on her head and upper torso with your other foot to steady the bootjack as you eased your booted heel between her grasping legs.

Bootjacks were a common functional household tool in frontier and Victorian America. Primitive bootjacks were often made of wood and essentially had two heel-grasping projections and a supporting wedge. The most frequent bootjack figural form, homemade and manufactured in all materials, appears to have been a fanciful beetle with two antennae seeing to the heel of your boot.

Most bootjacks are under a foot long (no pun intended), about four inches off the floor at the raised end, and are conventionally unimaginative. Naughty Nellie bootjacks are positively scandalous in some

5
Naughty Nellie from
the estate of Hugh
McCullough, c. 1860.
Hand-painted cast iron,
9½" high

6
Naughty Nellie with
chastity belt, c. 1870.
Cast iron, 10¾" high

incarnations. One Nellie is attired in blue-and-red calf-length stockings and a strapless red belted leotard with a split crotch. Her raised pubes, with sgraffito hair, is painted rather more flamboyantly than the hair on her head. She wears red garters and matching wristbands. This baby is from the estate of Hugh McCullough, Secretary of the Treasury under Lincoln and then Andrew Johnson. Maybe she never left his dressing room. I would have more likely expected a sedate and intricately carved Walnut beetle bootjack with an inset carpet step-down.

Who was the Nellie for whom these namesakes are monuments? Naughty Nellies invite aid in your

time of need; and when not actively employed, they moonlighted as doorstops. I have a Naughty Nellie wearing a chastity belt and another with a Caesarean scar. Relatively few casts have been struck; the creative expression is in the surface decoration, the paint job. Only reproductions have a casting mark and none of mine bear any maker's marks. Each Naughty Nellie speaks as articulately about her time as the Venus of Willendorf represents hers. It's just not politically correct to step on a woman's face to remove your boot these days. Naughty Nellies that remain are usually quaint paperweights, remnants of days long past.

7
Naughty Nellie with
Caesarean scar, c. 1875.
Cast iron, 9¾" high

8
Naughty Nellie, c. 1880.
Hand-painted cast iron,
9¼" high

HUNTSVILLE, ALABAMA.

HILLCREST MOTOR COURT

PHONE JE. 4-9184

FRENCH DRESSING

SWIPED FROM

9
Group of pinup ashtrays
with advertising, c. 1950.
4–5¼" high

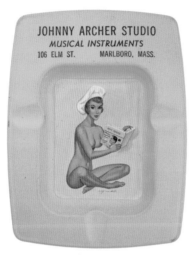

JOHNNY ARCHER STUDIO
MUSICAL INSTRUMENTS
106 ELM ST.   MARLBORO, MASS.

SWIPED FROM

BROCKPOR', NEW YORK

VIC'S ESSO

NE 7-9880

EDDIE'S CAFE

Hillsgrove-1-1099

CATCHY NUMBER

1288 Greenwich Ave.

Apponaug, R. I.

HOME COOKING

SWIPED FROM

RT. 69   GLEN GARDNER, N. J.

TWO SISTERS KITCHEN

AMERICAN FEMALE fantasy types have commandeered advertisements since the 1880s. Consider Coca-Cola trays depicting American beauties in a running series from 1892 through 1950 on their annually issued trays. During the 1940s, America churned out images of scantily clad generic white women in various stages of undress to call attention to the products or services being advertised on blotters, calendars, and ashtrays. The blotters and calendars found their way to the workshop or garage or the son's room, the expected place of idealized *femmes déshabillé*. These girlies stared unabashedly and alluringly at the would-be consumer. Given by a business as an inducement to grease the wheels of commerce, the susceptible gazer was likely more cognizant of feminine flawlessness than of the radio-parts distri-butor who presented it. The address and phone number were printed and at the ready, but I think classified listings are where one would look on the rare occasion that a concrete delivery might be needed. What does a gas station have to do with a high-heeled doll carrying armloads of groceries as her poodle wraps his leash around her ankles and her panties fall down? They both reside on the same ashtray. As the blotter absorbed and the calendar ran out, they were replaced, but what of the pinup ashtray?

I have collected these ashtrays for more than thirty years, and not one of them bears the blemish of hot ash. Since they are lithographed on stamped steel, their contact with a burning cigarette would be immediately apparent. These were gifts of complicity to teenage boys from their fathers, who kept them around referentially and reverentially, never to be defaced by a snuffed-out cigarette. My father smoked cigars and a pipe, and pinup ashtrays would never have been up to that ash task, so one never surfaced in plain view. We were more the heavy glass ashtray kind of household, with depressions to cradle the pipe and cigar. My mother humored my need to con-tribute large clamshells to the ash-catching campaign when I returned from visits to the seashore. Taste shifted, but these girlies live on in perfect synch with the time of their production.

ROXY EASTERN THREAD CORP.

Strip #1	Strip #2	Strip #3
8006 Bright Pink	8204 Neon Red	8923 Peach
8012 Pink	8211 Flame Red	8925 Tea Rose
8023 Baby Pink	8240 Lt. Marachino	8929 Salmon Pink
8053 Pink	8232 Jockey Red	8931 Peach Glace
8016 Dusty Pink	8234 Spanish Red	8934 Salmon
8057 Rose Pink	8218 Cherry Bloom	8953 Sp. Slm. Pk.
8030 Shell Pink	8225 Scarlet	8945 Lt. Carrot
8046 Lt. Pink	8245 Dk. Scarlet	8949 Sunset Sky
8098 Dk. Dusty Pk.	8235 Cardinal	8939 Crab Apple
8100 Orchid Pink	8260 Strwbry. Red	8959 Geranium
8101 Old Rose	8280 Capucine	8680 Totem
8076 Praline Pink	8275 Lt. Cerise	8689 Rustana
8109 Dory Pink	8285 Ex. Lt. Fu.	8691 Orangeola
8066 Bright Pink	8287 Zingo Pink	8666 Henna Rust
8070 Dk. Pink	8289 Swiss Beauty	8671 Luggage
8085 Dk. Pink	8305 Dk. Swiss Bty.	8686 Handicap Rust
8089 Pink Laurel	8294 Magenta	8656 Orange Glow
8160 Vivacious Pink	8302 Lt. Fuchsia	8471 Muscade Beige
8162 Violina	8308 Fuchsia	8633 Lt. Toast
8164 Pink Wine	8315 Persian Rose	8639 Musc. Beige
8177 Winter Apple	8321 Amer. Beauty	8644 Burnt Sugar
8180 Lt. Cherry	8355 Marachino	8636 Bark Tan
8166 Hot Pink	8348 Beauty Red	8525 Cocoa Brown
8184 Graperose	8341 Fire Glow	8650 Tile Rust
8121 Dusk Rose	8327 Radiance Red	8647 Sp. Spicetone
8039 Sweet Pea	8334 Dk. India Red	8530 Leather Tan
8146 Coral Reef	8369 Lt. Mt. Berry	8535 Cruise Beige
8153 Shrimp	8379 Spring Wine	8520 Dk. Polo Tan
8191 Castillian Red	8385 Winetone	8500 Cedar
8196 Majl. Rose	8392 Dk. Winetone	8663 Frk. Brn.

ALL HIS LIFE, my father was a wholesaler of threads, zippers, and notions to the coat, suit, and dress trade in New York City's garment center. I was the lucky claimant of the no-longer pertinent color charts when the year's fashionable names for colors were reshuffled and reprinted. The colors didn't change; only the names for them did. Jonquil became Turner's yellow, malmaison, glint o'yellow, daffodil, fustic, then nankeen, in seven years. The thread samples remained reliably present; you just had to call them by the right code name for that year. Poetry, fantasy, and giddy flights of verbal fancy crested and dipped from year to year, but each hue was stable.

10
Roxy Eastern Thread
Corporation color chart,
1952. Page one of six,
10" high

10

NOW, LINOLEUM sample books are visually revelatory. Each is an anthology of floor treatments and carpets, translated into the language of linoleum and visibly altered annually with stylistic adjustments. Tiles, stenciled floors and borders, braided, hooked, embroidered, knitted rag and tapestry designs were transfigured into all-embracing linoleum. Linoleum did not simulate, was not imitating, but created a unique vernacular. No one was meant to think an Aubusson carpet linoleum pattern was a carpet. Rather, these designs were adjusted year to year and offered up in serious bound volumes by manufacturers such as Armstrong, Quaker Standard, Sloane, Gold Seal, and Certain-teed. Octagonal tiles, tapestry facsimiles, medallions, still-lifes, flagstones, landscapes, animals, geometrics, florals, patchworks, bordered solids, wood grains, Oriental patterns, and novelties for children's rooms spoke clearly of the year of their adaptation. In the world of linoleum pattern books, a 1924 flower looks like other 1924 flowers; 1931 flowers look different. These anthologies are records that make stylistic changes in taste visually quantifiable from decade to decade. Each book has its dog-eared pages that communicate the consumer's preferences as well.

12

13

14

Group of three beauty shop magazine covers, 1939–41. Each 11½" high

AMERICAN HAIRDRESSER and *Modern Beauty Shop* magazines from 1939 through 1950 convey similar fervor. The how-to of feather bobs, marcelling, hair-piece magic, pin curls, puff curls, and scalp treatments are illustrated along with hair-show reports and association prize-winning hairdos.

14

IN 1946, in the Bronx apartment of my childhood, I was seated on the living room floor, drawing. My father leaned over to see what I was doing while lighting his pipe. On his matches there were men in suits, printed. He had just detached the one on the end from his fellows and struck it. Incredulous, I asked "What are you doing?"

Sucking on his pipe stem to get a good light, he answered, "Lighting my pipe. What do you mean?"

"How could you break up that set?"

"What set?"

"Those men."

"Let me smoke in peace."

"Can I see those matches?"

"A seven-year-old kid shouldn't have matches, but I know you won't light them."

This from a man who gravely demonstrated the dangers of fireworks to me and my brother, Bill, by way of a firecracker that I found. He did so by lighting it in the kitchen, calmly placing it on the white porcelain enamel top of our Robertshaw stove, and inverting an empty coffee can over it "to muffle the sound." Safety first. Then he peeked under the can to see what was taking so long.

The history and sociology of matches are complex and fascinating, and the big players in early manufacture were the United States and Sweden since phosphorus deposits had been an elemental necessity. The rest of the world was a ready consumer.

The first phosphorus friction wooden-stick matches were made in 1836 in the United States, and by 1875 there were seventy-nine match manufacturers here. These matches could be struck against any abrasive edge or surface for ignition, including a fingernail. The sparking ignition often caused the unintentional flaming of neighboring matches, eyebrows, and shirts; and, in 1892, Joshua Pussey devised the matchbook in which a specific striker, positioned away from the other matches, was required to produce a flame. In 1894 the Diamond Match Company bought the rights to make matchbooks.

Manufacturers' marks on matchbooks are called *manumarks* and are printed on the narrowest facet of the bottom fold. There are collectors of manumarks. A couple of the rare manumarks are *Owname Renewable Matchbook* and *King Midas Matchbook Company* in case you have any around the house. Many older matchbooks lack manumarks. The Lion Match Company began manufacturing matches in Brooklyn, New York, in 1917 and by 1922 began using *safety first* covers, which instructed the consumer to *close cover before striking*. Subsequently headquartered in Chicago, the Lion Match Company had a capacity for originality, creativity, and inventiveness that resulted in *feature* matchbooks. Feature matchbooks contained matches that were printed with figures, buildings, products, services, and/or text. There are 125 manumarks for features matchbooks, which means that by 1950 the Lion Match Company had

15
Group of feature figural matches, 1930–50. Printed with figures advertising men's apparel and restaurants, each 2" high (with cover folded back). Lion Match Company, USA

16
Safety matchbox (top and bottom), c. 1920. Printed cardboard slide box with abrasive strike strip, 1¾" high. Federal Match Corporation, USA

15

16

17

18

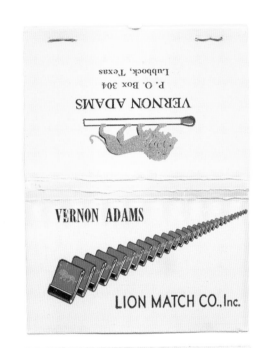

19

17
Group of four Lion Match Company feature figural matches, 1936–51. Printed with figures advertising apparel and nightclubs, each 2" high (with cover folded back)

18
Salesman's matchbook sample, 1947. Feature printed matches (open, outside), 3" high (open). Lion Match Company, USA

19
Salesman's matchbook sample, 1952. Feature printed matches (open, outside and inside), 3" high (open). Lion Match Company, USA

branch offices across America that handled the orders; the city in which the order had been placed followed the *Lion* on the manumark. Several U.S. companies followed Lion's lead in producing this kind of match. Lion was on the cutting edge of phillumenic inventiveness with the *knothole* cover and the *pop-up* cover. Both of these categories have robust collectorships. The knothole cover has a die-cut aperture that is an integrated element of the match cover advertisement, and through which the matches (sometimes figural) may be viewed. The pop-up cover displays a die-cut printed cardboard image attached to the upper inside of the matchbox flap and was popular with political candidates.

By 1976 there were only twenty-three American match companies, and by 1995 only three domestic match manufacturers remained.

I felt for the single match that I'd laid out in readiness. It wasn't there. I must have brushed it off when I was setting down the mug. No problem—I found the book of matches easily and opened it. Ah, but then my fingers felt nothing but cardboard stumps, like a row of children's teeth just coming in. It had been the last match in the matchbook.

Nicholson Baker, *A Box of Matches* (New York: Random House, 2003), 9.

There is a Lion Match Company in Durban, South Africa, a major area employer, formerly specializing in the manufacture and domestic sale of matches and their export to developing countries. In 2001, the factory announced its closing owing to rural electrification and the obsolescence of candles and paraffin, which required matches for lighting and cooking. An unemployed factory worker who was interviewed about the closing shrugged, showing the cheap plastic lighter he used for his cigarettes and said "What can we do? Progress."

In an age when smoking was a mark of sophistication, figural matches were a chosen advertising vehicle for restaurants, nightclubs, hotels, haberdashers, apparel manufacturers, and producers of vertical products such as bowling pins, beer bottles, and paintbrushes. Like the blotter and the pencil that sported advertising, the matchbook was ready for action on your behalf, with the advertiser at your service, and it nestled neatly in your pocket beside your hand.

20
Group of feature printed matches advertising specific foods, 1948–53. Each 2" high (with cover folded back). Lion Match Company, USA

21
Pop-up and peephole matchbooks with advertising, 1946–51. 3¾" high (open)

20

21

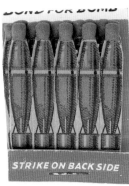

22

Back to my father lighting his pipe. I still have that book of matches and have collected the other 450 books of figural matches that I have ever seen. My mother didn't dump them. I guess she thought that safety matches could ignite only if struck. News of spontaneous combustion hadn't come to the Bronx yet. I regard these treasures with awe. Who at the Lion Match Company thought that something as ephemeral as a match should be adorned? After all, the advertisement was on the matchbook. Any text on the matchstick was gratuitous and destroyed in use. On what grounds did the person who came up with the idea sell it to his company? Surely manufacturing costs increased with the addition of the printed image to the matches.

When I regard the exquisite four-color lithographic images of five workers, each with a different facial expression, each in a different Sweet-Orr uniform, standing at ease looking straight ahead, I lose my composure. The simple elegance of five smiling chefs in identical white aprons unified by Longchamps in script across all five, wearing shaped chef hats formed of the igniting compound, causes my heart to beat faster. These matchbooks are as immediately informative about their time as is a medieval manuscript or *Les Tres Riches Heures* of the Duc de Berry is of its time. Their eloquence is eternal. Some even speak of patriotism. Ten yellow-complected Hirohitos stand in line, waiting to be ignited. A bending over, globe-clutching Hitler is on the match cover, striker on his butt, waiting to be struck by U.S. bomb-shaped matches.

Regiments of chefs, waitresses, delivery men, women turned out in fine fashion, vertical smiling shrimp and lobsters, hardware, jewelry, and industrial products reveal how we presented ourselves and how we wanted to be seen in a more innocent time when good was Good and the enemy was known. Then fickle taste went through changes that didn't include the figural match.

22
Feature printed matches with anti-Hitler propaganda (three views), 1940. Striker strip on Hitler's rear, 1½" (with cover folded back). Lion Match Company, USA

23
Feature printed matches with anti-Hirohito propaganda, 1942. 2" high (with cover folded back). Lion Match Company, USA

24
Feature printed matches advertising a blue-collar uniform company, 1947. 2" high (with cover folded back). Lion Match Company, USA

25
Feature printed matches advertising a restaurant, 1937. 2" high (with cover folded back). Lion Match Company, USA

23

24

25

I WEAR VESTS all the time. They are comfortable, serviceable, and generally underrated. They are a way to bring pockets along without the encumbrance of a jacket or purse. Descended from the earlier doublet and the jerkin, the waistcoat or vest, during the eighteenth and nineteenth centuries, provided portage for small, fragile necessaries such as a pocket watch, snuffbox, and toothpick. Something was missing if the illustration of a Dickens character or a carpetbagger lacked the gold chain and watch fob across an ample belly. The watch had not yet assumed its ultimately convenient place on the wrist. Another vest-pocket presence, the snuffbox, contained a powdered tobacco product that was commonly taken by the pinch, after meals. It was removed from the supply in the box to the back of one's fist and briskly inhaled. Other than having witnessed the immediate head-clearing sneeze, I have only my paternal grandfather's word proclaiming its "beneficial" effects. He never went further, even when pressed. The precise amount of a pinch of snuff must have been problematic to maneuver for a ham-fisted gent, so snuff scoops were invented. They were essentially pocketable handles with tiny spoon ends to aid in transferring the fine dark powder to the fist, especially when offering it around to your friends whose fingernails might not be too clean.

Speaking of fingernails, I assume that they were the first toothpicks. An astute caveperson must have discovered that a thorn did a better job and doubled as a sewing needle when not levering meat shreds from between molars. Generations later and generations ago, a French pillow maker discovered that the residue of goose down was the quill and that they made excellent writing instruments, drinking straws and, when cut at just the right angle, superlative toothpicks. The Soyez family, descendents of the pillow maker, currently supplies feathers to the Folies Bergères in Paris for their dancers' costumes. Talk about making the most out of what you have.

Oysters on the half shell can sometimes produce an intransigent fiber that lodges between teeth. In 1826, Charles Foster employed Yankee entrepreneurial ingenuity by placing wooden toothpicks imported from South America in his Oyster House in Boston. The fashion caught on and the canapé was the spin-off.

Back to vest-pocket tools. There was a marriage of the snuff scoop and the toothpick in that precursor to the jackknife, the vest-pocket compendium. These compendia were hand-carved and often took the forms of a bather, a geisha, a priest, a conquistador, or a Turk. I say often, but I have only eighty of these, and the aforementioned are repeated. I have not seen these in any other collection. Arms and legs fold into the torso to keep from breaking. The head also tucks in, the whole shebang neatly fitting into a vest pocket. They were made from ivory, horn, tortoiseshell, and later from celluloid and silver, from the sixteenth century through the early 1930s. Always a man's tool

26
Examples of ivory vest-pocket compendia (elegant and primitive), 1840. 3½" high (closed)

27
Swimmer toothpick and snuff scoop (open and closed positions), 1925. Articulated head, arms, and legs; enamel on sterling silver, 2¾" long (open). USA

28
Rabbi articulated toothpick and scoop (three positions), 18th century. Shows a tail that does double duty as a circumcised penis. Carved ivory and silver pins, 3½" high. England

29
Catholic cleric-demon articulated toothpick and scoop (six positions), 16th century. Carved horn and tortoiseshell, brass pins, 3¾" high. Reformation England

30
Walking character figural toothpicks and snuff scoops with articulated heads, arms, and legs, 1875–1915. Carved ivory, paint, teak, celluloid, and steel pins, 3–3½" high. France and England

31
Group of swimmer toothpicks and snuff scoops (diving position) with articulated heads, arms, and legs, 1890–1920. Carved ivory and teak, celluloid, silver and brass pins, 2–2¾" long. France and England

26

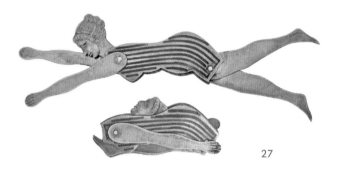

27

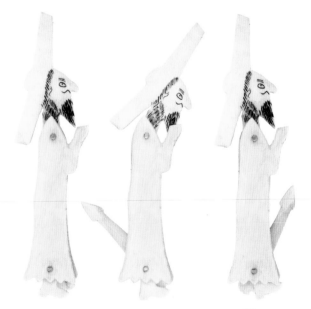

28

29

30

31

in the men's-club sense, they sometimes incorporated eye-winking innuendo into the imagery.

The oldest in my collection are four late sixteenth-century Reformation clergy with clearly uncircumcised genitalia that act as the snuff scoop and tooth-pick tools, which are exposed for use from beneath priestly robes by the feet of the figures. The heads on three of these swivel chinward, replacing the priest's head with a demon's head. These have been carved from tortoiseshell; the scoops and picks are ivory and horn. An eighteenth-century Orthodox Jew, made of engraved ivory, is presented as a bearded figure with stationary arms and hands raised to his face. His feet control the pick and scoop, which are circumcised

privates, arrow-shaped, that could also be positioned as a tail. That must have coaxed a chuckle in the drawing room. The characters portrayed vary through profession, gender, ethnic group, and activities, with no discernable pattern save functionality and compact portability. This tool form lasted until vests and snuff were on their way out and toothpicks became streamlined, standardized, clinically anonymous, and supereffective, some even sporting floss harps. After 1915, celluloid compendia simulated tortoiseshell and ivory in a giddy flapper idiom, and by 1930, figural compendia were passé.

32

33

34

35

36

32
Egyptian camel bookend,
1928. Bronzed pot metal,
5" high

33
Pelican bookend, 1930.
Patinated bronze, 4¾"
high. L. Artus

34
Lion bookend, 1926.
Cast bronze with
copper wash, 5½" high.
Metropolitan Foundry

35
Charles Lindbergh/
Propeller bookend, 1928.
Cast iron with a copper
wash, 6½" high

36
Indian chief bookend,
1926. Painted cast
iron, 5¾" high. Judd
Manufacturing Company

37
Group of bookends,
1920–40. Bronze, cast
iron, some with paint,
4¼–9½" high

THE BOOKEND came in with the book and I don't mean the Bible. Johannes Gutenberg set the tone circa 1455, and most bibles are substantial enough to serve as bookends. As slighter volumes were acquired by book consumers, keeping books upright became a necessity. The conventions of bookend themes seldom acknowledge bookish wisdom. The only one that comes to mind is Rodin's *Thinker* in miniature: if Rodin had known it would become such a prop, he probably would have made a variant pose for the other end of the book row. One might claim that the many bookend versions of praying hands have holy overtones, but they are only praying when together. Usually one hand is on each end of a line of books, and the hands are in the best position to keep the books upright. I'm not convinced that they were conceived as praying hands.

Bookends are about home décor and taste and about making personal selections from among safe choices. Bookend themes tend toward animals, mythological symbols, political and historical figures, sports, architectural details, modes of transportation, ethnic faces representing exotic civilizations, and reproductions of artworks. The first bookend was probably a stone, weighty enough to hold a row of books at attention.

Soon after, someone else likely discovered that a brick was heavy enough to do the job and had a serviceable shape. Considering bookend structure, there are really only a few ways to go. Something weighty with two contiguous flattish sides is desirable. The other choices demand right angles for both ends. The institutional model tends to be austerely functional and devoid of decoration, having one side flush with the end book cover and the other running beneath the book row, an *L* anchoring books in place. This system uses the book's tendency to fall against the bookend. The last version has its decorative panel-back flush with the end book cover and the support at ninety degrees to it in the shape of a backward *L*. This version is least effective in earthquakes and with books that have a natural tendency to tilt because they slide. They don't have much holdback conviction.

Lily S., an interior designer, owns a wide variety of configurations in the world of bookends. They show how taste changed throughout the nineteenth and twentieth centuries. All of the styles from traditional Realism, to Art Nouveau, Art Deco, Mission, and Arts and Crafts, through the 1950's Echo Deco, Folk Art, and all the subsets, abound in bookends. Beyond her collection, originality in conceptual format is seen in the vase bookend (the most cunning being the fan vase) in which the water or potting soil provides the ballast. Home décor has been the key in bookend choices. Considering that fashion is synonymous with changing tastes, bookend styles have been relatively enduring. How pertinent is a bronze Lindbergh to our present lives or a 1950s glazed ceramic steam engine? As the text age winds down,

bookends are often seen propping CDs, DVDs, and videocassettes. Will they always be called bookends?

Rodin's *Thinker*, acanthus-leaf volutes, and J.-B. Carpeaux's cherubs reproduced from the façade of the Paris Opera House imbue the bookshelf with un-questionably good taste in artworks. Horse, bird, and dog bookends, as well as sports themed bookends, passively identify our predilections. Steam-driven locomotives and sailing ship bookends refer to our musings and daydreams. Dragons and personifica-tions of exotic civilizations are about containability of the dangerous in the service of style. Political and historical figures such as Abe Lincoln and George Washington have established cachet and don't raise any issues at this time. This area of the bookend genre is the most likely of all to become an antique.

— No. 25 —
GERONIMO
Cruel, vicious Apache war chief, under whose leadership many hostile raids were made in New Mexico and Arizona. After hard fighting, was captured in 1886 by General Cook, only to escape with members of his tribe on the march to Fort Bowie. He then made his final desperate attack on white settlers, was captured and imprisoned by the government.

This is one of a series of forty-eight cards. More cards illustrating romantic America to follow.

INDIAN GUM
The World's Greatest Penny Value
Goudey Gum Co.   Boston

— No. 26 —
RED JACKET
Powerful Seneca war chief, known as "The Last of the Senecas." The Senecas were members of the once important "Five Nations," which also included the Mohawk, Cayuga, Oneida, and Onondaga, tribes, inhabiting what is now western New York State. RED JACKET was a dispatch carrier during the Revolutionary War.

This is one of a series of ninety-six cards. More cards illustrating romantic America to follow.

INDIAN GUM
The World's Greatest Penny Value
Goudey Gum Co.   Boston

38
Group of *Indian Chewing Gum* bubble gum cards, 1940s. Printed card stock, each 2¾" high. Goudey Gum Company, Boston, Massachusetts

39
Redskins in feather headdresses and war paint, bows and arrows at ready and knives in belts, 1947. Painted cast lead, each 2½" high

— No. 27 —
JOSEPH BRANT
Brave, devoted, diplomatic Mohawk Chief. His Indian name was Thayendanega. First engaged in battle at the age of thirteen against the French at Lake George in New York. Was an interpreter at Rev. Eleazar Wheelock's school in Connecticut, from which Dartmouth College grew. Fought with the British during the Revolutionary War and became a colonel.

This is one of a series of ninety-six cards. More cards illustrating romantic America to follow.

INDIAN GUM
The World's Greatest Penny Value
Goudey Gum Co.   Boston

— No. 29 —
OSCEOLA
OSCEOLA was not a real chief, but was looked upon as the master spirit and leader of the Seminole tribe, who inhabited the Everglades of Florida. In 1835 his wife was taken into slavery by the whites and, in his rage, he started the second bloody Seminole war. One hundred ten United States soldiers were massacred the first day of this war.

This is one of a series of forty-eight cards. More cards illustrating romantic America to follow.

INDIAN GUM
The World's Greatest Penny Value
Goudey Gum Co.   Boston

BETWEEN 1907 and 1930 Edward S. Curtis's portfolios of photographs and his volumes of *The North American Indians* were published. Shortly before 1900 he had set out to record what he could, in image and cultural information, of native North Americans. His study lasted more than thirty years in the field. The resulting twenty-volume set physically occupies almost five linear feet of bookcase, requiring the appropriate bookend or two. Curtis was an organized researcher, a tireless ethnographer, and a perceptive photographer with sensitivity to the telling details of expression and dress. His volumes are the literature of observation of North American Indian tribal customs, legends, song, oral histories, and personalities attested to by his forty thousand images of eighty tribes.

In the 1930s and 1940s the Goudey Gum Company of Boston produced rubber-based bubble gum in penny, then five-cent packages with which Indian cards were packaged. The gum was beside the point. The cards were the thing. They were sold in the two corner candy stores in my neighborhood, and a skinned-knee tomboy incarnation of me spent a substantial portion of her allowance on them. I still have my Indian cards. None of them are in mint condition because I flipped them for profit in an effort to complete a set. Except that completion of a set was not possible since there were successive sets with green backs and black backs and overlapping sets with red title bars and blue title bars on the front. Talk about futility.

Card flipping, my favorite of the card sports, required two participants. Simply stated, someone went first, holding one card by the long edges between thumb and middle finger; and with a flicking wrist motion (used for no other activity) the card was flipped downward and landed either face up or down. The second player had to match the card side, head or tail, to win both cards; otherwise the first player won both. There were usually five cards flipped in a round. My choice was to be the second player, if possible. I practiced at home alone and knew that if I kept the height and speed of my wrist flick consistent, I had a certain amount of control over the outcome, choosing a heads-up or heads-down handhold.

Indian card flipping was an early life lesson in cutting down the variables. Consequently, I have hundreds of Indian cards with rounded corners and creases down the center. I never attained the holy state of a complete set but was jubilant at opening a gum package to find a card that I didn't have. I was also crestfallen when I got my eighth Sitting Bull.

The graphics on the front of the card interested me. I read the card backs in search of titillating details of vivid cruelties but was never rewarded. These cards were tame by the standards of Gum, Inc. *Horrors of War* a few years earlier. *To Know the Horrors of War is to Want Peace* gave "educational" toys new meaning. Directly, uniformly, and homogeneously, Indian cards represented Indians as *the other*, not like us in the civilized world. I learned that Indians were athletic, shrewd, cruel, brave, prone to drunken violence, intemperate, scalping savages, and they had got what they deserved so they weren't coming to the Bronx. This opinion was shared by our own Theodore Roosevelt in his book *Winning of the West*, in which he characterized the Indian as a "lazy, drunken beggar [who] might at any moment be transformed into a foe whose like was not to be found in all the wide world for ferocity, cunning and bloodthirsty cruelty." By 1906, Roosevelt had changed his tune. In his foreword to Edward S. Curtis's oeuvre, he commends Curtis for his artistry and observation as a "great and real service . . . to our own people . . . and the world of scholarship everywhere."

The poses, expressions, hairstyles, jewelry, and clothing on Indian cards was taken directly from Curtis's portraits and probably set Curtis's findings back a couple of generations. More people read the importunate Indian cards than Curtis's expensive limited-edition books. The obverse and the reverse of the Indian cards were a sound bite of his photographs backed by written word. They were derivative in image and enhanced by cultural disinformation. They are what Classics Illustrated comic books are to literature. Taste has changed back and forth a couple of times on the representation of Native Americans and will probably do a few more pirouettes, with casinos coloring the picture.

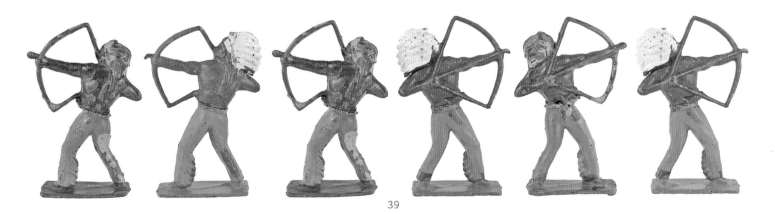

39

chapter 7

Owners Lost Faith

IN THE EARLY 1970s I was in the village of Chimula, Mexico, in the province of Chiapas, not far from San Cristobal de las Casas, near the Guatamalan border. The Chimula people are the closest living group to the Mayans and their direct descendants. I was interested in Mayan iconography as evidenced in the reliefs on ruins of stone buildings and in tribal weaving patterns, which vary from group to group within the context of their shirts, called *huipils*. Chimula, the place, was an important anthropological destination. The church on the *zocalo*, the large town square, seemed a good place to start on an overcast Christmas morning. I entered the building to a stupefying revelation. Forty-nine separate and various sized, homemade, and hauntingly primitive holy family groups of effigies were arranged throughout the basilica.

1

1
Santo, mid-19th century. Hand-carved and hand-painted wood with gold leaf, 14¾" high. Mexico

2
Santo, mid-19th century. Hand-carved and hand-painted wood with gold leaf, 8" high. Spain

3
Santo, 19th century. Hand-carved and hand-painted wood, 12¾" high. Portugal

4
Santo, mid-20th century. Hand-carved and hand-painted wood, 17" high. Mexico

2

3

4

These were not hasty carvings, but singular figures, carefully decked out in every aspect and infinite detail. All the pews had been removed, and the floor was covered with straw. Each Chimula clan was with its regaled holy family. Candles illuminated each vignette. Between festively garbed Indians and their mirror-eyed figures stood Fanta and Coca-Cola bottles that had been refilled with crystal clear liquor, the Mayan version of moonshine. Their particular version of Christian practice was inextricably mixed with paganism and Mayan myth, and the drinking of their offerings and audible supplication of favors had started early. I was conflicted, my riveted amazement offset by the feeling that I was witnessing tribal *in flagrante delicto*. I didn't linger. This remains my solo sighting of *Santos* in action.

There are *Santo* variations. Some are two-dimensional, painted on tin and processional figures; but my own collection of *Santos* are figures in the round, and all are less than twelve inches high. *Santos* are believed by the faithful to be intermediaries, capable of interaction with human beings and intercession with heaven on behalf of worthy supplicants on earth. My relics come from different places and live in a community with their fellows on a small English seventeenth-century tavern table in my home. I've never attempted to use them for their intended purpose, but I respect their potential. Their places of origin are Spain, Portugal, Guatemala, and Mexico. They range from high art, as striking as a fifteenth-century German misericord to the homely, inept, and sincere construction that is unequivocally poetic and usually Mexican.

He found her by accident. He was driving a nail into the adobe wall beside the kitchen stove when the head of the hammer broke through the thin layer of mud into air. The hole she stood in was not much larger than she, narrow and a little over a foot high. She was coated with dust and mud and woven with spiderwebs as if tied in place. Her hands came together at her chest; her eyes looked straight ahead. Her mouth was full and without a smile. The base she stood on was a piece of flat cottonwood. Much of the paint on her gown and from the robe that fell from her head to her feet had peeled away. He didn't know who had hidden her in the wall, only that she had stood there a long time.

Rick Collington, *Perdido* (Denver: MacMurray and Beck, 1997), 10.

6

5
Virgin of Guadalupe, mid-20th century. Hand-carved, stenciled, and hand-painted wood, with tin crown and remnants of rays at shoulders, 16" high. Mexico

6
Virgin of Guadalupe candle, 2002. Paraffin, printed paper, 5¼" high. Industrias Luz Eterna, Guadalajara, Jalisco, Mexico

5

Upon my return to San Cristobal de las Casas, I went to the market in search of old embroidered *huipils* and found a much-used Virgin of Guadalupe *Santo* that someone had, alas, given up on. What other reason could there be for the saintly to have entered the stream of commerce? Someone lost faith, again. This Lady of Guadalupe is old, wooden, and well-worn with handling by the desperate and sweaty-handed. She has seen it all. Triangular aura peaks, rising from her head and running down her mantle to her feet, had been made from a cut tin can, painted red, then pressed into her outline to enhance her. The points are mostly bent or missing and her paint is chipped and rubbed thin, but she is the "Queen of Heaven" in Mexico and wears her tin crown with majesty. She currently lives in retirement beside others of her ilk, with one Guatemalan penitent sinner rising from painted, carved wood flames. The Virgin of Guadalupe, dearest to the Mexican population of all the *Santos*, is most frequently depicted and implored.

On December 9, 1531, Juan Diego (an early Christian convert in the Roman Catholic conquest of Mexico), en route to mass, was halted on Tepeyac hill by music and a bright light in which the Virgin Mary appeared. She declared, in his native Nahuatl, that she desired to have a church built on this spot. The skeptical Bishop Zumarraga, to whom Juan Diego made his report, required verification and on

...he told the Lady that he knew she was here to protect the health of this house and those who lived here and that she'd done a rotten job of it.... He said that he would give her one more chance. If she failed, he would use her for fire in the stove, where she wouldn't throw enough heat for a pot of coffee.

Collington, *Perdido*, 206.

7
Penitent sinner, mid-20th century. Hand-carved and hand-painted wood, 9" high. Guatemala

8
Virgin of Guadalupe, first half of 20th century. Hand-carved and hand-painted wood, 10" high. Mexico

7

8

his next trek up the hill on December 12th, the Virgin reappeared. She instructed Juan Diego to bring roses to Zumarraga from the barren hilltop. Gathering the flowers in his cloak, he made the delivery with dispatch. During his presentation, an image of the Virgin appeared upon his cloak. A small church was soon constructed, which, coincidentally, required the destruction of an Aztec temple. In 1745, the Vatican recognized the miracle. The cloak-bound image is preserved in the basilica of the Tepeyac hill church, which has been rebuilt three times. Juan Diego was canonized in July 2002. Our Lady of Guadalupe, *La Reina de Mexico*, is still celebrated throughout Mexico on the anniversary of that fateful roseate incident that took place more than five centuries earlier. It has gained momentum, which speaks to paying attention to the little guy and his friends. Striking a sympathetic grass-roots chord goes a long way. *Vaya con dios*.

MORE THAN one form of faith can be lost. As a child growing up during World War II, there were a few unsteadying challenges that penetrated the secure arena of parental assurances and home life. One of them was the maternal mandate to "finish your food, the children in Europe are starving."

"How does my eating help them?"

"It's a sin to waste good food when others are dying of hunger."

"I hate lettuce and you always give me too much. Why can't you just send it to them?"

"It's not that easy. Besides, your body needs roughage."

"You wash lettuce, why can't we just put it into the ocean and it will float to them?"

"You don't know how lucky you are to have all the food and clothing you need."

"Are the Germans coming here?"

The Germans and the Japanese were the bad guys that my mother's brothers had gone to fight on European and Philippine turf. The Japanese were treacherous but too far away to worry about yet. The Germans were the imminent danger. My father, the air-raid warden, had booklets of airplane silhouettes. Every man on my street could be counted on to look skyward, hand to brow, shading the sun, at the sound of aircraft overhead, looking for the outline of the Messerschmidt 109E. The unspoken implication and fear was the possibility of evil trumping good. Fortunately, heroic radio adventurers such as Captain Midnight, The Green Hornet, Sky King, Straight Arrow, and the G-Men were savvy at decoding secret messages, delivering top-secret documents, and penetrating enemy ranks, so we had the edge. These radio serials were telling us that it wasn't easy but we would probably win. I cherish my five radio premium rings from those years. I would have had more if I didn't actually have to eat the food to snag the trademark off the box top as proof of purchase.

The mysterious and elusive Shadow, with his titillating and threatening laugh, was heard on Sunday nights in the car on the return trip from visiting my paternal grandparents. *Let's Pretend* was presented on Saturday mornings; I can still hear the theme song in my head. *The Lone Ranger, Li'l Orphan Annie, Jack Armstrong, All-American Boy, Archie Andrews*, and *The Inner Sanctum* were radio serials that I listened to irregularly. Most of them had sponsors who offered premiums that weren't sufficiently arcane to induce me to consume their product. Post Cereal's *Melvin Purvis G-man* serial/cereal offered Junior G-man rings. Post Toasties must have been palatable enough for me to be the owner of three. I didn't learn until recently that the real Melvin Purvis, who was famous for curtailing the careers of the criminally minded, was fired from the FBI by J. Edgar Hoover and died a likely suicide in 1960.

An inordinate proportion of 1940s radio serial heroes were ranchers. They were interesting to a city kid. Sky King was a pilot, a detective, and a rancher with a Palomino named Yellow Fury. As Skyler King, he owned a ranch equipped with an airfield and two planes named *Songbird* and *Flying Arrow*. Sky King's sponsors were Powerhouse candy bars and Peter Pan peanut butter, not too hard to swallow; but they must have required too many proofs of purchase because I have only one nifty Teleblinker ring with a telescoping view port. Powerhouse later sponsored early TV's *Captain Video*.

Straight Arrow was really named Steve Adams and was also a rancher. His Palomino was named Fury. Together with his young sidekick, Packy Mc-Cloud, he righted many weighty wrongs. They had a hideaway cave laden with gold nuggets. Nabisco was their sponsor, and you can bet that I have a Straight Arrow Golden Nugget Cave Ring with a lens and microfilm, which, when held to the light, reveals the minute, smiling Straight Arrow and Packy and an unsmiling Fury.

Captain Midnight was a fearless pilot who flew secret missions in service of America despite the great odds against him. Red Albright was his secret identity, and his ward Chuck Ramsay was a kid who child listeners wished to be. I remember Ovaltine as the sponsor. Since Ovaltine was more palatable than iceberg lettuce, I have the 1947 Code O'Graph Whistle, which taught me to use letters and numbers in new ways, in service of our country, if necessary.

General Mills sponsored *The Green Hornet* and I ate my share of their products in 1947, earning the Secret Compartment Glow-in-the-Dark Seal Ring. The brass Green Hornet seal pivoted to reveal its luminous interior, which could be used to silently reveal your presence to allies when hiding out or to transport hidden messages or deposit poison into the enemy's drink when the opportunity arose. This was a multipurpose ring. 1947 was a big year for building an arsenal, just in case the war wasn't really over. By 1948 our family had acquired an 8-inch Andrea television set. It was overall a massive contraption with a built-in radio and phonograph. The ratio of screen size to cabinet was about 1:80. Captain Video was on our side and his ray gun, etc., stunted my faith in the effectiveness of my radio premium gear. The flavor of one's loss of faith depends on one's biases.

15

15
Group of heart love tokens, lockets, and charms, 1850–1950. Made from silver, gold, ivory, crystal, mother-of-pearl, glass, malachite, agate, enamel, brass, and jasper, ½–2½" high

16
Group of heart love tokens, 1880–1945. Made from sterling silver, ½–¾" high

17
Campaign button, 1948. *Thomas E. Dewey for President*. Litho on steel with brass wire pin back, 1¼" diameter

18
Group of wedding cake toppers, 1900–2005. Painted plaster, plastic, and wax, 3–3¾" high

THINK OF ALL the heart lockets on the secondary market. Each was first given to someone as a token of affection. Now anyone can put them on and pretend, or collect them as trophies of so many broken hearts or lost faith in material proofs of love. At flea markets, if one has the patience and inclination to sift through and poke around in the jewelry boxes of other lives, there are more hearts to be found than any other single type of "charm." Engraved silver hearts abound as well as gold, gold-plated, and gold-filled lockets, many with pictures still inside. There are semi-precious stone hearts, carved ivory hearts, enamel, glass, butterfly wing-under-glass hearts, and brass hearts with centered "diamond" chips. So

many ways to say "I love you." If anyone still believes there is a special person fated for each one of us, lots of trial and error is represented here. These hearts represent an aggregate loss of faith.

LET'S TAKE THE commitment represented by the heart locket a step further, past the engagement ring (an object of intrinsic value) to the wedding. The frozen slice of wedding cake may have been consumed on the first anniversary, but why are so many bride-and-groom cake toppers (with clinging bits of dried icing) available to perfect strangers? Some have names and dates inscribed on their bases. I have about 125 and my artist-author friend John B. has about 350. They are made from painted plaster, plastic, glazed earthenware, and porcelain. The brides are clutching grooms and wearing white lace or white icing simulating lace, gold lamé and pastel shades for second marriages. There are black couples, Latino pairs, and mixed couples, grooms in uniform beside flags and brides holding bouquets and baskets of flowers. There are tiny pairs and large pairs, couples standing in sugar eggs and beneath wedding bells. There are dancing couples, stiff couples, and giddy and solemn couples. Each was selected as a symbolic hope that the marriage would endure. Now, John B. and I have them. Thomas E. Dewey was described by a journalist as "the little man on the wedding cake," an image he couldn't shake. He lost that fateful presidential election to Franklin Delano Roosevelt.

16

17

18

ALICE Z. IS a social worker and a collector of other people's Last Suppers. To date, she has 485, give or take a few. As crucifixes find their places over the beds of believers, Last Suppers materialized in the dining rooms and parlors of those who seemed to feel that they could imbue a paint-by-numbers kit with their special faith. Talent has nothing to do with this endeavor. A prediliction for oil paint on black velvet is a favored medium for the Last Supper crowd. Alice places iconic Last Suppers sold in European cathedral souvenir stores alongside commercial plaster-relief Last Suppers, salt and pepper shaker, ballpoint pen, and thimble Last Suppers. Central and South American Last Supper souvenir makers and vendors have very special thoughts about the menu of their Last Supper dioramas, which commonly include watermelon, doughnuts, and molé. There are hinged wooden triptychs with winged table extensions for the outermost three apostles, left and right. There are needlepoint, bargello, and tapestry Last Suppers and Last Suppers reverse-painted on glass. There are Last Suppers for knickknack shelves and Last Suppers glued to cross-cut tree slices, complete with bark. There is an elaborate painted, cast-plaster Last Supper with two angels hovering overhead, bearing a clock aloft. Is the message here that time is running out? There are illusional and holographic Last Suppers that project the scene into the viewer's space or the dining room of your choice, and there are collage Last Suppers that merge with the wall.

19
Last Supper folding fan (front and back), 1946. Litho on paper, 7" high

20
Last Supper fiber-optic lamp, 1996. Colored cast plastic, fiber-optic cable, and wood base, 12½" high

21
Last Supper lunch box, 2003. Printed steel with plastic handle, 5½" high. Accoutrements Company

20

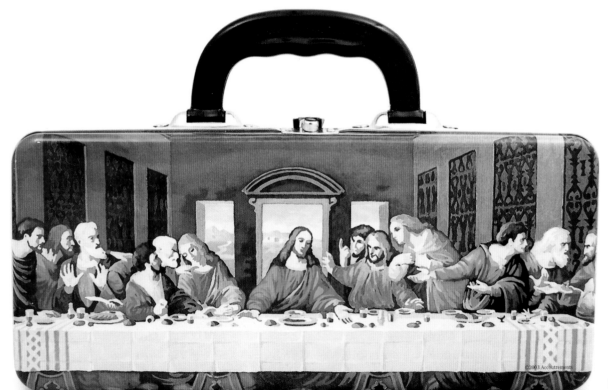

21

22
Last Supper embroidery
(*#500 EMBROIDER AS
STAMPED*), 1968. Linen
with cotton thread, 15"
high

23
Last Supper musical
pillow that plays "Hey
Jude," 1998. Printed
cotton stuffed with
kapok and key-wind
music box, 11"
high. Unemployed
Philosophers Guild

24
*Oil Paint By Number
Set* (*#11800, The Last
Supper*), 1993. Boxed set
and painting, 14¼" high.
Craft House Corporation

The Last Supper humidor is my personal favorite. The table goes 360 degrees and none of the disciples are interacting—the opposite of King Arthur's round table. There must be more than one kind of loss of faith going on here, one of them being the surmise of one's own skill level. Another might be one's ability to abide someone else's interpretation of a symbolic scene. I won't spell out the others.

24

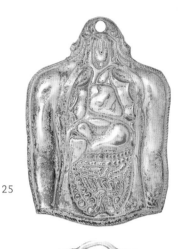

25

26

27

25
Group of ex-votos
(organs of digestion),
1900–1935. Silver,
4½–6¾" high. Italy
and Greece

26
Foot ex-voto, c. 1920.
Pressed silver, 6" high.
Italy

27
Baby ex-voto, c. 1910.
Pressed silver, 4" high.
Spain

28
Milagros at work in the
basilica, Toluca, Mexico,
before reaching the
secondary market, 2003.
23" high

SO MUCH FAITH attends the realms of belief. Particularly for the ardent, material tokens are essential. Ex-votos, *milagros*, and *cimaruta* are artifacts related to faith. Consequently, their appearance on the antiques and collectibles market indicates loss of faith in the petitioner's belief system so that the value of the artifact becomes pecuniary. Ex-votos are physical bids for specific divine intervention in return for an act of sacrifice by the petitioner. During the last two centuries they have largely been flat figures, symbolic of body parts, people, or animals that are in need of cure, salvation, or safe passage from various misfortunes. Made of embossed sheet silver, some are quite elaborate and voluted. Later, made of silver plate or aluminum, they represent a vow to pray or fast or otherwise deprive oneself of pleasure in return for results on an entreaty.

Ex-votos come from Italy and Greece where they originated in Etruscan, Greek, and Roman culture. In 2001, I visited the Museum of Epigraphy in Rome where I saw fine examples of small incised and inscribed terra-cotta body parts that had been left at sacred sites and thrown into the Tiber River in fervent hope, imprecating divine help or a cure. Most of these referred to infertility and venereal problems. In 2002, I visited Villa Giulia, the Vatican Museum, and several other museums in Rome where hundreds of terra-cotta and stone votive figures of arms, legs, genitalia, uteri, heads, ears, hearts, kidneys, and breasts were on display. The bid for celestial favor has not changed for a few thousand years; only the material format has become smaller and lighter. In many churches, donations of money have replaced the ancient custom. Ex-votos have surfaced on eBay and throughout secondary markets as church walls that were studded with the ex-votos of past years, were deaccessioned; old vows for sale.

28

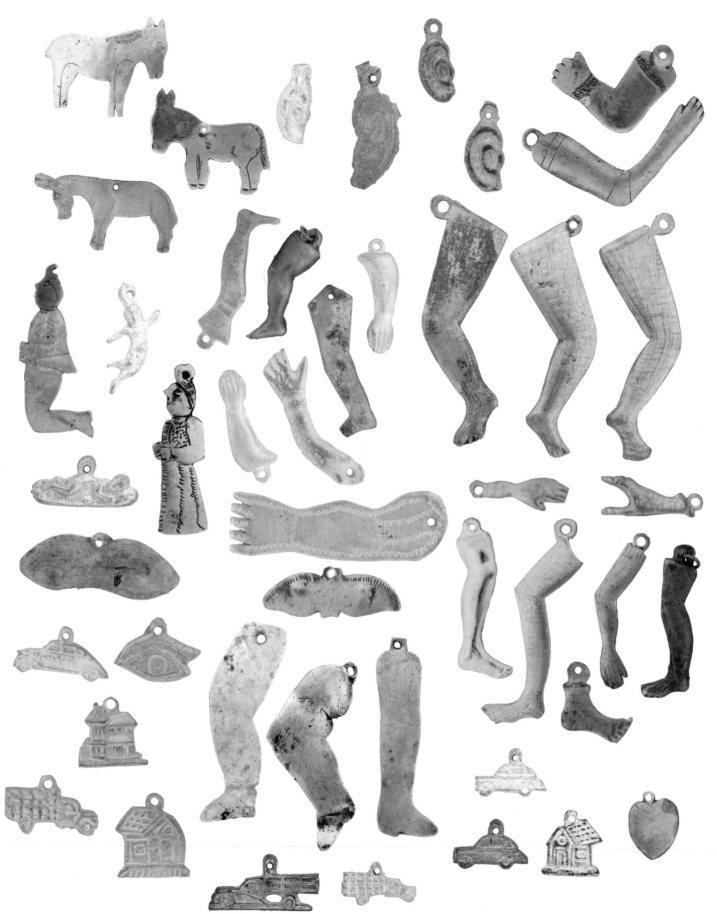

Mexico has its own version of the ex-voto called the *milagro*, or "small miracle." They are usually coin-sized to the ex-voto's cookie cutter's sizes. They seek to accomplish the same ends. On several trips to Mexico in the 1970s and 1980s, I stopped at churches, *libreria*, and those shops that sell unclassifiable necessities.

"*Tienes los milagros?*" I asked. Most of the time, they did. Small miracles abound all over Mexico. I built quite a nice collection. En route to Palenque in the early 1970s, right after the rainy season had destroyed the last remnant of passable rural road, I asked my husband to stop the car near a primitive lean-to in which an Indian woman was selling dried chilies, Fanta, vintage Lorna Doones, and mysterious herbs. I asked her if she had any *milagros*. She asked which part of me hurt. Figuring if there was only one *milagro* in the offing, it might as well be a head, "*Cabeza*" was my reply.

"*Cabeza*," she said, "*cabeza?*" She reached down beneath her counter and produced an outdated bottle of Bayer aspirin.

"*Aspirina*," she said.

Young gringas don't know what cures what. *Milagros* work on the ex-voto system. Faith still thrives in Mexico, and some *milagros* are available at primary sources.

There is an even more arcane relative of the ex-voto and the *milagro*. It is the *cimaruta*. It literally means "sprig of the rue plant" in Italian. Always cast in silver, it takes the form of an abstracted rue root system. In ancient times in Southern Italy, a sprig of rue was fastened to an infant's garb for protection from the *malocchio*, or evil eye. Not too much later the symbolic version became popular, and the attributes of silver strengthened the *cimaruta*. I had seen only three samples of this trinket until spring 2003 when I visited the Pitt Rivers Museum behind the Oxford Museum of Natural History in England. There in the midst of Lieutenant General Henry Lane Fox Pitt Rivers's (1827–1900) most numerous world-class stash of accumulated curiosity cabinet oddities was a showcase harboring sixteen *cimaruta*. The typed tag on yellowed card stock described "Southern Italian charms to ward off the evil eye." Yeah, and what else? The silver roots end in hands clutching a variety of things: a *mano fica* hand, a fish, a key, a rue fruit, a crescent moon, a serpent, a flaming heart, a bird, and male and female figures. Some had a vervain flower, a mermaid, an eye, an owl. In each *cimaruta* the symbolic objects were worked into a filigreed root system. They are double-sided, and the reverse shows a back view of the obverse. General Pitt Rivers bagged them with fifty thousand other trophies. Why were the Neapolitans willing to part with them? So much for faith in the face of lucre.

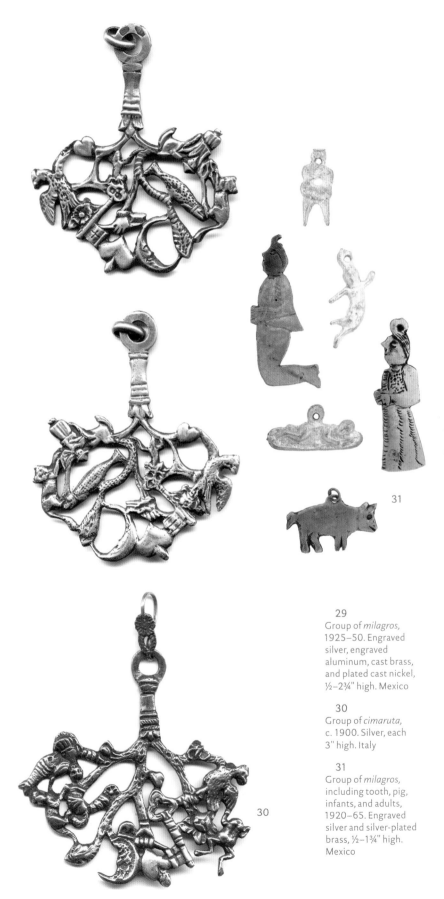

31

30

29
Group of *milagros*, 1925–50. Engraved silver, engraved aluminum, cast brass, and plated cast nickel, ½–2¾" high. Mexico

30
Group of *cimaruta*, c. 1900. Silver, each 3" high. Italy

31
Group of *milagros*, including tooth, pig, infants, and adults, 1920–65. Engraved silver and silver-plated brass, ½–1¾" high. Mexico

POLITICAL CAMPAIGNS inspire their own breed of short-lived faith that is signified in the campaign button. A campaign button is an emblem of personal conviction about a political party and its policies that are represented by a candidate engaged in the active pursuit of political office. There is an element of participation in spreading name and face recognition and the possibility of conversion by sublimation of the susceptible or the undecided. The wearer's overt faith is rewarded by the candidate's election, or it is dashed by the failure to persuade a majority. Either way, the campaign button, like the poster, isn't useful for its intended purposes after the election. Most constituents toss the buttons or drop them into catchall drawers or repositories of adrift buttons, old garters, and Tuberculosis Society lapel pins to be discarded by the next generation.

Like baseball cards, buttons from past campaigns stand for personae who were heroes and villains. Some of us just can't bring ourselves to discard them or to wear them in the first place. Many years after office, when the nimbus of a specific historic event is married to a politician, it's time to bring out old campaign buttons. What connoted a candidate's platform may or may not be congruent with his or her term in office. Wholly unforeseen events may have colored that course of office. Revelations about personal indiscretions may have enriched these emblems of our innocence. A candidate may have personally stretched and risen to high office or surprised us in other ways. Or transgressions of the public's faith may have ousted an office holder or nearly so. Campaign buttons are much more enjoyable in the aftermath, as an historical review given the perspective of distance, rather than at the time candidates are pertinent and one's own faith is at stake.

I've read of literal buttons, in George Washington's time, sewn or studded onto waistcoats, which, in a low-key manner, instigated name familiarity with candidates in a fledgling United States. The earliest pictorial campaign button that I've seen is in the Ford's Theatre Museum in Washington, D.C. It is Lincoln's 1864 re-election portrait with a silk ribbon lapel affix. It's an oval photographic likeness surrounded by an embossed brass daguerreotype frame about 1¼ inches high by an inch wide. There is no text. It was a Lincoln portrait in miniature; and the public, including John Wilkes Booth, knew what this presidential incumbent looked like. No previous president had to consider such a thing since photography hadn't been around. With photographic and technological advances, largely driven by fraternal orders, brotherhoods, and Masonic organizations requiring badges, celluloid and metal lithographed

41

42

41
Group of three campaign
buttons, 1898–1964.
Plasticized paper on
steel with brass safety
pin back, 1½–3½"
diameter

42
Campaign buttons for
Jimmy Carter, 1976.
Plasticized paper on
steel with brass safety
pin back, 2–3" diameter

buttons with slogans, images, and pin backs became the campaign buttons of choice. They still are.

Herbert Hoover's 1928 campaign buttons are now identified with the stock market crash of 1929. Franklin Delano Roosevelt's 1936 *Happy Days Are Here Again* campaign buttons are associated with the New Deal and the renewal of economic wellness. As with radio premiums, production of campaign buttons was reduced owing to raw-material shortages and were virtually unavailable in 1943 and 1944. I remember the *Do Your Part* collection bins on street corners. It was my job to step down to crush our empty tin cans and deposit them. The 1944 FDR-

Truman campaign buttons and the contra-campaign buttons *No Fourth Term* are part of my collection, which samples many subsequent electoral contests: Truman-Barkley, Eisenhower, Stevenson, JFK, Lyndon Johnson, Nixon-Agnew, Hubert Humphrey, Eagleton, McGovern, Barry Goldwater, Jimmy Carter, Ross Perot, Gerald Ford, Ronald Reagan, Bill Clinton, a couple of Bushs, and many governors and lots of mayors. Each name conjures the defining events of that hopeful's brush with high office. Each button represents the declaration of a side and a composite loss of faith by almost half the voting adults. Photographic technologies furthered the goals of political campaigns and were adapted to the photography of one's person as a form of record, sentiment, and art.

chapter 8

Owners Lost Interest

FROM THE 1850s through the 1870s, when photography was a
known but rare phenomenon, those who had access to it and the
means to afford it may have had one photograph taken in their
lifetime. Often that was a funeral-viewing image taken before the
likeness of the living person faded. Later, live studio likenesses
replaced the painted miniature portrait. These photographs were
usually printed on 5-by-7-inch heavy card stock with the name
and location of the photographer prominently featured. Too often
the date and subject's name were not inscribed on the back, so

1
Postmortem
photograph of a man,
c. 1880. 6⅕" high

2
Studio photograph
of a girl and boy
(anonymous), 1880. 6½"
high. Luidzley Studio,
Auburn, New York

3
Studio photograph of
brothers (anonymous),
1889. 6½" high. H.
Fallman's Parlor
Photo Car (railroad
car traveling studio
photograph business)

4
President McKinley
memorial portrait
button and bow, 1901.
5½" high

5
Group of portrait
photograph buttons
with brass and gold
frames, 1885–1904.
Each 2" diameter

the sitters' identities are lost though the photographer's are not. Some studio photographers offered *cartes des visites*, calling cards and commercial cards that necessarily recorded the subject's identity. When I visited the Ford's Theatre Museum, besides the 1864 Lincoln re-election campaign button, the photographic calling card of John Wilkes Booth was exhibited.

By the late 1880s, photo-button manufacturers had broadened the range of their wares to include festively beribboned commemorative models that are now highly collectible. America was infatuated with photography. It had moved out of the studio to fair grounds, to boardwalk concessions, to wherever people congregated at leisure. Photo-button manufacturers had adapted their offerings to round, coin-sized photographs with wire pin backs for lapels. Innovative companies such as Whitehead and Hoag proffered the "celluloid photo pinback button" in 1894. C. M. Wright's Pin Look Button Company patented a pin back for a miniature photo frame in 1898. Likenesses of oneself could be set into gold or brass frames with embossed, braided, or twisted wire and given to one's family and friends. Deluxe models were enameled. The photograph had become jewelry.

Someone cherished these small framed images of now-anonymous people to whom one feels connected; we know because people didn't wear photo

6

pins of themselves. These small likenesses were eventually set adrift by those to whom the gift was given, and there isn't a clue to the identity of any of them. There's no place for a name or inscription, and accompanying presentation notes have been long separated. Those pins were worn in the spirit in which we now show a wallet snapshot of a baby or a sweetheart to an acquaintance. When the baby grew up, the image must have been replaced because who would wear a baby photograph of their teenager? What to do with the photo button? It made a lump in the family album and dented the other photographs.

Many wound up in boxes of unmoored buttons. Interest dissipated, and those dear loved ones are now available to strangers. The recipients lost interest as photographic technology expanded into portable and affordable cameras that families pridefully owned and used to snap photographs of family and friends in action. As photography became more commonplace, people became more comfortable with it. The number of photographs grew exponentially as photographers became chroniclers of situation and collectors of their own frozen moments.

6
Group of portrait photograph buttons with wire pin backs and gold, brass, enamel, and tin frames, 1896–1910. 1–1¼" diameter

7
Portrait photo pins with gold and brass frames and brass pins, 1880. 1¼–2" diameter

8
Group of character wallets (cowboys, superheroes, comic strip characters, rock 'n' roll band), 1940–66. Printed leather and faux leather, 3–3¼" high

7

8

IN THE 1950S, photographs of Mom and Dad, siblings and friends, likely resided in a character wallet of embossed leather or impressed, printed plastic. My brother had a cowboy wallet; the edge was overcast in brown lanyard. Possession of a wallet was a coming-of-age rite. He meant that you had an allowance and could be trusted to carry it around and make discretionary purchases.

A new wallet usually came with a snap coin pouch, a printed identification card *in case of emergency call…*, and relatively clear plastic inserts with a movie-star card to demonstrate the photo insert's use. If you were a fan of a singer or a musical group, a cowboy or a superhero, you could select a wallet with your favored character emblazoned on the outside. Captain Video was the only personality that interested me. My mother advised me on my purchase of a sedate solid color as I'd soon lose my Captain Video

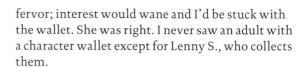

9
Cowboy character
wallet and box, 1949.
Embossed printed
plastic with zipper, 3¼"
high (box), 3" high
(wallet)

10
Cartoon character wallet
(front and back) and
box, 1947. Embossed
and printed leather with
zipper, 3½" high (box), 3"
high (wallet). S. Slesinger
Company, New York;
Fred Harman, cartoonist

9

10

fervor; interest would wane and I'd be stuck with
the wallet. She was right. I never saw an adult with
a character wallet except for Lenny S., who collects
them.

IN THE SUMMER of 1949, my mother had, unan-
nounced, saved forty dollars in household money for
the express purpose of taking Billy and me to Coney
Island. That was the equivalent of a week's salary
earned by my father. We were told that we could go
on any rides we wanted and to Steeplechase Park.
Fun house, Ferris wheel, Cyclone, scooter cars, hot
dogs, cotton candy, rolling barrel, distorting mirrors, Skeeball, and penny arcades were on the agenda.
Her only requirements were that we stay together,
in her sight. We would come home when the money
ran out. An ordinary weekday turned majestic. And
we had to agree to go to a freak show because, under
normal circumstances, we weren't permitted to stare
at anyone who looked strange, and she wanted us to
know about strangeness.

"Why can we stare at them and not others?" we
wanted to know.

"That's the only way that they can make their
living," my mother informed us with characteristic
empathy. So, education and charity were to be ingredients in this day, a small price to pay.

Chang and Eng were born in 1811 in Thailand,
then called Siam. Their Siameseness has come to
connote filial attachment regardless of nationality.
They were born with a documented ligament connection at the chest and who knows what else. They
had eight siblings when their father died in 1819, and
they sold small provisions to seamen, travelers, and
tourists to contribute to family survival. On one of
these vessels, a Scottish merchant passenger discovered them and encouraged them to exhibit their
uniqueness. In 1829, they sailed with him and an
American entrepreneur to Boston to be exhibited as
a paid *United Brother* exhibition. They subsequently
toured Europe and America independent of management until 1839, when they purchased a plantation
in North Carolina that they successfully farmed. In
1843, they married the Yates sisters and produced
twenty-one children. It's unproductive for Siamese
twins to be contentious.

In 1844 they became American citizens, adopting the surname Bunker. In 1860, they were seduced from retirement by Phineas T. Barnum's offer of a short exhibition in Barnum's American Museum in New York City. Financial setbacks caused by the Civil War instigated a second brief Barnum reunion. In 1870 Chang suffered a stroke, and Eng's support redefined weight bearing. In 1874 Chang died. Eng died four hours later. They are buried in North Carolina. While on the exhibition circuit, some of their $60,000 earnings came from the sales of fairings, glazed-china statuettes of the conjoined twins. What did spectators do with them when they brought them home? They're not sufficiently detailed or attractive to be interesting oddities to the folks back home. Like brightly colored trinkets from craftsy countries, they were purchased in the exuberance of the moment. What do you do with a souvenir of deformity? It doesn't sit well with the Bohemian glass or cup-and-saucer set on the bric-a-brac shelf. The owners must have put them out of sight quickly and wondered at the reasons for their purchase. Twenty-eight Siamese twin souvenirs from an earlier time nullify each other's negative potency, and become fascination with anachronistic enthusiasms. I have purchased every Chang and Eng fairing I've come across.

The sideshow to which my mother took us that day featured no exhibition as dramatic as Chang and Eng. The Bearded Woman was not more hirsute than some of our neighbors. The Fat Lady and her Skinny Man made a striking couple but nothing like the disparity depicted on the canvas banner outside. The Midget was small, but so was I. The Fire Eater held my attention, as did the Sword Swallower. They were the same man. Leopard Boy had a bad case of psoriasis. No one made eye contact. We stared. Mostly I learned that lots of things were not as adults described them. The best thing about that memorable day was that I increased my collection of penny arcade Fortune cards and Cowboy cards.

11
Group of Chang and Eng fairings, 1835–39. Glazed bisque, each 3½" high. USA

11

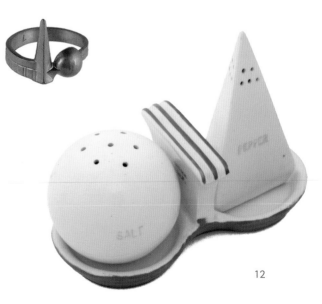

12

I WAS TOO young to remember my only trip to the 1939–40 World's Fair, but I have had a lifelong fascination with the Siamese twinned Trylon and Perisphere. The Perisphere was a 200-foot-diameter sphere that was the location of the World's Fair theme center. The Trylon was its 700-foot-high companion. The Helicline, a ramp that also led visitors back to the fairgrounds, joined the Trylon and Perisphere. Fair goers entered the theme center and ascended partway up the Trylon on the *World's Longest Escalator.* They were then directed to view the Democracity diorama of the *City of the Future,* which centrally occupied the Perisphere's floor and could be viewed from the perimeter or from a surrounding balcony. A six-minute film accompanied Democracity, showing happy farmers and workers of the future. The Fair's slogan *Building a World of Tomorrow* was epitomized here.

The Trylon and Perisphere were the only Fair structures that were permitted to be painted pure white.

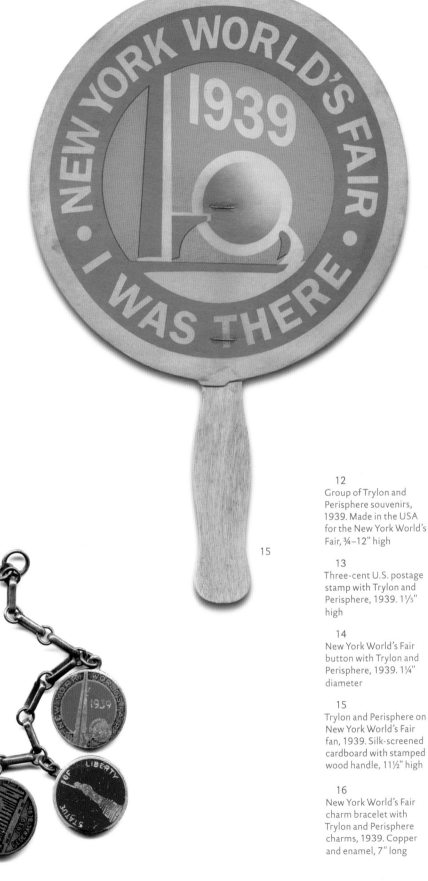

12
Group of Trylon and Perisphere souvenirs, 1939. Made in the USA for the New York World's Fair, ¾–12" high

13
Three-cent U.S. postage stamp with Trylon and Perisphere, 1939. 1⅕" high

14
New York World's Fair button with Trylon and Perisphere, 1939. 1¼" diameter

15
Trylon and Perisphere on New York World's Fair fan, 1939. Silk-screened cardboard with stamped wood handle, 11½" high

16
New York World's Fair charm bracelet with Trylon and Perisphere charms, 1939. Copper and enamel, 7" long

17

18

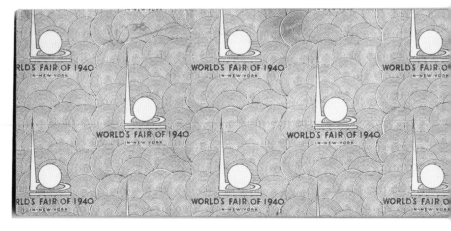

20

17
Trylon and Perisphere ashtray, 1939. Cast steel, 4¼" high. Made in the USA for the New York World's Fair

18
Trylon and Perisphere postcard, 1939. 5½" high. Miller Art, Inc., Brooklyn, New York. Made in the USA for the New York World's Fair

19
Trylon and Perisphere one-piece salt and pepper shaker set, 1939. Celluloid, 3¾" high. Eneloid Company, Arlington, New Jersey

20
New York World's Fair (1939–40) ticket book with Trylon and Perisphere pattern on back cover, 1940. 2¼" high

21
New York World's Fair poster made of 54 officially licensed stamps (detail),1939. 4½" high. Nicklin Company, New York

19

The architectural firm Harrison and Foulihoux designed the "pure forms" to "reflect an emphasis on purity embodied by industrial designers of today." The board of design directors—Norman Bel Geddes, Raymond Loewy (of Coca-Cola bottle fame), Henry Dreyfuss, and Walter Dorwin Teague, were unified believers in the clean lines and pure forms of the Bauhaus and Art Deco. They saw themselves as theorists with a mission to "regulate artistic and architectural organization against Manhattan's spires." They and corporate American organizers cooperatively influenced how things should look for an era. The Fair disseminated the style of American products from toothbrushes to airplanes, product packaging to automobiles.

The Trylon and Perisphere are the quintessence and symbol of the 1930s and 1940s. The twin forms were adapted to hundreds of uses: camphorglass bedside lamps, jewelry, silverware, dishes, fans, paperweights, ashtrays, coasters, suspenders, demitasse spoons, pencil sharpeners, serving trays, juice glasses, and, oddly antithetical to the theme, lace doilies. By far, salt-and-pepper sets outnumber every other incarnation, some cleverly in one piece, with perforations on opposing sides so that a wrist twitch produced only salt or only pepper. Most sets were manufactured in two parts. Sufficient numbers of fair goers purchased this form, then tired of it; so they may still be easily acquired.

21

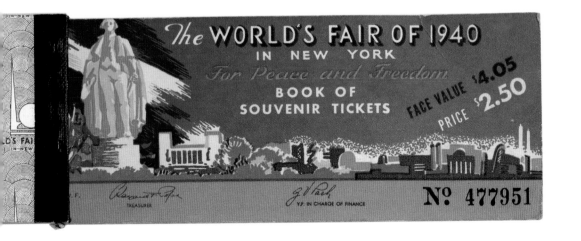

Red Shelton
METRO-GOLDWYN-MAYER

THOUGH eager for success, you are quick to realize that all good things take time.

COLLECT Engrav-o-links FORMERLY MOVIE STARS

Peerless Wghg. & Vendg. Mch. Corp., N.Y.

Ann Sothern
METRO GOLDWYN-MAYER

YOUR sunny attitude toward life is a constant inspiration to your friends.

COLLECT Engrav-o-links FORMERLY MOVIE STARS

Peerless Wghg. & Vendg. Mch. Corp., N.Y.

James Stewart
METRO-GOLDWYN-MAYER

QUIET, self-reliant and well informed, you make definite and sure decisions.

COLLECT Engrav-o-links FORMERLY MOVIE STARS

Peerless Wghg. & Vendg. Mch. Corp., N.Y.

Robert Taylor
METRO-GOLDWYN-MAYER

MEN like you for your frankness. Women like you for your ready sympathy.

COLLECT Engrav-o-links FORMERLY MOVIE STARS

Peerless Wghg. & Vendg. Mch. Corp., N.Y.

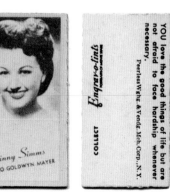

Ginny Simms
METRO GOLDWYN-MAYER

YOU love the good things of life but are not afraid to face hardship whenever necessary.

COLLECT Engrav-o-links FORMERLY MOVIE STARS

Peerless Wghg. & Vendg. Mch. Corp., N.Y.

With best wishes
Fuzzy Knight

MADE IN U.S.A.

Yours truly
John Wayne

MADE IN U.S.A.

Very truly yours
Gary Cooper

MADE IN U.S.A.

Cordially
Roy Rogers

MADE IN U.S.A.

THE FOUNDING father of today's video arcade was the penny arcade of the 1870s that offered various forms of mechanical entertainment for a cent. Strength testing, predicting the future, and watching Mutoscope peep shows were part of the fare. As arcade technologies advanced into the twentieth century, entertainment machines became more complex and sophisticated.

In 1909, Skeeball became a main attraction. The Skeeball Company still manufactures arcade games. The original and classic Skeeball game consisted of an alley with seven productive holes at the nether end and a long default slot. For a nickel, nine balls were delivered by means of a lever at one's knee. The target was the seven holes that diminished in size as their point value increased from ten to fifty. There was an automated scorekeeper in the hood of the apparatus. The player received tickets proportionate to the score at the end of each round. The tickets were redeemable for an array of prizes and were usually dispensed by a sour, stubble-bearded old man. If the hardwood ball was rolled up the center of the alley, in direct approach to the holes, it was inevitably deflected into the default slot or the ten-point hole. A score of 110 points was required for one ticket. By the 1950s, every aspect of the game had been calculated to appear a deceptive cinch. Weight and heft of the ball, thwarting of common trajectories, alley length and width, and rise and height of the hole surrounds for ricochet and deflection factors all contributed to your score. Where there's a will and a gaming spirit, there's usually a way to overcome poor odds. In 1956, my family spent the summer in a bungalow near the boardwalk at Rockaway Beach. My father commuted to and from the Garment Center with the other fathers. I took up the Skeeball challenge and discovered that if I rolled the ball with specific force at a point on the alley's sidewall just before the rise, the ball would, gracefully but with certain purpose, plop into the forty- or fifty-point hole. Another lesson in reduction of variables, shades of Indian card flipping. Earnest study has its rewards; I won two complete sets of china dinnerware, full service for twenty-four diners, although we never served banquets at home.

Penny arcades, along the boardwalks of my youth, contained archaic paraphernalia including Mutoscope peep shows, which had little vigor in the face of Technicolor movies. I searched out arcade mysteries as raptly as a seeker of animal traces in amber. I tried out every machine from pinballs to diggers, and acquired lifelong skill as an expert marksman at the shooting machines and live concessions. The most lasting material evidence of my arcade occupancy is my collection of VENDING MACHINE CARDS. Fortune cards, which described my character a dozen contradictory ways and my ninety Ideal Love Mates, stacked nicely. Salutations from my cowboy friends were delivered in one-color print jobs through a slot for two cents. A posse of cowboys, including

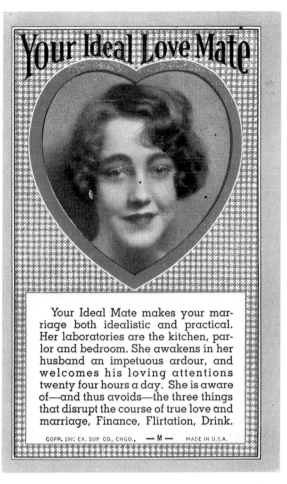

Your Ideal Mate makes your marriage both idealistic and practical. Her laboratories are the kitchen, parlor and bedroom. She awakens in her husband an impetuous ardour, and welcomes his loving attentions twenty four hours a day. She is aware of—and thus avoids—the three things that disrupt the course of true love and marriage, Finance, Flirtation, Drink.

COPR. 1941 EX. SUP CO., CHGO., — M — MADE IN U.S.A.

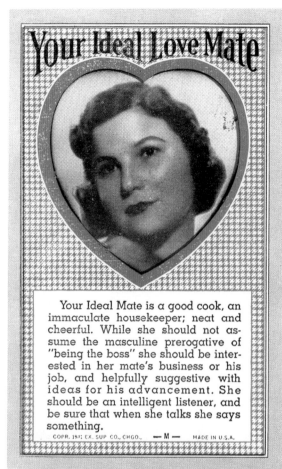

Your Ideal Mate is a good cook, an immaculate housekeeper; neat and cheerful. While she should not assume the masculine prerogative of "being the boss" she should be interested in her mate's business or his job, and helpfully suggestive with ideas for his advancement. She should be an intelligent listener, and be sure that when she talks she says something.

COPR. 1941 EX. SUP CO., CHGO., — M — MADE IN U.S.A.

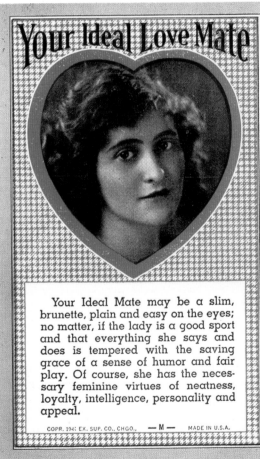

Your Ideal Mate may be a slim, brunette, plain and easy on the eyes; no matter, if the lady is a good sport and that everything she says and does is tempered with the saving grace of a sense of humor and fair play. Of course, she has the necessary feminine virtues of neatness, loyalty, intelligence, personality and appeal.

COPR. 1941 EX. SUP. CO., CHGO., — M — MADE IN U.S.A.

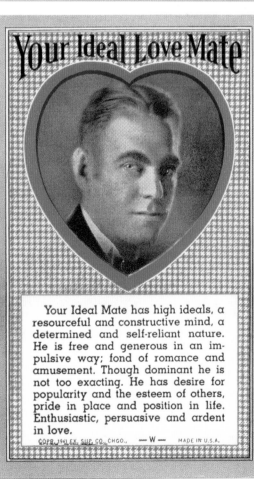

Your Ideal Mate has high ideals, a resourceful and constructive mind, a determined and self-reliant nature. He is free and generous in an impulsive way; fond of romance and amusement. Though dominant he is not too exacting. He has desire for popularity and the esteem of others, pride in place and position in life. Enthusiastic, persuasive and ardent in love.

COPR. 1941 EX. SUP. CO., CHGO., — W — MADE IN U.S.A.

22
Vending machine fortune cards showing your weight and an actor or actress for one cent, 1946. Each 2¼" high

23
Penny arcade cowboy cards, 1952–53. Each 5¼" high

24
Your Ideal Love Mate fortune cards, 1941. Each 5¼" high. Ex. Sup Company, Chicago, Illinois

24

Hoot Gibson, Fuzzy Knight, Tex Maynard, Buddy Roosevelt, and Roy Rogers in posed photos, not in action, offered salutations and autographs at the bottom of each card. My brother still has his penny black-and-white baseball cards. The card-vending machines were the last stop on the way out of the arcade. Residual pennies were inserted into circular recessed slots in a steel slide. As the slide was pushed machineward, a card emerged from the machine's innards into your hand. Many of these card stanchions were mechanical mutations devised by the Mutoscope Company. I never lost my fascinated awe with the tone of certainty with which these cards spoke, offering contradictory and wacky presumptions about where my life was headed as well as wholesome howdys from my equestrian friends. However, lots of my contemporaries did, so now I have their Ideal Love Mates all mixed up with mine.

WHEN I WAS a kid, games of skill included dexterity puzzles, particularly the ball-in-hole game. These games originated as portable novelties and pocket gimcracks in the 1880s. The earliest shop giveaways and product trinkets that I have are a pair, silver dollar-size and depicting ethnic heads on lithographed tin under glass. The player was expected to maneuver tiny white glass balls into eye sockets and smile indentations to complete the faces. One has a handy purse mirror on the reverse; the other has a grocer's address to remind the player who provided the fun. Later games are commonly rectangular 4-by-5-inch cases with glass tops, wood or cardboard game faces, and wood and paper tape framing that gave way to steel framing in primary colors. BBs, or steel ball bearings, provided the action that thwarted the kid.

The Golden Rod dexterity puzzle is no fun. Instead of steel balls, this puzzle requires that five graduated and virtually weightless squared rods be manipulated into snug corresponding slots in specific order. In Pin-U-Ring-It, five varicolored quoits must be coaxed onto elevated pegs bearing the name of each color. In Alice in Puzzleland, five BBs must be mustered into the doorway of a house, rolled down a path to an aerial view of the Mad Hatter's Tea Party and into five corresponding cups on the table. Instructions dictate that if any of the balls deviate from the tortuous path, the player must begin again. Five must be the digit for frustration.

25
Dexterity game (front), c. 1945. Printed cardboard, glass, paper tape, and wood, 5¼" high. R. Journet and Company, England

26
Dexterity game, c. 1945. Printed cardboard, glass, paper tape, wood, and brass rivets, 4" high

27
Group of dexterity games, 1810–1922. Printed cardboard, celluloid, glass, painted tin, and mirror, 2¼" diameter

28
Group of dexterity games (fronts and backs), 1929. Printed cardboard, glass, painted steel, and steel ball bearings, 3½–5" high. Bar Zim Toy Manufacturing Company, New York City

25

26

27

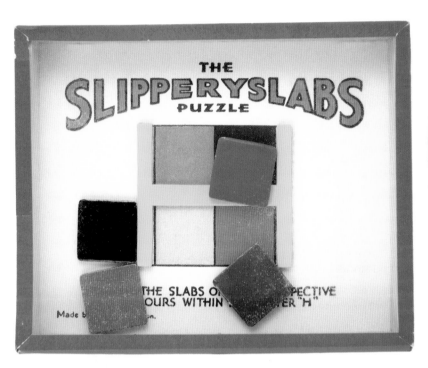

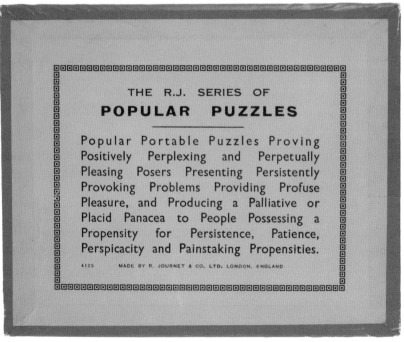

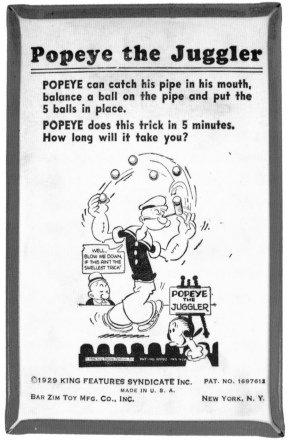

The tasks set by dexterity game manufacturers are iffy at best; it is in the nature of steel ball bearings to roll around uncontrollably unless they are captured in a motor. Bowling Green gets my most arcane dexterity-puzzle award. Like Skeeball, the far end has holes to receive the fruits of the player's skill. These holes, however, are arranged as ten pins in a triangular format: rows of four, three, two, and one. Bits of a quavering globule of mercury are to be deposited into each depression while avoiding the gutters on each side.

These games were never fun. As they aged, the lithographic image tended to separate from the cardboard backing and/or to warp from sweaty, angry hands or to suffer other disfiguring damage from being hurled across the room. These games represent another flavor of owners losing interest. I do not own any from my own childhood for all of the above reasons. But I have purchased many from the childhoods of less expressive others. All these games have been selected for their culturally revelatory images. They date from 1870 through 1950 and each orates a specific chapter within that time frame, expressing its pertinent attitudes, its heroes, its humor, historical events, and its perception of child fun.

FOUR WHEEL steel roller skates were my idea of a good time from my sixth to my twelfth year. These were steel skates that had a leather heel strap that buckled at the ankle and front clamps that grabbed the edge of the hard sole of my oxfords or saddle shoes. I was on skates whenever I had any choice in the matter. Chronically skinned knees were the attendant circumstance of races down Suicide Hill, neighborhood playground antics, adventure games, and journeys over amalgam surfaces that vibrated those uncushioned steel wheels, causing unpredictable jogs. Nothing could stop me except those clamps that required constant tightening. Every skating friend had skinned knees and the same maintenance problem. Outdoor shoe-skates and rubber wheels didn't come out until much later.

29
Group of World War II dexterity games, 1945. Printed cardboard, glass, painted steel, steel ball bearings in gelatin capsules, 3½–4¼" high

30
Group of roller skate keys, 1940s–50s. Steel, 2–3¼" high

31
Roller-skating illustration in *Elson-Gray Basic Reader*, Book II, 1936, page 3. 4¾" high. Glenview, Illinois: Scott Foresman & Company

32
Group of roller skate keys, 1947–51. Steel, 2–3¼" high

29

30

31

We weren't latch key children; we were skate key children. Skate keys kept skates on feet and knees off the pavement. With extra band-aids in my pocket and my skate key hanging on a cord around my neck, I'd be gone until dinner. The Chicago Skate Company made my skates, and my skate key said so. I still have it and my brother's Rollfast skate key and two unmarked blank replacement spares from the candy store. They were interchangeable, all fitting the squared shaft that tightened the clamps. The handle end of the key was a hex bolt-wrench through which my cord slipped. The hex wrench was infrequently called to mechanical performance. It was used to loosen the bolt that united or disengaged the slide to change the size of the skate. Skates could expand when you got new shoes and could be passed on to younger siblings with smaller feet. The other possible fate for old skates was the fruit crate scooter. All that was required was a 3-foot wooden plank, a fruit crate stood on its short end, old skates, a hammer, nails, and determination. Construction took supportive friends, much consultation, hours to construct, and about fifteen minutes to lose interest in. Scooters were extremely noisy in action, and they vibrationally challenged one's physical well-being. I can mentally re-create those vibrations fifty-five years later. Skate keys are the salient symbol of my childhood.

...an object of exceptional
ornament, one of the few such pieces extant.
The handle, worn smooth, indicates its use
in long-forgotten rituals, perhaps of a sacrficial nature.

It is engirdled with an inventive example
of gold interlacing, no doubt of Celtic influence.
Previously thought to be a pre-Carolingian work,
it is now considered to be of more recent provenance,
probably the early 1940s.

> Billy Collins, "My Heart" from *The Art of Drowning*
> (Pittsburgh: University of Pittsburgh Press, 1995).

32

chapter 9

Owners Grew Up

AS A YOUNG child, my daughter, Amie, collected dice, inspected-by-number tags, and miniatures of people waiting on benches. She used innate selective criteria and applied instinctive organizational principles to her collections and to the food that she admitted to her purview. In late June, incomparable Schoharie County strawberries appear on farm stands. For the last forty years, every June I have made a year's worth of strawberry jam, ice cream, and syrup. Amie was an excellent companion in sorting, hulling, and putting the most perfect strawberries into a bowl for eating with a bit of cream after dinner. She worked with me for hours, diligently, skillfully, and without hesitation, classifying and placing each berry into the respective receptacle that determined its destiny as a finished product.

At the dinner table one June night, at the age of three, she was seated beside the young daughter of our dinner guests, and both girls were served hefty plated portions of fresh strawberries for dessert. Amie selected each berry with purpose, following the standards of her inner muse, apparently saving the best one for last. Vanessa ate each berry as it came. They had two distinctly different styles of consumption. As Amie had put her next-to-last strawberry into her mouth, the other child reached for Amie's last one and put it in her mouth. It was a lightning strike and there was nothing to be done about it. Vanessa's appalled father, who witnessed the incident, immediately chastised the culprit. Amie's response was made in a near whisper. In an ages-old tone of resignation she said, "You can't take back time." The inflection in her expression of passive concession was the collector's sighing acceptance of the goneness of the one that got away, attended by silent self-recrimination about not having acted fast enough and about a lesson learned.

Every collector can tell a story about the one that got away. What is cherished is not friable, although it might be outgrown. Children are as different as adults in how they relate to their possessions. There are children for whom toys are items of interest as long as function or novelty last and there are children who bond with their possessions in a way that isn't exhausted by utility. Then there are the many permutations in between.

Amie's collection of miniature people waiting on benches is arranged in rows on a seventeenth-century English oak stand in her former bedroom. All the soldiers, civilians, children, fishermen, and farmhands are unified by their leaden and unmalleable seated attitudes, although not all are cast to the same scale of measurement. Many of these figures are awaiting the arrival of model railroad trains that will never come. The uniform face of acquiescent waiting captured Amie's interest when she was a young child visiting flea markets with me. She was in a stroller and, as a result, saw only what was on low tables or blankets on the ground. Her selections were always dice and diminutive people seated on Lilliputian benches. She still adopts sitters and their benches. Her amity for them continues; her perspective of larger experience causes her to regard them with an objectivity that is simultaneously close and distant. She follows the filament of a private continuity. Collectors mediate their own elevations.

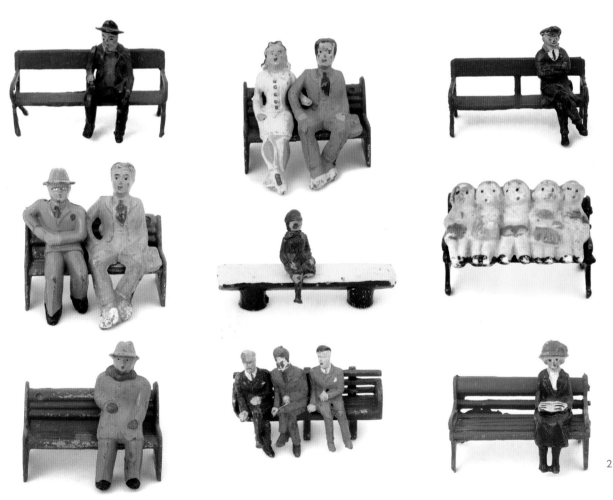

1
Toy figures waiting on benches, 1915–40. Painted cast lead, and bisque, 1½–2" high

2
Toy figures waiting on benches, 1915–40. Painted cast lead, and bisque, 1½–2" high

2

THE REGALIA surrounding electric trains of all gauges are varied and complete enough to assuage the most obsessive model railroad enthusiast. The range and detail of railroad-related signs and fixtures that are on the market prove live interest in their continuing manufacture. Besides trees, shrubs, distant churches, and snow-covered mountains, there are signs for the areas tangent to the tracks, railroad stations, waiting rooms (we know about the people waiting on benches), telephone poles, parking-lot light fixtures, and gas stations. It stands to reason that there were painted cast-iron gas pumps with vintage clock-face meters and shoelace hoses and *Don't Park Here* signs to support earlier diminutive realities. Those are the signs and gas pumps for which I search. Enough youngsters outgrew them that I find a couple every year. One sign and one gas pump have split personalities; their first was as glass candy containers. A decision had to be made about which collection would contain them.

MY SON, Jesse, collected action figures, robots, and comic books as a child. In 1972, when he was three-and-a-half years old, he was seated amid a group of superhero figures and robots. I was preparing dinner and glanced up at him as he sat uncharacteristically still within a teeming psychodrama that he had erected. I asked him what he was doing.

"Shhh, my mind is telling my brain what to do."

Robots and action figures were his proxies for dangerous strategic experiments. This one apparently had challenged the limits of his imagination. Superhero figures come with formulated characters, established responsibilities, clear moral codes, and strict social obligations. Their secret identities are the umbilicus to the willing child, if he/she is not a budding sociopath, and transference is easy. Excepting benign robots on the order of C3-PO and R2-D2, robots tend to be powerful and potentially danger-ous, lacking *our* moral code or ethical responsibilities to our community. A 1960s robot didn't necessarily come with a conscience, and unknown powers could be tailored to be a formidable and fitting enemy for the superhero. Solving knotty problems of good and evil with surrogate figures on the living-room floor helped pave the way to a law-abiding adulthood.

In the late 1940s and 1950s the Loews American movie theater offered *Junior Joy Shows* that lasted all day on Saturday. Comprised of twenty-five cartoons, *Movietone News* featuring the voice of Ed Herlihy, a travelogue or two, a couple of shorts, several episodes of serials that always ended with cliffhangers, and two feature-length movies. It was late afternoon by the time my brother and I crossed the street to Woolworth's lunch counter. We had a dollar for the day, a quarter each for the movies and fifty cents for a malted and sandwich split. In 1951, *The Day the Earth Stood Still* was one of those feature-length movies. Gort, a monumental robot with a disintegrating ray and unfailing aim, arrived with his keeper Klaatu, a few yards from the White House, in a flying saucer. Michael Rennie, who played Klaatu, announced early on that they came in peace, but the future of Earth was at stake. "Klaatu Barada Nikto" became my fluent mantra of welcome should the necessity arise. The phrase replaced the security of my radio premium equipment. At this historical juncture, flying saucers were a greater threat than Germans coming. The fifties were legendary for fear of outer-space invasion and for movies in which fears were played out, in black-and-white, in one-and-a-half-hour doses. Science fiction movies were simultaneously terrifying about the possibilities and comforting because dumb flaws in logic and clumsy visuals, coupled with extraterrestrial musical effects, recast them as fiction.

In 1956, *Forbidden Planet* was a Saturday feature film. Robbie was offered up as a helpful robot with a code of ethics and a *built-in safety device* that blocked killing the good guys when ordered to do so by Walter Pidgeon, who played the evil Dr. Morbius. By the standards of Japanese robots of the 1960s, armed with ejecting rockets and vehicular attachments, Robbie the toy robot looks like a whimsical, tubby, Echo Deco black enameled R2-D2.

Robot toys never really lived up to childhood expectations. Imagination had to provide cutting-edge thrills. Robotic moving parts didn't fare well in toy chests. Those that were relegated to the attic, garage, or basement are the ones that turn up at lawn sales and flea markets. Those still in their original boxes often wind up at auction. Either some kids saved just by instinct or were too daunted or uninterested to play with the robot in the first place. Jesse kept his robots and collected the robots of other kids who grew up.

5

5
Battery-powered robot (walks and shoots), 1960s. Printed steel, 9½" high. Horikawa, Japan

6
Key-wind Robbie the Robot (walks and sparks), 1956. Adapted from the movie robot in *Forbidden Planet*, 9½" high. Japan

6

7
Battery-powered Space Man robot (walks), 1950s. Printed steel and clear plastic viewing port, 7¾" high. Masudaya, Japan

8
Wind-up robot (walks), 1984. Printed pressed steel and plastic, 4¼" high. Masudaya Corporation, Japan

9
Crank-wind, friction motor robot (rolls), 1950s. Printed steel and clear plastic helmet, 7" high

10
Key-wind G Robot (walks), c.1980. Printed steel and plastic, 9¼" high. Japan

11
Key-wind Sparky Robot (walks), 1955. Painted pressed steel, 7½" high. Japan

12
Dial-wind robot (rolling walk with clicking), 1950s. Printed pressed steel and clear plastic viewing port, 9½" high. Yonezawa, Japan

13
Key-wind robot with astronaut face, 1950s. Printed steel and clear plastic viewing port, 8" high. Japan

14
Key-wind robot with easel back (walks), 1950s. Printed steel, 6" high. Line Mar Toys, Japan

15
Key-wind NASA robot (rolls as antenna and outer space screen in chest turns), 1960s. Printed steel, 7" high. Japan

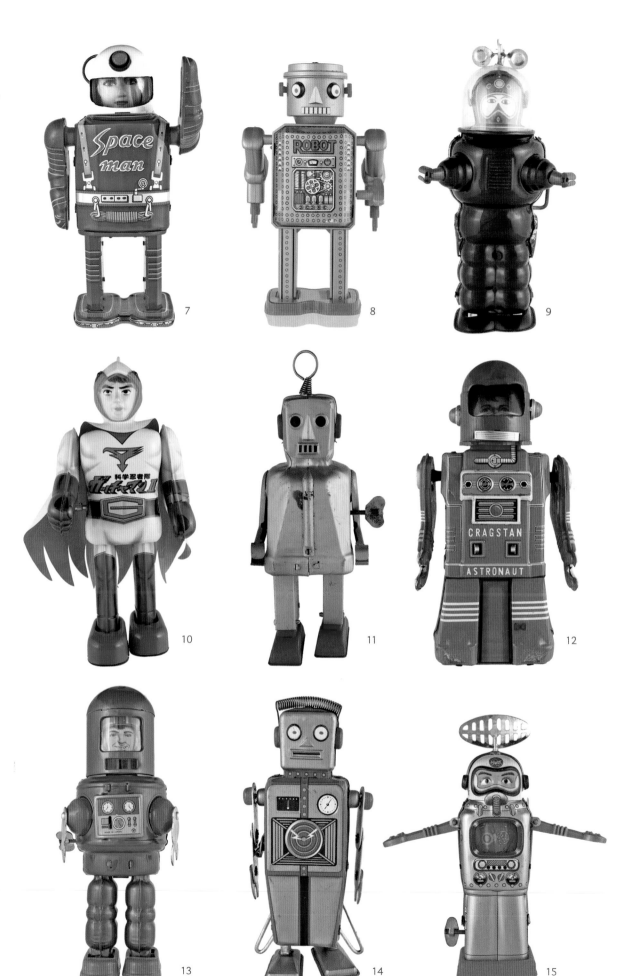

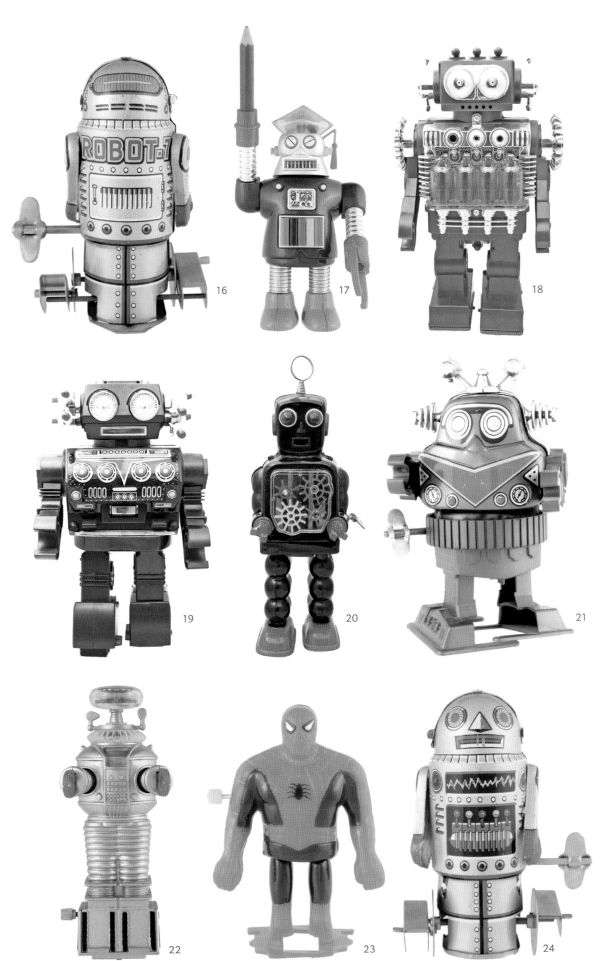

16
Key-wind Robot-7 (back) (rolls), c. 1970. Printed steel, 4" high. Japan

17
Scholar robot (articulated appendages with removable books in abdomen), c. 1980. Die-cast metal and plastic with pencil, 5" high. "GA42," Japan

18
Battery-operated Piston Robot (glides on wheeled feet with pistons at chest), 1968–75. Plastic with steel parts, 10½" high. Japan

19
Battery-operated robot (walks while torso rotates from side to side with four projectiles mounted on head with individual mechanical switches), 1965–70. Printed steel and plastic, 9½" high. Japan

20
Key-wind High Wheel Robot (walks and sparks with four turning gears), 1960s. Printed pressed steel and plastic, 9½" high. Yoshiya, Japan

21
Key-wind robot (walks with rotating torso), 1970s. Printed pressed steel and plastic, 5" high. "Yone 2219," Japan

22
Wind-up robot (glides on simulated treads), 1985. Die-cast plastic with steel works, 4⅕" high. Masudaya Corporation, Japan

23
Wind-up pseudo-Spider–Man robot (walks), 1978. Cast plastic with steel works, 3¼" high. Durham Ind Corporation, Hong Kong

24
Key-wind Robot-7 (front) (rolls), c. 1970. Printed steel, 4" high. Japan

IN MY HUSBAND Ivan's youth, toy soldiers were the cast of the battle between good and evil. We have an assortment of World War I and World War II survivors, mostly lead castings of soldiers engaged in activities specific to war: telegraphy, operating radios, sniping, carrying flags, aiming mortar launchers, or being carried on stretchers. Each is rendered in sufficient painterly detail to carry out his part in the narrative but shares the face of implacable neutrality with the person waiting on the bench for the train that never arrives. None are of the battle-accurate Britains caliber or are serious Civil War battlefield replicas intended for the hobbies of grown men. I have supplemented Ivan's collection with yard-sale finds over the years. Each is nicked and chipped, befitting a veteran of numerous boyhood coffee-table battles, and a few lack hands. There is a hefty, smooth, and tactile attractiveness about them.

In seeking lead soldiers scarred by evidence of use, I discovered a fine precursor group to the cast figures. These are World War I soldiers manufactured with moveable limbs. They are lithographed tin stampings about four inches high, with articulated limbs that are poseable. Even their rifles pivot shoulderward or toward action. Unlike the poseable action figures of the late 1960s and 1970s, they don't stand without help. Each has a rectangular green stand into which a tab on one foot locks. These soldiers show battle wear in their loosened joints and bends resulting from a child's impatience with a failed pose necessitated by plot. Robert G., who collects soap shards, tells me that he lost interest in his soldiers about the time that every TV program in California was about cowboys and he was backyard-war weary. He had gotten his hands on some firecrackers and staged a dazzling terminal battle before he turned to model cars and then girls.

Many chipped and nicked toy soldiers had been overrun by friendly toy-tank enthusiasts. Most of the toy tanks that I collected are friction-driven or wind-up and consequently have fulfilled their destinies by mowing down regiments of lead soldiers. Who owned enemy soldiers? In America, every boy had American soldiers. There were many stand-ins for the enemy and, in a pinch, even one of our own could try out for the part. *Friendly fire* hadn't yet entered the lexicon. Wind-up or friction action provided mobility and the possibility of unanticipated incidents (within limits). One could always call a do-over if the outcome was wrong. One wind-up lithographed steel tank combines Superman, emerging from beneath, and standing up, with an attractive rollover aspect. Indoor games in which hero and villain surrogates were used to enact scenarios were essentially lone activities in which a scheme was played out and a single will dominated all the roles. Children playing together typically engaged in more active games in which the plot unfolded in unpredictable ways.

25
Group of toy soldiers, c. 1937. Painted cast lead, 1½–3¼" high

26
Group of articulated
American World War I
toy soldiers, c. 1915.
Litho on tin, 5" high fully
extended

27
World War I tanks and
armored cars, c. 1915.
Painted cast iron and
printed steel, each
2¼" high

28
M-25 tank with
Superman rollover
feature, 1940. Key-wind
motor, printed steel,
3½" high with Superman
lifting. National Comics
Corporation Mar Line
Toys

JUMPING ROPE, roller skating, *ring-o-leevio*, hide-and-seek, punchball, stoopball, and bad guys vs. good guys were prime physical activities in a neighborhood where whoever was around was a participant. If lots of kids were outside, teams were formed. Punchball happened in the schoolyard because the wire fencing could prevent lost pink Spaldings. Stoopball necessitated a stoop on a dead-end street. Hide-and-seek required buildings with open doors, cellar ways, bushes, parked cars, and a tree base nearby. Jumping rope and roller skating demanded decent pavement. The requisite for *ring-o-leevio*, a hands-on game of capture, and bad vs. good guy games were areas of grass where rollovers could be enacted and shoot-outs and agonizing simulated wounding could be staged without incurring skinned elbows.

Cap guns aided our theatrics. Cap guns came in as many models as real firearms. The earliest, dating from the mid-1800s, were cast iron six-shooters and small single-shot pistols that resembled the guns that settled the Wild West. Later versions were nickel, then chrome plated with simulated bone grips. There was a spectrum of automatics as well. All were united in requiring caps for sound effects. Caps were small explosive dot charges enclosed in reddish paper that were set off by the hammer of the toy gun. They came in several forms, notably on discs, strips, reels, and as squares and single-round shots. All caps sounded identical, but caps were not interchangeable. Each gun required a particular shape of cap to ensure repeated firing or in fact firing at all. My brother had a Hopalong Cassidy six-shooter requiring reel-formatted caps. I had an elegant *Kilgore* automatic that worked off strip caps. These caps sounded like a gunshot, they smelled like gunpowder, and they sparked. Copious amounts of caps were used in a good shoot-out. The grass was strewn with spent and perforated red-paper fragments. The guns were durable, but there is no good reason that any caps for these pistols and revolvers should be extant. I must have been insecure about running out of caps because I still have multiple packages of each format. There are certain things that one doesn't want to think about running out of. I moved on to water pistols and penny arcade pinup cards but never outgrew my symbolic stash of caps. As an adult I have consistently purchased more than ample future supplies of paper towels.

29
Automatic pistol cap gun (closed and open), 1930. Cast iron, 5¼" long. USA

30
Automatic pistol cap gun (back and front), 1940. Cast iron, 5" long. USA

31
Revolver cap gun (closed and open), 1890. Cast iron, 5¾" long. USA

32
Revolver cap gun (closed and open to receive roll caps), 1950. Nickel-plated cast steel with plastic portrait grips, 9" long. USA

33
Automatic pistol cap gun (open to receive roll caps and closed), 1935. Cast iron, 5½" long. USA

34
Caps and caps packaging, 1915–85. Printed card stock, packages 1–1¾" high

35
Group of arcade
Mutoscope pinup cards,
c. 1945–55. Each 5¼"
high

I LEARNED about glamour and what men want from penny arcade Mutoscope pinup cards. The American Mutoscope and Biograph Company was established in 1895. I was established in 1939. By the time of my penny arcade summers, the company had two products. The first were painted cast-iron arcade stands, which harbored metal spool reels that held 850 frames of black-and-white still photographs of actors or action with sequential variation. The hand-turned crank shaft flipped the frames, creating the illusion of a motion picture that told a story about the slapstick antics of piano movers or a pie-eating contest or photographically reiterated a boxing match or the demise of the Hindenburg. For one cent I could stand on the child's step-up, watch the light bulb turn on, and see the action through a glass-covered oval peephole; hence the term *peep show*. The action could be slowed down or speeded up by manipulating the crank. This was my first experience with fast-forwarding, and I've never lost the knack. Those archaic machines were still around in the face of 1950s Cinemascope: I knew they were on their way out, but some of the reels like *Ladies' Night at the Turkish Bath* were still compelling because they were remotely enlightening about male-female behavioral mysteries. The flickering motion of those spool-reel frames is the reason we still call movies *flicks*. The other arcade Mutoscope product was related to my collections of 3-by-5-inch, one- and two-cent fortune, ideal mate, and cowboy arcade cards. The pinup, unencumbered by blotter ad copy or ashtray utility, could be had for five cents in four-color lithography on card stock.

On the pages of *Esquire* magazine in the 1940s and 1950s, Albert Vargas, Carl Moran, George Petty, Munson, Mozert, and others penned illustrations of idealized females in pert poses in panty- or garter-baring *accidents* with a cutesy accompanying phrase. These gorgeous, flawless, innocent, and dumb babes were the Barbie archetype. Unattached to ads, they were to be contemplated without the ruse of commercial purpose. They must have been important: my father had a subscription to *Esquire* magazine. The pinup found her way to drinking glasses, cocktail napkins, menus, and onto the fuselages of warplanes; I saw them on the *Movietone* newsreels. I was transfixed by the artful, in-your-face presentation of those dames. Nobody's mother looked like them. I knew they weren't real, but they certainly were popular. Their status was unattainably mesmerizing, and I collected them wishing to look as good as they did without having to play dumb. Neither Vargas, Moran et al., my father, nor I had an inkling that we were establishing a collectable tradition that would resound with a following trying to recapture (for big prices) what had been outgrown sixty years earlier. We sometimes relinquish our raw fractious youthful commitment to objects and grow back into them later with other motives.

DURING WORLD War II, Planters Peanuts were packaged in the kind of can that American soldiers ate out of in the field. It was thin tin with a key, dot-soldered onto the bottom of the can. The key was finger-pried off and a tab was inserted into the key slot. When the key was turned, a strip was wound around the key shaft, detaching the cover from the can. This left sharp raw edges and became my mother's lesson in bivouac dining—the reason for which she had used extra ration coupons to buy the can. Mr. Peanut on the can somehow belied the lesson's seriousness. Mr. Peanut became Planters' icon in 1916, which explains the top hat, monocle, spats, and cane.

36
Mr. Peanut nut dish (individual serving), 1951. Printed steel, 3" diameter. Planters Peanuts

37
Planters Peanuts bracelet, 1949. Brass links with plastic charms, 6" long

36

37

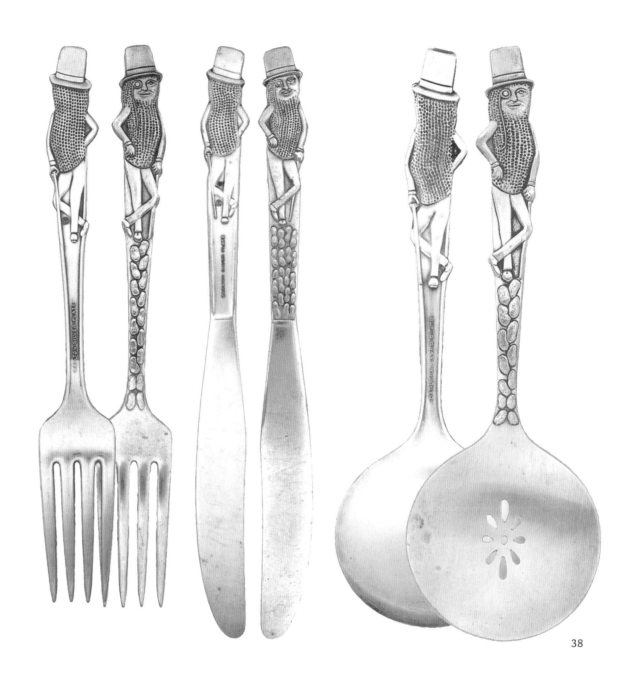

38
Group of Mr. Peanut
utensils, 1948–1950s.
Includes peanut
butter spreader with
perforations to lift off
oil in pre-homogenized
peanut butter, 4¾–5¼"
high. Carlton Silverplate

38

Cellophane snack-size sacks were a favorite of mine in the 1950s. As empties, ten of them were worth one Mr. Peanuts mechanical pencil or one silver-plate peanut butter spreader with a daisy perforation used to lift off the oil that plagued peanut butter in those days. I have six pencils and ten spreaders in their original wrappers. That represents my consumption of 160 Planters peanut packs. You could say that I grew up on Mr. Peanuts as well as with him. I wasn't interested in the mascot's tennis balls, banks, buttons, dolls, belt buckles, towels, or umbrellas. I

just thought the mechanical pencils and spreaders were the best ideas. I never opened one to use it. I just thought they were too good not to have. The peanut butter spreaders have a finely cast, classy Mr. Peanut on the end of the handle, and when turned around, his jaunty stance is conveyed in the back view. That was the magnetic nuance for me with character spoons: the best ones showed crystalline detail.

They are masterpieces, a word not often applied to promotional commercial items. Like decoder rings and badges, premium spoons were offered by

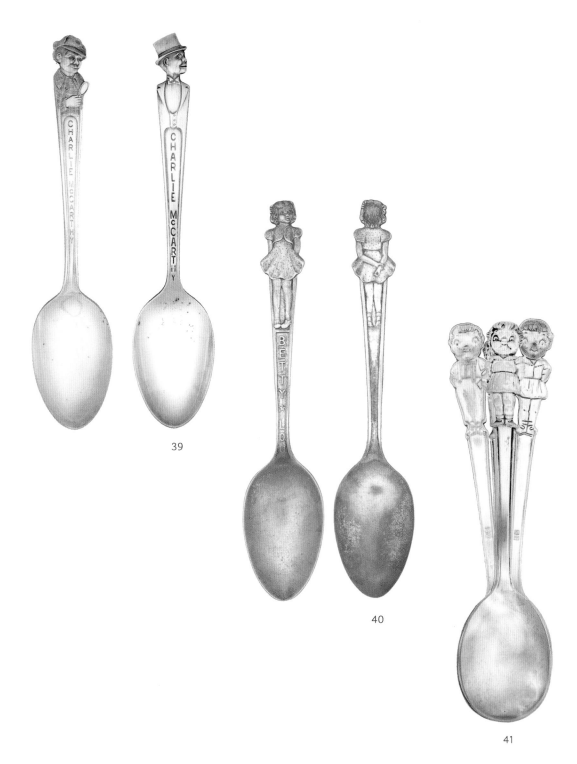

39

40

41

sponsors of radio programs as incentive for children to ask, cajole, insist, beg, and nag Mom to purchase their products. Product sales were definitively paired with the popularity of the radio characters that cereal, candy, milk, bread, and fortified beverage manufacturers sponsored. Oneida and Carlton Silverplate churned out Charlie McCarthy, ventriloquist Edgar Bergen's dummy, in tux and as sleuth and Betty Lou with hands joined behind. In the 1940s, five trademarks as proofs of purchase from Quaker Oats and fifty cents could be transformed into a Betty Lou spoon from NBC's *Girl Alone*. Stylistic generations of spoon handles bloomed thereafter, some of them representing the Campbell's Soup Kids, Mr. Peanut cutlery, and Log Cabin Syrup cabin spoons. Each has a flawless and accurate obverse and reverse. Later versions of these utensils marked with other radio and TV characters became simple, ordinary stampings on stainless steel. Did Campbell's chicken vegetable soup taste better from a Campbell's soup spoon? I never used mine but I still have them. They are harder to find on the secondary market than Dionne Quintuplet character spoons.

Nobody Cared

IN 1975, I found the shopping list of a previous user of a super-market shopping cart. It was short and simple: Clearasil, M&Ms, chips, baloney, orange soda, and dog food. It told a story, and I became a collector of this voyeuristic residuum. Purpose spent, these paper scraps transform into scenarios. Their only common physical trait is the occasional crossing out of what was found on the market shelves. Why weren't these lists taken home to transfer what was not found to the next list? Presumably that's what the authors of lists that I didn't find, did. If these lists tell a collective tale, it is that in recent years people are eating more salads. Some lists are weighted toward dairy products, others toward starchy comfort foods. My most recent acquisition leans heavily toward the laundry and personal-hygiene product aisles: detergent, Downy, Clorox, toilet paper, paper towels, Neutrogena shampoo, wetting solution, hair color, hot oil, bathroom cups, and breast pads. What's a nursing mother with contact lenses, in need of a touch-up, going to do with hot oil?

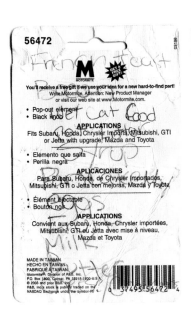

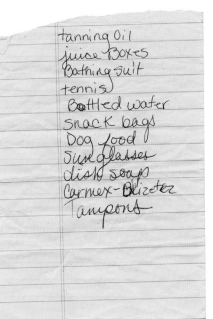

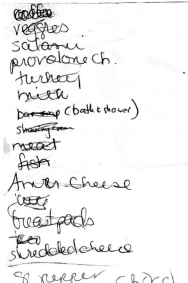

1
Group of shopping lists,
1991–2004. Ink on
paper, 3½–4" high

2
Group of shopping lists,
1987–2004. Ink on
paper, 3½–8½" high

2

3
Group of shopping lists,
1988–2004. Ink and
pencil on paper, 3–7"
high

BASIL
ROSEMARY
THYME
PARSLEY
cilantro
APPLES
BANANAS
ginger
RAISINS
APRICOTS
LEEK
SCALLIONS
SML RED POTS
jalapeno

Fish

Freezer bags
Kleenex
scrubbers

capers
p.nut butter
rice

o PAM -2
BOTTLED WATER
Bread Flour
(King Arthur blue)
Honey

MILK
MOZARRELA cheese
or GRUYERE

Zip lock bags

3 HOLOGEN BULBS
for kitchen

PRESCRIPTIONS

Bread
Grapes
Milk
—
dye hair

4 ROSES

BANANAS
CEREAL
MILK
DIAPERS
SNACKS

the
Clove Tip
for Gelleylul
Toilet Paper
paper Towels
Bounty + Charp

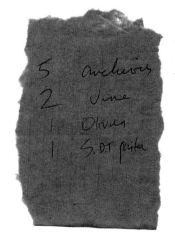

5   anchovies
2   Vine
1   Olives
1   S. DT pasta

BAKING SODA

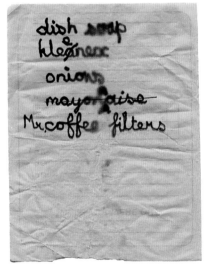

dish soap
kleenex
onions
mayonaise
Mr.coffee filters

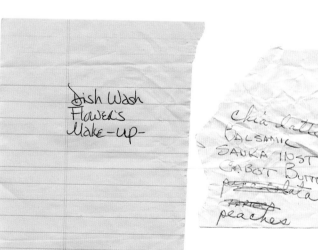

Dish Wash
Flowers
Make-up-

Chia latte
BALSAMIC
SAUKA TOST
CABOT Butter

peaches

Bagels
little yogurt
advantix film

3

Will it affect her milk? Will she do the laundry before or after she dyes her hair? Is she stocking up on toilet paper and paper towels or did she run out of them at the same time? Why is she using disposable paper cups in her bathroom? They are a needless expense, and the print design is not biodegradable. Does someone in her home have trench mouth?

Shopping lists run the gamut of naïve to sophisticated, mundane to poetic, stodgy to flamboyant, offhanded to earnest, vague to obsessively specific. Written for oneself, there is no self-conscious reserve. A sufficiently legible memory prompt is the only requirement. As shoppers abandon their exhausted lists, I harvest and cherish them. No residual fragment is too trivial to collect if you're drawn to it.

I HAVE MULTIPLE fidelities to incidental ephemera. As I linger awhile longer in the supermarket, come-ons beckon and *win instantly* invitations abound on cleaning-product labels and under soft-drink caps. The categorical competition is stiff, and the products are near equally effective. Impulse purchases, based on consumers eager for a lucky hit, probably attract enough sales to keep the game around. *Win Instantly! Dream Kitchen Plus 600 Other Great Prizes* was a recent offer on 409 Glass and Surface Cleaner. Is their dream kitchen my idea of a dream kitchen? Do people who already have their dream kitchens avoid this product? What are the other six hundred great prizes? This side of the game piece doesn't say, but there is an 800 number for further inquiry.

I buy products offering an instant win for their *Sorry Try Again* messages. They are constructed to transmit sympathetic commiseration and not to alienate. The rules section says *no purchase necessary*. These game pieces are not just suspended from the neck of the bottle by a paper loop. They are sufficiently fused with the packaging that extraction would attract the attention of every shopper in your aisle along with several stockboys. "Sorry, I don't want the soda, only the disk married to the underside of the cap" doesn't fly with store security personnel. In 1965, I was handed a postage stamp–size game piece with my change from a Mobil gas station fill-up. I opened it to find that I was a *25 cent Instant Winner*. The prize went unclaimed, since turning in the game piece was required. That was the beginning of my INSTANT WINNER OR NOT collection.

4

5

6

4
409 *Win Instantly!* coupon (outside); *No Purchase Necessary* (inside); *Sorry, Try Again*, 2003. 6" high

5
Mobil gas *You are an Instant Winner*, 1965. Printed card stock, 1½" high

6
Instant Winner lid label (closed and open), Kraft Philadelphia cream cheese, 2004. 4" diameter

MY DAUGHTER, Amie, collects hotel and motel *Do Not Disturb* signs. She has collected them since she began to read. Mastering their simple message was an early milestone. The sameness of their content is like studying the growth pattern of mosses. Their variation resides in format and language. Some are written in one language, others in many languages. Some signs have split personalities, and their reverse sides do double duty to alert room staff to attend to the mess in your room ASAP. Amie is multilingual in these two messages. Doorknob hanging configurations, color, and graphics were main attractions. Twenty years later, linguistic distinctions in command expressions have become informative, although none is guaranteed to keep a determined chambermaid from checking your room while you are abed. Taken singly, the message is direct and clear. Built over a span of years, layer upon layer, the collection is like geological sediment, revealing continental formation of styles of communication.

7
Do Not Disturb hotel doorknob hangers, 1938–89. 6½–14" high

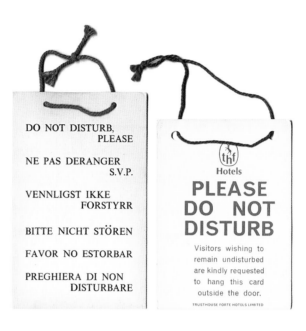

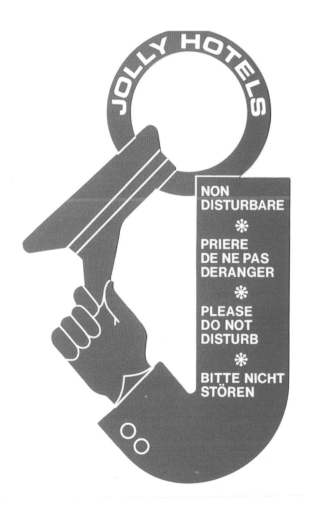

7

IMPERATIVE DIRECTIVES that are riders on a purchase command my immediate attention. *Keep This Coupon* tickets with a six- or seven-digit number printed on an edge have been handed to me over the years in return for admissions paid. Was there a raffle that I missed? How long should I keep this coupon? Lots of these tickets bear the imprimatur of Rogers or MMF Industries in tiny print along the bottom edge. They've been torn off a reel from perforations at the short edges; most have notched corners. They are inevitably red, off-white, orange, or blue, with black and red print. Have the manufacturers of *Take A Number* deli-line tickets evolved from numbered *Admit One* and *Keep This Coupon* tickets? Do vast stores of these tickets remain from carnivals long gone, and now find their way up the cultural chain to rural church breakfasts?

AS A CHILD, I spent lots of time on our living-room floor. I also helped my mother change our sheets and pillowcases. What is the common factor here? The underside of our living-room furniture, our mattresses, and our pillows had white, rectangular pendant tags with black print that read *UNDER PENALTY OF LAW DO NOT REMOVE THIS TAG*. Our coffee table and dining-room furniture didn't have tags. My mother couldn't tell me why these tags had to stay on, and they did stay on. Were the furniture police coming to check? What would happen if they did? As an adult, my first act of possession is to remove all tags; it's a ritual of ownership. Recently, *under penalty of law* tags have evolved to read

#03

UNDER PENALTY OF LAW
THIS TAG NOT TO BE REMOVED

ALL NEW MATERIAL CONSISTING OF
100% POLYESTER FIBER

REG. NO. PA-24368 (NE)

Certification is made by the manufacturer
that the materials in this article are described
in accordance with law.

MADE BY
PAHRUMP PILLOWS
PAHRUMP NEVADA USA
PRODUCTS UNLIMITED, INC. USA
OMAHA, NE 68102

FEDERAL REQUIREMENT
RN 105975
COVERING : 65% POLYESTER/
35% COTTON
SHELL: MADE IN CHINA
FILLED AND SEWN IN USA

8

LAPZ0054A-1

UNDER PENALTY OF LAW THIS
TAG NOT TO BE REMOVED

ALL NEW MATERIAL
Consisting of
100% POLYURETHANE FOAM

Reg. No. PA 24833 (RC)

Certification is made by the manufacturer
that the materials in this article are
described in accordance with law.

SOLD BY
GRACO CHILDREN'S PRODUCTS INC.
Exton, PA 19341

MADE IN CHINA

10

8
Under Penalty of Law This Tag Not To Be Removed, 1994. Printed fabric, 4" high

9
Group of *Keep This Coupon* numbered tickets, 1991–2001. Printed paper, each 1" high

10
Under Penalty of Law This Tag Not To Be Removed, 1996. Printed fabric, 4" high

evolved to read *UNDER PENALTY OF LAW THIS TAG MAY NOT BE REMOVED EXCEPT BY THE CONSUMER*. It's a nice recent addition to the tag collection; however, a course in surgical tag removal is still a necessity to leave all cushion seams intact. I can understand the *Do not remove this tag until you are sure you want to keep this bikini* command. If fiber content is the issue for furniture cleanability, the tag should say so; and it should be inconspicuously attached rather than a flag tag. If upholstery guardians want to see my tags, they're in a loose-leaf binder.

11
Under Penalty of Law This Tag Not To Be Removed Except by the Consumer, 2000. Printed fabric, 4" high

12
Under Penalty of Law This Tag Not To Be Removed, 1997. Printed fabric, 3½" high

13
Under Penalty of Law This Tag Not To Be Removed Except by the Consumer, 2003. Printed fabric, 3½" high

---

c

UNDER PENALTY OF LAW THIS TAG NOT
TO BE REMOVED EXCEPT BY THE CONSUMER

ALL NEW MATERIAL CONSISTING OF POLYESTER FIBER

REGISTRY NO. NC 277

Certification is made by the manufacturer that the materials in this article are described in accordance with law.

MADE BY
PERFECT FIT INDUSTRIES, INC.
201 Cuthbertson Street
Monroe, NC 28111

Date of Delivery . . . .

FULL
Fin. Size 53 x 75 in (135 x 191 cm)
FEDERAL REQUIREMENT—RN15881
FILLING: 100% POLYESTER
COVERING: TOP: 100% COTTON
BACK: 100% POLYESTER
SKIRT: 100% POLYESTER
Made in U.S.A. of Imported Fabric from China
100795

11

LBL#   485 00500-03 291027-01-01 14304240   396

UNDER PENALTY OF LAW
THIS TAG NOT TO BE REMOVED
ALL NEW MATERIALS CONSISTING OF

BODY:

SEAT CUSHIONS:3
   POLYESTER FIBERS 100%
BACK CUSHIONS:3
   POLYESTER FIBERS 100%

REG. NO. PA-25485 (NC)

CERTIFICATION IS MADE BY
THE MANUFACTURER THAT
THE MATERIALS IN THIS
ARTICLE ARE DESCRIBED
IN ACCORDANCE WITH LAW

SOLD BY:

DATE OF DELIVERY:

MADE BY: LANEVENTURE CONOVER, NC USA

TE OF DELIVERY:

12

UNDER PENALTY OF LAW THIS TAG NOT
TO BE REMOVED EXCEPT BY THE CONSUMER
ALL NEW MATERIALS CONSISTING OF BONDED
100% POLYESTER
REGISTRY NO. PA 869 IKYI
CERTIFICATION IS MADE BY THE MANUFACTURER
THAT THE MATERIALS IN THIS ARTICLE
ARE DESCRIBED IN ACCORDANCE WITH LAW.
MANUFACTURED BY
LOUISVILLE BEDDING CO.
LOUISVILLE, KY 40299   50M
DATE OF DELIVERY
FULL FOR MATTRESS
FIN. SIZE 53 IN. X 75 IN. [134 CM X 190 CM]
STYLE NO. 213C-W   068452   Jul 03
RN 16000-MADE IN THE U.S.A. OF IMPORTED AND U.S.A.
MATERIALS. TOP: 100% COTTON, FILLING, BACK & SKIRT: 100%
POLYESTER. HECHO EN EE.UU DE MATERIALES IMPORTADOS DE
E.U. PARTE SUPERIOR: 100% ALGODON, RELLENO. PARTE DE
ATRAS Y FALDA: 100% POLIESTER.

13

INSPECTED BY NUMBER tags accompany a wide variety of products from clothing to gas ranges to boxes of cigars. They are usually the size of fortune-cookie fortunes and printed in black ink with text that reads *Inspected by #*. Some are printed in two languages. Infrequently a first name is printed in lieu of a number. Rarely do first and last names appear. Both of my children collected these tags with me. As youngsters, they learned their numbers from them; each tag was a happy gift in the pocket of a new garment. The most numerous of the tags is *Inspected by #1*. I guess many factories have only one inspector and his/her anonymity has value. We keep these tags in clear plastic loose-leaf slide sleeves. The quantity of specific numbers diminishes as the numbers get higher. Our GE refrigerator tag reads *Inspected by #313,646*. I suspect a pseudonym rather than a head count, but who knows?

STIRO A MANO

6

WE HOPE YOU'LL ENJOY THE COMFORT, WEARABILITY AND QUALITY OF THESE SHOES THAT I HAVE INSPECTED.

3

THIS QUALITY GARMENT
EXAMINED BY
 # 10

7 | In caso di reclamo Vi preghiamo ritornarci il presente tagliando.
In case of complaint, please return this coupon.
Bei Beanstandungen bitten wir Sie, uns diesen Abschnitt zurückzusenden.
En cas de réclamation, veuillez nous retourner ce coupon, s.v.p.

This Garment Has Been
Thoroughly Examined
By Inspector No. 44

This Garment Has Been
Thoroughly Examined
by Inspector No. 27

INSPECTED BY
426

QUALITY IS MY RESPONSIBILITY
IT'S ESSENTIAL FOR THE SUCCESS
OF OUR COMPANY
EMPLOYEE *Patty*

This garment has been thoroughly examined.
It meets the high standards of tailoring at my final inspection station.
Elvira Riccio

Inspected by SANDRA

Taylor Fladgate & Yeatman –Vinhos, S.A.R.L.
Postal Address: P.O. Box 24 – 4401 Vila Nova de Gaia Codex – Portugal

Com o fim de manter os n/serviços de controlo de qualidade em constante actuação, agradecemos aos n/clientes que sempre que verifiquem qualquer anomalia nos n/produtos nos informem referindo o nome/código indicado e respectivo número de etiqueta. | In order to maintain our quality control level we would be grateful if customers would inform us whenever they notice any deficiency in our product, quoting code name and label number. | Avec la finalité de mantenir notre controle de qualité actif, nous remercierons à tous nos clients de nous faire parvenir chaque fois qu'il y a un problème avec nos produits, mentionnant le code/nom du produit et numero d'étiquette.

Etiqueta Label Etiquette { N.° 36951 | Nome/Código Code/Name Code/nom | MANUELA

SHIPPED BY
117
at
115 Brand Road
Salem, Virginia 24156

14

14
Group of *Inspected by Number* tags, 1976–91. Printed paper, ¾–2¼" high

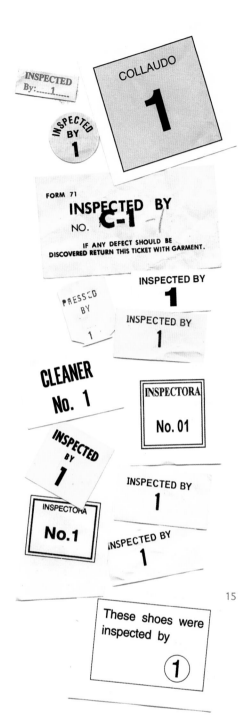

What other tags does the Inspector have at his disposal? When a product doesn't meet the standards for dispatch to a ready market, what are the inspector's other tag alternatives? Are there *reject, scrap it, try again, leaky, faulty, nonconforming, shabby workmanship, hold for adjustment*, and *return to assembler* tags? What about irresponsible, depressed, perverse, or jerky inspectors or those who don't see eye to eye with company standards. Are there inspectors of inspectors? This collection represents many unnerving possibilities. These tags are as much evidence that the manufacturer applies a standard to the product as they are tacit disclaimers that, if your purchase is flawed when you opened the factory-sealed box, it's not their fault. Did you drop this carefully wrapped item on your way home from the store? Did the shipper get rough? It left our factory in perfect shape.

Tacit disclaimers are a mental collection of mine. *Your canceled check is your receipt*; *void where prohibited*; *while supplies last*; *subject to change without notice*; and *parental guidance advised* put the ball squarely in the consumer's court. The provider abdicates responsibility. *The post office will not deliver without postage* message on the return envelope for my electric bill really means that for whatever reason, if they do not receive payment soon (no excuses) and my electricity is turned off, it's my fault—they warned me. *Avoid contact with skin*; *may contain traces of nuts*; *slippery when wet*; *if this condition persists, see your physician*; *beware of the dog*; and *objects in mirror are closer than they appear* ratchet up to the next level of disclaimer—injuring yourself with a product, service, or pet. *Keep your seat belt fastened until the plane comes to a complete stop* really means that in case you're less well-balanced than our stewardesses, you could fall on a third party from whom we don't want a lawsuit. *One size fits all* could be more sensitively worded, perhaps as *We only make one size*. I'd like to suggest one for hotel and motel showers: *Don't apply soap to the bottoms of your feet*. My all-star favorite, hands down, is *Sanitized For Your Protection*.

15

Group of *Inspected by Number 1* tags, 1982–2004. Printed paper, ¼–1¾" high

16

Tacit warning (parking lot), 2004. Printed paper, 2½" high

17

Tacit warning (hot product), 2004. Printed paper, 2" high

THE PORTENTOUS printed *Sanitized For Your Protection* band around hotel and motel toilet seats raises questions that might never have otherwise come up. What about the less than fastidious chambermaid who thinks that the toilet looks clean and just applies the band as casually as she folds the torn toilet-paper end into a neat arrowhead to reaffirm her presence on your behalf? *Disinfected* on a toilet-seat band raises related issues. Why is the management telling me this? What product, exactly, was used? And can it kill Ebola virus? Isn't the bathtub even more dangerous than the toilet: What if the cleaning staff used

DESINFECTÉ DISINFECTED DESINFIZIERT

18

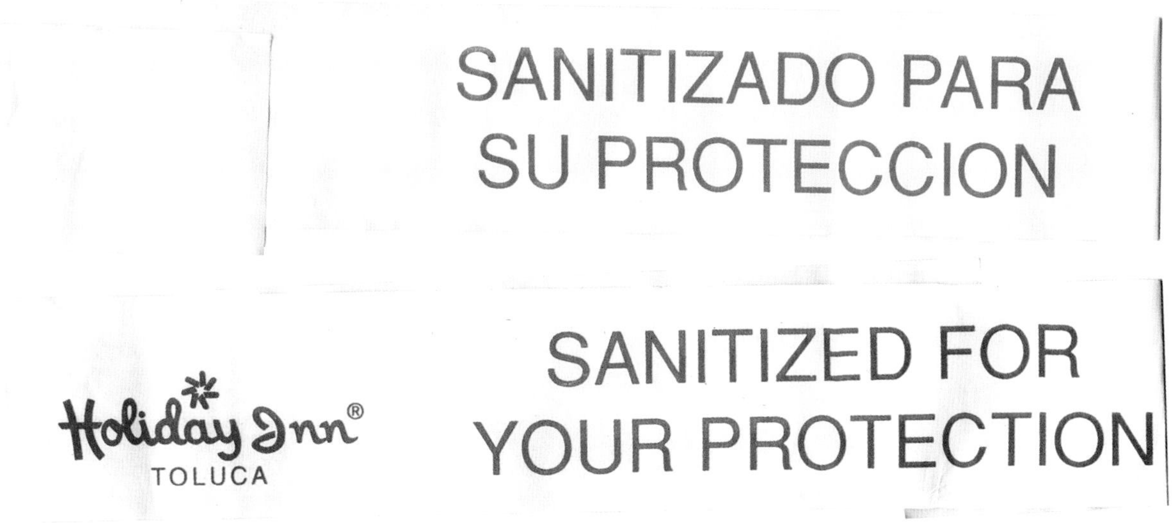

SANITIZADO PARA SU PROTECCION

SANITIZED FOR YOUR PROTECTION

Holiday Inn®
TOLUCA

19

Hotel Virrey de Mendoza

Esterilized for your security

Esterilizado para su seguridad

20

18
Sanitized For Your Protection toilet-seat band, 1988. *Disinfected,* printed paper, 2½" high

19
Sanitized For Your Protection toilet-seat band (bottom and top views), 1999. *Holiday Inn,* printed paper, 2" high

20
Sanitized For Your Protection toilet-seat band (top and bottom views), 1979. *Esterilized for your security,* printed paper, 2½" high

GARANZIA D'IGIENE
SANITARY SAFETY
GARANTIE D' HYGIÈNE
GARANTIERT HYGIENISCH

21
Sanitized For Your Protection band (top and bottom views), 1988. *Sanitary Safety*. Printed paper, 2¾" high

22
Sanitized For Your Protection band around Supersuckers' album *Sacrilicious*, guaranteed "clean" for in-store play, 1995. Printed paper, 2½" high. Sub Pop Records, Seattle, Washington

a sponge to clean the bathtub that also had been used to clean the toilet? Will complimentary bubble bath kill skin-eating bacteria? Sanitary safety toilet bands don't inspire confidence, and I prize them. My formula for hotel/motel safety is to use the shower cap to cover my toothbrush so cleaning personnel don't spray it with disinfectant or insecticide while cleaning the bathroom countertop. I throw toilet and bathtub caution to the wind, carefully saving the *sanitized for my protection* band.

Sub Pop records issued a promotional CD by Supersuckers in 1995 to introduce their album *Sacrilicious*. This CD was wrapped in a *Sanitized For Your Protection* band, guaranteeing that it was "clean" for playing in stores. A couple of tracks had been edited. The sanitized band has taken on cultural significance.

AIR SICKNESS bags are manufactured in profuse variety. Even generic versions, without benefit of airline name or logo, abound. *Do Not Disturb* signs and airline sickness bags have a clear and immediate intended message, and both occasionally have a secondary function. Some airline sickness bags may be used as *seat occupied* markers when not in primary use. Others become mailers for the development of your trip photographs; or, if you care to carry the bag around, handy phone numbers are printed for use at your destination and to confirm your return flight.

Sick bags appeared on the airline scene in the mid-1930s and have progressed through graphic and text improvements. Many are necessarily multilingual; some instruct to fold toward the user after use, some to fold away; others have drawstring pull ties, and some have tabs. It's hard to imagine why they all don't have flat bottoms, especially when the fraught user might have to set the bag down momentarily, to recompose or unfasten the seatbelt and rise. A goodly number include directive peculiarities such as *Please, No Refuse!* Some sick bags have odd mottoes such as *Going to great lengths to please* and *Wings of Comfort*, while others have structural anomalies such as a plastic liner that does not reach all the way to the bag bottom, disguising the actual capacity of the receptacle. Questionable pictorial choices occur, the most noteworthy being an African woman mid-childbirth. Might the unwritten message be *Works for morning sickness too*? A bright orange bag comes with no text, only a flying elephant, the airline logo. A few are so laden with international pictorial symbols that the passenger might not be able to determine or comprehend what the sick bag is for: *No Liquids! Solids Only!* What about mixed media and chunks? What if you don't know in advance? What's a person to do? Probably the best course of action is to check your sick bag before take-off when you're locating the nearest exit.

23

24

23
Thai Airlines air sickness bag. Printed paper with laminated plastic liner, 9½" high

24
El Al air sickness bag (Israeli airline). Printed paper with laminated plastic liner, 8¾" high

25
Air sickness bags, 1990s.
Printed paper with
laminated plastic liner,
9½" high

26
Maersk air sickness bag
(Danish airline) (back
and front). Printed paper
with laminated plastic
liner, 9½" high

27
Aeroflot air sickness
bag (Russian airline).
11" high

28
Korean Air air sickness
bag. Printed paper with
laminated plastic liner,
10" high

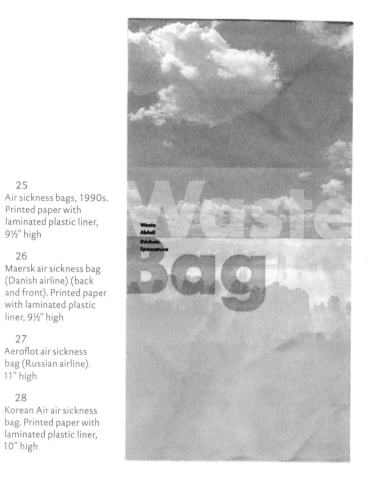

Air sickness bag
Spuckbeutel
Sac vomitoire
Sacchetto emergenza mal d'aria

swiss
+

25

26

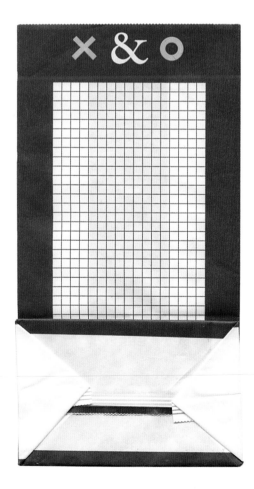

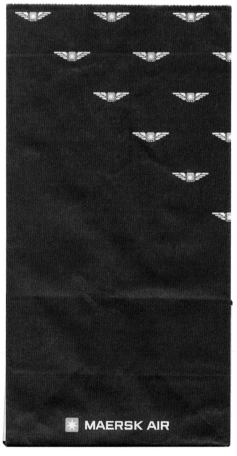

MAERSK AIR

27

28

Crooked or straight, poets mortgage their prospects
for an improbable goal: to make objects
carved in the abiding stone of language;
to leave, when they die, durable relics.

 Donald Hall, "It Was Sigmund" from *The Museum
of Clear Ideas: New Poems by Donald Hall* (New York:
Ticknor & Fields, 1993), 89.

1
Shamrock stanhope,
1870. Carved soapstone,
brass, glass lens, six views
within *Memories of Rhyl*,
¾" high. Made in France

2
Bear stanhope, 1880. *A
Memory of Swanage with
six views* is seen through
the belly aperture;
carved bog oak, glass
eyes, glass lens, and silver
rings, 1" high

3
Heart stanhope, 1910.
Glass, glass lens, with
brass hardware aperture
view of St. Maria Brettfall
church, Zillertal, Austria,
1" high

4
Drum stanhope, c. 1925.
Souvenir of *the Niagara
Falls;* quartz, gold, glass
lens, with six views with-
in the aperture, ½" high

Got Lost

chapter 11

We find the miniature at the origin of private, individual
history, but we find the gigantic at the origin of public and
natural history. The gigantic becomes an explanation for the
environment, a figure on the interface between the natural
and the human. Hence our words for the landscape are often
projections of an enormous body upon it: the mouth of the river,
the foot-hills … the heartlands, the elbow of the stream.
    Susan Stewart, *On Longing* (Durham, N.C. and London:
Duke University Press, 1993), 71.

LORD CHARLES Stanhope lived from 1753 to 1816, leading an active life as a politician and inventor. He was a friend to William Pitt and, in 1774, married Hester, Pitt's sister. He opposed war with the American colonies while sitting in Parliament, before he succeeded to the peerage. Scientific curiosity and finesse guided his experiments. He investigated methods of fireproofing stucco as well as raising and lowering water levels for the expediency of canal boat travel. He created two calculating machines, the printing press that bears his name, a duplicating device, a steam vehicle, and a minute lens that enlarged transparent objects. Stanhope's lens was a quarter-inch long (8mm) and a tenth of an inch in diameter (3mm), a cylindrical glass-rod microscope lens with one flat end and one concave end.

Great works notwithstanding, if it weren't for this tiny lens, I would not know Charles, third Earl of Stanhope. When a transparent bit such as an insect wing was applied to the flat end of the lens, and viewed through the concave end toward a light source, the specimen was impressively enlarged. The lens brought the mysteries of minutiae into plain view. Devised for microscopy, the lens—with its crucial focal length—was applied to photography a century later. David Brewster and John Dancer are credited with the application of microphotographs to the flat end of the lens. The results were microfilm for wartime messaging and a trinket called the *stanhope*. By 1865, having caught Queen Victoria's fancy, stanhope watch fobs, pendants, brooches, rings, charms, stickpins, bookmarks, letter openers, and sewing regalia were in vogue. The lens could be inserted into any appropriate piece of jewelry, souvenir, desk or pocket tool and trinket, made of the finest carved ivory, wood, horn, bone, silver, gold, brass, jade marble, meerschaum, jet, vegetal ivory, glass, gutta-percha, and even bakelite; you name it. Stanhopes were produced through the early 1950s and occasionally occur as a nonvintage souvenir rarity today.

The outer casings of pieces in my STANHOPE collection include miniature binoculars and monoculars, buildings, animals, hearts, locks, thistles, thimbles, hands, faces, ships, pencils, umbrellas, knives, whistles, compendia, books, cameras, pens, vehicles, and rings. With the exceptions of the Lord's Prayer in crosses and views of Niagara Falls in barrels, there is infrequent relationship between the stanhope's outward form and the private view within. An aspect of the stanhope's charm resides in the titillating secrecy of the internal image. Often the stanhope was an ornament that dangled from a gentlemen's vest-pocket watch chain. Commonly, the private image was a seemly French actress viewed for amusement over brandy and billiards. It went along with the figural toothpick. Vest-pocket culture is rife with erotica. My Straight Arrow Golden Nugget Cave ring was a last gasp of the stanhope, which had its widest audience in the 1930s when it became a mass-produced novelty for everyman in Johnson Smith catalogues. Even trick stanhopes, which squirted water faceward when the rube viewer turned the adjustment to see more of the lovely lass than her face and shoulders, were unleashed on a ready pre–World War II market.

The stanhope exemplifies the intensity of the miniature, a temple to the small. For about a hundred years, its diminutive fineness was prized, its contents preciously treasured. The trouble with small things is that they are easily misplaced.

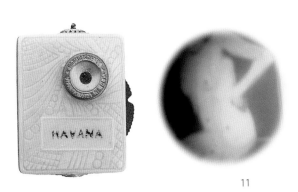

11

12

5
Group of stanhope telescopes and monoculars, 1875–1930. Brass, paint, plastic, and glass lens, 1–1¾" long

6
Group of pig stanhope watch-fob charms, 1893. Apertures in rear of pig. Cast lead and soapstone with carnelian eyes, ½" high

7
Easter egg stanhope, 1935. Bunny, basket, and *Happy Easter* shown in aperture. Painted cast silver and glass lens, ½" high

8
Stanhope binoculars, 1880–93. Each offering two views. Ivory, gilded cast brass, cast lead, and glass lenses, approximately ¾" high

9
Carved ivory cross stanhope, 1900. View within reveals an image of St. Mary, with text *O Mary conceived without sin* in four languages, 1½" high

10
Viking ship stanhope, 1900. Aperture shows a view of Liverpool. Engraved cast gold and glass lens, 1¼" high

11
Camera stanhope, souvenir of Havana, Cuba, 1921. One of three nudes seen in rotating viewer. Plastic and glass lens, 1" high. Czechoslovakia

12
Stanhope trick viewer with novelty ad and view within, 1940. 2" high. Johnson Smith & Company catalog, Detroit, Michigan, page 196

13
Group of cups depicting children playing marble games, 1820–30. Transferware with hand-applied color, each 2¾" high. England

14
Opaque swirl marble, 1888–1910. Glass, 1½" diameter

15
Spongeware marble, c. 1860. Cobalt glazed stoneware, 2" diameter

16
Kraft American cheese box with apertures, 1946. Used for marble games after reconstruction. Printed pine, 4" high

WHATEVER INEFFABLE signal causes Monarch butter-flies to migrate to Morelia, Mexico, hummingbirds to fly to Brazil, and salmon to swim upstream, also caused a bevy of Bronx kids to show up every spring in the playground at the circumference of the still-dry wading pool with pouches and cigar boxes of marbles. There was no announcement; everyone just turned up. The concrete curb around the wading pool was the ideal backboard for marble entrepreneur-ship and seat for each concessionaire. Marble season began, and skilled contenders tamely availed them-selves of the inexperience of the innocents.

The main games were about wagering your marbles by shooting them from a chalked line that was appropriately distanced from the target marble to win five, ten, or twenty-five marbles. The chalk lines were approximately ten, fifteen, and twenty-five-feet long respectively. One also could have rolled a shooter across the playground at a comic book to hit it and win it (or not). The wading-pool curb was the optimal backstop for the wagered marble. All failed shots were lost to the shooter and collected by the waiting novice dealer. Another main game in early marble season required the donation of a rectangular wooden cheese box from the local grocery store. The box was modified with one's father's coping saw to make three arched sequential apertures on the long side; then the box was inverted and the holes were labeled 5, 10, 20. The size of the hole was inverse to the quantity that could be won if the shooter suc-ceeded in getting the marble into the entry hole. Marbles were shot from a chalk line about ten feet from the inverted cheese box. Marbles that did not enter the lucky hole and stay there were kept by the kid with the cheese box. Experienced shooters did some checking before gaming, to make sure that the

14

13

15

16

holes were large enough to admit a marble and that the impresario had marbles on hand to pay off if necessary. The Bronx was a tough place even then.

I was a fair shooter at marble targets and at cheese-box apertures. I practiced on our parquet dining-room floor. I was not after quantity but a variety of different perfect marbles, and I soon became a committed entrepreneur, gambling only the imperfect, duplicates, and marbles of no particular distinction or interest. I amassed *clays*, *bennies*, *aggies*, *cabolas*, *puries*, *cat's eyes*, *swirls*, *spirals*, *snowflakes*, *onionskins*, and *steelies*, and even traded for a *comic* and a *sulphide*. Clays were unglazed ceramic, bennies (Bennington Pottery Company) were glazed. Steelies were ball bearings by another name. Comics were an opaque color, with a comic book character transferred on one side; and sulphides were clear glass, with a small, usually white figure within. The rest were glass orbs that had vivid, magical internal colors.

Pee Wee Reese, the legendary Brooklyn Dodger shortstop, was a champion marble shooter. Some boys I knew played marbles with the intensity of war games. They came to the playground to make their grubstake and then retired to a flat piece of earth in an empty lot where they would incise a circle or chalk it on cement or asphalt; they played hard. Their marble games were based on bowling and pool and territory (a pen-knife game) and were adapted to cracks, holes, and other irregularities in their playing field. No novices were allowed; theirs was serious business. From recalled observations, their game was about concussion. Largely the object was to knock opponents' marbles out of the ring, while keeping theirs within its precincts.

PLAYING AT MARBLES

17
Group of blue and brown Bennington marbles, 1850. Glazed ceramic, ½–¾" diameter

18
Group of *steelies*, nickel-plated ball bearings, c. 1920. ¼–½" diameter

19
Group of *swirls*, including split cores, Lutz, lobed core, Latticino core, ribbon core, clear and transparent swirls, 1888–1910. Glass, ½–2" diameter

20
Transferware cup depicting children *Playing at Marbles*, 1840–60. Transfer on ironstone, 2½" high. England

21
Swirl marble, 1840–75. Glass, 1¼" diameter

22
Lion sulphide marble, 1850–80. Glass with sulphide salt figure, 2" diameter

23
Swirl marble, 1850–80.
Glass, 2¼" diameter

24
Group of *melon balls* and
cleareys, 1889–1910.
Glass, ¾–1" diameter

25
Brown Bennington
marbles, 1850. Glazed
ceramic, 1¼–1½"
diameter

26
Group of unfired *mibs*,
19th century. Painted
clay, ¼–1" diameter. USA

Stone-pebble marbles have been excavated from archaeological sites around the world. Metal and wood marbles existed as early gaming pieces, along with glazed and unglazed crockery and porcelain marbles. Romans carried marbles to all parts of their empire. Glass marbles evolved beside the Venetian glass-bead industry. The Dutch imported marbles and marble game boards to Nieuw Amsterdam. Marbles were produced in America from about 1800; and in 1846, a tool called marble scissors revolutionized marble fabrication, enabling quickened production. In 1888, the Akron Marble Company began mass machine production, making a rich and wide palette of intricate and appealing designs. Glass marbles are made by melting glass in a furnace and injecting colors; then, as the glass is poured out, mechanized scissors cut short cylindrical sections and rollers shape and convey the marbles as they harden. Mal & Jack's candy store and soda fountain had penny candies, egg creams, comic books, sparklers, wax lips, and marbles for sale in sacks of fifty and boxes of twenty—if you ran out or lost your marbles from one season to the next. It's the nature of marbles to roll. Marbles roll away.

In this place and at this time,
Which is not time, I could take
the long road back and find it all.
I could even find myself.
  Philip Levine, "A Poem With No
Ending" from *New Selected Poems* (New York:
Alfred A. Knopf, 1991), 26.

23

24

25

26

MARBLES CAN be seductively beautiful. Gaming with them is not subtle and can be likened to the directness of checkers. Addition and subtraction calculate marble games. Dice are as old as marbles. They are cubic and, on a level surface, do not roll of their own volition. Dice games require a purposeful toss at a target area. The side on which they land, rather than what they hit, determines the outcome of the game. Dice games are cerebral, layered, and graceful. They are about multiplication and division and higher mathematics.

In casinos around the world, six-sided dice are *shot*. They are made of resin, molded and drilled to micrometer precision, exactly balanced and weighted. In the game of craps, if the shooter accidentally tosses a die off the table (onto the carpeted floor), it's held back from play, examined by the box man to see if it has been injured or surreptitiously switched for a loaded die. The shooter may request the same die, reclaiming it after house scrutiny. Overall the odds

are only very slightly in favor of the casino, so the house is very careful with its dice. Loaded dice have been weighted to land on a particular number and have been around as long as dice. Craps may be played as many ways as there are players around the table; all methods are dependent upon the outcome of the same dice toss. Whatever number is the sum of both dice, different players will be paid off according to varying odds, and some players will win while others lose. It is an elegant and complex game.

Dice aren't always six-sided. My daughter Amie's collection contains pyramidal dice of four sides and dice with a hundred facets. As a young child, she watched the dice roll in her brother's role-playing and board games and did her earliest sums. Her collection grew from conventional forms to include spherical dice; seventeenth-century ivory barrel dice; poker dice; thirty-sided Victorian auguring dice; an ancient Mesopotamian chipped stone die; and miniature Czechoslovakian glass dice. She has silver

27
Six-sided die, c. 1900. Hand-carved vegetable ivory (coquilla), ¾" high. USA

28
Six-sided dice, 1949. Printed in-painted Bakelite, each ¾" high. USA

29
Six-sided die, c. 1958. Cast, drilled sterling silver, ½" high. USA

30
Six-sided casino die, 1985. In-painted printed resin, ¾" high. USA

31
Six-sided casino die, 1990. In-painted printed resin, ¾" high. USA

32
Six-sided die, c. 1880. Hand-carved gutta-percha, ¾" high. USA

33
Round die, 1992. In-painted plastic, ¾" diameter. USA

34
Ten-sided die, 1979. In-painted resin, 1" high. USA

35
Eight-sided barrel die, c. 1850. In-painted incised ivory, each ¾" high. China

36
Thirty-two-sided die, c. 1880. In-painted glass, 1" high. USA

37
Thirty-sided die, 1981.
In-painted resin, 1½"
high. USA

38
Mesopotamian die,
second century B.C.
Chipped hard red stone,
1¼" high

39
Six-sided die, 1900.
In-painted wood, ½"
high. USA

40
Six-sided die with a
fumbled *two*, 1865.
In-painted horn, ¾"
high. USA

41
Six-sided poker die,
1965. Printed resin, ¾"
high. USA

42
Six-sided advertising die,
1970. In-painted printed
plastic, ¾" high. USA

43
Dice cup, c. 1915.
4" high. USA

44
Dice ads, 1940. 1½–2"
high. Johnson Smith
& Company catalog,
Detroit, Michigan, page
379

dice, lead dice, eighteenth- and nineteenth-century bone sailors' dice, dice from bazaars in exotic lands, and dice from flea markets in the United States. In 1992, the Children's Museum of Manhattan exhibited Amie's dice collection.

The ancients cast roughly cubic knucklebones of sheep. Each side was marked, and tossing specific sequences as well as high numbers were scored. Romans used pairs and trios of dice that were thrown by hand or from leather dice cups. As in craps today, bets could be made on one toss of the dice or on the outcome of a round. In twelfth-century England, the board upon which an unmarked die landed determined the score. The Koln Museum exhibited a pair of fourteenth-century six-sided dice in the forms of a man and a woman, with the face side marked with one dot and the bottom of each figure marked with six spots. They are tiny, intense cast-clay votive figures.

Dice usually come in pairs, so it is easy to misplace one and end up with a single, which preempts many games. My father's singlet dice and cufflinks were kept in a small box in his shirt drawer. He had a hard time giving them up, or maybe he was ever hopeful of the twin turning up. I've always had a soft spot for loner dice and cufflinks.

37   38

39   40

41   42

God does not play dice with the universe.
Albert Einstein

God not only plays dice with the universe, but sometimes throws them where we can't see them.
Stephen Hawking

43

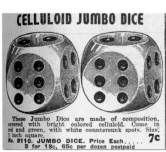

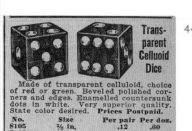

BEGINNING AROUND 1875, jewelers put decorative faces on French cuffs, linking them in ornamentally functional ways. The fashion caught on, and men's shirt cuffs since have been festooned with ballerinas *en tremblant*, miniature roulette wheels, enamel and mother-of-pearl snaps, glazed porcelain flowers, black enamel and gold scrolls, photographs of loved ones, *cloisonné* emblems, silver zeppelins, reverse-painted glass half-dome horses, Masonic symbols, *Bleriot* airplanes in relief, ruby studs, dice in miniature cages, stanhopes, and ancient coins. Cufflinks have four expressive opportunities, two for each cuff, although sometimes the backside of each cuff is simply a functional anchor to keep it in place. This is no guarantee; it's still easy to lose a cufflink.

BUTTONS ARE the prototypical tiny necessity with ancient roots. These early clothing fasteners are directly efficient and we still use them. Button forms appear in many cultures and styles. They evolved beside the bead and the marble. I own a nineteenth-century sulphide button with a lady's head inside a field of clear glass with red and cobalt blue flecks. It could easily be mistaken for a marble except for the looped shank on the back.

Buttons are generally disks, or spherically shaped fasteners with perforations or a shank to affix it to one side of a garment by means of thread. They fit through a slit or a hole or a loop on the garment's opposite side. Closure is simple and usually secure. When a person is buttonholed, he is corralled or captured or immobilized as a button might be. Bursting buttons with pride or bluster must have happened with some frequency, as there seem to be more un-moored than anchored buttons. Button boxes exist because buttons spring loose. If the owner doesn't find it, someone else does. It's nearly impossible to discard a button; you never know when you might need it. Shirt buttons are predestined to outlast shirts. Old shirts make great rags; their buttons are stowed in button repositories. What a triumph when you find that matching button that had been dormant for years.

45
Group of singlet cufflinks with stud backs, 1870–80. Each ¾" diameter

46
Group of singlet cufflinks, 1910–29. Glass, ¼–½" high

47
Group of Victorian buttons, 1875–90. Pressed brass, tin, paint with steel and celluloid insets, ¼–1¼" diameter

48
Group of common buttons, 20th century. Plastic, mother of pearl, shell, and horn, ¼–1" diameter

> My mother had been sewing a button on my shirt. She kept her buttons in a chipped saucer. I heard the rim of the saucer in circles on the floor. I heard the spray of buttons, little white teeth.
> Anne Michaels, *Fugitive Pieces* (New York: Vintage International, 1998), 7.

45   46   47   48

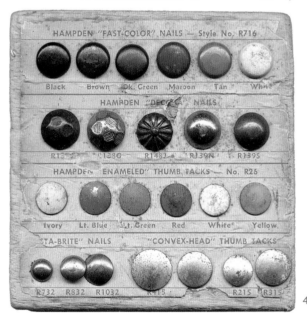

TACKS ARE another kind of fastener. As a testament to how often they are lost after dropping, I offer the tack in shoe-sole image. As an artist and teacher of studio art, I have perhaps experienced this phenomenon more than most; but thumbtacks and pushpins are taken for granted. Few mourn their loss. Dropped tacks are not generally retrieved until after a posting mission has been accomplished. Since they often land point up, they may no longer be apparent (unless you're barefoot) when the job is finished. Post-its have greatly reduced thumbtack drama in the workplace, but standard-issue thumbtacks are only a sliver of the picture. Decorative and austere tack heads have been produced in grand profusion and useful variety, from tiny multicolored orb map tacks (popular in marking serial-killer strikes in detective movies) to floral curtain tieback tacks popular in the 1940s. Fluted brass half-dome upholstery tacks and number tacks, clamp tacks, hook tacks, tacks with geometric solids for heads, and specialty tacks all have the same underside in service of a larger purpose, which, when it is fulfilled, doesn't necessarily find them back in the tack box.

49
Group of carded tacks, 1930s–40s. Each 3" high

50
Group of decorative tacks, 1947. Stamped steel, glass, and paint, each 2¼" diameter

51
Tacks sample card, 1947. 9' high. Huebel Bros., Inc., San Francisco, California

49

He showed me something small, no bigger than a hazelnut, lying in the palm of my hand, as it seemed to me, and it was round as a ball. I looked at it with the eye of my understanding, and thought: What can this be? I was amazed that it could last, for I thought that because of its littleness it would suddenly have fallen into nothing.

Julian of Norwich, *Revelations of Divine Love* (c. 1405).

50

Safepin Tacks

UPHOLSTERY NAILS — FURNITURE GLIDES

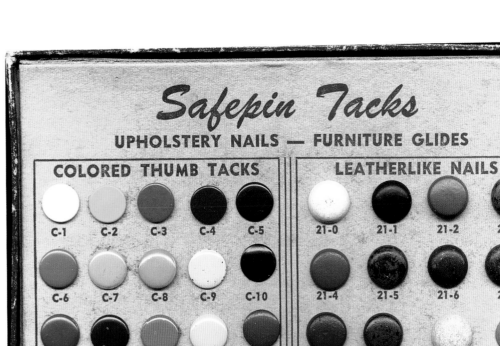

COLORED THUMB TACKS

C-1	C-2	C-3	C-4	C-5
C-6	C-7	C-8	C-9	C-10
C-11	C-12	C-13	C-14	C-15

LEATHERLIKE NAILS

21-0	21-1	21-2	21-3
21-4	21-5	21-6	21-7
21-8	21-9	21-E	21-G

NICKEL PLATED THUMB TACKS

2-S	2-SLP	3-S	5-S	5-SLP	6-S	2-XX	2-X	3-X

FANCY STEEL NAILS

42	43	19-1	19-2	38	39
9-1	9-2	9-3	34-1	34-2	34-3

FANCY BRASS NAILS

31-0	31-5	31-7	31-9	32-0	32-1	32-7
33-0	33-3	33-5	33-7	33-9	27-1	27-2

ESCUTCHEON PINS

5/8-13	3/4-14	3/4-16B	3/4-16N	5/8-18

THREE PRONG FURNITURE GLIDES — NICKEL PLATED

1/2"	5/8"	3/4"	7/8"

HUEBEL BROS., INC.   SAN FRANCISCO 5, CALIF.

51

chapter 12

Part of Something Bigger

1
Group of vehicle hood
ornaments, 1929–55.
2¾"–5½" high

2
Mack Truck hood
ornament (front),
c. 1954. 4" high

IN 1964, we purchased an 1847 farmhouse in
New York State in the midst of a pastoral
paradise. About one mile west, among functional dairy farms, there was a six-acre
vehicular graveyard. I felt like the great white
jodhpured hunter in a 1940s B-movie discov-
ering the proverbial elephants' dying ground.
There were no stacks of ivory tusks, but generations of hood ornaments affixed to long
dead Terraplanes, and rusted hulks of Kaiser-
Frasers that were no longer a source of spare
parts. Defunct vehicles had been deposited
here. There were Plymouth clipper ships of
many vintages entangled in hedge bindweed.
Hornet rockets and Pontiac Indian chiefs
stood amid pearly everlasting. Whippet
radiator caps and Mack Truck bulldogs were
harvested in fields of feathery golden rod.

When one dispatches an automobile or
truck to its next stage of utility, whether by
sale or junking, the hood ornament usually
goes with it; it's a small part of something
bigger. Usually little passion is expressed by
car owners about their last car's hood ornament.

2

3

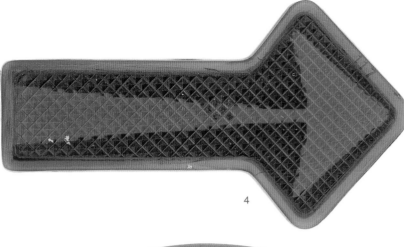

4

5

6

There is, however, lots of sentiment for these logo gems expressed by collectors of hood ornaments. Hood ornaments started out as radiator caps on early autos. They gradually developed into the identifying symbol of the car manufacturer. From the 1930s through the 1960s, the hood ornaments of American cars symbolically conveyed streamlined speed and modernity in the particular idiom of each producer. They were stylistically adjusted, as car models were, from year to year.

Beginning as the actual trademark, hood ornaments acquire stylistic value following years of successive changes. A hood ornament is the symbol of an automobile from a specific time, which is imbued with the culture of the manufacturing company; Cadillacs and Fords were worlds apart. Hood ornaments evolved into today's sterile logos from rich figurative metaphors and mythological themes. Most mascots from the golden age of hood ornaments had a date with the crusher when the car was scraped, and that's why they're scarce.

MOST OF US know reflectors from the rears of our childhood bicycles. They were usually red disks that glowed because they were made of faceted, highly saturated, red transparent plastic with a reflective backing. They let vehicular traffic behind us know that we were there. Automobiles and trucks also have reflectors that, these days, are technological

3
Generic round red reflector with steel frame and slotted bracket, 20th century. 5¼" high

4
Generic arrow reflector, 20th century. Glass and paint, 4¼" wide

5
Generic arced *Stop* reflector, 20th century. Amber glass, 4½" wide

6
Federal 95 reflector, 20th century. Steel and glass, 6½" high. Federal Stamp Company, Brooklyn, New York

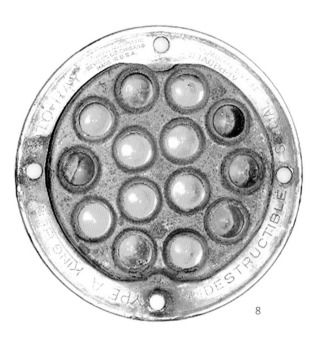

8

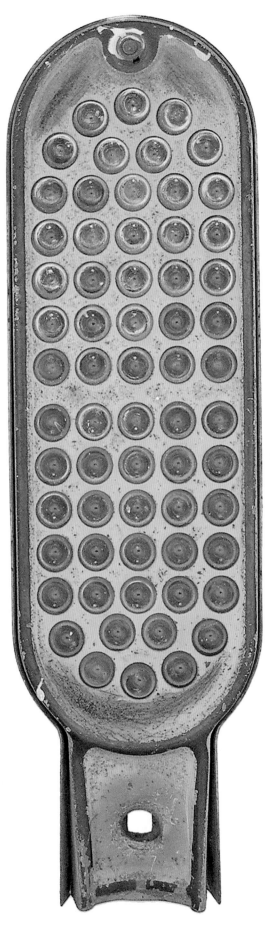

7
Group of car, truck, and bicycle reflectors, 1915–57. Glass, steel, and aluminum, 2¼–7¼" diameter

8
Foto-Ray reflector, 20th century. *Type A King Bee, Indestructible.* Aluminum and glass, 5¼" diameter. American Automotive Devices, Chicago, Illinois

9
Generic two-sided reflector, 20th century. Glass and painted steel, 10" high

wonders. At the least they are illuminated, but most often they are electronically adapted to sequentially blip and flash according to hazard light or slow-moving vehicle codes. In the gentler and more innocent days of spirit of flight hood ornaments, car reflectors were simpler, less dazzling affairs. They were usually intensely colored glass marbles or textured disks set into cast steel, later stamped aluminum. The arrow symbols and words were surrounded by textures that varied among manufacturers. These were not commonly electrified until the 1930s. They were designed to reflect vivid patterned light from vehicles to let drivers to the rear know the location of the preceding vehicle. The rounded glass tops of the marble types glowed brilliantly. Textured reflectors with arrows or word messages had tiny facets on the underside of the colored glass. Their glow could be likened to that of a stained-glass window. Both methods did the job. Reflectors largely shared the fate of hood ornaments but were easier to remove and sometimes saved for other uses. There are also more reflectors on the secondary market than hood ornaments because autos had one hood ornament but at least two reflectors.

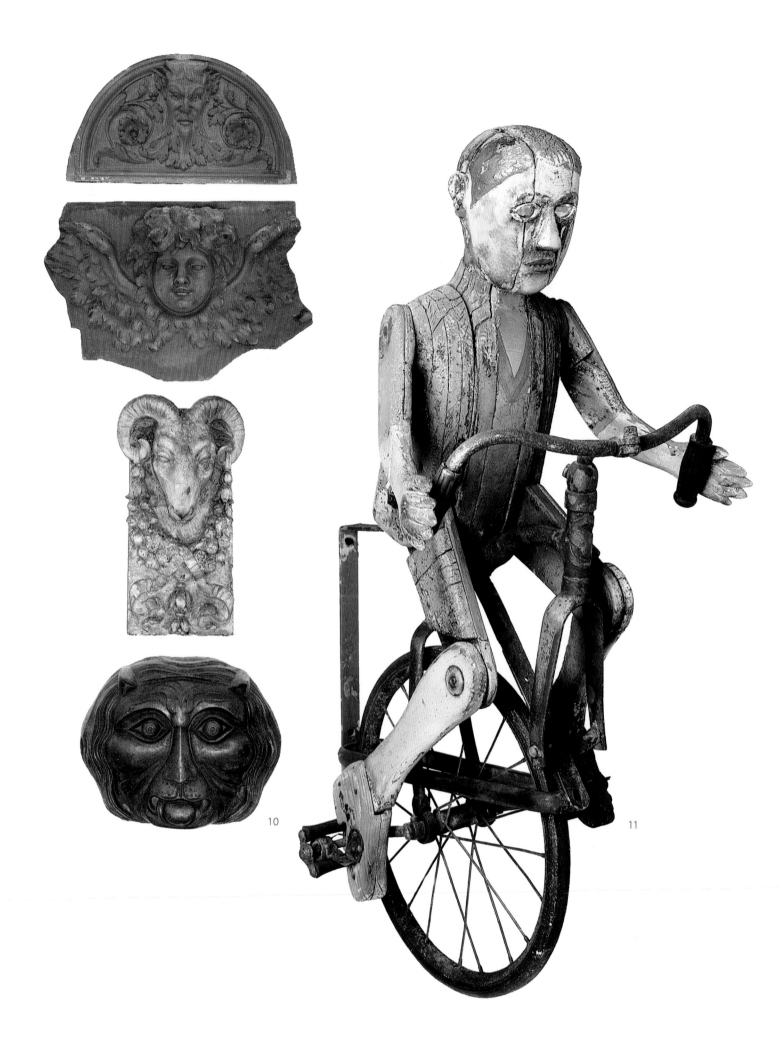

10

11

IVAN AND I enjoy driving through the nether regions of Brooklyn to look around at neighborhoods. In particular, we are observers of durability and change. In 1964, we were finely tuned to building demolition sites on which there were decorative carvings and castings. The Brooklyn Museum had been, since 1956, under then-director Tom Buechner, the main repository of the collection that Ivan deemed "rubble without applause." I was his "rubble queen." We gave the Brooklyn Museum hundreds of pieces of unsigned architectural ornaments from demolished buildings for public exhibition in a sculpture garden at the rear of their building. Some of it was installed directly into the south façade of the building proper, where it currently resides. Our organization is called the Anonymous Arts Recovery Society.

In the 1950s and 1960s many ornamented buildings were demolished for new construction. During demolition, when there was a foreman at the site, Ivan would ask that friezes, column capitals, a plaque, or a keystone be dropped "easily." Ten dollars usually ensured that we could collect the prize with its parts intact before the dozer and dump truck turned everything to grit. Building ornament is the quintessence of "part of something bigger."

On a fall day in 1964, we were driving down Greenpoint Avenue reconnoitering and I yelled, "didyouseethat?" The sign on the neighborhood bicycle shop featured a weathered, life-size wooden boy emerging centrally, seated on the front half of a bicycle. His hands gripped the handlebars and his marble eyes stared straight ahead. We entered the shop and began talking to Louis Simon, a wizened veteran who had fought in the Sino-Japanese War. I knew all about that war from my "Horrors of War" cards. I also knew about Jane Eyre from Classics Comics. Practical information often comes from unorthodox sources.

Louis had owned the bicycle shop since coming to Greenpoint, Brooklyn, from provincial Russia many years before. We could have the sign for a modest sum and "pick it up tomorrow" so he could give it a coat of fresh paint.

"Thanks, we'd rather take it with us today, if that's okay."

Wrench and ladder in hand, he disengaged the boy and half-bicycle, apologizing that he would be cutting the wires that had long ago electrified the boy's articulated legs to turn the pedals and illuminated his marble eyes. He explained how to rewire if we desired. He said that he would be carving a replacement: he'd been meaning to do so for some time and the boy we were carrying off was the second he had made. He didn't ask why we wanted it and very matter-of-factly handed it over. It was just a transaction, goods for *gelt*. I don't know if he ever remade the figure. Last time we drove past the location of the bicycle shop, it had become a bakery, although most of the buildings in the neighborhood looked as they had in 1964.

The Boy on the Bicycle lived on the wall in our home for years. In 1974, a dealer in Folk Art asked Ivan if he would sell it; he had a client who would be interested in a figure of that scale. The boy had a haunting, disquieting quality in our interior space. I was reluctant to give him up but had learned that if Ivan and I were not in tandem about deaccessioning a work, life would be easier (storage too) if I named a consolation price that was so high that it was doubtful the work would be purchased. The work could rest in limbo if necessary. I said that I would agree to sell it for $1,200. The piece was purchased; the dealer was secretive about the identity of the client.

Subsequently, we attended the opening reception of the Brooklyn Museum's "Folk Sculpture" exhibition. The feature piece in the exhibition and on the cover of the catalogue was the Boy on the Bicycle trade sign. The Brooklyn Museum had purchased the work for $7,500, not an inconsequential part of its acquisition budget for that year. We would have given it to them; after all, our names are engraved as "Founders" in the marble wall in the lobby of the Brooklyn Museum.

The Anonymous Arts Recovery Society has given works for public exhibition to the New York State Museum in Albany, the Museum of the City of New York, and the New York State Historical Association in Cooperstown. Awareness and a sense of the importance of historic preservation has grown; and ornamented buildings from 1875 to 1910 that survived the 1960s and 1970s scourge are now hopefully prized for their style and rarity.

10
Group of architectural ornaments, c. 1885. Cast terra cotta, carved granite, and cast iron, 19–30"

11
Boy on the Bicycle trade sign, c. 1946. Painted wood, steel and rubber bicycle parts, and marble eyes, 41" high. From Louis Simon's bicycle shop, Greenpoint, Brooklyn

12
Ornamental beam tie, c. 1880. Painted cast iron, 26" high. New York City

12

13

> "The house was a breccia of affections. Everything was wind-worn or sea-worn. Old and odd, mostly only of personal value.... A dozen ships in bottles, a map of the moon. An old sea chest of black iron ribs arching across the lid. A glass case across one wall with a jumbled collection of fossils. Sills with fantastic shells, stones, bottles of blue glass, of red glass. Postcards. Driftwood. Candlesticks made of ceramic, wood, brass, glass. Oil lamps of every size and shape. Doorknockers of different sizes, each shaped like a hand."
>
> Anne Michaels, *Fugitive Pieces* (New York: Vintage, 1998), 264–65.

DOOR KNOCKERS in the form of a shapely feminine hand holding a ball, made of cast iron or brass, have been common throughout Europe, North Africa, and the Levant since antiquity. Walking the back streets of English cities, Turkish towns, and villages in India, knockers that are ages old are still in place. Knockers are easier to remove for salvage than the keystone from an arched doorway, and in that sense they are analogous to reflectors, but there aren't so many that they are commonplace. They are in dwindling supply.

PARLORS ARE no longer commonplace, and cigar-smoking, brandy-imbibing gents rarely enjoy their postprandial activities engaged in male bonding around the billiard table. Billiard-table pockets haven't been fabricated in figural cast iron since the end of the nineteenth century. Even then, only high-end tables had dimpled babies' hands or inscrutable mandarins or classical beauties on a fulcrum that released the pocketed ball into replay. Robert L., a physician, collects these rare billiard-table parts. When the table itself was unwanted, someone had to say, "wait a minute, save those pockets." This had to happen for each varying billiard-table pocket he has in his possession. The chance of that not happening is greater than vice-versa. What happened to the massive tables themselves? After their fates were sealed, were they dismembered and burned? Does someone collect ornamented billiard-table legs?

13
Group of door knockers, 1840–80. Ladies' hands holding fruit. Cast iron, 6–7" high. Italy, Greece, and England

14
Billiard table pocket, c. 1880. Child's hand in closed position. Cast iron with paint, 7½" high

15
Group of billiard table pockets (closed and open positions), 1870–85. Cast brass with patina, paint, and oxidation, 9½–10½" high

14

15

THE EARLIEST origins of paper playing cards have been traced to China, where paper domino-related cards with coin and bamboo suits were shuffled and dealt. The cup and sword as suit symbols entered Europe through Islamic card games. By the mid-1300s, France, Italy, Spain, Germany, and Switzerland had developed fifty-two card-deck games with four suits designated by *pips*, which included cups, swords, acorns, fruit, bells, and others. The French codified hearts, spades, diamonds, and clubs. Court cards depicting royalty with specific designations were also a gift of the French; the king of hearts was Charlemagne, the king of spades was biblical King David, et cetera. Early French cards were hand-painted and expensive, and simplified forms were perfected for mass manufacture. Popular demand resulted in the export of cards and games, which quickly became part of English culture and found their way to England's colonies. England favored red-and-black printing, an enduring vernacular preference.

American inventive spirit made several significant and lasting adjustments to the playing-card format. The faces of American playing cards have double-sided printing so that cards could be immediately read in whichever direction they were dealt. This was a quantifiable convenience, as were the index denominations printed on the corners that were rounded. American cards were coated for durability and smooth handling, and in the mid-1850s, the Joker was added to the deck to facilitate the game of euchre and, successively, poker.

By the 1870s the Joker, a *wild* card, was widely depicted as a prankish jester, a puckish buffoon, and a roguish clown. The Joker is an immeasurable and unpredictable quantity that can change the outcome of some games. The Joker is a chameleon. Unnumbered and unsuited, the Joker's value depends upon the cards he is dealt with, not unrelated to the Tarot fool card. In some games the Joker has a sliding scale of values; in others it is unused or simply used to cut the deck. There are two Jokers in every American fifty-two-card deck, and my son Jesse has collected them since he was a tot. The playful Joker character, with high naughtiness potential, was attractive to him and was orphaned from the children's card games that he played. War, Slap-Jack, Go Fish, Rummy, and Casino don't require Jokers, and Jesse gave them safe quarter.

16
Playing-card Jokers, 20th century. Printed card stock, each 3½" high

17
Group of playing-card Jokers, 20th century. Printed card stock, each 3½" high

16

17

A MISSING Joker does not break a deck, but a missing ace of spades does. Amie began collecting aces of spades when she was about six years old. She did not know that in England every pack of cards had been taxed a shilling, levied on the ace of spades as it was printed. She was unaware that in fortune telling, the ace of spades relates to love affairs, malice, misfortune, and ambition, or that when inverted it portends death. She was ignorant of the fact that aces and eights in draw poker are a *dead man's hand*. She thought they were the most interesting cards and that they differed from deck to deck as variously as Jokers. They included pictorial devices within the ace and/or surrounding it. The cartouches, scripts, and identification text were not part of any other card.

Picture cards were uninteresting by comparison. Amie harvested aces of spades from every weary deck she encountered. Both Jokers and aces of spades are the only cards that bear the manufacturer's logo, identification and, on occasion, commercial advertising, sponsorship, pictures of products, slogans, service announcements, and place images. Both aces of spades and Jokers have reinvented themselves in novel forms, while all the other cards, including the court cards and the other aces, remain very much their medieval selves. Jokers aren't immediately missed, but aces are; an abducted ace of spades is a death sentence for the deck. Aces of spades and Jokers are integral components of card decks and of something even bigger—gaming culture.

18
Joker and ace of spades playing cards, 20th century. Printed card stock, each 3½" high

19
Ace of spades playing cards, 20th century. Printed card stock, each 3½" high

20
Ace of spades playing cards, 19th and 20th centuries. Printed card stock, each 3½" high

A♠

R.W. HULL
CARD MAGIC SUPREME
CROOKSVILLE, OHIO, U.S.A.

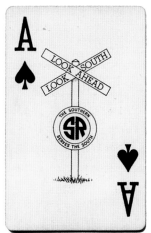

A♠

LOOK SOUTH
LOOK AHEAD

THE SOUTHERN
SR
SERVES THE SOUTH

A♠

·U·S·PLAYING·CARDS·
·999·

999

THE UNITED STATES PRINTING CO.
RUSSELL·&·MORGAN·FACTORIES
TRADE MARK REG'D B.303 · CINCINNATI, O. U.S.A.

A♠

A♠

A♠

F6911

A♠

RUSSELL'S PLAYING CARDS
2

Willis W. Russell
90K   TRADE MARK
Blue Ribbon

COPYRIGHT 1907 BY
WILLIS W. RUSSELL CARD CO.
MILLTOWN, N.J., U.S.A.

A♠

DE LUXE

THE NEW YORK
CONSOLIDATED CARD CO.

F 3604

A♠

"BEE"

THE NEW YORK CONSOLIDATED

CARD COMPANY

59

A♠

DUTY THREE PENCE

THOMAS DE LA RUE & Co. Ltd.

LONDON.

A♠

A♠

HOWARD JOHNSON'S
PENNSYLVANIA TURNPIKE

A♠

GEDEPONEERD
FABRIEKSMERK

EXCELSIOR

A. DOUGHERTY

26 BEEKMAN ST.

MANUFACTURER

NEW YORK

A♠

20

JACQUIE A. IS a textile historian who collects World War II home front textiles. Fabric and the clothing and household goods that have been constructed from it aren't the usual medium for expounding political doctrine. She explains that these textiles interest her because they "express patriotic ideas and feelings that serve as visible markers of national unity and support for military and political goals." These propaganda textiles convey more aggressive commitment than Victory gardens or sending salami to your boy in the army. Home front textiles showed solidarity with nationalistic purpose and bolstered civilian morale. They are irrefutable memoranda of the active motivation and belief of three countries: Britain, the United States, and Japan. Each textile exhibits a breadth of vivacious and spirited imagery and a range of colorful, animated pictorial design in bulletins from three cultural traditions.

There is crossover between American and British home-front textiles; subtle nuances of national usage and references are conveyed in expressive graphic imagery and shades of text. Japanese textiles are unequivocal in their visual statements. Propaganda textiles are a lasting by-product of war that kept nationalistic goals in common view, on your table, on your person.

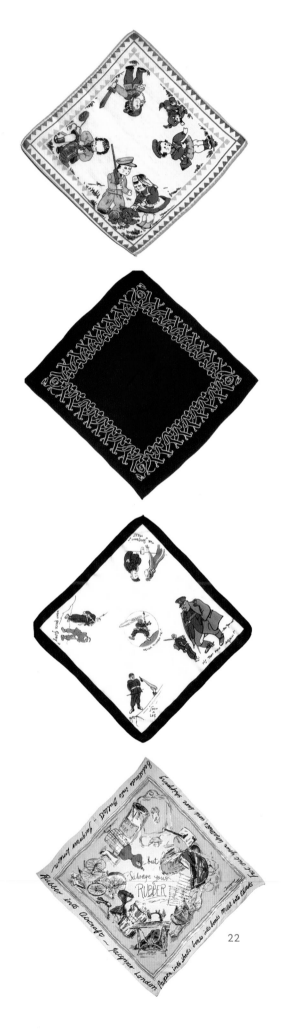

21
American home front fabric, 1944. Printed rayon and woven cotton, 16" high

22
Group of British homeland scarfs and handkerchiefs, 1939–44. Printed cotton and rayon, each 26" high

23
Showing the colors on printed cotton home front handkerchiefs, 1943–44. Each 12" high. USA

24
American homeland dress fabric, with military vignettes including paratroopers, tanks, airplanes, P T boats, and marching soldiers, 1941–44. Printed rayon, 28" high

25
Detail of home front tablecloth with World War II football allegory, 1941–44. United States vs. Axis Rats. Printed cotton, 25" high

23

In the stylistic idiom of the 1940s, the British mass-produced silk scarves, cotton handkerchiefs and tablecloths, and fabrics for items of household utility that glorified Winston Churchill and recommended *Run, Adolph, run, we're gonna hang out the washing on the Siegfried line*. Their propaganda notably supported home-front mandates such as *Rubber into Aircraft*, *Metal into Tanks*, *Bones into Bombs*, and *Paper into Shells*. More fervent than design savvy, these laden messages often appeared in unlikely pastels with tame greeting-card visuals. There are sincerely drawn and dowdy designs in which red and blue dominate a white background as well as a few masterpieces of graphic design exemplified by one in which a single fluid white line on a navy blue background good-naturedly caricatures Churchill repeatedly in a running border.

American home front textiles range from red, white, and blue emblematic geometrics of stylized fighter planes flying in formation to hand-embroidered handkerchiefs commemorating specific fighting groups such as the U.S. Navy or the Twelfth Air Force. We produced woven *V for Victory* feed sacks, pictorial and graphically patterned scarves and handkerchiefs, cotton apron and napkin fabrics, and rayon dress fabrics. Tablecloths were printed with vignettes of battles (Guadalcanal, Iwo Jima, and the Battle of the Bulge) that were notable for our losses and our eventual triumph. Were these ever used to eat upon? We made war-scoreboard tablecloths with Hitler taking a beating at football and dress fabrics depicting stylized descriptive scenes, bordering on caricature, of our forces doing what troops do—dropping bombs, tank driving, parachuting, and the like.

Japanese propaganda textiles were both hand-painted on silk and mass-produced in yardage for *kimono*, *obi*, and ceremonial robes. Clearly, winning the war was tied directly to divine mission. The images are incisively provocative in their aggressive spirit, albeit artfully designed and poetically executed. There is no ambiguity or equivocation in these single-mindedly serious tidings. High cultural artistic standards rendered the imagery and iconography of practice and wishful thinking.

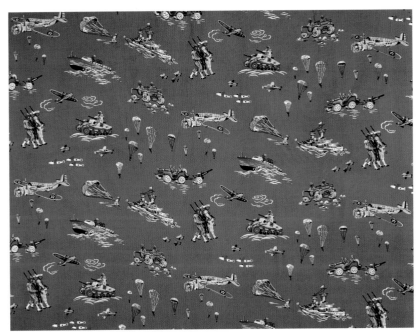

24

25

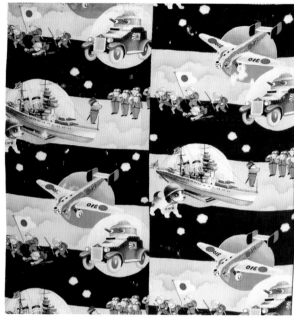

27

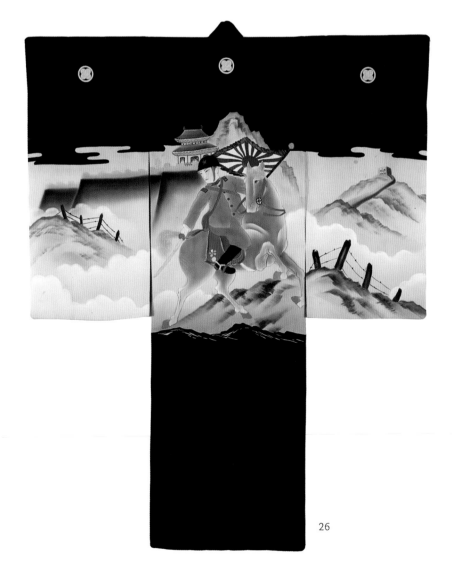

26

28

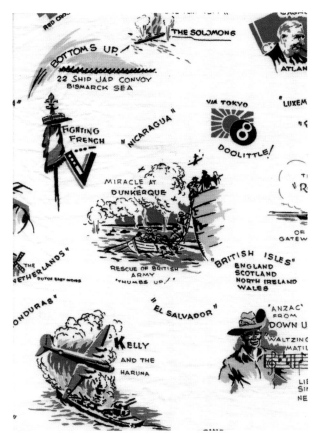

Most home front textiles were not about verbal assertion, although text may have been a graphic-design element. They were public signposts of patriotic enthusiasm and sentiment as expressed in one's personal clothing choice and in dressing children. That was an era that we tend to regard as more innocent than today, when the demarcation of friend and enemy was blatantly clear.

These textiles shouldn't surprise us. Many of us wore the stars and stripes adapted as clothing in the 1960s, and we have surely become accustomed to the marketing of consumer products under the red, white, and blue umbrella. After 9/11, the American flag blossomed on T-shirts, belts, tote bags, earrings, and underwear as a fervent showing of the colors, worn by conservatives and liberals alike, in a surge of unity against an enemy that would destroy our democracy. It was a way to articulate the inexpressible when the nation was all choked up.

The propaganda textiles of World War II are about a nation engaged in a war that permeated every aspect of civilian life. In America, there were many products that were packaged as propaganda. The purchase of Yanks bubble gum on occasion was one of my contributions to national well-being.

26
Man's or boy's Japanese homeland *haori* lined with tanks, helmets, guns, et cetera, 1940–44. Printed cotton, printed wool, and muslin, 38" high. Japan

Boy's *omiyamairi* (shrine-visiting kimono) with mounted cavalry officer in front of the Great Wall of China, 1930s. Yuzen dyed and embroidered silk, 48" high. Japan

27
Detail of *nagajuban* (slip under kimono) with boy soldiers, armored cars, airplanes, battleships, and helmeted dog, 1940–44. Printed muslin, 16" high. Japan

28
Japanese homeland *obi* with battleship, song, and *sakura* (detail), 1938–44. Printed synthetic silk, 11" high. Japan

29
Kent's *Cloth of the United Nations*, 1944. Home front fabric, printed cotton, 36" high. USA

30
American home front fabric, 1943. Printed rayon and woven cotton, 30" high

31
Elizabeth Arden pamphlet for the *Victory Red* cosmetic line (outside and inside), 1941. 5¾" high

29

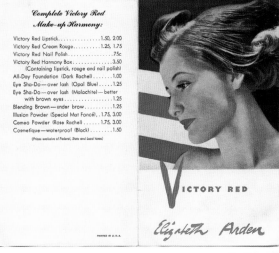

30

31

LUCKY STRIKE cigarettes announced that its green package color had *gone to war.* In 1943, Elizabeth Arden introduced Victory Red lipstick that harmonized with *Army Tan . . . and our own beloved Navy blue.* The Gem Razor Company offered "Voices of Victory" records, the mailers of which endorsed War Bonds and stamps acquisition, announcing *You Help America, You Help Yourself.* Text and voice ads were permeated with reminders of civilian responsibility to the wartime effort.

At that time, I regularly shopped for groceries with my mother and remember clearly the tan booklets of ration coupons that were necessary for the purchase of many foods that the U.S. Office of Price Administration (OPA) regulated as part of the homefront war effort. Violating OPA regulations was a seditious act that undermined the national purpose to *conserve vital goods.* As a child I knew that the purchase of something we didn't really need could cause hardship in the Bronx and abroad, and that our hardship encouraged the enemy. Food, gasoline, and goods made scarce by war were rationed because they were needed by our troops, my uncles. I remember my mother trading sugar coupons for canned-fruit coupons with another shopper. My brother loved canned pineapple.

Shopping for food took considered thought on a daily basis. I understood that prices had ceilings for everyone's benefit; the back of the booklet said so. *Never Buy Rationed Goods Without Ration Stamps* and *Never Pay More Than The Legal Price* to discourage black-market activity. Ration books were never to be discarded, even when empty or expired, because *you may be required to present this book when you apply for subsequent books.* I didn't perceive this as a tacit disclaimer. I still have our ration books. The minute pictures of fighter planes, cannon, aircraft carriers, tanks, cornucopia, and Statue of Liberty torches in hand are arranged in mesmerizing squadrons of perforated stamps that bring back some vivid memories. I also kept three dozen dime-sized embossed composition red and blue OPA points that were part of the rationing system. The length of World War II is temporally relative. Japan's war endured fifteen years, from the occupation of Manchuria in 1931. Britain's war spanned six and a half years. America's war lasted four years, but I still have my ration books.

32

33

34

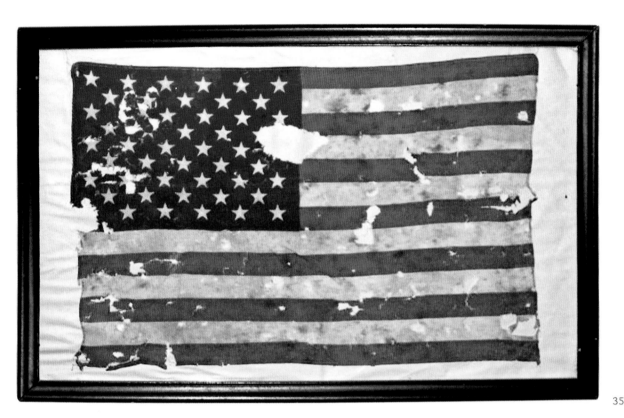

35

NOTHING RALLIES strong universal sentiments like the concepts of *Mother* and *Flag*. Flags are part of something bigger even than war. They are symbols of a nation's identity. In peacetime, the flag is subject to petty factional symbolic manipulations; but given an instance of national threat, it's a signal to call the entire population to patriotic, self-righteous attention. Technically, a flag is the symbol of a country, rendered in specific proportion, design, and colors, and which has a particular history, symbolism, and etiquette. It commands the attention of a particular group of people. It is the symbolic artifact through which allegiance to a country is pledged.

A flag is an emblem, a standard, a pennant—the colors. Under specific and loaded conditions it may be damaged or destroyed because it is part of something bigger.

> . . . And the rockets' red glare, the bombs bursting in air,
> Gave proof through the night that our flag was still there . . . .
> Francis Scott Key, "The Star Spangled Banner
> (The Defense of Fort McHenry)," September 20, 1814.

36

37

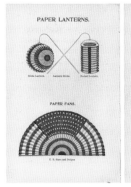

38

Keep Democracy at Your Finger Tips

GAME OF FLAGS

McLOUGHLIN BROTHERS N.Y.

UNCLE SAM SHOE POLISH
MAHOGANY STAIN
WAX POLISH
OXBLOOD

VILLAGE IMPROVEMENT SOCIETY
SO. SHAFTSBURY, VT.

happy life and a dear little wife

39

Flag etiquette and praxis are codified and printed in hometown newspapers every Flag Day. The protocols for the honorable and correct destruction of damaged flags by burning are as specific as the holiest religious rituals. In "Ragged Old Flag," his only poem, Johnny Cash enumerates the meaningful ways in which an American flag might have been damaged.

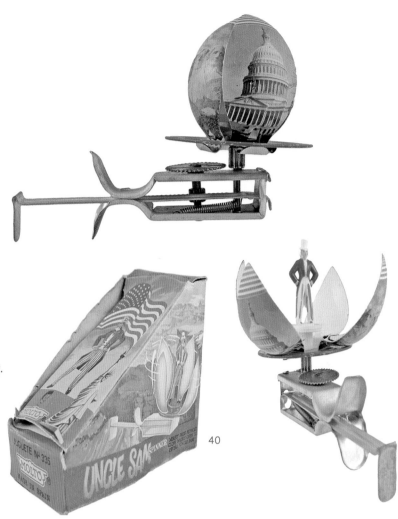

> You see, we got a little hole in that flag there
> When Washington took it across the Delaware.
> And it got powder-burned the night Francis Scott Key
> Sat watching it writing "Oh Say Can You See."
> And it got a bad rip in New Orleans
> With Packingham and Jackson tuggin' at its seams.
>
> And it almost fell at the Alamo
> Beside the Texas flag, but she waved on through.
> She got cut with a sword at Chancellorsville
> And she got cut again at Shiloh Hill.
> There was Robert E. Lee, Beauregard, and Bragg,
> And the south wind blew hard on that Ragged Old Flag.
>
> On Flanders Field in World War I
> She got a big hole from a Bertha gun.
> She turned blood red in World War II
> She hung limp and low by the time it was through.
> She was in Korea and Vietnam.
> She went where she was sent by her Uncle Sam.
> "Ragged Old Flag," Johnny Cash

40

The design of a flag changes for constituent adjustments (for example, the addition of a state) or for political reasons of secession, conquest, or independence. Flag symbols change after revolution and sometimes alter postwar. I collect American flags as well as sincere and innocent images of American flags from the past. They include flag embroideries memorializing *My Trip to the Philippines and China*; stitched state seals; flag-painted fish decoys; thirty-one, thirty-six, and forty-eight stars and stripes; hand-held parade flags; flag fans; children's collages of flags; crocheted *Old Glories*; game boards with flags; flag puzzles; flag paintings; feather flags; and all manner of flag lapel pins. I draw the line at flag air fresheners and flag depictions that are not beautiful or convey messaging beyond sincerity and innocence.

In times of actual or implied threat, the flag inspires passion. In peacetime, it inspires sentiment. Both are aspects of emotion ranging from general nationalism to more specific patriotism. Expressions and shades of these feelings range from gentle poetry extolling the virtues of her colors to wartime marching songs meant to raise adrenalin on the first note. We are all susceptible to some of these feelings. Some of us are susceptible to all of them.

> One good flag lasts a very long time.
> Verlyn Klinkenborg, *The Rural Life*
> (New York: Little, Brown & Co., 2002), 101.

39
Group of flag incarnations, 1880–1977. 2½–15" high

40
Flag and Uncle Sam spinner toy with box (three views), 1969. 3" high. Molto Corporation, Spain

41
Uncle Sam, 1910. Celluloid and paint, 7" high

41

Used Up

chapter 13

ONCE UPON a time the postman actually collected the postage due on mail; milk was delivered in glass bottles to your door at dawn; wax crayons were the brightest colors a child could draw with; Halloween costumes were made of crepe paper; and sewing needles came in needle books.

My musings about the history of needles envision a thorn as the first tool for puncturing animal-skin clothing, through which sinew or vegetal fiber was coaxed for fastening. The second step must have been a calculated perforation through the widest part of the thorn, through which flora or fauna fiber was passed to enable the first act of stitching.

1

2

Gliding through history to the mid-1850s, machinery had just been invented that transformed wire into needles with perforated "eyes," through which cotton or silk thread could pass. This machinery preempted one of the grave industrially related diseases of the era. Pointer's disease was the main hazard of hand-grinding needles caused by inhalation of finely ground steel dust. England led the world in needle production and Pointer's disease.

Prior to 1910, needles were contained in paper packets and leather sewing wallets. After 1910, sewing needles were commonly packaged in paper needle books, which were roughly the format of today's greeting cards with an attractive bit of usually pictorial advertising on the cover, needles contained within. The needles were stuck through cloth swatches or bright foil paper, or were placed within affixed packets of labeled black folded paper. All needle books proffered needles at the ready, occasionally with a wire needle threader. From 1915 through the 1920s, needle book advertising giveaways were as common as advertising blotters. From the early 1930s through the 1950s, they often came as a bonus with another purchase or as an inexpensive peddler's item or as a "gift" with a donation to a charity.

1
Two needle books (outside and inside), 1936, 1953. Printed paper, 3 and 3½" high. Made in Germany and Japan

2
Needle packets, 1876, 1880. Printed paper, each 2¾" high

3
Two needle books (outside and inside), 1876–1919. Printed paper, each 2¾" high

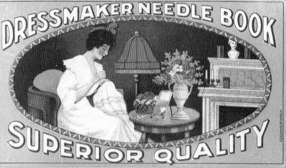

3

Betsy Ross, the assumed seamstress of our first flag, was a frequently celebrated needle book cover personality. She was rendered in the graphic traditions of each decade of needle book production, ranging from austerely representational to voguish chic to cutesy stylized outline. She is the natural historical selection of the American goddess of the needle, and she came with a red, white, and blue sales pitch.

Some needle books simply represented a product; others included its virtues and a vendor. Many depicted cozy scenes of family life, flowers, sunrises over water or bucolic landscapes, landmark skyscrapers, sports successes, a world's fair, or the Twentieth Century Limited. Others portrayed the high-life, perhaps with imagery offering a rosy future to the housewife mending her husband's blue collars. What does Gatsby or a flapper in a speedboat have to do with darning? The iconography of needle books is rich and mysterious.

But somewhere in my soul, I know
I've met the thing before;
It just reminded me—'t was all—
And came my way no more.
    Emily Dickinson, *The Poems of Emily Dickinson*
(Cambridge: The Belknap Press of Harvard University).

4
Needle books, 1933–54. Printed paper, 3¾–4¼" high. Made in Germany and Japan

5
Army and Navy needle books (fronts and back), 1909. Printed paper, 2¾" high. Made in Germany

6

time as we get. Pink rubber erasers commonly reside in the metal ferrule situated on the shoulder of a pencil. Small rectangular blocks with slanted short ends often vary bilaterally in color and texture—one side embedded with fine grit—as they tackle the difficult job of ink erratum. Soft art gum and soap erasers are used by those who draw to remove soft graphite, charcoal, pastels, and conte crayon without abrading the paper. Pink Pearl erasers were my preferred tool for changing sums and quotients. Whatever their composition or design, with each use erasers are worn down and eventually out of existence.

6
Needle books, 1933–54. Printed paper, 3¾–4¼" high. Made in Germany and Occupied Japan

7
Group of erasers, 1935–55. Rubber, aluminum, and bristle, ¾–3½" high

Most needle books were printed on cardstock. During and after the 1930s, most sported a glossy lacquered finish, were rectangular in shape, and folded along the long side. The edges of many needle books are die-cut, and earlier examples are gilded. Needles are slight and bend with ardent use; they are easily lost or misplaced. My mother taught me to thread all needles taken out of a packet, even those used for splinter removal, so that they might be more easily located if dropped. Needles eventually vacate the needle book and the books expire; they're used up, but not as quickly as erasers.

ERASING, RUBBING out, *removing, expunging, deleting, effacing, eliminating, obliterating*, and *scratching out* are verbs used with erasers. An eraser is usually a specially fabricated piece of rubber employed to remove all traces of something that was written or drawn. The act of erasing is as close to taking back

7

THE DISTINCTIVE paraffin, pigment, printer's ink, and paper smell of Crayola crayons, according to a Yale University study, is one of the twenty most recognizable aromas to American adults. I remember the colors in Chuckles candies as being red, yellow, green, orange, and black, and the colors in the small Crayola box the same with blue, brown, and violet added. Both candy and crayons had the same saturated hues to my child's eyes. In 1949, I was awarded the forty-eight-crayon box. I visually devoured the rainbow for a week before I violated the sanctity of the arrangement and the virgin points. I used them only for drawing edges at first, employing older stubs and peeled nubbins where a sharp line was not required, thereby saving the points. I just caught the mental whiff of Crayolas as I wrote the last line.

During my crayoning years, I received well-intentioned gifts of other crayon brands from uninformed relatives. The crayons, after trial, inevitably failed one or more of the hue, luminosity, hardness, residue-when-pressure-was-applied, smoothness, or fluid-use tests. The colors in these sets were oddly tinted and shaded, not the strong, fully saturated Crayola spectrum. They were relegated to the value of stubs and kept in reserve on the theory that *you never know when you could need them*. The boxes that these strange crayon sets came in were another story. The second-rate crayons were expendable, but their boxes were not. They were more interesting than the Crayola box. They were exotic, made of lithographed tin, cardboard, or wood; and they taught tacit or aggressive lessons about color and form, and occasionally used the name of a famous artist.

The Crayola line expanded from the eight-crayon box to their forty-eight crayon assortment in 1949, to sixty-four in 1958, and to seventy-two in 1972. In 1993, ninety-six colors were produced; and in 1998, they offered one hundred twenty colors. Chuckles stuck with the original five colors.

Joseph Binney founded the Peekskill Chemical Company in 1864 and was the inventor of life-lengthening rubber blackening for automobile tires as well as barn-red iron oxide paint. He had a son named Edwin. In 1885, Edwin Binney and his cousin C. Harold Smith partnered up in the Binney & Smith Company, which produced shoe polish, printer's ink, pencils, and chalk; they experimented with adapting their black wax crate-marking crayons for school use. Binney & Smith is now a subsidiary of Hallmark Cards, Inc., and the lore of their corporate chromatics informs that Edwin's wife, Alice Binney, conflated *craie*, the French work for chalk, and the prefix of *olea*ginous, for oil, to arrive at the word *Crayola* in 1903.

8
Crayon box, c. 1930. Printed cardboard, 4" high. Binney & Smith Company, USA

9
Crayon box, 1940. Printed cardboard, 3¾" high. Milton Bradley Company, USA

10
Crayon box, 1940. Printed cardboard, 3¾" high. American Crayon Company, USA

11
Crayon box, 1925. Hinged printed steel, 3" high. Binney & Smith Company, USA

12
Crayon box, 1925. Printed cardboard, 4¾" high. The Ullman Company, USA

13
Crayon box, 1930. Printed cardboard, 3¾" high. Milton Bradley Company, USA

14
Crayon box, 1935. Hinged printed steel, 4½" high. American Crayon Company, USA

15
Crayon box, 1935. Hinged printed steel, 4½" high. American Crayon Company, USA

16
Crayon box, 1925. Printed cardboard, 3¾" high. Creston Candle Works, Inc., USA

17
Crayon box, 1937. Hinged printed steel, 4½" high. Standard Toycraft Products, Inc., USA

8

9

10

EIGHT STICKS

Colored
DRAWING
CRAYONS

•

BINNEY & SMITH CO. NEW YORK
MADE IN U.S.A.

11

JUMBO
CRAYONS

BIG CRAYONS FOR LITTLE PEOPLE
No. 540   THE ULLMAN MFG. CO.   MADE IN U.S.A.

12

PAUL REVERE
First Steps in Art
WAX CRAYONS
STANDARD COLORS
WITH BLACK AND BROWN

COLOR MIXING SHOWN BY
WINDOW STEPS
MILTON BRADLEY
COMPANY
SPRINGFIELD MASSACHUSETTS

13

Crayonart

Colored Drawing Crayons

14

Blendwel

SUPER QUALITY - BRIGHT COLORS
16 HEXAGON CRAYONS
THE AMERICAN CRAYON COMPANY   SANDUSKY · OHIO   NEW YORK

15

No. 8

CRESTON
TRADE MARK

SCHOOL CRAYONS
· EIGHT COLORS ·
for
SKETCHING and EDUCATIONAL WORKS · WATERPROOF

MANUFACTURED BY
CRESTON CANDLE WORKS INC.
NEW YORK, U.S.A.

16

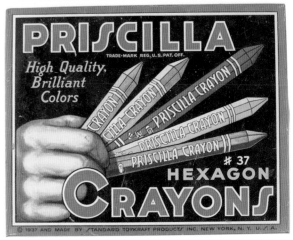

PRISCILLA
TRADE-MARK REG. U.S. PAT. OFF.

*High Quality,
Brilliant
Colors*

37
HEXAGON
CRAYONS

© 1937 AND MADE BY STANDARD TOYKRAFT PRODUCTS INC. NEW YORK, N.Y. U.S.A.

17

18
Crayon box, 1915.
Printed cardboard, 4"
high. Standard Crayon
Manufacturing Company,
USA

19
Crayon box, 1937.
Printed leatherette snap
wallet, 4" high. Standard
Toycraft Products, Inc.,
USA

20
Crayon box, 1930.
Printed cardboard, 3½"
high. Milton Bradley
Company, USA

21
Crayon box, 1915.
Hinged printed steel, 3¾"
high. American Crayon
Company, USA

22
Crayon box, c. 1910.
Printed cardboard, 3¾"
high. Binney & Smith
Company, USA

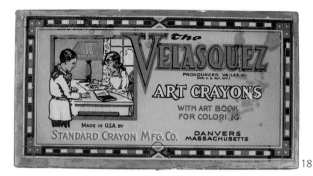

18

19

> Children can accomplish the renewal of existence in a hundred
> unfailing ways. Among children, collecting is only one process
> of renewal; other processes are the painting of objects, the cutting
> out of figures, the application of decals—the whole range of
> childlike modes of acquisition, from touching things to giving
> them names.
>   Walter Benjamin, *Illuminations* (New York: Schocken
> Books, 1985), 61.

21

22

Recently, I went to a toy store to buy a gift for a child and passed an audacious and astonishing arena of Crayola products including crayons that glow in the dark, that are aromatic, that glitter, and that change color, in large, regular, and "kids' first" sizes. I saw a toy Crayola Factory intended to compress nubbins into integrated, revivified amalgam crayons. I also glimpsed a stupendous array of colored Crayola markers that are destined to make crayons obsolete. They're easier for little hands to use and yield fully saturated colors. I should have stopped to smell the crayons. My box of fragments is gone, but I have lots of crayon boxes, the contents of which were used up every time I made a mark.

20

THE DENNISON Company of Framingham, Massachusetts, manufactured a variety of paper tags, mucilage-gummed paper labels, sealing waxes, birthday and holiday candles, lithographed and silk-screened holiday novelties, disposable tableware for special occasions, sham cloth tablecloths, and all manner of crafts supplies. Dennison's store on Fifth Avenue between Thirty-fifth and Thirty-sixth streets contained running yards of regimented printed labels that varied minutely from size to size, arranged by message from bordered blank address labels to *Assorted, Special, Personal, Please Rush, Dictated but Not Read, Insured, Past Due!, Air Mail, Duplicate,* and *Please Remit,* along with countless other labels. There were mucilage-backed letters and numerals for the creative sign maker, waiting to be moistened. There were colored foil stars in various sizes and boxes of red and cobalt blue certificate and diploma seals for graduates to come through the ages. Most of these labels, in boxes of multiples of ten, twenty, twenty-five, thirty-five, and fifty were used up after they were moistened and affixed to their final contexts. I still have a few small boxes of labels, stars, and seals from this wonderland of raw materials, a favorite destination for me from the late 1940s through the 1960s. But labels were not the most memorable Dennison's product.

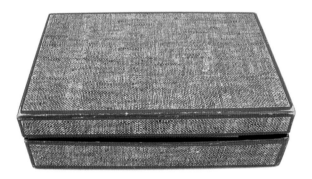

24

25

26

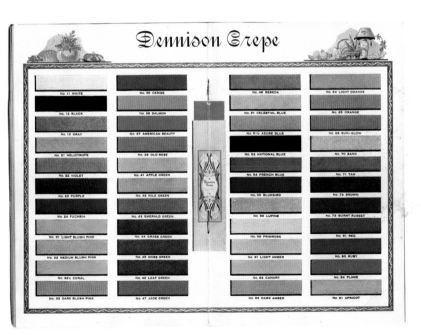

27

23
Three booklets of forty-eight gummed-back decorative seals, c. 1955. 3" high. Dennison Manufacturing Company, Framingham, Massachusetts

24
The Handibox No. 20 (closed and open), 1948. Comprised of assorted Dennison's labels and stationery products, 2" high

25
Crepe paper decorated car, 1916. Photo postcard, 3½" high

26
Packages of Duplex and Duo-Fold crepe paper to duplicate nature's loveliest flowers and delight your friends, 1948–52. 10 x 5" long

27
Crepe paper instruction booklet, *How to Make Paper Costumes*, 1925. Centerfold color chart, 7¾" high. Dennison Manufacturing Company, Framingham, Massachusetts

THE RAIL SPUR that sided the Dennison's factory distributed crepe paper across America from circa 1880 for sixty years. Unique among papers, crepe paper looked like its namesake fabric and actually stretched sufficiently to be molded into ruffles and flower petals. It had the integrity required to be sewn by hand or machine into detailed costumes, lampshades, and fanciful hats. It came in a wide variety of subtle pastels, brilliants, and metallic colors that changed annually. Detailed *How to Make . . .* catalogues materialized as holidays approached. Sumptuous colors such as *Flame*, *Nile Green*, *Dark Amber*, *Light Blush Pink*, and *American Beauty* were annually in the offing. Of the twenty-eight colors offered in 1948, four were subtle variations of blue: *Bluebird*, *National Blue*, *Light Blue*, and *French Blue*.

28
Dennison's crepe paper
wrapper section, 1922,
and Woolworth's price
tag, 1931. 7" high

29
Lampshades and *"How
to …" Crepe Paper Lamp
Shades: Art and Decor-
ation in Crepe and Tissue
Paper,* September 1902,
page 11. Each lampshade
4" high. Dennison
Manufacturing Company,
Framingham,
Massachusetts

30
Crepe paper necklace,
1950. 20" long

31
Crepe paper Santa Claus
Christmas tree ornament
(front and back) with
printed paper, twig, and
string affixes, c. 1895.
8" high

Strong enough to endure energetic bouts of trick-and-treating as well as Easter-parading of *chapeaux*, crepe paper had a culture and dedicated following that exceeded all the materials of childhood with the exception of Crayola crayons. Not including coarse, unstretchy party streamers, crepe paper was manufactured 20 inches wide by 10 feet long, first on rolls and later in soft packets held by a paper sleeve. Originally developed for window dressing and bazaar and party decorations, it was quickly adapted to costume and artificial flower construction. The Dennison Manufacturing Company provided free booklets of instruction, with diagrams, to teachers and window decorators—booklet lessons in crepe paper utility. *How to Make Crepe Paper Flowers*, *How to Make Crepe Paper Costumes*, and *Decorating Halls, Booths, and Automobiles* cost the rest of us ten cents but were self-described as "brimful of practical ideas." How

many practical ideas can there be for crepe paper automobile enhancement?

My special interest was the fabrication of carnations, poppies, roses, and daffodils. These were generic flowers that rarely grew in whatever colors I had on hand. I got a special frisson from cutting across the short edge of the packet that yielded a 2-inch-by-10-foot-long strip of amazing fringing and stretching potential. A basic vocabulary of cuts and stretches spawned a garden of results. The only crepe paper liabilities that I recall are that once wet, crepe paper products are irredeemable; intensity faded with exposure to the sun, and, once used, it could not be satisfactorily recycled into other constructions. These lessons were learned in the school of hard knocks. Otherwise, crepe paper flowers lasted somewhat longer than nature's cut blooms. The manufacturer made no claims of permanency.

28

ART AND DECORATION IN CRÊPE AND TISSUE PAPER. 11

CRÊPE PAPER LAMP SHADES.

Empire, either size. Price, $4.00.
For Empire Shade Wire Frames, see page 18.

Dennison's
DECORATED
CREPE PAPER
Dennison Manufacturing Co.
THE TAG MAKERS
FRAMINGHAM, MASS., U.S.A.
10 FEET LONG   20 INCHES WIDE

16—613
CREPE PAPER
10 Feet Long
Fold 5¢
F. W. WOOLWORTH CO.

29

30

31

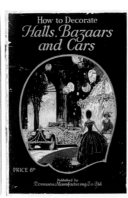

32

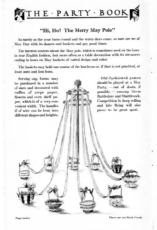

32
Group of crepe paper
instruction booklets,
1910–27. 8" high.
Dennison Manufacturing
Company, Framingham,
Massachusetts

33
Dennison's crepe paper
instruction booklet
centerfolds, 1910–27.
Approximately 7¾" high.
Dennison Manufacturing
Company, Framingham,
Massachusetts

33

34
Trylon and Perisphere sugar cube, 1939. Sugar and printed paper, ¾" high. Domino, American Sugar Refining Company, for Hotel Taft and the New York World's Fair

35
Domino sugar packet, 2001. Printed paper, 1½" high

36
Casino sugar packets, 1985–96. Printed paper, each 1¾" high

37
Kennedy for President sugar packet (back and front), 1960. Printed paper, 2½" high. C & H Sugar Company

38
Advertising sugar packets, 2001. Printed paper, 1¾" high

39
C & H sugar packet, 2003. Palm tree (standard reverse side), printed paper, 1½" high

IN THE HOME of my youth, sugar was purchased in boxes of unwrapped cubes, except the sugar used for baking. My grandparents sipped hot tea through a sugar cube clenched between their teeth. Like whistling, that was a skill I never mastered. My parents dropped small cubes into cups of coffee or tea and stirred well as a prelude to drinking. The local lunch counters had individually paper-wrapped rectangular solids of Domino sugar called "cubes," with which I practiced building brick walls while awaiting sandwich delivery. In upscale restaurants the wrappers were usually imprinted with the name of the eatery on one side and the sugar company on the other. The cubes were the equivalent of a teaspoon, and if one wanted more or less, the little hard block had to be divided. This was accomplished by the brute breaking or chomping with canine or molar, since division by knife tended to send a sugar projectile across the room. Sometimes the eroded cube was spooned up before complete meltdown. None of the processes were delicate, mannerly, or accurate, and all wasted a portion of sugar. I imagine that this is why the sugar packet caught on. I only cared to save packets of sugar depicting U.S. presidents and I collected all but James Monroe (1748–1831, Republican, Virginia), from George Washington through Dwight D. Eisenhower. The sugar-packet producer replaced the series with state birds before I located Monroe. Finding Monroe is something to live for.

34

35

36

37

38

39

Packets equivalent to a teaspoon of sugar were a practical adaptation of the sugar cube and one that lent itself to a larger graphic field for name, product, or logo recognition than the little blocky cube. There are thousands of sugar packets produced and shipped worldwide, and some of them are used in tropical climates. Sugar packets are usually laminated with a satiny humidity-inhibiting liner. Most are pliant and rectangular. Some European packets are tubular. Like air-sickness bags, sugar packets are fabricated in generic styles as well as custom models. Although I haven't needed to collect more widely than the U.S. presidents, I imagine others collecting museum, restaurant, airline, bowling alley, or hotel categories. I can envision a collection of packets from every country governed by a dictatorship or from every amusement park in the world. I see a multifaceted set of possibilities here. There is a further conundrum: whether or not to tear off the top of the packet for use and then bring home the prize; or to operate on the packet with a surgical blade to preserve its relative intactness in the café; or to save the sugar in the packet, perhaps necessitating the capture of two packets so that both may be seen in a two-dimensional exhibition format. Whatever the choice, sugar packets are an ideal packaging concept for their contents. One might easily tear off the packet end, pour the sugar, and crumple the submissive packet, dropping it into the saucer of your latte without further thought.

40
Group of scenic New England sugar packets, 2005. Printed paper, 1¾ and 1¼" high. Domino Sugar Co.

41
Babe Ruth sugar packet (front and back), c. 1960. Printed paper, 2½" high. I.A.M. Packing Company, Perrysburg, Ohio

40

41

43

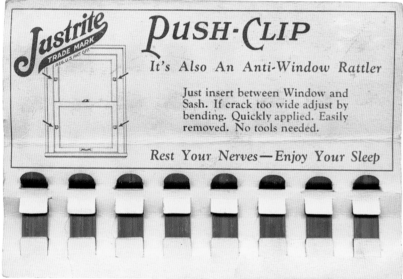

42

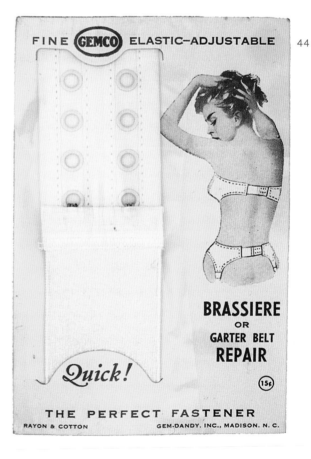

44

42
Carded Push-Clips (front and back) to fasten electric wires to baseboards and stop windows from rattling, 1928. Printed cardboard and painted steel, 4" high. Justrite Company, Chicago, Illinois

43
Carded zipper-repair slides, 1951. Steel with printed paper and cellophane wrap, 5½" high. Snag-Pruf Company, Inc., New York City

44
Carded brassiere and garter belt repair, 1951. Printed cardboard, cotton, rayon, painted steel eyelets, and stainless-steel hooks, 5¼" high. Gem-Dandy, Inc., North Carolina

BOTH CLEVERNESS and economy of design figure into flawless packaging. Often simplicity is a partner. When clear wrappers are employed, an odd or otherwise compelling product is a sure seller, as with Gemco's expander and repair kit for brassiere or garter belt. Arresting visuals demonstrating the product's use on its display card provoke impulse sales, as may be seen on the Tip-Top Broom Holder, Snag-Pruf zipper slide, and Mendets pot repair patches.

PAINTED INSULATED STAPLES 40 No.5

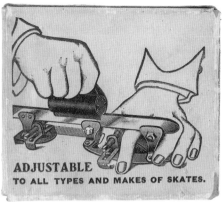

ADJUSTABLE TO ALL TYPES AND MAKES OF SKATES.

J. & P. COATS Darning and Mending MERCERIZED

DOLLY'S OWN DINNER SET

MADE IN GT. BRITAIN

MATCH BOX Construction Set

MADE BY LOUIS MARX & CO 200 5TH AVE. N.Y.C.

ONE PIECE COLLAR BUTTON

ILLUSTRATED CUBE Spelling Blocks

TIGER. EAGLE. PIG. BIRD. COCK. OWL. LION. PELICAN. ZEBRA.

No. 41-A ENLARGED Colored Sticks J. L. Hammett Co. Cambridge, Mass. Newark, N.J.

45
Perfect packaging group, c. 1870–1967. 2½–8" high

45

46
Carded broom holders with whisk broom hook, 1924. Printed cardboard and steel, 3¼" high. Tip Top Manufacturing Company

47
Pearl Shirt Button card with seven buttons, c. 1915. Printed paper with seven mother-of-pearl buttons, 4½" high

48
Carded bobby pins, 1938. Printed cardboard and steel, 4¾" high. Pin-up Girl Manufacturing Company, USA

49
Matchbox gas station set, c. 1950. Printed cardboard sleeve simulating a matchbox with side friction strips and cardboard inner-slide box, 1½" high. Made in Western Germany

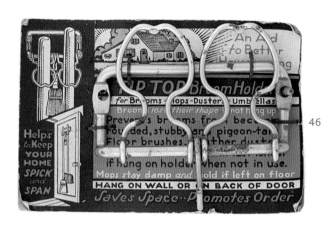

46

PEARL SHIRT BUTTONS

47

SMOOTH FITTING
Pin-up Girl
BOB-PINS
TRADE MARK REGISTERED   MADE IN U.S.A.
10¢

48

Button cards exhibit classic design economy. The cunning aesthetics of the direct and spare lithographed cardboard box containing an adjustable ice skate blade sharpener with instructions for use is exquisitely integrated. Great packaging may be as simple as three 1870 slate school pencils tied with red, white, and blue silk ribbon or Dolly's Own Dinner Set on a slotted, printed cardboard place setting. There are many instances of selling by over-packaging, in which the product itself becomes an anticlimax. There are abundant instances of insensitive packaging. Excellent packaging jumps out if you're tuned in. It's usually destroyed getting to the contents, so I save the whole thing and, when possible, buy a second package to use.

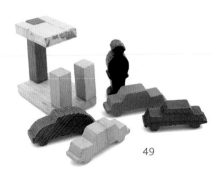

49

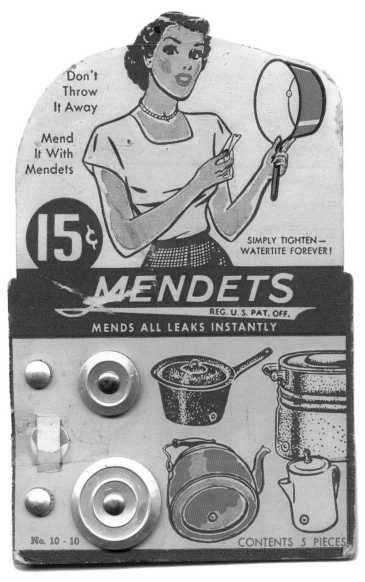

50

51

52

50
Carded pot-repair patches, 1945 and 1954. Printed cardboard, aluminum patches, and steel screws, 6" high. Collette Manufacturing Company, Amsterdam, New York

51
Button card with flag-wrapped smiling woman with ten buttons, 1941. *Miss America Pearls*. Printed card stock, 3¼" high

52
Cat's eye marbles in original *Five-Star Brand Pride of Young Americans* package, 20th century. Package, 3½" high; each marble, ¾" diameter. USA

1

chapter 14

Better in the Afterlife

His wife left in the middle of the second
summer. In the morning she put two
suitcases into the car and drove away,
but not before she'd taken every lure
out of the tackle box and thrown them
off the front porch into the trees. There
were lures everywhere, gaudy and
sharp, some in the ferns, some up in
the white birches by the wall, others
hanging festively off the pine.

Mark Slouka, *Lost Lake* (New
York: Alfred A Knopf, 1998), 13.

SOMETIMES OBJECTS made in the past later
seem surprising and unexpected. The
impetus for their conception is remote and
the spirit in which they were made could
not be as rich as the spirit in which they are
now observed. Both picture postcards and
toy zeppelins acquire a patina with temporal perspective.

Upon receipt, a picture postcard has the
immediacy of a written message and the
context of the location or other image that
is pictured. When I read the backs of my
vintage postcards, I know that most were
saved because of sentiment for the sender,
or for the recipient to relive the echo of a
specific feeling. Saving postcards by pictorial category, regardless of message or
archaic stamp, is an objective act embarked
upon with an aesthetic of distance. The
collector of HOMES OF THE STARS postcards or postcards of defunct Las Vegas
Casinos or of patriotic valentine postcards

2

3

4

is zealous about the cards' afterlife. One card doesn't have large significance. A group of categorically gathered postcards can be central and revelatory.

From 1910 through the 1950s, exaggerations were a picture-postcard idiom. Images of two giant strawberries or one ear of corn filling a railroad flatcar were printed, inscribed, and mailed. Chromolithographed mega-trout were landed beneath the caption *The way we catch them here.* Texans were depicted riding saddled jackrabbits, and one canteloupe filled a wheelbarrow that four people couldn't push. A colossal object pictured beside dwarfed and dazzled people trying to fathom or manipulate it was a postcard genre. America, land of plenty, couldn't have been the only message when you consider that these cards were printed right through the Great Depression and World War II. Victorian humor postcards, *Welcome to Dixie* postcards, and postcards of pool halls across the United States are all best viewed standing at the tip of the wedge, looking back from a distance toward the past so that they may flash the queer exuberance of another time.

1
Melon exaggeration
postcard, 1912. 3½" high

2
Fish exaggeration
postcard, 1932. 3½" high

3
Fish exaggeration
postcard, 1943. ½" high

4
Fish exaggeration
postcard, 1949. 3½" high

5
Corn exaggeration
postcard, 1927. 3½" high

6
Grape exaggeration
postcard, 1931. 3½" high

7
Tomato exaggeration
postcard, 1932. 3½" high

8
Strawberry exaggeration
postcard, 1910. 3½" high

9
Potato exaggeration
postcard, 1937. 3½" high

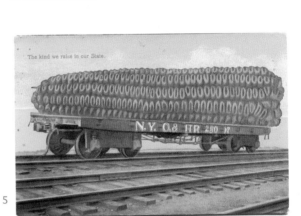

5

6

7

8

9

10

11

EMPIRE STATE BUILDING - NEW YORK CITY

12

10
Zeppelin postcards, 1909, each 3½" high

11
Zep pocket watch (front and back) commemorating the Graf Zeppelin's twenty-one-day trip around the world, 1929. 2¾" high

12
Postcard of a zeppelin approaching the Empire State Building mooring mast, 1935. 5" high

13
Group of zeppelins as objects and as emblems on products, 1907–35. 1½–7" high

ZEPPELINS ARE also better in the afterlife. Toy zeppelins are much better than the real thing was, considering that the toys were highly maneuverable and didn't explode. Zeppelins were rigid, aluminum-framed airships with motors, propellers, and inflated hydrogen cells. They were named after Count Ferdinand Graf von Zeppelin, foremost German builder of dirigibles, credited with the first successful untethered two-engine airship flight in 1910. By the time of his death in 1918, Germany had constructed sixty-seven of the airships, of which sixteen survived World War I. Zeppelins were used to bomb London and Paris. But airplanes could ascend to higher altitudes, were more maneuverable, and could survive storms. Zeppelins were large targets and comparatively slow and clumsy. Their crews were susceptible to oxygen deprivation above ten thousand feet, and the ships were uninsulated from frigid temperatures and heat. Worst of all, hydrogen-inflated zeppelins were highly flammable.

In 1928, the *Graf Zeppelin*, the finest and second most famous airship, entered commercial service, carrying more than thirteen thousand passengers in

ten years to destinations in the United States, Japan, South America, the Middle East, and the Arctic. In 1936, when the *Hindenburg*, the most famous airship of all, entered commercial service, zeppelins were becoming competitive with ocean liners for long trips. In 1937, landing in Lakehurst, New Jersey, after completing its tenth trip, the *Hindenburg* airship exploded, killing thirty-five of those on board and one member of the ground crew.

The hydrogen explosion was captured on film and widely publicized on the airwaves, in newspapers and magazines, and in movie-theater newsreels. Images of the fireball effectively terminated zeppelin travel. Zeppelin toys have represented both their fulfilled and unrealized potential in their afterlife.

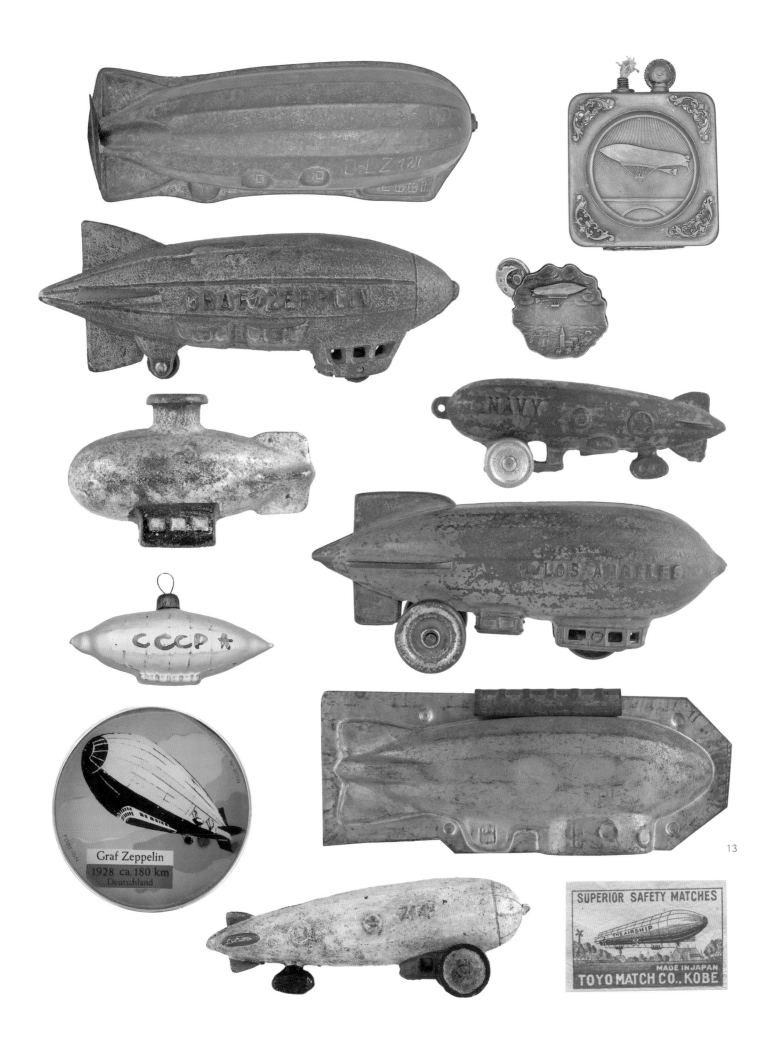

SUPERIOR SAFETY MATCHES
THE AIRSHIP
MADE IN JAPAN
TOYO MATCH CO., KOBE

Graf Zeppelin
1928 ca. 180 km
Deutschland

13

14
Photograph of zeppelin
approaching airfield in
reverse painted glass
frame with steel back,
c. 1930. 8½" high.
Germany

15
Zeppelin Valentine
card, 1922. Printed card
stock, glassine, 9" high.
Made in Germany for the
American market

16
Skylark needle book
(open, exterior and
interior), 1933. Printed
paper, 4½" high. Made in
Germany

15

I'M COMING
TO YOU DEAR VALENTINE

Printed in Germany

16

SINGLE CIGARETTE and cigar silks, like tangible instances of leaps of faith, are adrift fragments, each singular in its primary existence but unanchored to a larger significance. They were often set aside; yet when later moored to others of their ilk, they have an engagingly substantial vitality. Each cigarette silk was a premium received as a bonus with a package of cigarette tobacco. Paper trading cards with masculine subjects such as famous sports figures were their precursor. Bookmarks and lightweight scrapbook fodder at best, the cards were comparatively unappealing to the woman of the house. By the early 1900s, attractive pictorial silks had succeeded them. These silks had sumptuously printed images of flowers, flags, actresses, maps, birds, butterflies, bathing beauties, biblical heroines, fruit, and animals. While men smoked, women embroidered, crocheted, tatted, and quilted the silks into table scarves, pillow slips, doilies, and crazy quilts.

CIGAR SILKS were almost always a spectrum of yellow ribbons, about twenty inches long, that held bunches of cigars together and upright. Most cigar bundles were printed with the name of the tobacco company and/or a particular cigar's specific designation and/or its place of origin. Elaborate typefaces were unique to specific cigars and were centered along the length of the silk ribbon. *London Dog*, *Exorbitantes*, *Flor de Aromas*, *Exquisitos*, *Victorias*, and *Regalia Conchas* printed on golden ribbons were surely used singly as an expedient bow around long tresses. But when accumulated to enter a full second life, they were plain-stitched to backing or embroidered into a pattern and the result was far greater than the sum of its parts.

17
Group of cigarette silks, c. 1890. Printed silk and cotton thread, each 2¼" high

18
Clutch of cigar silks and a pillow top of embroidered cigar silks, c. 1880. Printed silk ribbon and silk thread, 10½" high

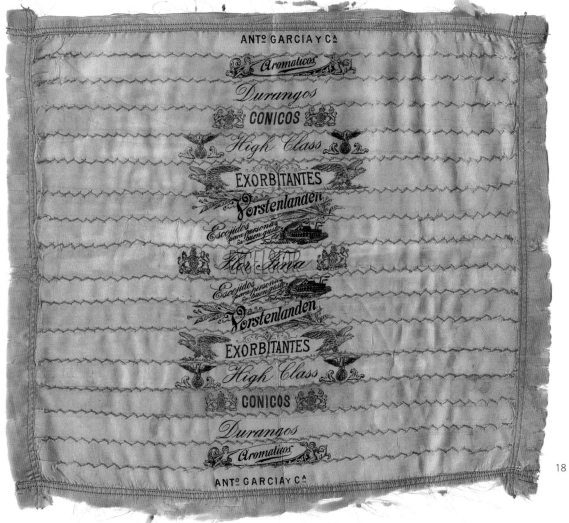

18

MY LEAPS OF FAITH collection is also greater than the sum of its unlikely parts. It has grown from the bellwether postcard of the mid-leaper and the third-class relic to include a package of Fan Tan chewing gum that boasts *Royal Flavor* and a box of purple Victorian mourning pins announcing that *None Are Genuine But Those Bearing This Label*. Both require a leap of faith on the part of the consumer.

I've also added photographic artifacts that record a leap of faith by an action or intention captured, the outcome of which will never be known. One is an airborne horse and rider at full extension over a hurdle. They could have made it, although I have my doubts about the flaccid stream of water arcing from a red hose toward a raging house fire. A reverse-glass painted heart-shaped frame with a reflective silver *Remember Me* surrounds an angry, scowling, very unlovable face that raises as much skepticism in this third party as does the horseshoe-shaped arcade pocket charm with an inlaid Indian Head penny that reads *Keep me and never go broke*. The penny, worn down with rubbing, is now worth less than when it was new. The converted sardine can oil lamp has equal chances of illumination or explosion. It requires a leap of faith to light it. Separately these relics are odd and dismissable. Each could be tossed out or remanded to a desk drawer with the bent paper clips, glueless recycled stamps, the dead calculator, and your last movie stub. Together they are a telling testament to the extremes and ironies of human nature and an afterlife.

19
Photographic postcard of airborne horse and rider on racecourse in Spain, 1914. 3½" high

20
Package of *Royal Flavor* chewing gum, 1950. ¾" high. Bee Bee Confection Company, Inc., Ohio

21
Box of mourning pins (top and bottom), 1870. *None are Genuine but those bearing this label.* Printed cardboard and paper, 1½" high. Kirby, Beard & Company, London

22
Kodachrome print showing inadequate stream of water used to combat a four-alarm fire on Columbus Avenue, Boston, July 5, 1965. 5" high

20

21

19

22

23

24

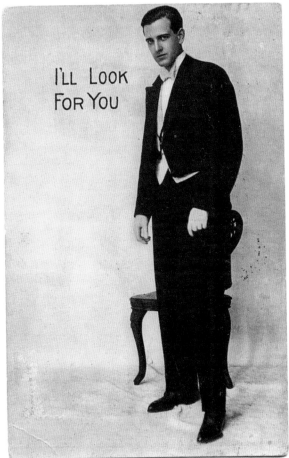

25

23
Photograph in reverse painted glass frame, 1946. Pocket mirror on back, 3" high

24
Never Go Broke lucky charm (front and back), 1903. Pressed aluminum and Indian Head penny, 1½" high

25
Commercial flirtation postcard meant to romantically encourage the recipient, 1912. 5½" high

26
Oil lamp (side and back views), 2000. Sardine tins, solder, and kapok, 4½" high. Ethiopia

26

ANIMAL TRAPS made from adapted Mason canning jars and lids could only have been humbly conceived in dreams of grandeur and riches born of the invention of the better mousetrap. During the eighteenth and nineteenth centuries, many foods were preserved in salt-glazed stoneware vessels stored in earth cellars and cool breezeways. This was an iffy proposition, and the 1858 patent of the screw-top Mason glass canning jar revolutionized home canning. It was a major improvement on stoneware jars and the various clamp-top and plunger contraptions meant to seal and keep the vacuum in home-canned fruits and vegetables, jellies and jams, and canned venison, if you were so inclined. One dreamer must have been in his cellar, staring at a rack of empty canning jars, mouths agape, awaiting next summer's bounty, perhaps harboring a desiccated mouse or two, when the proverbial light bulb of inspiration illuminated.

"Well, hot-diggety-doo . . . if I cut out the center portion of the lid and rim the circumference with sharpened wire spikes that are clustered tightly in a wasp-waisted configuration extending well into the jar, a mouse, lured by a bit of food (or not), could squeeze into the jar but not out." If passive, it would starve to death. If aggressive and frantic, it would

27
Mason canning jar with lid converted to make a mousetrap, c. 1865. 7¼" high

28
Glass canning jar converted to make a minnow trap (two views), c. 1915. Lid perforated, and steel wire brace for legs and handle, 14¾" high

27

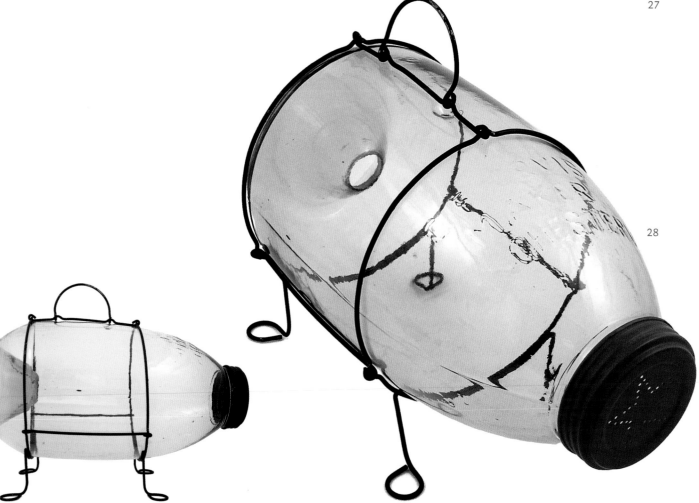

28

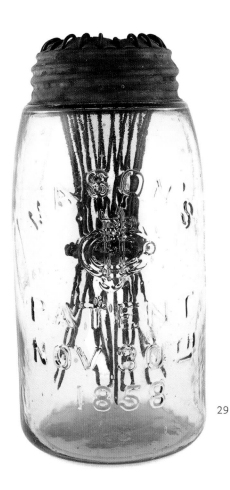

29

impale itself. The devil makes home industry for idle hands. Kindred spirits to this ingenious soul adapted clear glass jars into minnow traps. Inverted conical apertures pierce the body of the jar, the larger circular opening on its exterior wall, the tiny circular opening on the tip of the cone within the jar. When set into a stream or riverbed, the jar quickly fills with water and becomes invisible to minnows, except for the metal Mason jar lid and handle frame the fisherman would require for retrieval. Minnows swim in and do not exit. Someone in Checotah, Oklahoma, devised the minnow trap with three apertures. These traps are evidence of the epiphanies of inventiveness that are better in their showcase afterlife.

29
Mason canning jar with lid converted to make a mousetrap, c. 1865. 7¼" high

30
Mason canning jar with lid converted to make a mousetrap, c. 1865. 7¼" high

31
Glass canning jar converted to make a minnow trap, c. 1900. Mason jar lid, 12" high. Checotah, Oklahoma

30

31

THERE ARE artifacts of bizarre senses of humor in the Whoopee Cushion, cigarette loads, electrical hand buzzers, and spritzing lapel flowers. Other humorous gimcracks are a segue from the calling card or the acquaintance card, which invited the familiarity of responsive strangers; an example is the slogan button. Celluloid buttons from the 1920s showed text and rebus figures identical to the content of earlier puzzle and humor acquaintance cards: *O U [monkey]*, *You Are the [apple] of My [eye]*, and *Will You Be My [deer]*. They evolved into cigarette-button premiums and metal pins through the 1930s, 1940s, and 1950s, with messages that were more direct such as *Shimmie and I'll Do the Rest*; *Come to Papa*; *Take Me in Your Arms, I'm Not Married*; *I Love My Wife, But Oh You Kid, Let's Go*; and *Kiss Me I'm Polish*.

The sales pitch for these buttons was the provision of "pleasant jokes" and opportunity for "amusing conversation . . . smoothing the way for more familiar acquaintance and cordial friendship. They are wittily worded and quite unobjectionable." What was the producer thinking? The concept of the "pickup" was unaddressed. Was the possibility of white slavery gaily laughed off? Slogan buttons are certainly best served up with an aesthetic of distance in order to observe the merchandiser's peculiar expectations of complicity or naiveté from the consumer.

32
Advertisement for Motto Cards, 1929. 7½" high. Johnson Smith & Company catalog, Detroit, Michigan, page 320

33
Slogan buttons, 1935–55. Celluloid on tin frame and printed steel, with brass pin backs, 1–1½" diameter

34
Slogan button ad, 1940. 8¼" high. Johnson Smith & Company catalog, Detroit, Michigan, page 183

32

33

34

SIMILAR ADVERTISING techniques pushed the purchase of books that retooled the gullible toward new and lucrative careers. For between ten and thirty-five cents in 1936, you could *Become a Star Electrician*, *Learn to be a Detective*, garner *The Secrets of Ventriloquism*, receive *Twenty-Five Lessons in Hypnotism*, learn *How to Love and Be Loved*, take *The Five Minute Harmonica Course*, *Become a Fortune Teller*, and master *How to Win at Draw Poker*. The expectations instigated by these books flourished in publishers' ad copy and perhaps in the dreams of desperate teenagers, but could not be fulfilled in real life. They remained small forgettable ads in the back pages of romance and movie magazines through the 1950s.

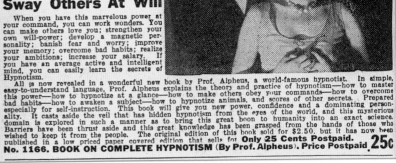

35

36

37

35
Misinformation book ad, 1935. 3¾" high. Johnson Smith & Company catalog, Detroit, Michigan, page 40

36
Misinformation book ad, 1940. 7¾" high. Johnson Smith & Company catalog, Detroit, Michigan, page 324

37
He: The Magazine for Men (front cover) offering misinformation about women and dice, September 1953. 6" high

A significant subset of these misinformation books related to the subject of food. *Dishes Men Like* is one example. The pitch is: If you can't cook honey, you can fool him. *The way to a man's heart is through his stomach*, as we all know, and these recipes for macaroni camp-style, pork 'n' beans, and London Loaf will snag him. Was there a companion book called *Dishes Women Like*? Was there a sequel called *Dishes Women Like to Cook*? *Unusual Recipes* promises that Mystery Pudding dessert, made of breadcrumbs and nine spices, will guarantee skating-party successes. *The Sunny Side of Life* book recommends planning colorful meals such as "*white* celery, *green* lettuce and *red* beets that my family will enjoy."

How to Have Good and Avoid Bad Luck offers many recommendations, which include finding a four-leaf clover or two chairs accidentally placed back to back for the former, and not spilling salt, breaking a mirror, or cutting your nails on Sunday for the latter. *Atomic Attack! What To Do* recommends dropping to the floor and getting under a heavy table after turning off all appliances as well as not rushing outside right after an atomic explosion. The advice is to "Wait at least an hour to give lingering radiation a chance to die down."

38

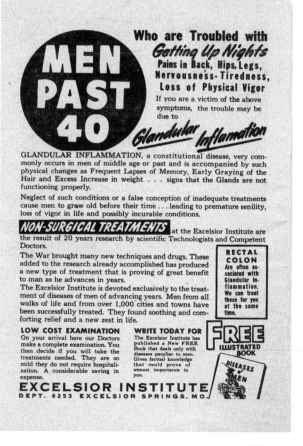

39

OUR DELICIOUS COD LIVER
BEEF PEPTONE AND IRON TONIC
(Contains No Oil)

A MODERN TONIC

IT WILL BUILD YOU UP AND CREATE STRENGTH

Luck
How to have good
How to avoid bad

Good luck to you

MORGAN DRUG CO.
Piedmont   W. Va.

40

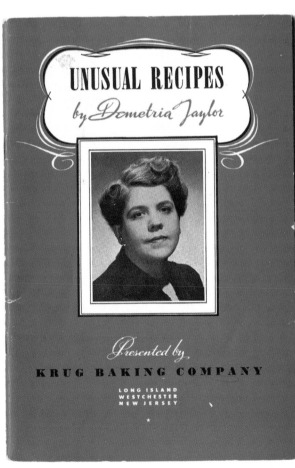

UNUSUAL RECIPES
by Demetria Taylor

Presented by
KRUG BAKING COMPANY

LONG ISLAND
WESTCHESTER
NEW JERSEY

41

ATOMIC ATTACK!
WHAT TO DO

42

FIVE HUNDRED epitaphs bridge my MISINFORMA-TION BOOK and my LEAPS OF FAITH collections, but the prize for best of all in the afterlife goes to Gum, Inc., Philadelphia, Pennsylvania, for its 1938 issue *Horrors of War* cards packaged with bubble gum. Card No. 1 starts the set with Japan's invasion of China. The first set was comprised of 240 cards. An additional 48 cards subsequently brought World War II to Hitler's annexation of the Sudetenland, making the complete set 288 cards featuring the war's anti-heroes and starring their victims.

The cards, meant for gum chewing, bubble blow-ing American kids, presented war scenes in graphic detail, showing bloody wounds, dismembered bod-ies, bombings, beheadings, and hasty, incomplete mass burials. Specifically, they represented the most extreme and vivid occurrences of war from a child's view. What I mean by this is that they were depicted the way a child draws—outline drawings filled in with unsubtle primary and secondary colors. Be-neath the pulp narration of the picture on the back of each card, there was a line in bold type that read *To know THE HORRORS OF WAR is to Want PEACE.* In their first life, these cards were terrifying and titillating. In the afterlife they graduated to blatant, stylized, zesty propaganda, turning a spotlight on the specific flavor of sympathy, naiveté, and enthusi-asm of a past moment.

43
Horrors of War No. 1 and No. 2 bubble gum cards (fronts and backs), 1938. Printed card stock, 2¾" high. Gum, Inc., Philadelphia, Pennsylvania

44
Horrors of War No. 3–No. 6 bubble gum cards (fronts and backs), 1938. Printed card stock, 2¾" high. Gum, Inc., Philadelphia, Pennsylvania

No. 1   Marco Polo Bridge Is Scene of First Fighting
The Marco Polo Bridge, ten miles west of Peiping, had been the scene of the first fighting between Chinese and Japanese troops. A truce was made, and Japan agreed to evacuate. On July 10, 1937, however, the Chinese declared the Japs had broken their truce agreement and had moved back to the Marco Polo Bridge-Wanpinghsien district. The Japanese attacked Wanpinghsien about 5.30 P. M. When the Chinese saw them attacking, troops of the Twenty-ninth Army, which had deserted the village the day before, returned by crossing the Marco Polo Bridge. There the Chinese and Japanese met for some of the bloodiest fighting of the war. Automatic rifles were brought into action behind sandbags. Snipers got to work. The troops of the Mikado returned fire, and hand grenades exploded all around the troops at the bridge. Some met horrible deaths at the point of the bayonet or the broadsword. Meanwhile Japanese were being reinforced by the arrival of troop trains from Manchukuo.

To know the HORRORS OF WAR is to want PEACE
This is one of a series of 240 Picture Cards. Save to get them all. Picture and Text Copyright 1938, GUM, INC., Phila., Pa.

No. 2   Chinese "Big Sword" Corps Resists Jap Forc
The "Big Sword" Corps of the famous Twenty-ninth of China was active in the fighting in the area sout Peiping in the summer of 1937. These warriors, many them armed only with their great, broad, two-handed swc cast terror into the ranks of the Japanese. With a despe determination they opposed the Japanese superior battle mach consisting of machine guns, tanks, and airplanes! The Chin slaughtered 600 of the enemy troops at Fengtai and killed an captured many others at Tungchow, east of Peiping. Chinese casualties in the fighting were great, as may well be imagined. Two Japanese airplane squadrons moved around the battle-front bombing the Chinese at points even where they were not in actual battle. The big bombers rained down death, but the Chinese sullenly refused to give in and abandon their posts. Then the Japanese infantry attacked, and the fighting became general all around Peiping.

To know the HORRORS OF WAR is to want PEACE
This is one of a series of 240 Picture Cards. Save to get th all. Picture and Text Copyright 1938, GUM, INC., Phila., I

No. 3   U. S. Marine Shot While Aiding Americans

Savage fighting had been going on for some days outside the city of Peiping's ancient walls. At dawn on July 28, 1937, Japan had opened a general attack and the fighting persisted all day. Inside the city, air raids were a constant threat to the lives of the citizens, and a feeling of anxiety led many to seek the safety of the legation quarter. U. S. Marines were directing Americans to the security of the American Embassy. All of a sudden angry firing broke out within a few hundred yards of the Embassy. Undaunted, Private Julius F. Flizar, member of the detachment on duty, stuck to his post. As he hurried to help another party of refugees, an unaimed bullet caught him in the right thigh. As he dropped, spectators discovered that the cause of the shooting was a venomous encounter between Chinese Military Policemen, barricaded on Hatamen Street, and Japanese Plain-clothes Operatives near the Legation Quarter.

To know the HORRORS OF WAR is to want PEACE

This is one of a series of 240 Picture Cards. Save to get them all. Picture and Text Copyright 1938, GUM, INC., Phila., Pa.

No. 4   War Planes Over Tientsin

The battle which centered on Tientsin was being fought from Tangku to Fengtai, Japan's field headquarters. At mid-afternoon on July 29, 1937, Japanese war planes began bombing the city. The great bombers droned low, dropping tons of explosives. First target of the raiders was the huge Administration Building of the Peiping-Mukden Railroad. Then school buildings were wrecked; the law courts bombed; entire streets gutted. Soon Tientsin's City Hall was aflame. Thousands of non-combatant men, women, and children were killed or injured. The lives of Americans and other foreigners were imperilled. The savage attack from the skies was the signal for Japanese ground troops to drive against the Chinese concentrations at barricades in various sections. Artillery was rushed into position, and both sides began shelling. When the shades of night fell and the great bombers finally withdrew, they left a flaming and destitute city in their wake.

To know the HORRORS OF WAR is to want PEACE

This is one of a series of 240 Picture Cards. Save to get them all. Picture and Text Copyright 1938, GUM, INC., Phila., Pa.

No. 5   Chinese Pursuers Shoot Down Jap Planes

On August 14, 1937, a Japanese squadron of twelve heavy German-type bombers made a raid along the Yangtze River. In their attack they hit the Air Base at Nanking and destroyed several Chinese military airplanes. During the attack, anti-aircraft batteries rocked the city with their fire, but the bombers soon wiped them out. Before the Japanese could make their escape, however, Chinese pursuit planes were hot after them. A couple of Japanese pilots were killed instantly and their bodies hurtled from their plane, their clothes in flames. The fuselage of one of the bombers fell 300 feet away from the rest of the plane. A Japanese pilot, found dead, had tried to bandage himself—contrary to the imperial ruling that air pilots kill themselves to prevent capture, after setting fire to their planes. Chinese bragged that the Japanese flyers seemed in a daze when a pursuit plane started after them!

To know the HORRORS OF WAR is to want PEACE

This is one of a series of 240 Picture Cards. Save to get them all. Picture and Text Copyright 1938, GUM, INC., Phila., Pa.

No. 6   Suicide Squad of Japs Is Blasted at Woosung

In the darkness that preceded the dawn, late in August 1937, Japanese warships were assisting in the landing of reinforcements of troops for their hard-pressed numbers in the International Settlement. Chinese positions were silent until an advance guard of Japanese warriors was lowered in a small armored launch. Then, as though this had been a signal, the blackness became an inferno of flame and noise. Chinese machine guns and artillery blazed. But the launch with its death-defying Japs kept on. In it were seventy picked men. The only color they wore was a white sash around their backs and shoulders—traditional guard of Japan's proud Samurai, who enter combat prepared to die. As the bottom of the launch scraped the Yangtze mud flats, the band of death leaped into the waist-deep water and waded ashore in the face of withering fire from machine guns and hand grenades. Then, as they scrambled up the bank, a Chinese land mine was touched off. The few survivors closed in bloody hand-to-hand combat with the enemy.

To know the HORRORS OF WAR is to want PEACE

This is one of a series of 240 Picture Cards. Save to get them all. Picture and Text Copyright 1938, GUM, INC., Phila., Pa.

44

chapter 15

A Bad Idea in the First Place

AS A CHILD, I expended a share of my nervous energy fondling, pressing, and molding candle wax, softened by the warmth of my hands. The corner candy store offered bright red "cherry"-flavored caricature wax lips, with a horizontal support at the back to be gripped between a child's teeth in an exaggerated crimson pout.

Fat glossy-black wax moustaches were made for boys, not too popular as they were licorice flavored in a bid for some kind of authenticity. Both the lips and the moustaches were two cents each, and the peach/orange wax *Pipes of Pan* with indescribable artificial flavoring cost a nickel. They came with printed paper instructions stuck to the back, offering many kids their first music instruction along with their first carcinogen. Play with them and, when the novelty receded, chomp them: double bang for your money. All were meant to be chewed to extract the flavors of these dyed petroleum products. There were also tiny colorless foggy wax bottles filled with red, orange, yellow, or green sweet syrup.

JOY BUZZER
(Hand Shaker and Tickler)
FUNNIEST JOKER'S NOVELTY EVER INVENTED!

☞ Use the ring as a key to wind it.

Wear it as a ring —the Buzzer in the palm. ☜

☞ It "shocks" them when they shake hands.

It makes them jump if they are ticklish. ☜

☞ They will hit the ceiling if they sit on it.

Under a sheet it feels like a mouse. ☞

With one of these little contrivances you may have no end of fun. Attached to one end of the Joy Buzzer is a brass ring that slips over the second finger, allowing the Buzzer itself to be concealed unobserved in the palm of the hand. Inside the Buzzer is a clock-work mechanism that is wound up. Projecting from the center of the Buzzer is a brass point, and a little pressure upon this point releases the mechanism. Shake hands with someone and see the shock the person receives when he unconsciously releases the mechanism of the Buzzer. If he is ticklish, watch him jump. Place it on a chair and watch the commotion when someone sits upon it. Place it under a pillow—under a sheet it feels like a mouse. You can use it as an ordinary "tic-tac" on a door or window—use it to awaken a sleeper by holding it on the sole of the foot or just behind the ear—try it on the window of an automobile just as the gears are shifted; they will think the engine is "busted." Dozens of other uses will suggest themselves to you. It is well and strongly made, entirely of metal, and it is certain you will get more than your money's worth of fun out of this little contraption............**28c**

No. 2955. JOY BUZZER, Price Postpaid.................**28c**

238 ★ Johnson Smith & Co., ★ Detroit, Mich. | YOU HAVE MADE THIS CATALOG POSSIBLE. Please keep it for future reference.

2

3

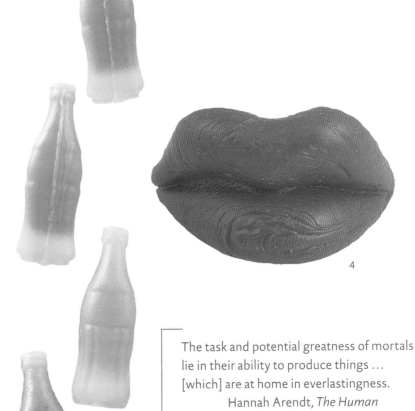

The task and potential greatness of mortals lie in their ability to produce things … [which] are at home in everlastingness.
Hannah Arendt, *The Human Condition* (Chicago and London: University of Chicago Press, 1965).

5

1
Joy Buzzer, 1935. Steel, 1½" diameter

2
Novelty ad, 1940. 8" high. Johnson Smith & Company catalog, Detroit, Michigan, page 238

3
Nik-L-Nip fruit-flavored drink, 2004. Wax Bottles penny candy, 2¾" high. Concord Wax Company, Selma, Alabama

4
Wax lips penny candy, 1947. 1¼" high. Concord Wax Company, Selma, Alabama

5
Luckyettes Candy Cigarettes (box, front and back), 1948. *Smile with Smiley's, five cents.* Printed card stock, 3" high. Tasty-Bits Fine Foods, Easton, Pennsylvania

You had to bite off the top of the wax bottle to sip the syrup and then chew on the empty if you wanted the last bit of residual flavor for your cent. In the early 1960s, wax-impregnated paper milk containers were replaced by those we use now, and most former wax eaters now comprehend the error of their ways. If you desire a glance at the wax-bottle phenomenon, for old time's sake, Nik-L-Nip manufactured by Concord Wax in Selma, Alabama, still offers them up. The label informs that *the container is made from fully refined wax and has no nutritional value.*

For an object made in the past to have been a bad idea in the first place is definitely worse than for it to be better in its afterlife. It means that, from the get–go, the object was something inspired by an ill-conceived conviction or a blunder made in innocence. From the vantage point of hindsight, it was a mistake and it cannot be undone; there is material evidence in hand. These items can only be observed, regarded as evidence of shafts of misplaced zeal, bad taste, or the downright crude insensitivity of another age.

232 ★

THE RIGHTS of nudists to freely live natural lives in the open and the elimination of the illegality of social nudism are proclaimed in that "without a stitch" manifesto, the *Magna Carta of Nudism*. Nudists of the 1950s declared their rights to sun and sand. If I trust my eyes, the magazines that document their activities are subjective vehicles for promoting a way of life. One could call them vanity publications, but it seems an odd word to use about photographs in which no one seems to have the slightest interest in glamour. These magazines are about the functionality of nudism. There isn't the remotest connection to the pinup. Cheesecake magazines of the same period are about the sexuality of the female body; they are about ideal forms, allure, and aspirations to perfection. They have entirely different motives than the self-righteous, serious nudity touted in these nudist-colony recruitment vehicles.

Nudist-colony magazines are proselytizing publications; their unretouched photographs are nudism with a vengeance. The nudists' self-conscious unselfconsciousness is their most constant and exposed nuance, aside from their sensible shoes. These bodies are not attractive and their poses are surprisingly stiff for a group desiring to convey naturalness, radiant health, and candor. The photographs are a parade of badly composed stills produced by nudists who happen to have a camera. Their captions are unenlightening, unenlightened, humorless, and sophomoric. Browsing these magazines is rather like watching other people's endless, dull home movies. Elysian fields are not all they're cracked up to be. One person's arcadia is another's existential nightmare. Not too many people saved these magazines, and their afterlife is their high moment.

6
Group of novelty ads from the Johnson Smith & Company catalog, 1940. 1¼–2¾" high. Detroit, Michigan

7
Nudists at Yuletime. *Sunshine and Health: Official Journal of the National Nudist Council*, December 1960, page 7. 4½" high

8
Nudists have a ball. *Nudism et Beauté: Revue Naturaliste*, September 1951, page 7. 4" high

9
Nudists at Yuletime. *Sunshine and Health: Official Journal of the National Nudist Council*, December 1960, page 7. 4½" high

10
Nudist cookout. *Sunshine and Health: Official Journal of the National Nudist Council*, April 1959, page 32. 11½" high

8

9

7

10

ON MAY 28, 1934, before the era of fertility drugs, Marie, Cecile, Emilie, Annette, and Yvonne were born at home to Elzire (Mom) and Oliva (Dad) Dionne in Corbeil, Canada. Two midwives and Dr. Allan Roy Dafoe delivered the only surviving quintuplets to 1934. They had a combined birth weight of thirteen pounds and five ounces, and they were not publicly regarded or referred to as individuals until the printed obituaries of Emilie in 1954, Marie in 1970, and Yvonne in 2001.

Their improbable birth catapulted them to celebrity as the most famous children in the world. An onslaught of spectators came in constant droves to see the farmhouse shrine, the place of their birth. Tourist support services thrived and Papa Dionne autographed postcards and souvenirs for a fee, bringing home the bacon. In September 1934, the Canadian government declared the quintuplets wards of the Province of Ontario to counter and impede their commercial exploitation, thus writing the script for the opposite. The quintuplets were moved to a specially constructed nursery in Dr. Dafoe's hospital. A February 1935 newspaper clipping reports that the Dionne parents were suing for guardianship and a share of the quints' trust fund fortune. They wanted to use some of the trust monies for the benefit of their six older children. The parents deposed that they were threatened with denial of welfare funds and so were forced to sign away their guardianship to the state. Furthermore, their visits to the quints were regulated; they were "treated brusquely" by hospital staff, and the quints' siblings were enjoined from visiting.

The government had appointed five guardians for the sisters, including Dr. Dafoe, who was mythologized in articles of the moment and later in books and movies as the archetypical noble country doctor. Between 1936 and 1938, the quintuplets starred in three movies: *Reunion*, *Country Doctor*, and *Five of a Kind*, and were the subjects of numerous newspaper and magazine articles. Tourists clamored for a glimpse of the girls. Vigilant photographic exclusivity was maintained by the guardians for a hefty fee from one syndicated news service. A half million dollars was turned down for an appearance at the 1939 New York World's Fair, too much of a free photo opportunity. The king and queen of England came to Toronto in 1939 to see them where they were photographed out of the nursery.

11
Dionne Quintuplets books, 1936–37. 10" high. N.E.A. Service, Whitman Publishing Company, Racine, Wisconsin

12
Glazed ceramic Dionne Quintuplet cups with photographic transfers, 1934. 2¾" high

13
Dionne Quintuplets paper dolls, 1937. Litho on paper, each figure 4¼" high. Palmolive Soap division, Colgate-Palmolive-Peet Company, Jersey City

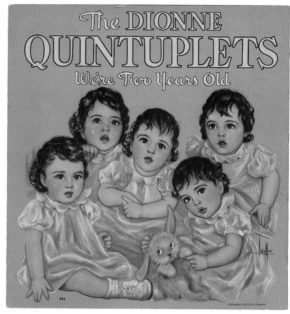

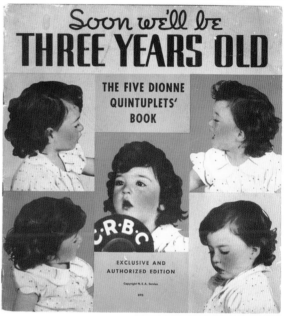

11

12

The names on the dress tabs read: MARIE, ... E, EMILIE, YVONNE, ANNETTE

In 1943, Canadian courts returned the guardianship of the nine-year-old quintuplets to Elzire and Oliva Dionne. Raised in a clinical setting and estranged from the Dionne family through their formative years, they did not find serenity and contentment. They left a very unhappy home life when they were eighteen. Each of them entered a convent at various times. Cecile and Annette are still living.

In the days of their early childhood, quintuplet memorabilia had taken on a life of its own. Throughout the 1930s and 1940s, the quints' united visages were used to champion Lysol disinfectant, Palmolive soap, Colgate toothpaste, the National Hockey League, and Quaker Oats, with many premiums in the offing. Cloth, composition and paper dolls, blocks, ball-in-hole games, calendars, handkerchiefs, dishes, cups, postcards, books, and silver-plate character teaspoon sets showing the quints' likeness may still be found on secondary markets for ascending prices. I've never seen a quintuplet decal, but wouldn't be surprised if one turned up as the images on their cups are transfers. There is a Dionne Quintuplet museum in Canada, a Dionne quintuplet newsletter, and a Dionne Quinvention at which collectors convene to trade and sell quintuplet collectibles. The event of their birth caused the celebrity that made the quintuplets a collectible product. Independent of the five girls, these depersonalized objects represent the curious awe of another time and unify a group of people bound by an anachronistic interest and a ready market.

14
Dionne Quintuplets dexterity game, c. 1936. Printed cardboard, glass, painted steel, and steel ball bearings, 3½" high

15
Set of Dionne Quintuplet spoons (front and back), 1941. Silver plate, each spoon 6" high. Carlton Silverplate Company

16
Dionne Quintuplets on a pocket mirror advertising Palmolive soap, 1942. Litho on celluloid, 3" diameter

14

15

16

IN STAFFORDSHIRE, England, during the Industrial Revolution, potteries made a great deal of the world's ironstone, earthenware, and paste dishes. Designs were hand-painted in intricate patterns on expensive colored ironstone. William Hogarth's popular, satirical lithographic subjects of the mid-1700s were adapted as transfer ware in the early 1800s. These linear images on paper, when pressed onto unglazed clay dishes or cups, imprinted themselves there. This new process revolutionized dinnerware design. The outlines of the transfers were roughly filled in with colored glazes by Dickensian child laborers who hadn't the skill or coordination of the decorators of high-end painted china dishes. Much has been written on the occupational diseases, hazards, and working conditions in these potteries. Not many children lived to develop the skills required to move on careerwise. Ironically, many transferware dishes were gifts to more fortunate children, since they conveyed lessons in the form of illustrated homilies and maxims, alphabets and animal images, temperance and life lessons, in text, and perhaps a child's name.

17

17
American transferware pitcher with two-sided images of *The Young Artist,* 1886. 9½" high

18
Transferware scales plate, 1870. Ironstone, 7¼" diameter. England

19
Staffordshire transferware dish with *Gambling* image, 1830. 5¼" high

20
Staffordshire transferware dish with endless-knot puzzle message, 1830. 5" diameter

18

19

20

IN THE MID-NINETEENTH century, the horizon of women's hobbies broadened from beading flowers, making waxed and woven memorial hair bracelets and brooches, embroidering Ben Franklin's sayings, and honing their shuttlecock skills to a craze for covering the surfaces of household objects, small pieces of furniture, and gifts with transferred images. Technical printing advances enabled the provision of rich and colorful images that were made for conveyance from one material to another. They were transferred and collaged to a multitude of surfaces that called out for decoration. The application of these visuals became so popular that the operative verb *decalcomania* was coined. *Decal* is the noun that has been adapted for the actual picture.

From around 1910 through the 1930s, steamship line, railroad, hotel, and tourist-destination decals were all the rage among sophisticated travelers. Valises and steamer trunks told a story of worldliness. Later in the twentieth century, decals went awry. Billowing masts of clipper ships sailed across bathroom tiles; pendant vermillion cherries dangled from the front of flour canisters; serape-clad Mexicans bordered enameled kitchen cabinets, snoozing against cacti beneath sombreros; and movie stars seductively glanced from the tops of jewelry boxes. Debonair teddy bears surrounded baby's crib; graduated fish swam in tandem around glass shower stalls; little Dutch girls with pert caps and shoulder yokes carried milk pails across refrigerators and flashy pinups lolled on the lids of metal-fishing tackle boxes.

Decals were sold in hardware stores, novelty stores, and at Woolworth's. They were meant to decorate your home if you weren't predisposed to wallpaper. They were intended to spruce up your kitchen, bedroom and bath, baby's nursery, and mirrors. Instructions came on the glassine envelope. The only mistake one could make would be to soak the decal too long, losing the fugitive water-base glue. This was an era of stereotyping and stylizing, both qualities foundational to the decal world. The ease of application and the crassness of the images appealed broadly to children and those who needed a dancing Chinese couple on the sink backsplash. Artful handcraft slipped to an all-time low. Decals are the granddaddy of the sticker and have recently been applied to sticker books and automobiles.

21
Cigar decalcomania applied to glass dishes, c. 1885. Felt back, 4–6" diameter

22
Decal sheet and instruction card for applying Duro Decals, 1950. 5" high

21

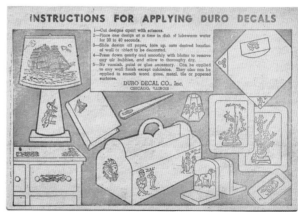

22

23
Decal below its glassine envelope with printed instructions and suggestions for applying Duro Decals on many surfaces, 1946. 7½" high

24
Brooklyn Dodgers decal, 1950. Printed transfer on paper, 3¾" high. USA

25
Decal of movie star Tony Martin (back and front of package) recommending use on waste basket, mirror, skate case, lunch box, windshield, and drinking glass, 1950. 5" high. The Meyercord Company, Chicago, Illinois

26
Group of decals, 1952. Each 8¼" high

27

28

29

27
Paint by Numbers
painting, 1960. Oil on
canvas board, 18" high

28
Paint by Numbers
painting, 1958. Oil on
canvas board, 10" high

29
Paint by Numbers
painting, 1953. Oil on
canvas board, 12" high

30
Paint by Numbers
painting, 1954. Oil on
canvas board, 14" high

31
Paint by Numbers
painting, 1959. Oil on
canvas board, 21" high

32
Paint by Numbers
painting, 1963. Oil on
canvas board, 10" high

33
Paint by Numbers
painting, 1961. Oil on
canvas board, 16" high

34
*How the Artist's Brain
Paints A Picture*, Collier's
Encyclopedia, 1917, page
489. 10¾" high

30

SUCCESSFUL DECAL do-it-yourselfers must have empowered their more dexterous minions to try painting by numbers. There is a related aesthetic here. In the 1950s, if you had a modicum of hand-to-eye coordination, someone probably suggested that your potential as an artist be auditioned on a *Paint by Numbers* set. These constructive hobby kits were offered up in your choice of subjects including floral, still life, landscape, seascape, farm scene, biblical vignette, animal, or presidential portrait. Each kit contained a printed line rendering, sectioned off, bit by numbered bit, *on genuine canvas*. The numbered sectors corresponded to the numbers on the lids of the small paint containers that clustered with brushes at one end of the box. Predetermined tints and shades preempted any decisions and left no question about the final image. Like jigsaw puzzle recourse, you could always check your version against the box lid to make sure you got it right and then pat yourself on the back for a mechanical job well done.

Alan H. is an artist and a set designer. He has collected *Paint by Numbers* paintings for twenty years from yard sales and Salvation Army stores. He has never paid more than two dollars for a picture. The most creative act that could have been performed with a *Paint by Numbers* kit was to use the wrong colors in unordained places or to render the small canvas in large scale and leave it unfinished. Andy Warhol did both.

31

32

33

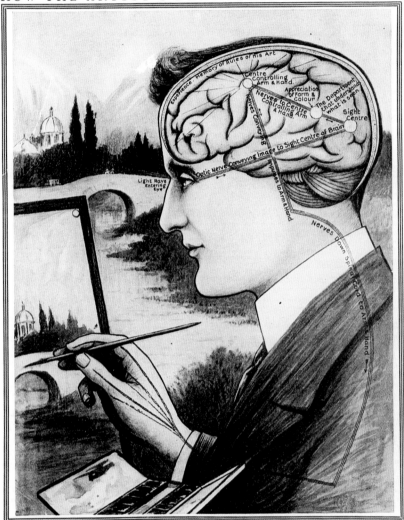

Perhaps you have thought that the clever fingers of the painter should get the credit for a beautiful masterpiece. But here we see how the picture is first painted in the brain and then transferred to the canvas by that well-trained servant—the hand. As the artist sits down before his easel, the picture of the landscape is photographed through the lens of his eye upon his retina. There the image is picked up by the sensitive ends of the optic nerve and conveyed back to the sight center of the brain, where it is registered. So far, everything is mechanical, just as a new-born baby's vision is mechanical, for while it can *see* as well as the artist, it cannot *understand* what it sees. But now the mental image of that landscape is carried to the intelligence center, where its colors and shapes, its distances and perspectives, are interpreted and given a meaning. That meaning is telegraphed on to the controlling center of arm and hand. There the artist calls upon his experience and the memory of the rules of his art to give new shape and color to his picture-thought. He really paints it in his imagination, and then sends the details one by one down the nerves to his hand, which puts them on the canvas.

contained in the Easy Reference Fact-Index at the end of this work
489

34

Kate H. is a costume and children's-clothing designer who has page 489 of an unidentified volume of Collier's 1917 encyclopedia framed on her wall. It is a full-page illustration of *How the Artist's Brain Paints a Picture*. The caption explains:

> Perhaps you thought that the clever fingers of the painter should get the credit for a beautiful masterpiece. But here we see how the picture is first painted in the brain and then transferred to the canvas by that well-trained servant—the hand. The artist sits down before his easel, the picture of the landscape is photographed through the lens of the eye upon the retina. There the image is picked up by the sensitive ends of the optic nerve and conveyed back to the sight center of the brain where it is registered. So far everything is mechanical, just as a newborn baby's vision is mechanical, for while it can see as well as the artist, it cannot understand what it sees. But now the mental image of the landscape is carried to the intelligence center, where its colors and shapes, its distances and perspectives, are interpreted and given meaning. That meaning is telegraphed to the controlling center of the arm and hand. There the artist calls upon his experience and the memory of the rules of his art to give new shape and color to his picture thought. He really paints it in his imagination, and then sends the details one by one down the nerves to his hand, which puts them on the canvas.

The caption skirts the hard-to-pin-down issue of creativity but alludes to its residence in the artist's "intelligence center" and "imagination." Did anyone who painted by the numbers ask if there were facets of creativity that went beyond parochial outlines and preordained colors? Did they humbly accept the plaudits of family and friends and move on to conquer other professions? Was the person who conceived of *Paint by Numbers* kits a failed artist? From a temporal perspective, why are the inept, dull, and graceless products of this genre fascinating? Does distance convey an appreciation of misplaced painterly confidence and a naïve self-image?

SELF-SERVING recipe booklets were produced by the manufacturers of a specific food product or food-preparation aid to unabashedly promote their products by clearly self-seeking means. Recipe booklets from the Sternau Chafing Dish Company, the Walter Baker Chocolate Company, and the Spry Shortening Company's famous *Aunt Jenny's Favorite Recipes*, are a few examples. In a way they are like the Paint by Number kits; these recipe books want you and the people in your immediate sphere to see you as a professional, courtesy of their product.

Jell-O recipe booklets from 1900–1930 gracefully and insidiously, making use of exquisite graphics, guided the housewife of the white-collar family to the illusion of "robber baron" status, with Jell-O assisting her through all the important occasions of her life. Each of these booklets is a visual prize and insists: *Even if you can't cook, you can make a Jell-O dessert.* These booklets feature colorful crenelated castles and bright, luminous cathedral spires of Jell-O fantasies. Various household service personnel, in the background, advise and automatically elevate the user's station in life while warning that *anything sold in any other package is not Jell-O.... the famous Jell-O desserts cannot be made with anything but Jell-O.* The implication is that the choice of Jell-O indicates the housewife's choice of a better life for her family. Knox's gelatine recipe booklets are quite simply just *Dainty desserts for dainty people.*

36

35

37

38

35
Selected pages from Jell-O recipe booklet, 1916. 5½" high. Ottmann Publishing Company, New York City

36
Self-serving milk recipes from the Borden Company, 1936. 6½" high. New York City

37
Self-serving recipes from the Minute Tapioca Company, Inc., 1934. 6¾" high. Orange, Massachusetts

38
Selected pages from Jell-O recipe booklet, 1916. 5½" high. Ottmann Publishing Company, New York City·

39
Selected pages from Jell-O recipe booklet showing Jell-O as intrinsic to the "good" life, 1916. 5½" high. Ottmann Publishing Company, New York City

The Perfect Treat

Surprising Father and Mother

The Birthday Party

Prepared for Emergencies

Another Caller Wants Jell-O, Too

Who Knows Better what's Good?

A Treat for Old Schoolmates

The Jell-O Girl Talks to her Class

39

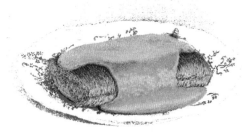

WELSH RAREBIT. RECIPE Nº 50.

RASPBERRIES IN BISCUIT BASKET.
RECIPE Nº 136.

MUSHROOMS IN SHREDDED WHEAT   RECIPE Nº 65
BISCUIT BASKETS.

JELLIED APPLE SANDWICH.
RECIPE Nº 249.

OYSTER PATTIES. RECIPE Nº 42.

FISH SANDWICH. RECIPE Nº 255.

SHREDDED WHEAT FISH CHOPS
RECIPE Nº 16.

POACHED EGG ON SHREDDED WHEAT BISCUIT.
RECIPE Nº 26.

40

1528. Home of "Shredded Wheat."

41

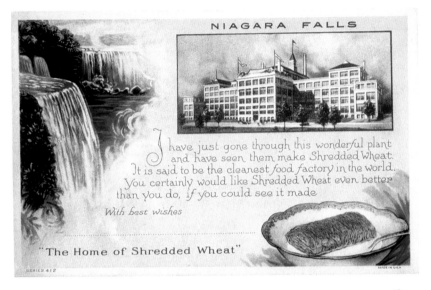

NIAGARA FALLS

I have just gone through this wonderful plant and have seen them make Shredded Wheat. It is said to be the cleanest food factory in the world. You certainly would like Shredded Wheat even better than you do, if you could see it made

With best wishes

"The Home of Shredded Wheat"

42

In 1899, the Cereal Machine Company produced *The Vital Question*, a Shredded Wheat recipe booklet that begs description. The fineness of the illustrations is almost as astonishing as the food combinations. Shredded Wheat Welsh Rarebit, Shredded Wheat Fig Loaf, Shredded Wheat Jellied Apple Sandwich, and Shredded Wheat Fish Balls get my vote out of the 262 Shredded Wheat dishes. In this booklet, Augustus Murray, railroad worker on the New York & Boston line, states:

"I have been employed on the railroad for more than 20 years, and I feel safe in saying that all railroad men will concur with me that the chief evil that befalls men who continuously ride is constipation. Can you find a railroad man who will say he has not tried almost every remedy prescribed by the school of medicine? Shredded Wheat Biscuit has produced the most wonderful results with us."

It takes a blue-collar worker to shed light on irregularity. Social conundrums live on, but there is marketing genius in these booklets that are married to a time and place.

The hostess in whose kitchen Frigidaire is an assistant, greets her guests unworried and with an air of perfect assurance. She knows that her problem of refreshments is simply that of transferring them from Frigidaire to table. In the meantime, Frigidaire is imparting to the food that Quality that only refrigeration can produce.

Jessie M. DeBoth, *Frigidaire Frozen Delights* (Dayton, Ohio: Frigidaire Corp., 1927), 11.

HOPEFULLY NOT A note of onion. *Frigidaire Frozen Delights* is primarily a black-and-white publication that lacks the charm of the earlier prototypes. The clumsily retouched color dessert pictures are printed in lurid hues with only a very basic attempt at detail. This booklet is the beginning of a subset of booklets by self-serving producers that should be scrutinized in person to fully appreciate the remarkable grotesquery of these brazen and embarrassing documents. Take my word for this observation until you are able to hold one in your hands.

40
Selected pages from the Cereal Machine Company's Shredded Wheat recipe booklet, 1899. Each 1" high

41
Home of "Shredded Wheat" postcard, 1925. 3½" high. Niagara Falls, USA

42
The Home of Shredded Wheat postcard, 1915. 3½" high. Niagara Falls, USA

Their heyday was the 1950s, and they have titles like *Hamburger & Hot Dog Book* featuring Glamour Dogs, Hamburger Pie, Corkscrew Dogs, and Stuffed Franks. The Borden's Company published *Money Saving Recipes with Milk*, which offers Ham Custard, Veal Supreme, and Pimentos au Fromage. The c. 1952 *Frigidaire* salad book suggests Chop Suey Salad and Paradise Salad Supreme. The Krug Baking Company presented (c. 1955) *Unusual Recipes*, which brings to light Stuffed Spare Ribs, French Toast Corinthian, Mulled Cider Sandwiches, and Fish Flakes New-burgh. Talk about fancy dishes. In 1938, the Kraft-Phoenix Cheese Company featured Wonder Salad. A picture is worth a thousand words.

Unlike the Jell-O and Shredded Wheat publications, these garish and unappetizing presentations were meant for anyone who would pay any attention and buy the product to try it out. Their lasting power

43
Self-serving recipes from the Frigidaire division, General Motors, 1938. 7" high. Dayton, Ohio

44
Self-serving recipes from General Foods Corporation, 1932. 6¾" high. New York City

45
Self-serving recipes from the Diamond Walnut Company, 1938. 7" high. Los Angeles, California

46
Bottoms-Up glass in glazed white ceramic, c. 1920. 3½" high. White Cloud Farms Pottery, New York State

43

44

45

is in the peculiarity of their realization. It is aston-ishing that anyone would make one of these dishes; nothing looks like you could eat it and live to see your next meal. Of course, people got rid of them. John B. has a library of these ghastly wonders. He's never tried a recipe.

TOASTING BY DIPPING scorched bread into wine or mead figures into the early origins of saluting, com-memorating, or honoring with an alcoholic drink. Drinking customs dictate special shapes of glasses to clink that vary from country to country and region to region. They are as nuanced as dialects. There are also common toasts that cross cultures. "To your health," "cheers," "peace," "long life," "prosperity," and "good luck" are generic wishes issued around the world upon raising a glass of wine or spirits. The Asian "dry your cup" is as standard as the Ameri-can "bottoms up" and essentially means "down the hatch" or "drink up." I have seen Victorian glasses etched with York Rite Masonic symbols, the bot-toms of which are rounded so that the contents must be consumed swiftly following a ritual. Generally, their form defines the Bottoms-Up glass, a glass that cannot rest on its bottom; it must be emptied and inverted on the rim of its mouth to be set down.

IN THE LATE 1920S, White Cloud Farms, a New York pottery, cast white-glazed ceramic Bottoms-Up drinking glasses that featured a nude female figure draped over the base of the glass, literally bottom up. This idea was unabashedly appropriated by the McKee Glass Company of Pennsylvania (a foremost Depression glass manufacturer), which infringed on White Cloud's patent for the design. Rather than settling the lawsuit, McKee acquired the pottery and continued making the design (patent # 77725) in opalescent beige, or *Custard*, and light green *Skokie*, or *Jadite*, glass through the 1930s. In the 1950s, the Jeanette Glass Company bought some of McKee's molds and produced many of their glass forms. In c. 1985, the design was reproduced in dark amber glass in Mexico by the Berreteaga Rum Company.

These are not glasses from which to sip and savor fine wines or single-malt scotches. The supple, languid, smooth, and streamlined Art Deco nude fits nicely into one's palm, and McKee's glass has subtle beauty and refinement in its color; but they were glasses from which to drink a toast or toasts in succession, which is why not too many survived the ever loosening of the drinker's grasp and inhibitions. Those that remain are specimens meant to be admired on a shelf, not used. Currently they are savored for their form and stylistic reference to past contexts (in which nude ladies draped over glasses weren't surprising) rather than for their contents.

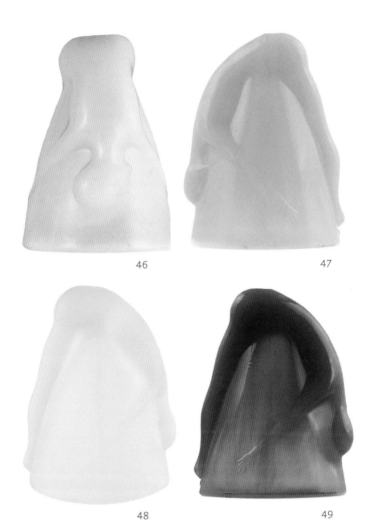

46   47

48   49

But things hung from the trees, things that had never hung from trees before. A bent black umbrella, its handle carved like a duck's head. A limp embroidered felt sombrero, rinsed pink, and a huge green lamp-shade, one side caved in. A blue tablecloth draped like bunting from one tree to the other, gold threads in it sparkling in the headlights. A white plastic doll stroller, a dish drainer, a flowered bathrobe hung as neatly from a spruce branch as if it had been on a bathroom door, a throw pillow with its stuffing dangling like a cloud, a work boot, part of a fishing rod . . . on the path itself a gray portable typewriter driven half into the ground; the top of a pressure cooker, its round gauge like a monocle; silverware; a glass doorknob; the round wire cage from a Bingo set.
Beth Lordan, *And Both Shall Row* (London: Picador, 1997), 38.

47
Bottoms-Up glass in *Skokie* green or *Jadite*, c. 1930. 3½" high. McKee Glass Company, Pennsylvania

48
Bottoms-Up glass in *Camphor* glass, c. 1930. 3½" high. McKee Glass Company, Pennsylvania

49
Bottoms-Up glass in dark amber, 1985. 3½" high. Berreteaga Rum Company, Mexico

50
Bottoms-Up glasses in opalescent beige or *Custard*, c. 1930. 3½" high. McKee Glass Company, Pennsylvania

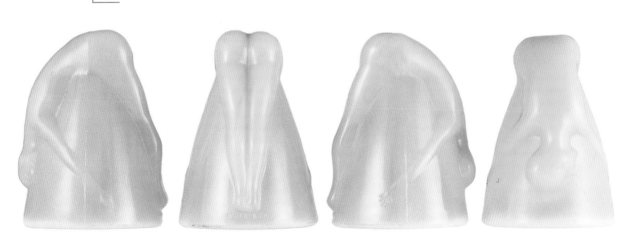

50

Never Made Enough

chapter 16

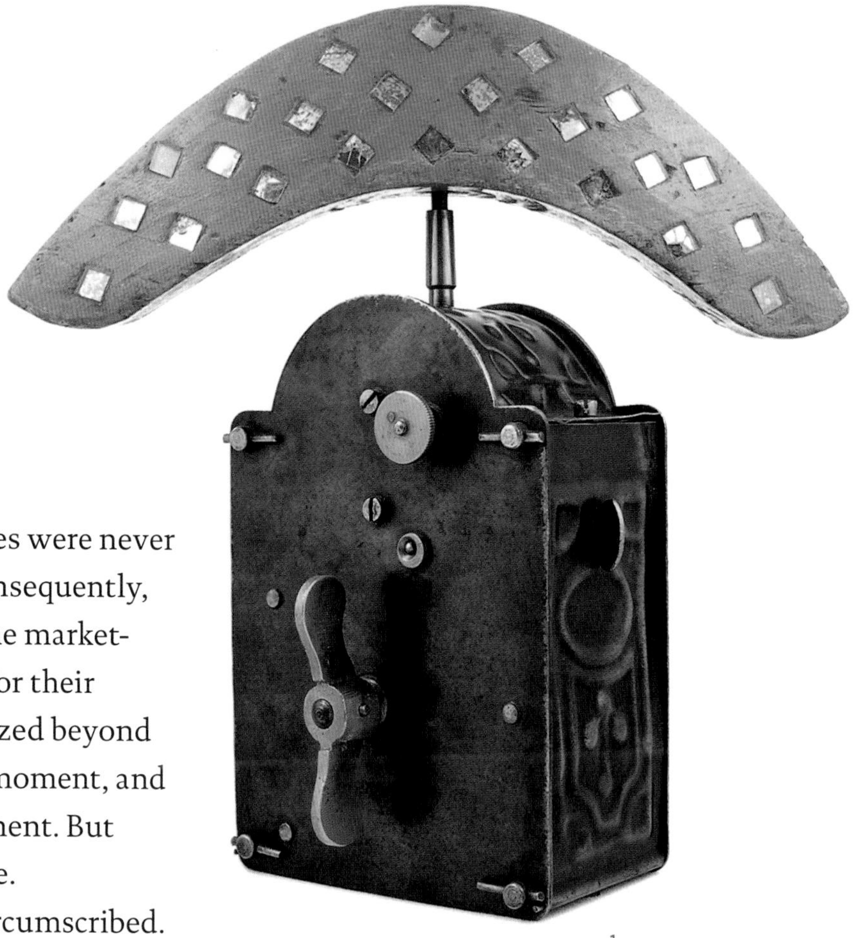

1

CERTAIN OBJECTS from past ages were never produced in quantity, and, consequently, they appear infrequently in the marketplace now. A few were saved for their functional use, some were prized beyond their short-lived fashionable moment, and others were kept out of sentiment. But they were never commonplace.

The utility of lark lures is circumscribed. Larks are exemplars of songs of strength and sweetness on the wing, and they are found in temperate zones worldwide. As ground nesters and feeders, they are innately curious about small motions in close proximity to their habitat. As gregarious creatures, they approach elusive glimpses and flashes of light. In rural France and Italy, this social response is often terminal. Larks range in size from four and a half to nine inches; they make an ample meal, if you're so inclined. They are a delicacy in regions where, coincidentally, strong wine and heady cheeses are made.

Alexandre Cochet made my lark lure in Morbier, France, in the last quarter of the eighteenth century. Its business end is an orange boomerang-shaped treen crescent that has been inlaid with small diamond-shape glass mirrors and sits on the stem of a steel and brass key-wind clockwork mechanism. When wound, the mirror-studded finial turns, catching facets of sunlight and converting them into elusive, nuanced reflections. Arrow or net capture song and transform it into food.

Pound in a mortar the flesh of two larks; add some butter, some chopped samphire, some breadcrumbs soaked in milk, some Malaga raisins and some crushed Juniper berries. Stuff a third lark with the mixture and roast it covered with samphire leaves and a strip of bacon, on a spit. Serve on a crouton soaked in gin and then toasted and buttered.

Sarah Bernhardt's recipe for Larks (Vol. 2, No. 18, *Food Reference Newsletter,* foodreference.com/html/larkssarahbr.html)

Morbier is renowned for its larks and for a raw cow's milk cheese—tangy, cheeky, and semi-soft with compound flavor. The cheese is, not surprisingly, called Morbier and has a two-layer antique-ivory interior and a toast-brown rind. Each round is comprised of morning and evening curds, left over from Compte Gruyère production. A finely spread ash delineates and keeps the bottom layer from drying out. The French have been resourceful and obsessive to the benefit of the culinary world.

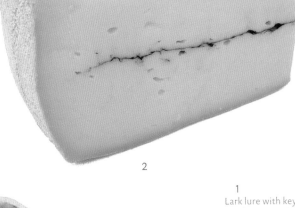

2

LARK AND YOUNG ONES

3

1
Lark lure with key-wind mechanism, c. 1790. Steel, brass, hand-carved, painted wood, and mirrored glass, 8¾" high. Made by Alexandre Cochet, Morbier, France

2
Wedge of Morbier (raw milk cheese) showing the layer of fine ash separating the morning from the evening curds left over from Compte Gruyère production, 2004. 3" high

3
Staffordshire transfer-ware dish depicting two farmers harvesting with sickles, revealing a *Lark and Young Ones,* c. 1830. 6¾" high

Radical focus on the finite details of food preparation in tandem with intrepid venturing curiosity have defined French food preparations. Etang de Capestang in Langedoc-Rousillon is a noted wet grasslands habitat of lark and ortolan bunting. Ortolans are tiny yellow birds with a soft tremolo song. They are an endangered species and it is a punishable offense to hunt, buy, or eat them. On January 1, 1995, François Mitterand, dying of cancer, commissioned his last dinner. Designated ortolans were force-fed grapes, millet, and figs and, according to the classic recipe, drowned in Armagnac, then roasted for eight minutes. Ritual consumption requires placement of a velvet hood over the diner's head (Mitterand used white table linen)—not for modesty's sake, but to infuse the senses with ornithological vapors. The bird, straight from the grill, is inserted head last, whole, into one's mouth. The diner rapidly inhales the essential vapors, cooling the bird before chewing. Here a schism in the school of ortolan appreciation occurs among those who prefer incisor separation and discarding of the head/handle with the first bite and those who prefer to consume it. Once past this point, both schools agree that the trickle of fat, the vapors, the textures and crunch of bone against yielding flesh, the unique and separate flavors of the organs separated by tongue, palate, and cheek should be consumed in twelve to fifteen minutes before beginning on the second bird. This is not a taste acquired late in life. Thirty family members and friends joined Mitterand in this ultimate repast. He consumed oysters in preparation for his two ortolans.

Ortolans are enjoyed in Italy as *ortolano*. During their annual migrations, ortolano have been netted to near extinction. In 1970, at lunch in Frascati, Italy, in an undistinguished restaurant, I ordered *Spiedini Rustica* thinking it was *Spiedini Romano*, a baked cheese, bread, and anchovy dish. A skewer arrived beneath a silver dome carried by white-gloved wait staff. The skewer pierced three tiny lumps with miniscule charred claws. In an instantaneous act of selfless devotion, my husband said that he would prefer my *piatti prima* to his. He consumed them in my stead, refusing the hood that we thought a bib.

You can make a meal out of a lark, but an ortolan is merely a bite. Ortolan nets are not special to look at, although they may appear on the antiques market in the future. My lark lure is beautiful to regard. I've seen a few other lark lures, all singular and handmade, which leads me to deduce that larks were not a mainstay of too many diets and that per capita lark consumption was probably satisfied by a handful of provisioners.

4
Matchbox label, depicting lark, 1906–7. Printed paper, 1¼" high. Japan

5
Matchbox label, depicting lark, 1906–7. Printed paper, 1¼" high. Japan

6
Thorburn's illustration of the male Ortolan (1915–18). *The Complete Illustrated Thorburn's Birds*, vol. 1 (New York: W. H. Smith Publishers, 1989), plate 18. Actual size of bird is 1½" high by 2½" long

7
Ortolan illustration and description from the *People's Cyclopedia*, vol. 2 (Washington, D.C.: Phillips & Hunt, 1879), page 1295

4

5

6

Or'tolan, a species of Bunting, much resembling the Yellow Hammer, and not quite equal to it in size. The adult male has the back reddish-brown, the wings dusky black and rufous brown ; the tail dusky black, some of the outer tail-feathers with a patch of white on the broad inner web ; the chin, throat, and upper part of the breast yellowish-green ; the other under parts reddish buff-color. The O. occurs in great flocks in the S. of Europe and N. of Africa.

Ortolan.

7

SAMSON BRIDGE TABLES

STRONG

WILL SUPPORT 200 LB. MAN

FIREPROOF:
CIGARETTES
CIGARS
MATCHES
WILL
NOT
MAR IT

WASHABLE!
TOP NOT AFFECTED
BY HOT WATER
BEER OR
WINE GLASSES
LEAVE NO
RINGS

STRONG ENOUGH TO STAND ON

8

MILITARY
BUTTON POLISHING KIT

COMPLETE WITH
POLISH · BRUSH · CLOTH · BOARD

9

LIKE LARK lures, self-promoting bridge tables had singular utility. The statement and illustration of its attributes constituted its purpose. *Strong Enough To Stand On. Will Support a 200 LB. Man.* How many Bridge players stand on the table? *Washable! Top Not Affected By Hot Water or Beer. Wine Glasses Leave No Rings. Fireproof. Cigarettes Cigars Matches Will Not Mar It.* What about the wooden legs? A woman in a red dress, one arm on her hip, pours a tea kettle full of steaming water on the tabletop, right next to the foot of a stout, three-piece blue-suited, cigar-smoking man depicted centrally, standing on a Samson bridge table. What about the water running toward his shoe? He doesn't look agile enough to jump off. How many women poured boiling water on Mah-Jongg tables? If all these things are true, how come my table is scratched, scarred, and nicked?

Made by the manufacturer for self-selling in a competitive retail situation, this bridge table is related to the salesman's sample. There can't have been too many of them, silk-screened by hand. Of course, the customer ordered one without any lettering or imagery. I wouldn't pay $7.99 for a bridge table, but I paid $300 for this gem.

MILITARY BUTTON POLISHING shields had a singular function and a limited market—to keep button polish off a uniform while keeping the button stationary, allowing polish application, energetic brushing, or rubbing and brisk buffing of the brass or nickel-plated buttons. To pass inspection, those buttons had to shine. Also called button sticks or button guards, they slipped between the button back and the uniform. They were usually made of a flat sheet of brass and, consequently, were polished along with the button. I have seen some fairly elaborate button-guard shapes, meant to do their jobs on buttons in places that are difficult to access; those are even less common than other button shields.

10

11

WHILE ON THE subject of dressing aids, shoe horns come to mind. Bootjacks assisted in boot removal; shoe horns accommodate putting on snug shoes and are more comfortable than a teaspoon for that job. Cultures that thrive in climates favoring sandals and moccasins know little of shoe horns. In most of the world, the shoe horn is a common tool. All shoe horns have heel cups and a handle. Frequently they are imprinted hotel giveaways. When I was growing up, shoe stores that sold Indian Walk, Enna Jetticks, Red Goose, and Buster Brown shoes gave away shoe horns with every purchase to remind you of where your shoes had came from when they were outgrown. The number of shoe horns manufactured narrows as categories are defined. Many display some form of advertising. Some are decoratively hand-painted. Comparatively few shoe horns have a second tool on the handle, such as a clothes brush, a whiskbroom, a bottle opener, a shoe buttonhook, or a backscratcher. The rarest category is that in which the form of the shoe horn is translated into a figural leg. Sometimes the heel scoop is an engraved bloomer leg. I have a collection of these made in brass, silver, and celluloid. They are hard to find; not too many were made.

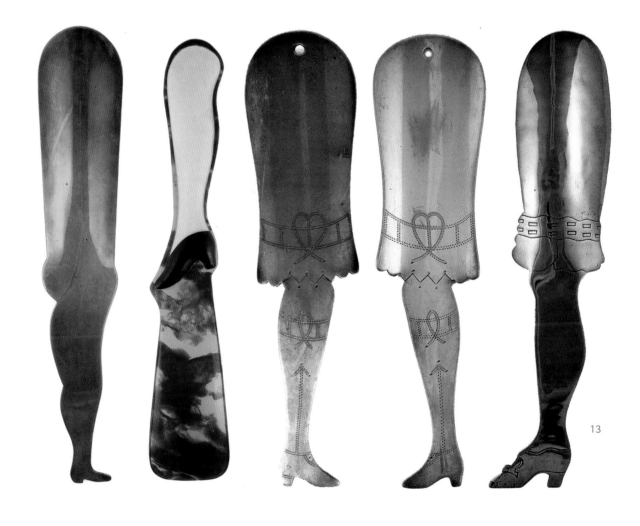

12

13

12
Shoe horn and button hook (folded and unfolded), c. 1910. Pressed steel, 6¾–15" long. J & J Slater, New York City

13
Group of leg shoe horns, c. 1880–1920. Silver, brass, and celluloid, 9¾–10" high

CALIPERS ARE tools used by loggers, automobile mechanics, woodworkers, and machinists to precisely measure inside and outside dimensions of pertinent parts. Calipers are usually indexed for exact numerical readings. However, sometimes they aren't indexed and are simply meant to transfer the adjustable literal space between the caliper's two legs from one physical object to another, as in reproducing a specific wood form. In primitive circumstances, where craftsmen did little mathematical figuring and lots of transferring from situational circumstances, calipers were handmade, precise tools. Caliper legs became literal legs, or legs and arms, or legs and torsos. The toe tips made inside measurements. The heels or arms made outside measurements, unless the connecting pivot had a 360-degree radius, in which case heel and toe roles were reversed. Figural calipers are made of steel or brass and are rare.

14
Group of legs calipers, 19th century. Steel, 3½–5½" high

15
Legs calipers in six positions, 19th century. Brass, 4" high when closed

14

15

NOT ENOUGH mummy pencils, mummy jackknives, or Moses baskets were made. They were a case of enthusiasm for an event that ignited a fashion that peaked. And then the world turned its fickle head again.

Georgian, Victorian, and then Edwardian England were infatuated with and fascinated by the material evidence of the mysterious and exotic culture of ancient Egypt. The practice of tomb breaking and violation flourished despite sealed portals and false chambers. Pillage of ancient Egyptian tombs kept up with a ready market for archaeological artifacts, including mummy cases, scarabs, jewelry, furniture, Canopic jars, dishes, tools, cosmetic implements, unguent bottles, anything with hieroglyphics, and actual mummies.

Hot, arid, desolate Thebes was the burial place of Egypt's pharaohs and royal attendants. By 1922, the Valley of the Kings had been pretty well denuded of the coveted necessities of pharaonic afterlives. British Egyptologist Howard Carter located the tomb of Tut-Ankh-Amun, after a seven-year search, in just the place that orthodox archaeological judgment had excluded. On November 26, 1923, he and his patron, Lord Carnarvon, entered the anteroom to the burial chamber of the tomb and revealed the consummate horde of Egyptian antiquities. Excavation and cataloguing of the contents of the four rooms took ten years. Popular attention anticipated progress reports from Luxor in a renewed wave of spellbound attachment to the mysteries of ancient Egyptian culture.

By 1925, miniature silver versions of mummy cases with precisely enameled hieroglyphics were being manufactured in France and England for the affluent sector of a waiting world. These mummies were produced in the form of pendants, pocket-projecting/retractile pencils, and jackknives. They were exquisite functional ladies' jewelry. Diminutive hinged vermeil mummy-case charms harboring miniscule enameled mummies were produced. Minute gold Moses babies resided in tiny silver, reed-textured, oval baskets with velvet linings and lids enameled with biblical scenes.

16
Mummy pocket/purse knife (back, front, and open), c. 1923. Enamel, silver, and vermeil, 2½" high

17
Lord Carnarvon (left) and Howard Carter open the stairway to the sealed burial chamber of King Tut-Ankh-Amun, 1922. By permission: Getty Images #50690030 Time and Life Pictures Collection

18
Mummy case (top and bottom, closed), c. 1923. Silver, enamel, and vermeil, 1¼" high

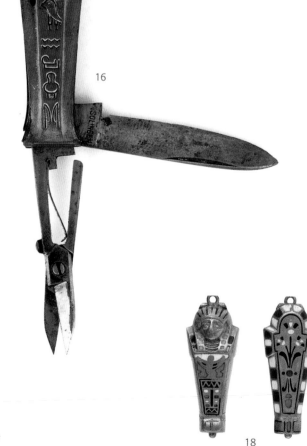

16

17

18

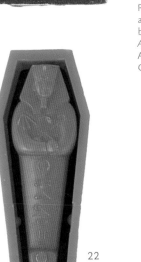

19
Mummy and mummy-case fob charm (open, exterior and interior), c. 1923. Silver, enamel, and vermeil, 2" high

20
Mummy and mummy-case fob charm (open, exterior and interior), c. 1923. Silver, enamel, and vermeil, 2" high

21
Group of mummy retractile pencils; pocket/purse knives; and Moses baskets, c. 1923. Silver, enamel, and vermeil, ½–2½" high

22
Plastic mummy novelty and printed cardboard box, 1950. *King Tut Arises,* 2¼" high. Franco American Novelty Company, USA

Amid a tidal wave of trinket flotsam, these objects resound as the finest tangible responses to Howard Carter's discovery. They were carefully made, and production did not exceed demand. Consequently these exquisite rarities speak of another time with optimal eloquence. They don't speak of ancient Egypt but of perceptions of ancient Egyptian culture during the 1920s and early 1930s. They are artifactual expressions of temporal enthusiasm.

I have collected these artifacts since the early 1960s, and they are hard to find. Undamaged mummy-folding pocketknives still turn up. There's not much to break unless someone imprudently forces the blade sideways to lever something very weighty. The retractile mechanisms on the pencils tend to malfunction with use. Hinges and clasps on the Moses baskets and mummy cases probably loosened with wear because the tiny figures are usually gone, if you can even find one these days. Popular attention turned toward the more compelling events of 1933. Mummy fascination picked up again after World War II in the form of mummy movies.

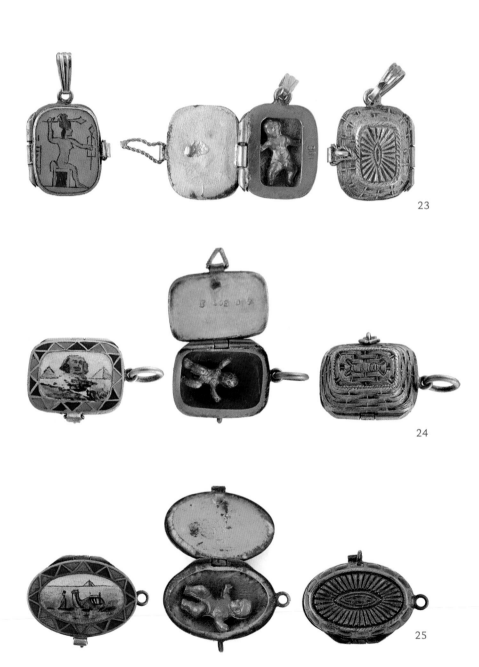

23
Moses and Moses basket fob charm (front, open, back), c. 1923. Enamel and silver, 1¼" high

24
Moses and Moses basket fob charm (front, open, back), c. 1923. Silver, enamel, and vermeil, ¾" long

25
Moses and Moses basket fob charm, (front, open, back), c. 1923. Silver, enamel, and vermeil, ¾" long

LACE BOBBINS were passed on to successive generations of family lacemakers as precious tools. They incisively connect any interested person now living to another historical period. During the eighteenth and nineteenth centuries, bobbin lace was made at home for personal use, for gifts, and for sale. In England it was a cottage industry. The making of bobbin lace began by drawing a design on a vellum or parchment sheet that covered the small cushion upon which the lace was worked. Steel pins were thrust into the pattern as points around which to wind and weave the thread on each bobbin. The pins were moved to keep the threads sufficiently taut. A bobbin identified one thread in the lace design, which required a number of threads. Consequently, each bobbin had to be visually unique so that the correct thread could be easily selected and the outcome of the design would be as intended. Bobbins lend weight to the threads and keep them in place around the pins; they are the source of the thread and the handles by which threads are manipulated. I have a bobbin-lace tablecloth that must have required 150 bobbins. Each bobbin controls the path of a thread the length of which starts out about three times as long as the finished piece will be. Bobbins are worked in pairs with two simple motions—a cross and a twist around the preset pins.

The bobbins that I know best are from a small section of England and are made of carved and engraved horn, ivory, bone, or wood, with glass beads on one end and an indentation around which thread was wound on the other. The singular decoration on each bobbin occurs along the length between both ends and followed certain conventions. Many have incised names and dates with ringed ridges along the length, or concentric circles, or are dotted with circular punchwork designs. Some lace bobbins have spiral inscriptions and designs. Brothers, fathers, and sons carved many lace bobbins. Bobbins were love tokens as well. During the centuries of home-industry lace-bobbin work, there were public executions, drawing considerable audiences as events. Names of the executed sometimes found their way to bobbin shafts. My favorite lace bobbin is made of incised wood, dated 1701. In a double winding text spiral along the shaft, in blue and red encaustic, it reads (in Middle English) from top to bottom: *In the midst of mirth remember death.* If you read it from bottom to top, it reads: *In the midst of death, remember mirth.*

Bobbin lace is no longer a home industry; virtually no one makes it anymore. Lace bobbins are not adaptable to any other use save recycling the beads. There is no functional reason that these objects survived to the twenty-first century.

26
Hand-carved, incised, and in-painted wood lace bobbins, 1701–1821. 4–4½" high. England

27
Hand-carved, incised, dyed, and in-painted ivory, bone, and horn lace bobbins with glass and semi-precious stone beads strung on wire, 1720–1845. 4½" high. England

28
Hand-carved, incised, and in-painted wood lace bobbin, 1701. Text spirals around bobbin; 4" high. England

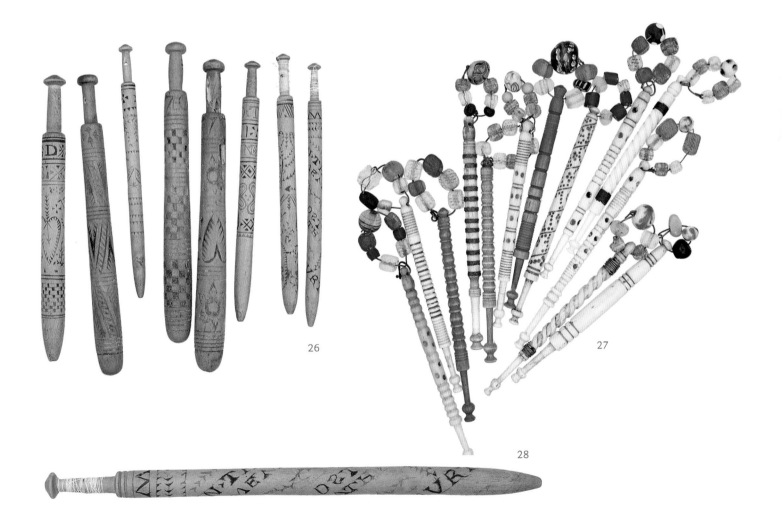

26

27

28

29

ONE CATEGORY of objects that was never produced in great numbers stands alone. It is a genre of unique artifacts. End of day pieces cross material lines and all classes of utility. Some of them have no practical function at all. There is a dearth of end of day objects because they were just that, the last piece made by a manufactory worker, at the end of a long tedious day, out of residual bits of materials from his day's labor. Most of the time all materials and personal spirit were gone by day's end, but not the "waste not, want not" mindset.

Consider the oppressive working conditions in a Staffordshire pottery in the late eighteenth century. British workers labored twelve-hour days, six days in a good week, for meager sustenance. Barbara M., a photographic historian, collects end of day Staffordshire pottery. She specializes in glazed cups and mugs that have a resident frog within, looking up at the drinker. This working class humor expressed a bit of whimsy in otherwise grave lives. End of day frog cups became an underground practice, as did end-of-day sewer tile artifacts. Unsophisticated workmen, using sewer tile clay that remained at the end of the workweek, made many uncommon products. Remnants of damp earthenware were usually fashioned into animal forms and tree stumps, as paperweights, doorstops, and match holders. Typically they were

brought home as a gift for a child or as a token of practical skill for a wife or mother. They are infrequently acknowledged because few people know about them. Sewer tile objects are English and American; immigrant workers must have brought the convention here.

End of day pieces were made from the ordinary materials of mass manufacture by occupationally

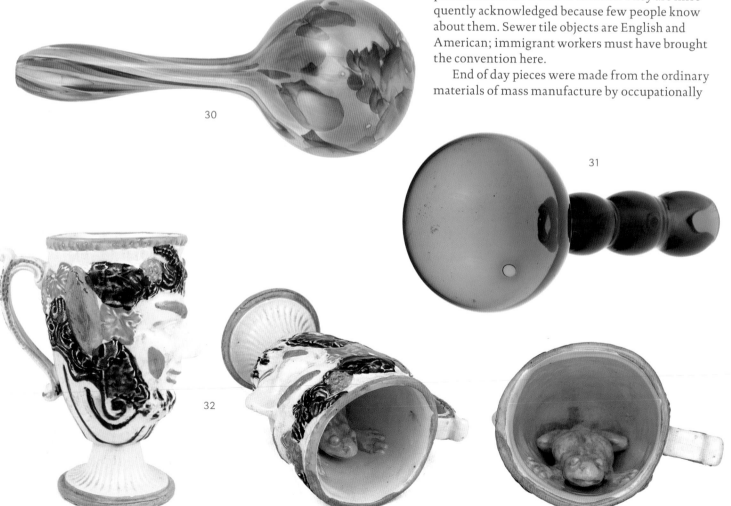

30

31

32

trained hands; the results are naïve and unconventional, sincere and earnest, wholehearted and often quaint, amusing, or droll. End of day marbles are confetti sprinkled with specks of colored glass, collected from the factory floor. I've seen a coreless sulphide; only clear glass had been left over. Glass slag end of day pieces occur in spatter patterns, swirls, and agate wannabe bowls and nonstandard vases. Serviceable enamelware pails and austere teapots become riots of turquoise and red using surplus material on the factory worker's own time. End of day pieces are surprising and unexpected transmittals of pride and sentiment and can be as quirkily astonishing as the triangular, galvanized tin, reverse-glass paint and foil pendant sign *To Betty from Grandpap*. It possesses poise and a grace of form rarely encountered. As a genre, these objects are never imperious or doctrinaire. They are off-center, unorthodox, offbeat, and eccentric.

The queerest end of day piece I know is a symmetrical, bunched barbed-wire bowl, perhaps a remnant of the "fencing the lower forty" cliché, in which case, it would be an end-of-the-month piece. It can't be used for a bowl's chief purposes: the barbs pierce apples and onions alike. If it were used as a colander, slashed pasta and nicked berries would flow out with the water. It's peerless; it surpasses any end of day whimsy I've ever seen for creative audacity.

33

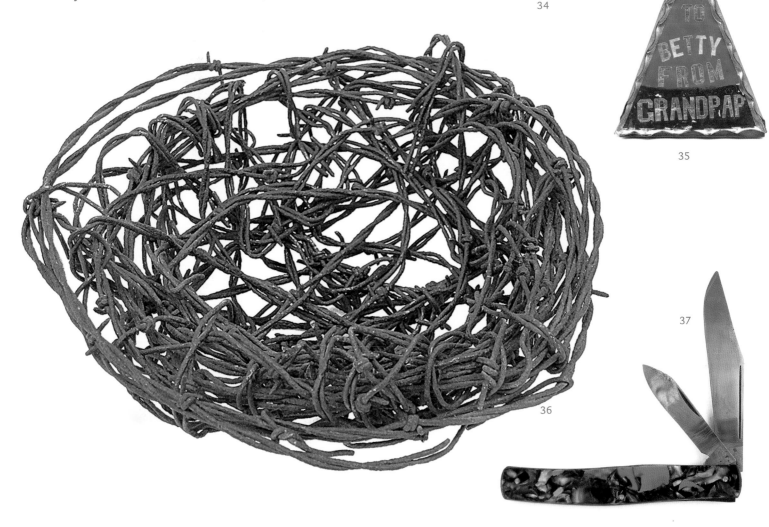

34

35

36

37

33
End of day marbles, 1900–1915. Glass, ½–1" diameter

34
End of day dental instrument tray, c. 1950. Glazed porcelain, 6" long. Shenango China Company

35
End of day sign made for Betty by her *Grandpap*, 1938. Reverse-painted glass, hand-cut foil letters, 5" high

36
Bowl made of barbed wire, c. 1940. 10¼" diameter

37
End of day jackknife (open), c. 1925. Celluloid and steel, 4" long

chapter 17

Conceived for Provisional Utility

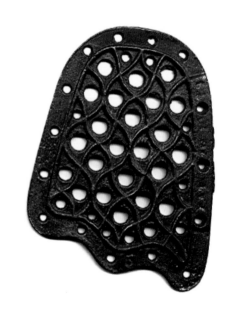

SOME OBJECTS were designed to extend the useful life of another object, or to contain, support, instruct, or identify something for a limited period of time, after which it will have outlived its purpose, unless, of course, you find its form or function sufficiently fascinating to acquire it and add others of its ilk to your holdings.

Leading this supporting cast are taps. Taps were not conceived for permanence, but to extend the functional life of a shoe, a small investment to protect a larger one. Postponing wear-and-tear in the shape of a little metal smile at the toe and a larger smile at the heel, taps put off the inevitable erosion of footwear that accompanies bipedal loco-motion. In pre–soft-soled running-shoe days, ordinary taps were designed to wear out before your hard-soled shoes.

1

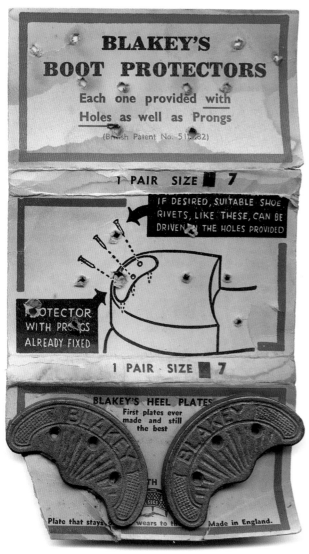

1
Clogging heel and toe
taps, 1955. Cast steel, 4
and 2" long respectively

2
Taps for shoes, 1947.
Blakey's, with packaging
and instructions, 6" high

3
Cobbler's tap sample
board, 1958. 9" high

2

In my family, taps were applied only when the heels and toes of our shoes had worn down a bit so that there would be no guessing at the exact location of wear spots and new shoes would not have an unnatural lift. Toe taps were ten cents each, heel taps were fifteen cents apiece, and my mother didn't anticipate wear spots; she acted on proof of their existence. One time only, when I was about eight years old, taps came in the shape of animals instead of smiles. The common shoe tap extends the life of hard-soled shoes. Someone thought tiny, perfect metal animal shapes might make life more amusing for a child than generic taps.

New taps always announced one's arrival. Tap dancing and clogging require large taps that basically share a shape. Tap shoes typically have one large tap on the sole—tip to arch—and one tap covering the entire heel. They are meant to articulate each step. Clogging shoes have two taps on the toe and two on

3

the heel, one beneath the other. Clogging shoes are much louder than tap shoes. Clog dancing lands with heavy, percussive heel steps. Tap dancing is primarily toe-stepping and fleet-footed. Clogging and danc-ing taps are affixed with screws, not nails. Nails and loose screws, no longer countersunk, wreak havoc on wood dance floors. Dancing taps probably outlast dance shoes. Maybe broken-in taps migrate through generations of tap shoes and dynasties of clogging shoes.

THE SHAPE and size of a crutch or a pair of crutches is less universal than a pair of taps, which needn't take the user's height or weight into account. Crutches support a person and enable locomotion until an injured leg or foot heals. The tap-related part of a modern crutch is its rubber tip, which is replaceable when it wears out. It protects the height of the crutch as well as parquet floors. Old crutches of homely ingenuity capture my attention.

Lucky Animal SEGS SHOE STUDS

2ᴰ

WET THE LEATHER BEFORE FIXING

LUCKY ANIMAL SEGS

"Oh look – ANIMAL SEGS
Dad's just fixed them to my shoes. Aren't they fine"

MADE IN ENGLAND.

LUCKY ANIMAL SEGS

LITTLE TOMMY AND MARY TOO
LOVE THE ANIMALS AT THE ZOO
HOW THEY'LL ADORE THESE–

ANIMAL SEGS

THE ONLY CREATURES WITH THREE LEGS

Essex, Connecticut, was an early American ship-building center. There is a crutch on exhibition in the Town Hall that has initials, text, and dates from 1801 through 1846 carved into it. These carvings support the belief that this is the Mack Shipyard crutch. Shipyard workers, who had been injured in a hazardous profession in which hewn timbers were cut with hand-axes and nails were stepped on, had successively used it. This crutch had been shortened, retiring its usefulness for tall laborers. Each set of initials was traced back to a Mack Shipyard employee within the incised time frame.

Light construction, adjustability, padding, shock absorption, and custom features do not characterize the crutches that I notice. My crutch preference is for those that were made from materials at hand, at times and in places in which comfort, mobility, and user fatigue weren't considered in current terms. Adjustment was final and meant that the tip was sawn off to shorten it so that a shoulder wouldn't be dislocated. These crutches didn't come in pairs.

Primitive crutches were commonly fabricated from a sound branch that was doweled into a carved wooden underarm rest. The users hand-clutched the stick support to keep it in place. Soldiers hobbled home from Civil War battlefields on an astonishing array of make-do crutches made from scavenged material, but most were a kind of tall cane without a handgrip. I have a crutch that was made from a sturdy bough, split along two-thirds of its length and reinforced at the crotch. The top ends are doweled into an armpit rest, and one-third of the distance from the top there is a hand rest that keeps the split open to prevent excessive strain on the top dowels. The handgrip is a stunning improvement in primitive crutches. Each elementary crutch served and supported an injured person for the time required either to heal or to die. Every crude crutch tells a practical story or serial stories of support for the infirm before formulaic solutions succeeded.

7
Hand-carved doweled crutches made from straight branches with reinforced tips and customized underarm supports, 1870–80. 42" high

8
Primitive doweled crutch made from a split branch with steel screw reinforcements and replaced handgrip, c. 1865. 48" high

… the man wore a giant yoke from which hung hundreds of small bottles on different lengths of string and wire. Moving as if part of a glass curtain, his body enveloped within that sphere. … Up close the glass was rough and sand-blasted, glass that had lost its civilization. Each bottle had a minute cork the man plucked out with his teeth and kept in his lips while mixing one bottle's contents with another's, a second cork also in his teeth. He stood over the supine burned body with his wings, sank two sticks deep into the sand and then moved away free of the six-foot yoke, which balanced now within the crutches of the two sticks. He stepped out from under his shop.
    Michael Ondaatje, *The English Patient* (New York: Vintage, 1992), 9.

FROM THE 1940s into the 1960s, annually and unsolicited, my father received a miniature of his license plate on a brass-beaded key chain. The back of this small replica commanded: *Finder—Deposit in any mailbox. Postage Guaranteed. Disabled American Veterans 2840 Melrose Avenue, Cincinnati, Ohio.*

"Dad, how do they know your name, your license plate, where we live?"

"They're veterans, they work for the government. It's all connected."

"If they're disabled, how can they make this tiny thing so perfect."

"Veterans with disabled hands do something else."

"What if someone finds your car keys and uses them instead of mailing them back?"

"That's why I'm giving this to you."

And so my collection of miniature license plates began. These Lilliputian tags had useful potential, like coins and tokens, but their practical utility expired each year as license plates changed. Biannual adhesive license plate tags didn't arrive until the mid-1980s. It was only a few years ago that license plate longevity was linked to the payment of your registration fees, and license plates could be transferred to your future cars in succession.

There were a few stylistic modifications to these diminutive symbols of car ownership. The early 1940s two-color, state-identifying version with a die-cut hole for the chain soon became a thin tabbed surround to which the keychain was anchored, giving it a framed look for several years. The 1950s and 1960s heralded clear plastics and laminated plate renditions with aluminum-edge encasements. License plate key chain tags surfaced at flea markets in the 1970s, and I added orphaned license plate tags from many states to my collection. Some early tags were all brass embossments made by the BF Goodrich Company. Key chain tags were conceived for the valid span of one's current license plate and, in the right hands, they are artifacts of automobile culture.

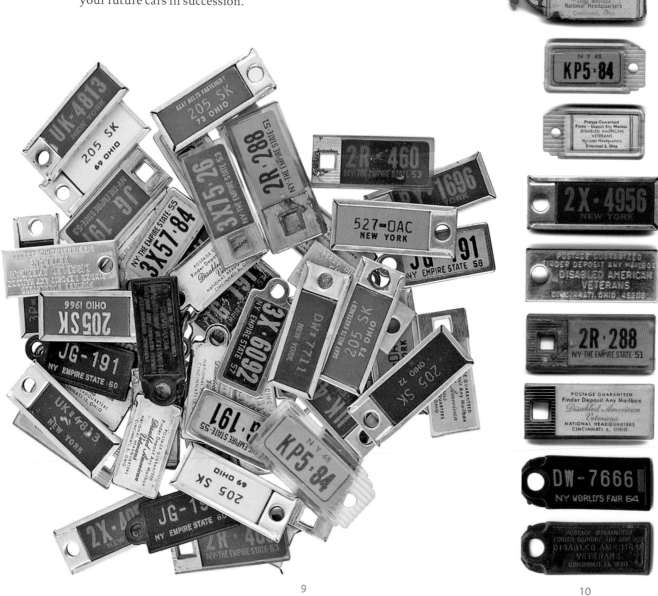

9
Group of license plate key chain tags, 1942–68. Brass, steel, plastic, and cardboard, ½–¾" high

10
Group of license plate key chain tags (fronts and backs), 1943–64. Steel, plastic, and cardboard, ½" high

I pushed open the drawer of the matchbox, feeling both sides of the inner sliding tray when it emerged to be sure that I wouldn't open it upside down and allow the matches to tumble plinkingly out, and I singled out one match and rolled its square shank between my fingers. When I struck it in the profundity of the dark I could see the dandelion head of little sparks shooting out from the match head and the eagerly waving arms of the new flame before it calmed down. The match flares more on the side away from where you slide it. Or am I wrong—is there more flare on the side that has touched the striking surface?

Nicholson Baker, *A Box of Matches* (New York: Random House, 2003), 11.

12

11
Matchbox labels,
1906–7. Printed paper,
each 1¼" high

12
Pocket sliding matchbox,
1919. Wood with printed
paper label, 2¼" high.
Capitol Safety Match
Corporation, USA

IN GERMANY, in the late 1600s, a glowing substance was concocted from the distillation of human urine. This concentrated substance ignited spontaneously and was called phosphorus for its light-bringing distinction. Great quantities of urine were supplied by the German army, which had interest in its potential. A few years later in Ireland, Robert Boyle discovered, through experimentation, that phosphorus rubbed against sulphur would burst into flame. In Sweden, in the mid-1700s, Karl Scheele formally identified phosphorus as a highly reactive, poisonous, non-metallic element. In the 1820s, the English market offered phosphorus-tipped, long wooden sticks, early matches, named *Lucifers* for the fallen angel of light. By the mid-1830s, England and the United States made small wooden phosphorus matches. Red phosphorus was identified in 1845, and Johan Edvard Lundstrom, a Swede, divided the combustible parts of matches between the match head and the striking surface. England, Sweden, and the United States led in the commercial development of match production. Phossy Jaw, or phosphorus necrosis, was the debilitating, face-collapsing, eventually fatal disease of the workers who manufactured, packaged, and sold phosphorus matches.

By 1855, small rectangular matchboxes were manufactured of wood, paper, a frictive strip on the side elevation, and a graphically engaging top label, ensuring brand recognition. This format became the disposable container for wooden matchsticks. The simple sliding boxes are still manufactured and used around the world for containing matches and safely striking them when igniting flame for heating, cooking, or for a smoke. These boxes were not displaced by Joshua Pussey's 1889 paper matchbook that is described in the figural match section. They share the market.

11

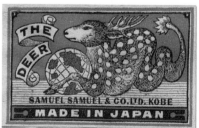

The striking graphic beauty of the labels on these basic boxes is their distinguishing characteristic. The labels produced in Japan, Thailand, and Russia for the world market during the first two decades of the twentieth century call out to me. They are defined by an economy of design in absolute service to a particular brand of matches. Three black birds poised in a divided yellow circle within a navy-blue square are flanked by block type on each end reading *MADE IN JAPAN, SAFETY MATCHES*. The Lion of Britannia strides across three globes on a red field beneath a lettered green scroll that reads *Lion Brand Safety Matches*. This imagery lies within a white text frame—*Do not glow nor heads fall off, impregnated*; *Gill Bros Company Sole Agents*; *Best Matches Trademark, Made in Japan*—on a label that is approximately 1¼ by 2 inches. Five suitably dressed cyclists synchronized on a bicycle built for five are poised in a red, ivory, pink, and black surround. Each of these labels depicts a logo that identifies a brand of matches. After the early 1900s, matchboxes went into wider advertising service, and manufacturers sold label space to a range of commercial enterprises. My interest is confined to about twenty years and is narrowly defined by the diversity of symbols, the patchwork of ornamental elements, pastiches of pseudo coats of arms, expressions of mythologies, and odd depictions from a multiplicity of cultures. Deftness of graphic rendering and mastery of craft are pure. These boxes were considered disposable when the matches were used up. Friends have given me later Swedish, Russian, Italian, Indian, Pakistani, Japanese, Chinese, and Hungarian matchbox labels. They are interesting referents. They are not in the same league.

"Next he brought out his bunch of . . . matches. But the tremendous cold had already driven the life out of his fingers. In his effort to separate one match from the others, the whole bunch fell in the snow. He tried to pick it out of the snow, but failed."
Jack London, *Klondike Tales: To Build a Fire* (New York: Modern Library, 2001), 267–68.

13
Group of matchbox labels, 1906–7. Printed paper, each 1¼–2¼" high

14
Group of matchbox labels, 1906–7. Printed paper, each 1¼" high

15
Group of matchbox labels, 1906–7. Printed paper, 2–2¼" high

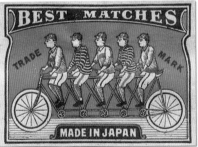

14

15

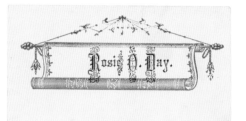

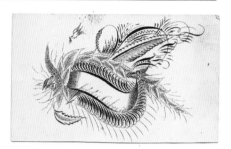

16

ABOUT THE same size as matchboxes, social calling cards announced that a visitor had called on
you while you were out or that one awaited your
availability in eighteenth- and nineteenth-century
worldly society. In early America, calling cards were
handmade, name austerely drawn by quill pen. If
adorned, decoration was a simple flower, wreath,
scroll, or bird drawing. Gradually calling-card fashion evolved into steel-pen calligraphed handwork
and colored printing and lithographed hidden-name
floral extravaganzas in the 1880s. In the late 1860s,
these cards segued into humor cards, puzzle cards,
and rebus cards, meant to reach out to a wider circle
than one knew well enough to visit and into acquaintance cards. *May I have the pleasure of escorting you home? If not can I sit on the fence and watch
you go by?* reads an example. They also spun off into
trade cards and business cards that are still in wide
use. The evolution of the social calling card into the
business card was not strictly a sequential process,
but overlapping. In each incarnation, these cards are
collectible. Together they tell a story of the greening
of American social and business outreach.

VOLATILE MORPHING occurred, from the tasteful expression of convention to creative declarations of
sincere sentiment to gregarious acquaintance and
then business cards that redefine social limits. One
present reality of the business-card form is the
brash XXX-rated offer of specific services. These
cards push the envelope of probity. They are usually
found tucked into a window gasket on one's parked
car, stacked on vending machines, or strewn on the
sidewalk. They are two-sided, so landing heads or
tails up is quite literal, and each side serves the same
purpose. Un-utterable wishes could be granted via
an impulsive, if expensive, phone call. The possibilities are printed out beside phone numbers fusing the
business card, the calling card, the phone card, and
probably the credit card in your very personal service.
These lusty invitations have transitory utility. Department of Sanitation street sweepers ingest more
than are put to use. However, they have evolved from
inexpensive one- and two-color print jobs in the
1990s to four-color portraits during the first years of
the twenty-first century; so scattergun merchandis-
ing has apparently repaid its investment and given
me another collection by which to chronicle American culture.

17

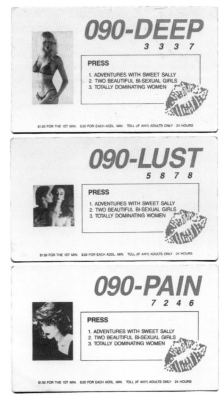

16
Group of social cards
(sentiment and calling),
intended to show artistic
accomplishment and
social place, 1800–
1890. Handmade and
commercially printed on
card stock, 1¼–2¾" high

17
Group of hot girls and
guy business cards,
1996–2004. Printed
card stock, 2–4¼" high

18
Group of hot girl calling
cards, 1989–94. Printed
card stock, each 2" high

18

UNLIKE AIRLINE sick bags, there is probably more than one use for an airline safety-instructions folder; but its utility is still provisional. They seem to be in endless supply as they usually look fresh and are meant for YOU.

> Preventing accidents from happening and preventing recurrence of accidents that have happened is a responsibility for everyone in the airline industry.
>
> Harro Ranter, *Access to Air Safety Information* (Paper delivered at CIS & Eastern Europe Airline Engineering and Maintenance Conference. Budapest, Hungary, October 9–10, 2002).

19
AeroMexico and Swissair *Safety Instructions* cards (front and back), 2003. Printed plastic, 10¼" high

20
American Airlines *Safety Instructions* (front and back), 2003. Printed paper, 11" high

Airline accidents are infrequent. Massachusetts Institute of Technology Professor Arnold Barnet has computed the odds of dying in a crash as one in eight million. Online *Airline Safety Tips from Dave and Dee* interprets these odds as follows: *If you were to fly once a day on a randomly chosen flight, you would fly 21,000 years without a fatal crash.*

All airline safety instructions, stowed in the seat pocket in front of you, are a sober approach to alerting you to responses to possible emergencies without causing panic among passengers. Scratch the surface of a passenger and you'll find a person who believes he's safer on the ground than in the air.

English may be the official language of air-traffic controllers and pilots worldwide, but pictorial clarity is the lingua franca of the passenger. Some of us have a pre–take-off safety instruction card look-see after we reconnoiter the nearest exits. Elaborate six-page cardstock foldouts with text have evolved into the universally unequivocal pictorial two-sided laminated card. These cards show exits and exit protocol, the how-to of life vests, oxygen-mask sequences, and crash positions using photographs of very calm models or stylized drawings. Then the flight crew gives an on-the-spot demo or launches an instructional video to reinforce the message, in pertinent languages, on international flights.

Half a century of air travel has given me a fair lay perspective on the evolution of air-safety guidance-card artwork that has the potential to cleave through the hysteria that accompanies imminent disaster. These neutrally communicated instruction cards speak in a standard code that is delivered in pictorial languages that vary from airline to airline. These graphic training manuals have fascinated my son, Jesse, since he was a youngster, even before our Sikorsky helicopter take-off from the Pan Am Building helipad to JFK, preliminary to embarking on a Pan Am flight to Guatemala when he was seven years old. Ours was the second-to-last flight from that heliport. The next one crashed onto Forty-second Street and Madison Avenue. No one had a chance to look at the card. Besides, it was mostly text—no time to read. His is a thirty-five-year interest in the wording and pictorial representation of staying calm and doing the right thing to save himself and others.

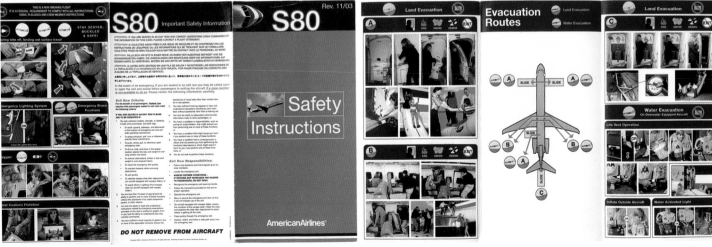

20

ANOTHER CATEGORY of objects of limited useful viability is the papier mâché Jack O' Lantern, a bail-wire-handled container for the tricks and treats of Halloween. Like Mexican sugar skulls for *La Dia de los Muertos*, Jack O' Lanterns are symbolic representations that have foundational connections to the antiquity of a specific culture.

My brother and I were not permitted to go trick-or-treating. We were well versed in its dangers, such as razor blades fiendishly tucked into apples. We were, however, allowed to purchase Woolworth's bright orange, papier mâché, grinning pumpkinhead Jack O' Lanterns with eye and mouth apertures covered by printed glassine eyeballs and teeth, which became quite terrifying when illuminated and animated by a flickering candle. This must account for the missing paper features in my three remaining Jacks. We were peripheral participants in Halloween festivities, handing out treats to the costumed kids who rang our doorbell. My mother even made the scary costumes in which we performed our benevolent acts. Ours was a cautious household in which our own candies remaining from All Hallows Eve filled Jack's post-flickering candle void. Not too many papier mâché pumpkin heads were sufficiently sturdy to

stand up to the evening's revelry, but some made it to the current marketplace; each may command several hundred dollars, which is the ultimate trick or treat, depending upon your point of view.

Woolworth's Jack O' Lanterns were the available commercial alternative to carving one's own pumpkin, which we did on occasion, also roasting the seeds. However, our hand-carved pumpkins never achieved the requisite titillating scariness level.

Recognition of a bountiful harvest, the anticipation of the onset of winter, and the appeasement of elusive and powerful spirits have a two thousand-year basis in Celtic and Druidic ritual that contribute to Jack O' Lantern mythology. Numerous versions of *Thieving Jack* or *Stingy Jack* legends have been recorded from European countries since the 1700s. They differ in detail, but all agree that Jack had committed too many reprehensible acts to pass muster with Saint Peter and, having tricked the devil, was even excluded from hell. Old Nick tossed Jack a burning ember to light his way in his nocturnal wanderings. Jack put it into a turnip carrier, and generations of Halloween carousers have imitated him with beets, gourds, large potatoes, and, recently, pumpkins and their ephemeral doppelgangers.

21
Jack O' Lantern in the making, 1938. Photo on paper, 11½" high. USA

22
Woolworth's price label on stainless-steel bracket for their glass shelving system holding Jack O' Lanterns, 1952. 1" high

21

22

23

24

23

Group of Jack O' Lantern
postcards, 1895–1908.
Printed card stock, each
3½" high

24

Papier mâché Jack O'
Lanterns, 1936–46.
Paint and printed paper,
4–8" high

TECHNICALLY, POLICE mug shots are viable for the active lifetime of a criminal, after which they become curiosities, records of past events onto which questionable attributes of personality may be thrust based on features and stance, expression, clothing, and posture. In recent years, photographed mug shots have been replaced by digitized identification systems that are distributed to law-enforcement agencies around the world at cyber speed. That identification triad—fingerprints, rap sheets, and mug shots, including a detailed subset of scars, tattoos, and other identifying marks—is no longer discrete. The virtual database assigns an identification number fusing scans of fingerprints, digital photos, and relevant information, backing it up to a network with uniform standards so that local police stations can input photos and data to a federal crime database. This is a far cry from recent six- to eight-week manual processing. This innovation is making strides to keep up with criminal mobility and is making paper photographic prints, which had been the mainstay of criminal identification for more than a century, obsolete.

In 1973, New York City Police Department headquarters moved to One Police Plaza, a fully equipped high-rise in close proximity to City Hall. Since 1909, police headquarters had been at 240 Centre Street, between Grand and Broome streets, in an imposing Edwardian baroque palace, designed by Hoppin and Koen, and meant to inspire respect for "the majesty of the law." In preparation for the move, the sorting process included dumping obsolete and "irrelevant" records, including many books of mug shots dating from the end of the nineteenth and early part of the twentieth centuries. I own a Staffordshire dish

25

that depicts a furniture-laden wagon with toppling household articles surrounded by the message: *Three Removes Are As Bad As a Fire.* Whenever I see that dish, I wonder who made the decisions about what to dispose of and what to move to One Police Plaza.

In the early 1980s, my husband exhibited, at OK Harris Works of Art, the canvas ledger pages from two of the officially discarded books of mug shots dating from 1916 through 1939 that had somehow survived the questionable disposition of archival records. Each page contained multiple glued paper photographs of America's most notorious criminals, including the cast of characters of Murder Inc., chronicling individual offenses. These photographs do not include scars and tattoos or the precise kind of information that is included in the new virtual database. Instead, early mug shots visually reveal the progression of criminal careers, escalating offenses, and transitional gang loyalties through the lens of hindsight. Many of these mug shots were full-length portraits, and many showed groups of perps who were arrested together red-handed. Handwritten charges such as *burglary*, *assault*, or *breaking and entering* are inscribed beside each photograph with the date of arrest. Later, *dead* or *deceased* had been unceremoniously scrawled upon the photographs of repeat offenders in whom the police department had ongoing interest. Posture and stance, in lineup context, runs from nonchalant to confrontational—rarely desperate. Stylistic changes in clothing and police methodology are archived in undercurrents. Taken together, this kind of documentation is unique and revelatory. The loss of those historical records in 1973 is testament to the fact that provisional utility is relative to the eye of the observer.

26

(4) FRANK MATTO

PATRICK MITCHEL ALIAS LINKEY

HARRY OYSTERHOUT STICK-UP (5) ALIAS OYSTERS

4982 JAMES EGAN

27

MOE MORRIS - TRUCK THIEF

FRANK MOTTO
GENERAL THIEF (9)

FRANK-COSTELLO   SAM   ARNOLD   GENO
ALIAS   ZUCKERMAN   WITTENBERG   CESAREO
FRANK   JOYA

TRUCK - STICK-UP

COSTELLO- 76756 - ZUCKERMAN- 1030- WITTENBERG-62

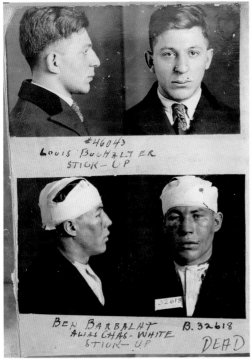

#46043
LOUIS BUCHALTER
STICK - UP

BEN BARBALAT   B. 32618
ALIAS CHAS- WHITE
STICK - UP   DEAD

DEAD   DEAD   PLATE 1184   1/29/26   DEAD

1- EDWARD DIAMOND- 2- JOHN DIAMOND- Plate # 1183
3- JOSEPH WALSH- 4- CHARLES LUCIANO
STICK-UP

Fabian FARBER, STICK-UP

HUGH DENOCHE, - STICK-UP

DEAD

EDWARD DIAMOND
STICK-UP- B. 59859

LOFT BURGLARS   Plate: 578
B. 70434   70435   70436
DEAD

JACK COHEN   JOE COOPER   SOL SAMUELS

28

29

chapter 18

Made for One Use Only

I THINK OF audiotape as singular in its function of recording and playing back audible sounds. In November 1976, while meandering through fields, forests, and orchards in upstate New York, observing seasonal changes, I found a curious bird nest in a tree denuded of its summer foliage. It was made of twigs, straw, leaf bits, horsehair—and a length of audiotape.

Objects devised or concocted for one particular serviceable mission are rarer than fungible articles that have adaptive utility. Twigs, horsehair, leaves, and straw are multipurpose materials. In a pinch, audiotape might be used as ribbon for gift wrap, but most tapes would be discarded once the audio messages were no longer pertinent. The scenario that ended with a bird's nest partially constructed of audiotape in my hands, deep in rural woods, is something I have mused on.

1

I considered the poise, beauty, and eccentricity of the nest against my curiosity about what the length of tape might reveal about the mystery if played. I opted for the intactness of the object on "the goose that laid the golden egg" principle, knowing that I never could have adequately rewoven the nest. The brown audiotape apparently met bird camouflage and nest drainage standards. Preempting many twig- and horsehair-securing flights, it probably shortened nest-construction time. The nest had been well used in its season, having passed the comfort criteria of fledglings. What species of bird was so notably resourceful? Was there any difficulty in communicating the audiotape idea to the other half of the bird pair? Had the fledglings engaged on a lifelong quest for audiotape with which to nest build? Had the tape been placed mostly matte side up, luster facing downward so that glints wouldn't attract predators? Was the length of tape wrested from the reel, in a flurry of feathers and beak action, or was it found as a ribbon? What happened to the rest of the tape and the cassette? It would be nice to interview this bird.

The elegant construction of this nest was enhanced by an iconoclastic material, evidence of International Style architecture in a bricks-and-mortar culture. Most things that were conceived for one use are very infrequently elevated to a higher calling when their purpose has expired. They are usually trashed. Forms that exceed the qualifications of function have occasionally been given a reprieve by those who look at material things fluidly and sideways; some are even compelled to collect them.

IN THE UNITED States since the 1950s, preprinted, sturdy, often waxed cardboard boxes have been used to ship fruits and vegetables to warehouses and sales destinations from their rural origins. From the 1870s to the 1950s, glossy, vivid labels adorned the ends of wooden fruit and vegetable crates; they had the purpose of attracting while informing. Stiff competition among produce growers required clear announcement by label in order to survive among myriad identical crates in wholesale distribution centers. A striking, surprising, or demanding image, a grower's or packer's singular expression, attracted notice, identified the product, the location of its origin, and told, by color or logo, the grade of the produce—all at a glance. The big rich images with references to historical figures, fruit grower's children, animals, exotic locales, patriotic themes, perfect idealized fruits, and wacky puns were produced by stone lithography until the 1920s, when they were superceded by less costly photolithographic plates. Both processes were no longer used for produce-crate labeling in the 1950s.

The crate label was the only brand signature of the fruit grower or packer. It was the great indiviualizer in the equal universe of uniform wooden crates. The all-purpose container for sturdy produce was a simply constructed rectangular box with thin wood

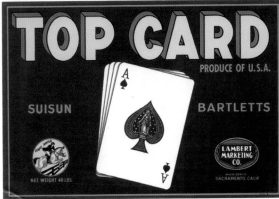

1
Four views of a bird's nest made from mud, straw, and audiotape, 1976. 5¼" diameter

2
Pear and orange crate labels, 1935–50. 7¼–10" high

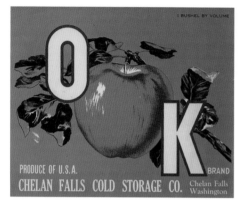

slat sides and a twisted wire support around the girth of the long sides that flexed with hefting the damp and heavy loads. The short ends of the crates were about 10 by 14 inches, and it was there that everyone had a chance to present distinguishing identifying logos for the contents of the standard container. The universal mission of the end labels was to announce a product by means of color, image, and text, thus attracting retailers to repeat purchases of the product. Attention-nabbing images, lush contrasting colors, and humorous wordplay established unique identities. These were labels that advertised themselves.

Fruit and vegetable crates were stacked at the greengrocers with the labels visible; the crates were the partitions that segregated the produce. The items that shoppers selected were speedily tallied by pencil stub on a brown bag. Crates were the shelving system on the horse-drawn fruit wagon that an Italian vendor brought to my Bronx neighborhood twice a week. Fruit crates figured into my first kindergarten assignment: to bring in the end of a fruit crate, cleaned, and a photograph of my five-year-old self. Each of my kindergarten fellows placed poster-paint handprints and their photographs on their fruit crate end and brought home a shellacked plaque memento

of our first school year. Three years later, my brother had the same assignment. His handprint was blue; mine was red. My mother had the pair of personalized fruit-crate ends on her wall to her dying day. My connection to the produce-crate world includes cherished construction memories of my tooth-rattling, bone-jarring, orange crate/roller-skate scooter and a collection of a few hundred fruit-crate labels, post-childhood acquisitions.

When produce-label technology moved on to printed cartons, the old unused labels were destroyed or languished in warehouses to be rediscovered by collectors. Although the labels are industrially obsolete, I've seen their images reproduced on T-shirts; ceramic tiles, quaintly mounted on wood for decorative hanging; on kitchen magnets; and on mouse pads for that refreshing antique-your-computer look. Remaining labels have an established collectorship. This dwindling commodity is ensured of a place among collectible graphic ephemera. There are rare images; yet, when warehouse quantities are found, rare pieces can become common. Printed phenomena are an iffy collectible if you're in it for the money instead of the astonishing visuals.

3
Fruit crate labels,
1930–52. 8¾–10½" high

4
Fruit crate labels,
1935–49. Each 10" high

5
Kindergarten Project,
Bronx, New York, 1944.
Fruit crate wood end,
paint, photograph,
shellac, and steel screw-
eyes, 9½" high

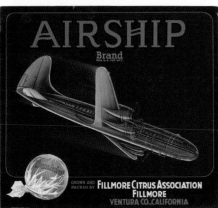

4   5

6

7

STONE LITHOGRAPHY is now used only in fine-art printmaking. The method was developed in Germany in the late 1700s, utilizing the nature of wet limestone to repel oil-based ink and the nature of damp paper to absorb it. Images were drawn on, pecked out on very smoothly sanded, three- to four-inch-thick Bavarian litho stones that had been covered with a thin, durable ground. These stones could convey thousands of nondegraded, sharp images to damp paper without wearing the stone down. One stone was required for each color, the aggregate of four to fourteen colors creating the final image. At its best, the result was breathtaking. The method was slow, time consuming, demanding, skilled-labor intensive, and expensive; yet it became the main method of producing commercial illustration during the nineteenth and early twentieth centuries. Label aesthetics reached a zenith of artistry, complexity, and precision in cigar labeling from 1880 to the 1920s.

Until 1870, cigars were sold in bundles of twenty-five or fifty, called *wheels,* which were tied with yellow cigar silks. Only the cigar silk was printed with the brand; the cigar ring had not yet been conceived. Cigar silks were easily reused to sell not strictly what the ribbon proclaimed. Post–Civil War taxation could not be regulated on cigar bundles, so tobacco taxes were levied on boxed cigars and regulated by a tax stamp sealing the lid. Early cigar boxes sported the brand burned into the lid—literally *branding.* Competition for consumers' attention went the same route as produce crate labels, leading to stone lithography.

In contrast to the two standard rectangular crate ends for high stacking in wholesalers' warehouses, cigar-box imagery appealed to the consumer directly, at eye level, on six outside box panels, the inside of the lid, on an inner sheet, on box edging, on nail seals, the back flap, the front flap, and on each cigar banded within the box. Cigar convention dictated that each of these labels was a subtle variant on the brand logo. The outside panels enabled the retailer to identify the box regardless of its stacked positioning. The most elaborate and complete illustrations were reserved for the *inner* lid so that the smoker or shopper would be induced to buy the product and, if satisfied, find it again in the shop's humidor case, on a vertical plane comprised of regiments of competing illustrated, open cigar boxes. The *top* label was also ambitiously illustrated as protection of the cigar's outer skin, or wrapper, from cover abrasion. It too was readily seen in open-box store displays on the horizontal plane, lightly covering the cigars.

Demand fired competition, and grand and majestic labels were produced by the stone lithography medium. Crystalline images from mythology and the classics, transportation triumphs, cowboy life, sporting events, gambling vignettes, views of foreign and exotic places, heroic exploits, political figures, stereotyped minorities, historical personages, patriotic subjects, royal portraits, biblical characters, theatrical personalities, and, most of all, copious bounty expressed through sumptuous females (clothed, half-clad, or nude)—all conveyed the lush extravagant promise of the five-cent cigar.

At first, labels had been printed on inexpensive wood cellulose papers that were later replaced by rag-based papers that could be embossed without breaking. Embossment gave volume and dimensional detail to already superior printed imagery; armored breastplates became palpable and lustrous, and curly hair rivaled the depictions by Renaissance masters. Exquisite craft and spectacular artistry currently defines this graphic cigar genre. At the time, these labels were simply wrappers to be discarded as cigars were smoked . . . and they were smoked and wrappers were discarded.

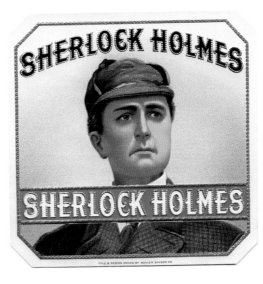

8
Cigar box labels, c. 1890–1920. Stone lithography on embossed paper with gold ink, 3¼–4¼" high

8

Historically, tobacco products have had the most compelling graphics, as shown in cigarette and cigar silks, cigar boxes, cigar labels and rings, cigarette tins, and plug-tobacco tin tags. Tobacco packaging is deeply rooted in tobacco culture, and its forms have been resoundingly inventive. The employment of graphic artists of exquisite skill and refinement by the lithograph companies yielded the many label types that adorned each cigar box. Cigar culture of the nineteenth and early twentieth centuries lives on in its residual paper images that convey rich information about the era.

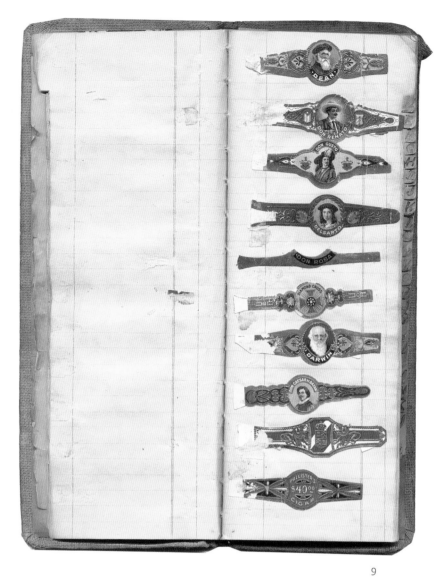

9

10

12

11

9
Ward Heinzman's Cigar ring book, c. 1908. Clothbound covers with ruled pages; rings produced by stone lithography on embossed paper with gold ink, and arranged alphabetically, 10" high

10
Cigar in sealed, labeled glass tube, 1892. Packaged in Havana, Cuba, for Denver's Brown Palace Hotel; cork and printed paper, 6½" high

11
Group of cigar bands featuring portraits of presidents of the United States, 1882–1909. Embossed printed paper with gold leaf, each 1¼" high

12
Group of cigar bands featuring portraits of heads of state, 1882–1910. Embossed printed paper with gold leaf, ½–1¾" high

ANOTHER TOBACCO form that delivers tokens of unique artistry is plug tobacco. In this format, tobacco leaves that have been flavored with molasses or other sweeteners, such as rum, prune juice, champagne, honey, or various fruits, are compressed into hard cakes, or plugs, for shipment to retail points of sale. There the vendors, with counter lever cutters, divided the pound plugs along score marks, producing pocket-sized plugs, for purchase by the chewer. After that, molar or knife loosed a chaw.

In the early 1870s, P. Lorillard & Company of New York, Pioneer Tobacco Company of Brooklyn, and Finer Tobacco Company of Louisville, Kentucky, pressed embossed-tin tags into sections of plug tobacco by means of two sharp, pointed corners of the tag folded at ninety degrees to the tag face. Tags ensured quality control, since cagey vendors who sold cheaper products masquerading as superior tobacco reused other types of labeling and boxes. Tags caught on and were used by Liggett & Myers, National Tobacco Company, Hanes, Drummond, R J Reynolds Tobacco Company, Florodoro Tobacco & Tag Company, Taylor Brothers Tobacco Company, American Tobacco Company, and Continental Tobacco Company, among others. In fact, from the 1880s through the early 1900s, about 40 tobacco companies manufactured about 3,500 different tagged tobacco brands. Tobacco companies made only a few types of tobacco, which were sold under many tag names. They were fiercely competitive, and a tobacco company might seem to have been competing against itself by offering from 35 to 120 different tagged products; but the tags were redeemable for gifts that ensured company loyalty while offering the consumer a great variety of flavor and product as an inducement not to drift away.

All of a company's various tags were redeemable for gifts listed in catalogues that can still be bought in secondary markets today. The 1903 *Florodoro Cigar Band and Tobacco Tag Catalogue of Presents* offered musical instruments, washing machines, bicycles, and suitcases. A child's dining-utensil set was available for 25 tags and a grand piano for 90,000 tags. Now there's an inducement to chew like mad. The 1910 American Tobacco Company's forty-six-page *Catalogue of Presents for Tobacco Tags or Coupons* offered to redeem 25 tags for a pair of scissors as well as 11,000 tags for a Davenport bed. Tag-redemption catalogues for gifts and presents instigated brand chauvinism since tags could be redeemed for tobacco paraphernalia, furniture, safes, tools, firearms, clocks, carpets, jewelry, and clothing through the 1930s, by which time many of the smaller tobacco companies had been bought by the larger companies. Plug-tobacco product lines dwindled in favor of cigarettes, which were regarded as cleaner in use; the constant spitting that accompanied chewing tobacco was seen as blue-collar or hayseed behavior, *déclassé* and unsophisticated.

13
Napoleon and horse lever-action plug-tobacco cutter, 1860. Cast iron on wood base, 5¼" high

14
Elf lever-action plug-tobacco cutter, c. 1870. Cast iron, 6½" high

15
Group of die-cut printed tin tobacco tags, 1872–1935. ¾–1¼" high

16
Group of die-cut printed
tin tobacco tags, 1872–
1935. ½–1¼" high

16

Coupons packaged with Raleigh cigarettes in the 1940s and early 1950s were the last gasp of tobacco coupons for redemption of goods on a grand scale. After that, tobacco companies began aggressive and competitive campaigns to market particular lifestyles as the bonus for using their products.

Like produce-crate labels, the smaller tobacco tags attested to the genuine product, announced the maker, and enlisted humor and clarity of logo in advertising the products they adorned. Most tobacco tags are well under an inch in either dimension; only a few are larger. The earliest tags were die-cut tin and embossed tin, some of which were stained red, blue, green, or gilt. Many featured stamped-out letters that identified the manufacturer, such as RJR or AT or TCJ. Others were die-cut objects, which named a brand, such as an anchor, an arrowhead, an apple, a canoe, a flat iron, an arm and hammer, or a shield. Of necessity, these miniature artworks were simple, articulate, and clear minute depictions that, by the 1880s, were enameled or colorfully printed, graphically enhancing each tag. By the 1900s, tobacco tags had evolved into less elaborate stamped shapes with sophisticated printed pictorial representations and text. There is no reason for tobacco tags to turn up at antiques and collectibles sources, but they do. Most were discarded as the plug was used or the tags were redeemed.

BAKEABLE CAKE charms possess the minute intensity and punch of plug-tobacco tags and similarly could be easily swallowed, but they grow out of religious custom originating in medieval France and the celebration of Epiphany on the twelfth night after the birth of Christ. Called *le jour des rois* in France and *dia de los reyes* in Spain, Mexico, and Latin America, the day is now standardized and celebrated on the Sunday preceding January sixth. Traditionally, a tiny token or figurine (*fève*) is hidden in *la galette des rois* (king cake), or *roscon*; a *frangipane* cake (flat puff pastry with almond paste) in Paris and New Orleans; a *brioche* in Provence; and all manner of sweet cakes, *rosca de reyes*, elsewhere. The lucky recipient of the charmed segment of cake becomes the representative of the three kings or three wise men, or Magi, and is paper-crowned "King of the Day."

17
Bakeable cake charms, 1946. Sterling silver, printed card stock with cotton thread, 3¾" high

18
Bakeable cake charms with box and instructions, 1920. Lead charms, printed paper, and cardboard; box 3¼" high

19
Bakeable cake charms
box with silver foil
charms inside, 1950.
Printed cardboard, 2"
high

20
Bakeable cake charms
box with lead charms
inside, 1938. Printed
cardboard, 3¾" high

21
Group of king cake
charms (*fêves* and
monitos), 1880–2004.
Glazed porcelain,
painted bisque, and
metal, 1–2¼" high.
France, Mexico, and USA

22
Galette des Rois and
Rosca des Reyes
(king cakes), baked
with charms (*fêves*
and *monitos*) inside
for consumption on
Epiphany Sunday, 2004.
Each 14" diameter.
France and Mexico

The charm, formerly the Christ child or a biblical figure, has evolved into a lucky charm that portends an important personal quality or event in the year to come. Charms have been made of china, metallicized paper, metal, and lately of plastic. They are now found in the forms of biblical figures, horseshoes for luck, a baby for a blessed event, a ring for marriage, and the like. Derived from Epiphany celebrations, the bakeable cake charm convention has, since Victorian times, become a wedding cake practice in which the half-inch charms have very specific meanings. A four-leaf clover or a wishbone presages good luck; a dollar sign is an omen of wealth to come. A pacifier or safety pin signifies children in the near future, and a globe or airplane foreshadows travel and adventure. A flower bouquet indicates a blossoming relationship and a frog portends kissing a prince.

> Find a pin, pick it up.
> All the day you'll have good luck.
> Find a pin, leave it lay,
> Bad luck will follow you all the day.
> *Nineteenth-century proverb*

Some tokens didn't outlast the Epiphany feast. Epiphany cake charms had been almonds and broad beans in their earliest incarnations and were often intentionally swallowed in the locales in which gaining the token brought with it responsibilities such as buying another king cake for the next turn or a round of drinks for companions. Small porcelain and metal figures discouraged on-the-spot consumption but weren't often saved beyond "you're it" phase.

19

20

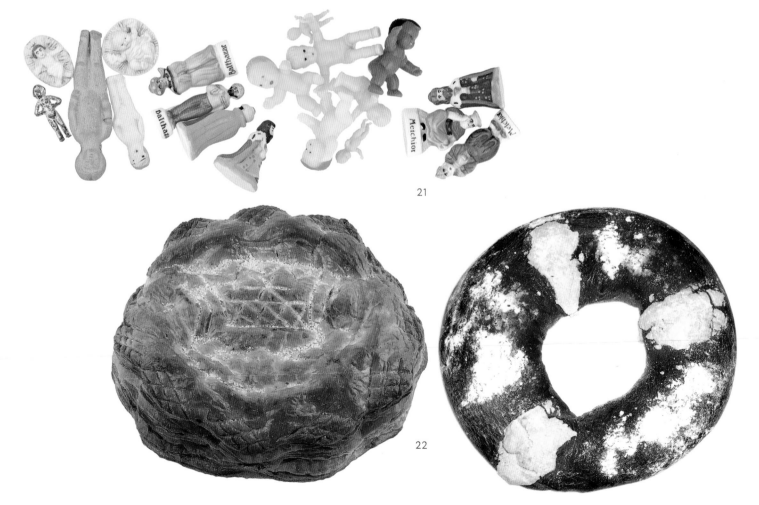
21

22

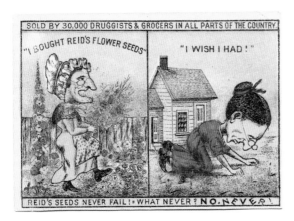

REID'S FLOWER SEEDS ARE SURE TO GROW.

Making as I do, a specialty of the Flower Seed trade, I am enabled by purchasing in large quantities to secure the very best, in quality, purity and freshness, to be obtained, which fact will explain the reason, that during the past five years the sales of my seeds, for each succeeding year, have more than doubled, so that last season over FOUR THOUSAND POUNDS OF FLOWER SEEDS, were used in my establishment making an aggregate of four million packets, and my list of Grocers and Druggists selling the same amounted to THIRTY THOUSAND, located in almost every town from Maine to California. These facts speak volumes for the popularity and consequent reliability of my seeds. A trial of them will convince you of their value.

Yours Resp'ly, W. H. REID.

23

SEED PACKET displays that are seen in urban hardware stores every spring are likely destined for indoor and outdoor window boxes, rooftop pots, and the infrequent yard. They are an abbreviated offering tailored for the city dweller. Rural farmstore presentations by the same seed producers offer a fuller variety, delimited for broad locales or growing zones. Observation of the salient details of current packaging reveals that the only real difference among seed producers or distributors is their logo. For flower, vegetable, herb, and fruit, each seed packet is an envelope with a plant name and lackluster photograph of the expected outcome of the seed on the face, minimal planting instructions on the back, and a few seeds nestled in the bottom seam of the envelope. The destiny of used seed packets is frequently impalement on a stick, stake, or twig demarcating the region of planting and plant variety for reference during pre-harvest growth. The envelope may be re-encountered the following spring when installing the next garden, if it is not long gone owing to gardener tidiness or the ravages of winter.

A few leeks remained in the ground from last fall, along with a clump of unbulbed Florence fennel and a broken row of carrots, one or two of them firm, the rest top-rotted. I had forgotten them, and the January frost had heaved them. I also dug up hickory nuts and old plant labels.

Verlyn Klinkenborg, *The Rural Life* (Boston: Little, Brown & Co., 2002), 39–40.

24

23
Reid's Seeds trade card (front and back), c. 1880. Printed card stock, 2¼" high

24
Group of lettuce seed packets, 1915–48. Printed paper, 4¾–5¾" high. New York State

The first seeds were proffered commercially in the United States in 1820 by James L. Belden, founder of the Wethersfield Seed Company in Connecticut. They were wrapped in folded paper with a scroll border. D. M. Ferry of the later Ferry-Morse Seed Company was the first, in 1856, to merchandise an assortment of garden seeds in small envelopes at retail points of purchase. He ensured quality control and repeat sales by removing leftover seed from retailers at the close of each growing season. He guaranteed his seed and believed that it could become unreliable if left in envelopes for more than a year. By the mid-1880s, Washington Atlee Burpee sold seed with gardening advice and stories through mail-order seed catalogues. From the end of the Civil War through the 1920s, large-scale seed production and stone lithography coincided to produce the greatest variety of seed types and detailed artist-rendered wrappers that, on the front, visually articulated images of the specific variety within each packet—first-class portraits of what the gardener might expect to grow from that envelope of seed. On the back were planting instructions and hints for bountiful cultivation.

25
Group of onion seed packets, 1910–48. Printed paper, 4¾–5¾" high. New York State

26
Group of radish seed packets, 1910–20. Printed paper, 4¾–5¾" high. New York State

27
Carrot seed packet, 1916. 4¾" high. Genesee Valley Lithograph Company, Rochester, New York

28
Celeriac seed packet, c. 1945. 5" high. Nicht's Seeds, Auburn, New York

27

28

29

30

31

There are seed envelopes that attest to twenty varieties of lettuce, sixteen kinds of onions, and twelve different radish types offered for sale within the same year from the same seed distributor. Variety seemed to be a means of satisfying a customer. Most of the varieties seen on vintage seed packets for flowers, fruits, and vegetables are not available to us today. Our choices have been limited by hybridization in the service of durability, shipability, and unsproutabilty, as well as by the acquisition of small seed companies by larger seed companies. In the late 1950s, an article was published in *Scientific American* about corporate cultivation of a hearty, durable, easily shipped square tomato. The hybridizer's insurmountable difficulty was that it was tough-skinned and tasted like cotton.

Leonard D. and Lee S. bought a 170-year-old farmhouse that borders my upstate New York farm. After four years of residency, they had to install a septic system since the ancient plumbing system was no longer serviceable. The excavator asked whether they wished to have the residuum carted off. They opted for spreading the rich, friable soil at the edge of the field west of their house. The end of the following summer, without having planted any seed, they had a magnificent and varied crop yield of heirloom tomatoes. Apparently tomato seeds survive human digestion and dank storage for scores of years. Seed arousal from dormancy is a lengthier version of birds spreading wild berry seeds over the countryside.

Johnny Appleseed notwithstanding, apple seeds do not produce offspring of consistent character from pips. Eighteenth- and nineteenth-century farms in New York State had cider orchards, in which many seeds had been planted; the juice of the ripe fruit was crushed and mingled for cider, a staple food that is good fresh and when fermented. Hard cider abetted survival through long, cold winters. Only when a sapling was proven to have good eating or baking fruit was it transplanted to a location near the farm kitchen door. In our area, most farms have a farmer's-wife's apple tree and a cider orchard with heirloom apple trees. The fruit is biannual and the seeds are there to be cultivated. In theory, we are not stuck with the same eight disease-resistant, storage-surviving apples.

29
Group of cabbage seed packets, 1915–50. Printed paper, 4¾–5¾" high. New York State

30
Watermelon seed packet, 1928. Packet, 5¾" high. Burt's Seed Company, Dalton, New York

31
Peas seed packet, 1928. Packet, 5¾" high. Burt's Seed Company, Dalton, New York

32
Seed sower, c. 1940.
Painted cast lead, 2¾"
high

33
Water-pumping
gardener, 1940. Painted
cast lead, 2½" high

34
Seed-watering gardener,
c. 1940. Painted cast
lead, 2½" high

35
Flower-watering
gardener, c. 1935.
Painted cast lead, 2½"
high

36
Watermelon seed packet,
1928. Packet (back),
2¾" high. Burt's Seed
Company, Dalton, New
York

32

33

34

35

Seed envelopes that endure pictorially attest to
what we are missing. Heirloom tomatoes, grown
from seeds gripped back from the maw of oblivion,
have survived outside the boundaries of agrochemi-
cals to grace the plates of *haute cuisine* restaurants.
They are fashionable anomalies that don't ship well
since their shapes are not standard; they must vine-
ripen and they bruise easily. The spirit of agribusi-
ness is to take marketable characteristics of produce,
say, corn varieties, and bioengineer them to arrive at
one reductive model that is tasty, herbicide-tolerant,
disease-resistant, and shipable, with transgenetic
pesticide-producing properties if necessary. Apparently, variety is no longer the spice of life. Clues to
the panoramic spectrum of edible plant varieties, a
panarchy of veggies, are harbored in throwaway
paper seed packets from yesteryear, semi-wild and
overgrown cider orchards, and in reviveable mum-
mified seeds. My seed packets from the past came
from stored printer surplus and never made it to the
seed-filled stage or I would have planted them. Likely
some would have germinated since the seeds would
not have been sprayed with post-1950s anti-sprout-
ing and anti-fungal agents.

During World War II, many people in the Bronx
planted "Victory Gardens." The Works Progress Administration (WPA) hired artists to illustrate posters
urging civilians to grow vegetables in home gardens
in order to relieve the burden of supplying our troops
and the consequent food rationing. "Fighting with
Food" became a marker of self-sufficient patriotism,
and much of the produce that was consumed during
the war came from home gardens that originated in
retail-store displays of seed packets.

Seed envelopes were made of an ephemeral material. They were printed on wood cellulose paper; and
if they were not used as out-of-door plot markers,
they would have been discarded upon emptying or
would have self-destructed unless pains had been
taken to preserve them. Acid in the paper itself
would have yellowed the envelope and made the paper brittle enough to fragment and disintegrate over
time. Inadvertent warehouse storage in dark, cool,
dry locations spared packet and label surplus, saving
them from extinction.

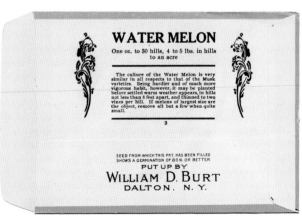

36

RARER STILL are Civil War propaganda envelopes, letterpress-printed on the same wood cellulose papers. Seed packets were produced in plenty, but comparatively few of these pro-Union envelopes were ever printed. Only half the country was pro-Union, and letterpress printing was a hand process from carved relief wood blocks, the press imprinting one envelope at a time. These envelopes are approximately 3 by 5½ inches, standard letter size at the time; and the left side or entire face of the envelope (reserving a place for the address) conveys the symbols and slogans of pro-Union propaganda. Printed in one, two, or three colors in New York, Boston, Connecticut, Philadelphia, and Ohio, they represent vehement Union loyalty in a number of genres.

Flag, shield, and fierce-eagle depictions, along with lightning, political figures, and Union generals with memorable quotations, are categorical images. State seals in support of the *Union Forever*, and patriotic representations in cartoon and symbol with aggressive and uncompromising slogans of *Death or Victory* are the other general categories into which the envelope images fall. The last category includes disparaging and provocative caricatures of Confederate leaders behaving badly; Union compromise is depicted as a smoking cannon.

Union propaganda envelopes came into my possession as three carefully preserved collections over a period of eleven years. I passed on the only other examples that I have seen; the envelope faces had been cut out and glued to file cards, a travesty of the first order. I don't think many firsthand material indicators of how people really felt during the Civil War survive. They connect us to our counterparts more than a century ago. Most of them were mailed envelopes and as such were containers for messages; consequently they were torn open and discarded.

37
Union envelope, 1863.
Letterpress-printed
paper, 3" high

38
Union envelope,
1862. Hand-colored
letterpress-printed
paper, 3" high. McGee,
Philadelphia

39
Union envelope,
1862. Hand-colored
letterpress-printed
paper, 3" high. McGee,
Philadelphia

37

Columbia awake at last.

38

Three Cheers for the Red, White & Blue.

39

ONE FLAG AND ONE GOVERNMENT.

RICE STRAW!
Effect of " feed " on the Cavalry Horses in the Secession Army.

Rebel Army " Rations."

Did'nt I tell you so? Jeff. Davis.

The Union is as Good as Wheat.

OUR COMPROMISE.

DEATH OR VICTORY.

Stiring him up.

Uncle Sam cutting down the
"Secession Tree" just as it is in
full bloom, against the wishes of
the planter.
S. C. Upham, 310 Chestnut St.

J-ackass Davis and G-asconade Beauregard backing each other.

JEFF DAVIS GETTING TO THE WHITE HOUSE.
With his eyes on Washington, Jeff is unconscious of the
way in which he sits in his saddle, or in what direction
his lean nag "Secession" is carrying him.

Cease Viper, you bite a file.

Uncle Sam sends his bird after
TRAITOR JEFF.

The End of Rebellion.
Uncle Sam—Now, boys, I want you to be good
in future.

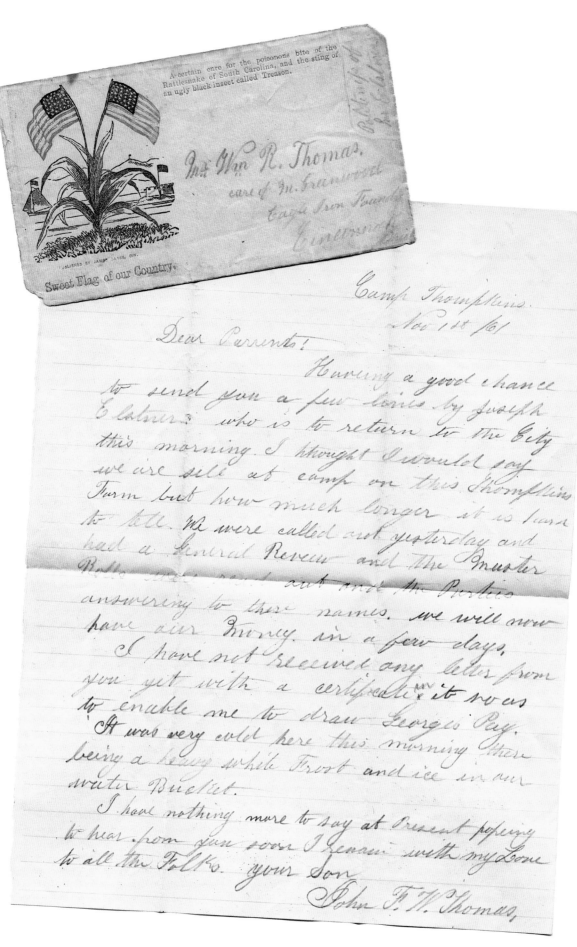

A certain cure for the poisonous bite of the
Rattlesnake of South Carolina, and the sting of
an ugly black insect called Treason.

Mr Wm R. Thomas,
care of M. Greenwood
Eagle Iron Foundry
Cincinnati

PUBLISHED BY JAMES GATES, CIN.

Sweet Flag of our Country.

Camp Thompkins.
Nov 1st /61

Dear Parents!

Having a good chance
to send you a few lines by Joseph
Elstner who is to return to the City
this morning. I thought I would say
we are still at camp on this Thompkins
Farm but how much longer it is hard
to tell. We were called out yesterday and
had a General Review and the Muster
Roll was called out and the Parties
answering to their names. we will now
have our Money in a few days.

I have not received any letter from
you yet with a certificate in it so as
to enable me to draw Georges Pay.

It was very cold here this morning there
being a heavy white Frost and ice in our
water Bucket.

I have nothing more to say at present hoping
to hear from you soon I remain with my Love
to all the Folks. your Son
John F. W. Thomas,

40
Group of Union
envelopes, c. 1863.
Letterpress-printed
paper, each 3–3¼" high

41
Union envelope,
1861. Hand-colored
letterpress-printed
paper, 2¾" high.
Published by James
Gates, Cincinnati, Ohio;
and handwritten letter,
1861. Pencil on lined
paper, from John F. W.
Thomas to his parents

41

My cane, my pocket change, this ring of keys,
The obedient lock, the belated notes
The few days left to me will not find time
To read, the deck of cards, the tabletop,
A book and crushed in its pages the withered
Violet, monument to an afternoon
Undoubtedly the unforgettable, now forgotten,
The mirror in the west where a red sunrise
Blazes its illusion. How many things,
Files, doorsills, atlases, wine glasses, nails,
Serve us like slaves who never say a word,
Blind and so mysteriously reserved.
They will endure beyond our vanishing;
And they will never know that we have gone.
         Jorge Luis Borges, "Things" from *Selected Poems*
(New York: Viking, 1999), 277.

chapter 19

Unintended Survivors

IN 1959, I was walking downtown along the west side of Second Avenue. It was a sunny day in early spring and the weather was chilly. Passing the Ukrainian National Home and the Deutsches Dispensary, I noticed in the bright sunshine that the cold air had caused the interior of B & H Dairy Restaurant's window to cloud and trickle with condensation. The steamy sight was a welcome residual of winter. B & H was, and still is, the bastion of potato pierogi, respite from the cold for the hungry on a budget and those just craving lima bean soup. Tiny and narrow, its counter seats about eight diners and its cooking side is purposeful and productive in cramped space. As I ambled south, I passed two Yiddish theaters, Ratner's Bakery, Block's Drug Store, and Schacht's Smoked Fish Shop. This neighborhood was unyielding to change and I was just taking it all in.

I got to the variety store between Sixth and Fifth streets and stopped to look at the casually and causally arranged window. The display hadn't been changed, in a commercial sense, in years. The proprietor's sole gesture toward public outreach meant that something was added to the window, but nothing was ever replaced. The interested passer-by could observe dynasties of dead flies and dust, defining the edges of generations of added wares. The previous summer's addition to the window had been an inflated beach ball, now a sagged pouch. In a fit of pre-Christmas zeal, someone had put a miniature Christmas tree atop a corner pile. The tree was about three feet tall. It was actually a tree branch painted white, positioned vertically, imitating the stance of a tree. Its support was an embossed domed steel base that had been enameled glossy green in the spirit of the season. New York City apartment dwellers celebrate inventively, usually taking into account the ratio of dwelling space to Christmas tree. Looking at the tree, I realized that tiny green buds had emerged at the crotch of each white branchlet. Was there a nurturing condensation phenomenon on the west side of lower Second Avenue that nourished living branches masquerading as dead trees as well as hungry people? Had sufficient condensation seeped into the domed base to start a new life cycle? What was going on here? If ever there was an unintended survivor, this was it. What a quiet and unattended resurrection. I had a moment of cosmic consciousness. I wanted to stand in the middle of the sidewalk and yell, "Stop! Come over here. Would you look at this?" At the same time I realized that the object of my epiphany was something no one else on the street would care about.

I have since thought about unintended survivor objects. Tangent to the budding branch, there is a realm of excellent objects of unimpeachably stately form that were manufactured to be destroyed. The survivors here under consideration were conceived to possess considered grace and striking beauty that was never meant to last. From the get-go, everyone knew that the express function of these objects would reduce their handsome forms to ash, fragments, rubble. Those that survived did so because they were never used. They may have been put away as gifts, but were never given or opened, or were squirreled away for emergencies that never occurred. Stashed away so well, some of these things may not have seen the light of day for decades, perhaps were never thought of again or were put away in a spot later forgotten, or maybe the occasion for their use never arose. In the case of others, they may have been used, landed in a safety zone after missing their mark, or were narrowly missed themselves. Some of the forms were to be terminated in one dramatic flash, for example target balls, projectile fire extinguishers, figural fireworks, and lightning-rod balls. The dissolution of others is slightly more gradual. Nonetheless, the forms of figural soaps and candles, mosquito coils, wax sewing fruits, and sugar skulls are conspicuously altered with use. With the passage of time and use, less and less of their material substance remains.

THE GREATEST fiesta in a country of fiestas, *Todos Santos*, is Mexico's collective *Los Días de los Muertos* (Days of the Dead): October 31, November 1, and November 2. Church relics are displayed throughout Mexico, and death is portrayed humorously, in every

1
Sugar skull packaged for transport from vendor's stall at La Feria Azucar, Morelia, Mexico, 2003. 8" high

2
Coffin with sugar skeleton (closed and open), 2003. Sugar paste, royal icing, and paper hinges, 3" high. Morelia, Mexico

3
Swaddled sugar skeleton resting on sugar coffin, 1995. Sugar paste, royal icing, 2½" high. Oaxaca, Mexico

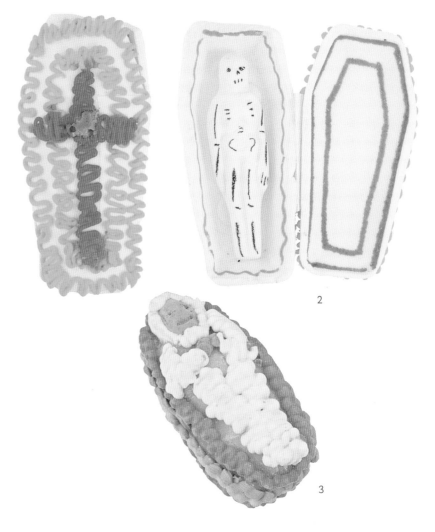

2

3

conceivable stance and activity of the living, in folk artifacts found in the markets. The vanities of life are portrayed in the spirit of the continuity of life and death. In a merger of present and pre-Christian times, the dead are welcomed back to their families. Family-centered graveside reunions and feasting with music were folk-religious practices of pagan Rome, early Christianity, and the pre-Columbian Indian cultures that coalesce in Days of the Dead. They reaffirm the interactive connection of the dead as intermediaries with the divine on behalf of the living. What the austere inscription on the lace bobbin dictates, Mexican culture advocates, remembering *death in the midst of mirth* and vice versa. However, in Mexico there's no asceticism. There are formal categories of observance.

Sugar-paste skulls are unique artifacts of *Los Días de los Muertos*. Part social history, part material culture, part religious narrative, these objects are so physically exigent that they must be celebrated. Called *calaveros*, the edible skulls are staples of *ofrendas* or *altares de muerto*, the table of offerings composed by families to welcome the spirits of their departed ancestors for annual tribute by means of favored foods, personal mementos and photographs, incense and candles, flowers, tobacco, liquor, fruits, and sweets.

Remarkable grace and excellent artistry, in distinctive regional variety, is uniquely conveyed in the short-lived *Alfenique* consumable *calaveros* and *calaveritas*. *Alfenique* is both the style and the method of working confectioner's sugar, egg whites, and lemon juice into an edible moldable paste that is cast into ceramic molds and subsequently elaborately iced. The craft is learned by children working at home beside their parents in a cottage industry that is passed on generationally; it is practiced by men and

women. In April, artisans begin laying down the supply of *Alfenique calaveras* for markets in late October. Lemon juice keeps the white sugar paste from oxidizing yellow before the *calaveras* reach the *altares de muerto*. The term *Alfenique* is also used to describe small sugar animals and a baroque, wedding cake style of architectural decoration; but its most notable application is the extravagant edible rococo skull that symbolizes the life-death continuum.

4
Group of sugar skulls, 1995–2003. Sugar paste, royal icing, and metallic foil, 1¾–3¼" high. Ocotlan, Puebla, Patzcuaro, and Morelia, Mexico

5
Group of sugar skulls, 1975–2003. Sugar paste, royal icing, and metallic foil, each approximately 1¾" high. Ocotlan, Puebla, Guanajuato, Atlixco, Oaxaca, Toluca, Patzcuaro, and Morelia, Mexico

4

It has a bronze covering inlaid with silver,
originally gilt;
the sides are decorated with open work zoomorphic
panels depicting events in the history
of an unkown religion.
The convoluted top-piece shows a high
level of relief articulation
as do the interworked spirals at the edges.

The ball at the center, visible
through the interstices of the lead webbing and the elaborate
copper grillwork,
is composed possibly of jelly
or an early version of water,
certainly a liquid, remarkably suspended
within the intricate craftsmanship of its encasement.
    Billy Collins, "My Heart" from *The Art of Drowning*
(Pittsburgh: University of Pittsburgh Press, 1995).

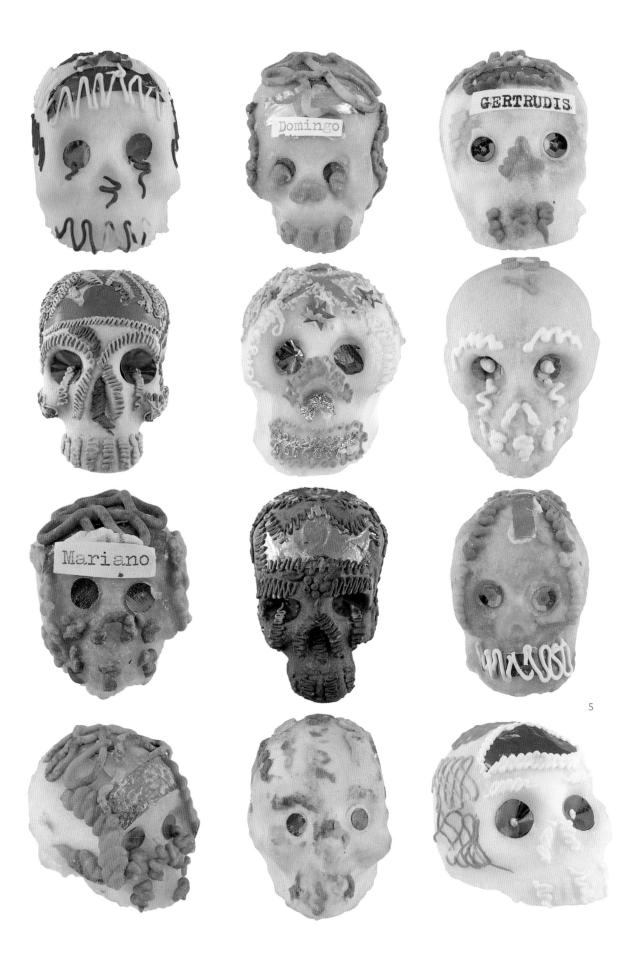

5

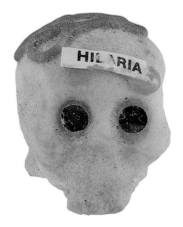

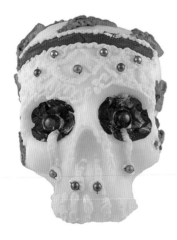
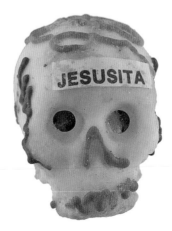
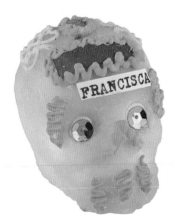

Respectful preparations for the traditional rituals of communion with deceased family members begin in late October with the cleaning, repairing, painting, and decorating of family graves. Weeds are pulled, decorated crosses are set, *ofrendas* are built, and *cempasuchil* (orange marigolds) and *mano de leon* (magenta cockscomb) are placed in anticipation of All Hallows' Eve (October 31), All Saints' Day (November 1), and All Souls' Day (November 2). For special acknowledgement, with local variations, the dead return in categorical groups: those who died in accidents, by violence, by drowning, warriors, women who died in childbirth, children who died without baptism, baptized children, and all other adults. Those who died within the last year are given special reverence and often their own *ofrendas*. The *ofrendas* are constructed with careful attention to what pleased the dead in life. The sequential formality of arrival is not echoed in the *ofrenda* styles, which tend to be creatively individual and idiosyncratic, reflecting family tastes. The dead visit, absorbing the essence of the feast, and then the family partakes. Some parts of the feast are carried to the graveside. Golden *cempasuchil* petals mark the path from cemetery to home.

Alfenique calaveros are edible memento mori of exquisite beauty and exacting craft that reflect the interface of the living and the dead. They are the quintessence of the feast of family remembrance, bittersweet devotions, which are given to children to eat with their names written on the *calaveros* forehead in flavored icing; and from lover to lover, much as candy valentine hearts are given in North America. There is surpassing intricacy and transcendent grace in the mounded *calaveros* at the markets against a backdrop of tons of marigolds and cockscombs and thousands of decorated wax votive candles to be illuminated, one for each soul.

6
Group of sugar skulls, 1975–2003. Sugar paste, royal icing, and metallic foil, each 1¾" high. Ocotlan, Puebla, Guanajuato, Atlixco, Oaxaca, Toluca, Patzcuaro, and Morelia, Mexico

7
Sugar skull, 2003. Sugar paste, royal icing, and metallic foil, 14" high. Toluca, Mexico

8
Sugar skull, 2003. Sugar paste, royal icing, and metallic foil, 22" high. Toluca, Mexico

7

8

WAX IS A resinous substance, allied to fats and oils; it is solid until heated to its melting point. There are animal, vegetable, and mineral waxes. Wax is found in the secretions of insects (beeswax) and plants (palms, myrtle, bayberry), and in spermaceti (the waxy ingredient resulting from crystallizing sperm-whale oil); it is derived from petroleum. It is used for casts, ointments, emollients, laxatives, and is most familiar as the principal ingredient of candles.

Wax has long been used to coat sewing thread. Usually it is contained in a small box that is slotted so thread may be drawn through the wax without coating fingers or becoming embedded in foreign matter. Generally, textile conservators, fabric restorers, and bookbinders prefer beeswax to paraffin (petroleum-derivative wax). Wax strengthens sewing thread against breakage, it eliminates twisting and knotting, and it lubricates, assuring thread tension and minimizing friction so that thread easily slips through what is stitched. A cube or small block of wax is ideal for the job, and with use becomes terminally perforated and thread cut. Pieces fall away and wax crumbles. Each drawing of thread diminishes the substance of the wax. In 1939, fine little wax fruits were made, to cheer the seamstress, in boxes of a dozen. The fruits were meant to be pierced and sliced into oblivion, unless, of course, they were never used.

IN ANCIENT times, rush lights were the archetypal candles. In ancient Egypt, they were made by impregnating the pithy center of papyrus-related reeds with melted tallow that had been rendered from the suet of cattle and sheep, enabling a modicum of light. Bundles of these reeds became the first torches for use in temples, homes, and for guidance in traveling through darkness. They provided clouded, smoky illumination accompanied by malodorous effusions. Ancient Romans also used tallow torches, and later olive oil, in their clay oil lamps. In the Middle Ages, beeswax was discovered to burn cleanly when a wick was inserted within a wax block. In Colonial America, the annual task of dipping tallow candles was replaced, in some locations, by bayberry wax and spermaceti candles, all of which were harder than beeswax and, when compared to tallow, smokeless, sootless, and odorless, and made by pouring into tin molds rather than repetitious wick dipping. In the 1830s, Joseph Morgan invented a candle-molding machine, taking the tedious responsibility of candle making out of the kitchen. In the 1850s, paraffin wax was distilled from crude-oil residues, making it the most economical clean-burning candle fuel, to which stearic acid was added to raise its melting point and hardness. In 1879, the light bulb put the candle into the shadows for general illumination purposes.

9
Segmented box of sewing wax fruits to coat sewing thread, 1932. Colored cast wax, printed paper label, and cardboard, 4" across. Germany

10
Thanksgiving Day turkey candle, 2000. Painted wax, 3" high

11
Boy birthday candle, c. 1950. Wax with paint, 2¾" high. Tavern Novelty Candles, Socony Vacuum Oil Company, Inc.

12
Muerte Santisima votive candle (to be lit on each of the first nine days following a death with an accompanying prayer), 2002. Painted wax, 4¾" high. Mexico

9

10

11

12

Votive lights were among the candle's first uses, and they are still used in churches and cemeteries throughout Mexico on October 31. Candles also set the stage for romantic dinners, symbolize ceremony, and mark celebrations as well as mourning. Tapers, column candles, and figural candleholders have at times given way to literal figural candles. Stearic acid is essential to the production of figural candles, since it causes wax shrinkage upon cooling and aids release from the mold. It also increases opacity and intensifies dye colors. The acrid smell of burning tallow has been substituted by myriad cosmetic and aromatherapeutic fragrances. The addition of Crisco to candle wax during the molten phase facilitates scent throw for that gift-shoppe smell.

In the late nineteenth and early twentieth centuries, folk-magical, colored figural candles, principally made in New York and New Orleans, were advertised throughout the United States, along with pamphlets on how to employ them. Spiritual suppliers offered male and female forms, hands and other body parts, paired figures, and animals with an amalgam of instructions and spells drawn from the Kaballah, Christian practice, and African, European, and Caribbean magical traditions. Many figural candles are uniquely hand-worked and exquisitely beautiful. They vaporized with use. The only survivors are unused.

The wax figure longevity award goes to a nine-inch ancient Egyptian striding male. He is a survivor from 1580–1085 B.C. of the lost-wax process, also called *cire perdue*, or bronze casting. In this process, a detailed three-dimensional wax model is sculpted and then encased in clay, gypsum, or plaster. This mold is then heated, the wax melts and drips out of the mold, and is "lost," leaving the sculptural void to be filled by molten bronze. As the bronze cools, it hardens. The mold is then broken to reveal an exact metal form of the ghost footprint of the wax. This figure never made it to the encasement phase and continues to stride into the future.

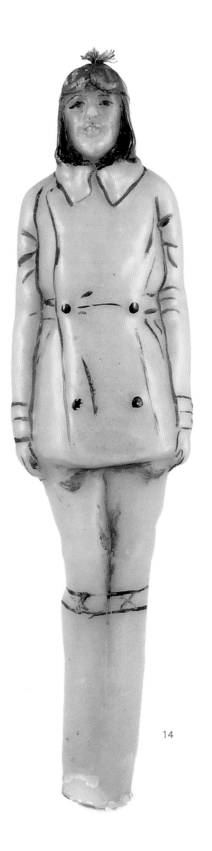

13
Ancient Egyptian striding male figure, 1580–1085 B.C. Wax, 10¾" high. © Christie's Images Limited 2003

14
Amelia Earhart candle, commemorating her solo transatlantic flight from Newfoundland to Ireland, c. 1932. Painted wax, 8" high

Figural candles have been used in religious ceremonies and magical rites as well as celebratory events (birthdays) and occasional commemorative incidents (Amelia Earhart's Atlantic crossing in 1928). Both figural candles and figural soaps can be objects of extraordinary beauty and grace. They have different purposes but share a common ingredient and outcome—their material presence dissipates with each use. Although wax is primarily composed of fatty acids, it differs from fat in that it is harder and less greasy. Both wax and fat tend to be yellowish and remain solid when not heated to their melting points. Both are less dense than—and are not soluble in—water.

INSCRIBED CLAY containers from 2700 B.C. have been unearthed in Babylonian excavations. Their inscriptions spell out the ingredients of the soap contained within: fat and ashes, boiled. Archaeological finds from ancient Israelite sites include soapy mixtures of oil and ash. The Ebers Papyrus of medicinal recipes from 1500 B.C. includes a topical soap concoction of vegetal and animal oils mixed with alkaline salts. In Ancient Rome, around 300 B.C., Mount Sapo was a principal site of animal sacrifice. Rain washed both wood ashes and tallow down into the earthy clay along the shore of the Tiber River. Washing soil from one's person or garments was easier here than elsewhere, aided by the soapy clay.

Improvements on basic soap-making formulae were guarded local secrets. In France, Italy, Spain, and Portugal, saltwort ashes were used for making lye (a concentrate of potassium or sodium) and olive oil was plentiful. Consequently, a finely defined soap craft thrived there from the seventh century A.D. through today. In America, those who remember their grade-school history lessons will recall that Colonial women performed the tedious annual task of rendering and straining animal fats, mixing the decoction with potash (wood ash), stirring and stirring for homogeneity, then pouring and cutting soap cakes. The two basic ingredients of soap were, and still are, lard and lye.

The commercial soap industry has synthesized a vast array of cosmetic ingredient additives from which to choose your own indulgence. Although the ingredients are not listed on Ivory soap packaging, they are available from the Food and Drug Administration. One needn't wonder any longer: *99 and $^{44}/_{100^{ths}}$ percent pure* what? The "what" is tallow, palm and coconut oil, and three sodiums. Ivory soap floats because the mixture is aerated before hardening. Procter & Gamble keeps the price of a bar of Ivory soap low by leaving out glycerin, a natural moistur-izer, sodiums are caustic and dry the skin. Commercial soaps generally contain petroleum products, synthetics, cosmetic fragrances, and dyes (that are periodically banned as carcinogens). The more

expensive the soap, the greater the number of ingredients appearing on the label, or the fewer in the case of small companies that offer environmentally friendly, usually handcrafted soaps, made only from pure, vegetable-based ingredients.

A book of puzzles and crafts projects called *Fun for a Rainy Day* occupied some of my eighth year. One activity to which I returned repeatedly was carving polar bears out of cakes of Ivory soap. The Ivory ursine was not possible to carve from harder soaps that chipped away and cracked in unintended spots. The sculpture was never as perfect as the illustration, nor as sleek and flawless as molded figural soaps, but the project taught lessons in fortitude and subtraction.

Most soap is sold as an oval or rectangular solid cake, sized to be easily graspable when wet and slippery. One bar is hardly distinguishable from another in a lifetime of hand washing . . . except for figural soap. In 1896, the Andrew Jergens Soap Company of Cincinnati molded soap figures for William McKinley's presidential campaign. The figure is a standing child with an adult face, wearing only a printed string tag that states in green ink, *I am for McKinley and sound money. Ain't you? No 16 to 1 for me.* The pinkish soap was a figural campaign giveaway. This one was stashed at its peak moment, unused. Literally, figural soaps are poised, intense little sculptures in the round, representing people (usually nudes, children, babies) posed so that heads and limbs don't break off but wear away, eroding smoothly. If not used, they harden with age and become visually indistinguishable from ivory or bone or hard rubber.

15

16

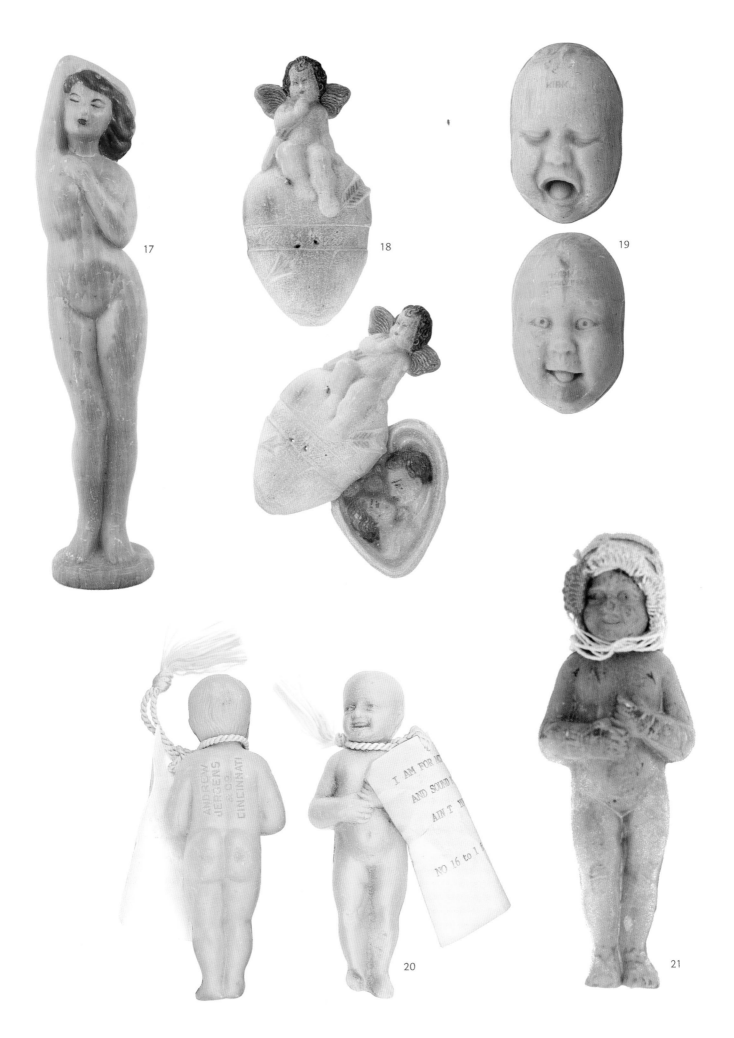

17

18

19

20

21

MOSQUITO COILS, like incense, are burned to release aroma for an effect on one's environment. Incense comes in sticks and other forms that are not unusual. Mosquito coils that are made in Asia are packaged in boxes with a graphic character and iconography that refer to the matchbox labels of the late nineteenth and early twentieth centuries. Two green disks are inside, and each disk neatly separates into two pre-formed, nested spirals. The perfect economy of form rivals the egg. The box also contains a tiny aluminum stand with a pointy tab that balances the sperm–headed innermost bit of the spiral mosquito coil by means of a pre-formed slot. These short-lived coils and their packaging are needlessly superior in their format. When the outermost tip of the tail of the coil is ignited, the coil smolders to a fine residual ash within eight hours, protecting all within range of its vapors—usually slumbering—from mosquito-borne diseases.

As an efficient mosquito repellent, the coils are used for months, but the non-pesticide material of a single coil releases particulate matter the equivalent of more than one hundred cigarettes. The active pesticide agent is octachlorodipropyl ether, or S-2,

which, when inhaled, exposes users to bischloromethyl ether BCME, a potent lung carcinogen. Neither S-2 or BCME are listed ingredients on the packaging, and both are banned in the United States, yet the coils are sold for use here . . . in packaging of rare appeal. Seeking to avoid mosquito-borne illnesses, millions worldwide are trading in a chance at West Nile virus for lung cancer.

Besides going up in smoke, mosquito coils and candles have petroleum vapors in common. Smoke and exhaust from petroleum products emit carcinogenic vapors. Simple paraffin candles contain eleven compounds that are toxic air contaminants; consider their mixture of synthetic fragrances not necessarily intended for combustion with chemical fixatives, bleached fiber wicks, and synthetic glosses that exacerbate the hazards of a romantic evening by candlelight. Dangerous over time, in comparison to being engulfed in a cloud of poisonous smoke, mosquito coils and paraffin candles have gradual poisonous effects. Toxic objects in elegant presentations and irresistible packaging should never meet their dates with fate. They should be the souvenirs of another age.

22
Mosquito coils and box (front and back), 2000. Vegetal and chemical compound, and printed paper box, 4¾" high. Blood Protection Company, Ltd., Hong Kong

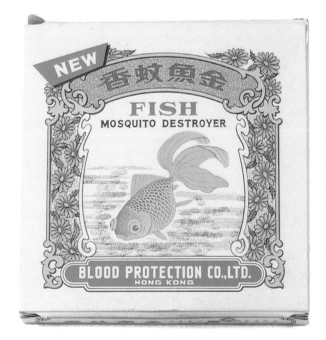

PROJECTILE FIRE extinguishers are artifacts of striking fairness of form and radiant beauty that were meant to be used in one explosive moment. Projectile fire extinguishers were stored in wall-mounted holders in stores, homes, public buildings, factories, government institutions, schools, hotels, and wherever visible and handy remedy to the danger of fire was needed from 1860 through the 1940s. Also called *fire grenades* and *dowsers*, they were ornate colored glass orbs of rare delicacy and beauty that were conceived to be expended in one explosive, fire-extinguishing, hurling motion. One surprising advertisement shows a female figure smashing two grenades together over a parlor fire. The fluid chemical contents were either carbon tetrachloride or salt water (with ammonia or bicarbonate of soda). Both types had an airtight seal on the globe to prevent evaporation and dissipation over time. Instructions directed the user to *Throw at Base of Flames!* Advertising from an 1884 dowser label states that the contents of the smashed grenade immediately vaporize into *immense volumes of fire extinguishing gas in which combustion cannot possibly exist.*

23

24

25

23
Harden star fire grenade, c. 1895. Blown molded glass with whetted lip, 8" high

24
Clyde Glass Works fire grenade, c. 1870. Blown three-mold glass with whetted lip, 6½" high. Geneva, New York

25
Harden's fire grenade, 1888. Blown molded glass with whetted lip, 4" high

Carbon tetrachloride is extremely toxic in one exposure. As steaming vapor it produces phosgene gas and is readily absorbed through the lungs and skin, affecting the liver, brain, and kidneys. Formerly used in fire extinguishers, as a dry cleaning agent, propellant, and in refrigeration coolants, carbon tetrachloride is currently banned from these uses in the United States. Ammonia vapor is no less toxic. The glass dowsers came in blown, blown-molded, or pressed glass in intense stained-glass colors. Some are ribbed or faceted, with impressed-glass messages that glow, gem-like, from their holders. They are among the finest examples of beautiful objects that were made to be destroyed.

Occasionally, when an old industrial building, abandoned warehouse, or unused factory is rehabilitated, these singular luminous, chromatic, patterned orbs or smooth pear-shaped glass vessels are still in place in metal wall hangers, brass mounting brackets, or wire racks. Meant to be *Functional, Safe, Handy, Portable, Powerful, Ever Ready and Cheap . . . the Irresistible Conqueror of Fire* (H. H. Gross Company, 1882 AD), they turned out to be works of art.

ROUND, COLORED, lustrous, individually crafted glass spheres that are scaled to fit in the palm of one's hand have great visual and tactile appeal. The fragility of Christmas tree ornaments is simultaneously seductive and off-putting, as are fire grenades for other reasons. Target balls and lightning rod balls are close cousins to projectile fire extinguishers, but they are rarer. Although less fragile, they were put directly into harm's way, expected to be smashed concussively by the impact of ammunition or shattered by a lightning strike. Around 1866, in the Boston area, glass target balls for sportsmen were used competitively to replace animate bird and bat targets. Glass target balls were mechanically tossed sixty feet high, in a consistent arc, by a trap that equalized competition, particularly when multiple hidden traps were employed, adding unpredictability to the mix.

In the 1920s, clay pigeons, which could be clearly seen to be fragmenting, replaced glass balls for skeet or trap shooting; but during the tenure of the glass target ball, it was made in grand variety and pattern. Target balls were all blown or blown-molded glass in colors that range in rarity from amber to olive green, blue-green, cobalt blue, clear, purple, and yellow, roughly the colors of blown and blown-molded glass inkwells. Blown-molded balls have a rough uneven neck that confirms their separation from the blowpipe. Blown balls have pontil marks. The patterns and lettering on blown-molded varieties reduced the possibility of ricochet and uneven thickness,

26
Hayward fire grenade, c. 1895. Blown molded glass with turned lip, 6" high. New York State

27
Target ball with a shooting man pictured in a circle, c. 1875. Two-part blown-molded light green glass in a quilted pattern, 3" high

28
Target ball, c. 1870. Olive green blown glass with aperture at pontil mark, 2" high

26

27

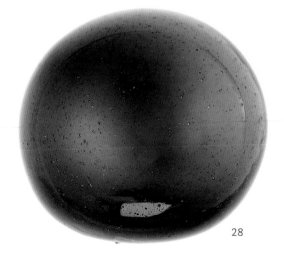

28

29

increasing the chances of scoring breakage on contact. Feathers and sand filled some target balls for that realistic sensation of shooting a bird in flight. Filled balls were corked and cemented at the neck or pontil mark. Annie Oakley's targets of choice were glass balls filled with silk ribbons that Buffalo Bill chased on horseback and sometimes caught as they fluttered earthward. She targeted streamer-filled glass balls while standing on the back of a galloping horse. She extinguished flames on a swiftly revolving wheel and shot glass target balls behind her, aiming at reflections in her Bowie knife blade.

Glass target balls that remain have been found stored in warehouses or barns, packed in sawdust in the barrels in which they had originally been shipped. They have also been recovered at the bottoms of lakes or ponds on the grounds where competitions were held, and where water cushioned the landing of balls that had been missed. And they were stored in boxes of Christmas tree ornaments that have been passed down through generations.

29
Bogardus-type target ball, c. 1877. Two-part blown-molded cobalt blue glass in a quilted pattern, whetted lip, 3¼" high

30
Target ball, c. 1870. Two-part blown-molded clear glass with whetted lip on fill hole, 2¼" high

31
Post Toasties Annie Oakley badge, 1947. Press-printed steel, 2" high

32
Target ball, c. 1870. Two-part blown-molded clear glass with whetted lip on fill hole with silk streamer fill, 2¼" high

33
Feather-filled target ball, c. 1885. Blown glass, dyed feathers, and wax stopper in pontil hole, 2¾" high

30

31

32

33

IN AUGUST 1963, my husband and I were driving through Vermont, looking for the country property that we found two weeks later in New York State. As we entered a candidate farmhouse, a violent summer storm materialized. The air in the room in which we were standing literally turned blue. A smell or feeling of ozone lodged between my eyes and a smashing crack shook the house. The house had been hit by lightning. No fire ensued because the house had been protected since the 1850s by a lightning-rod system that conducted, by means of copper wires, the blast of electricity into the ground. After his kite and key experiments, in 1789, Benjamin Franklin wrote: "the power of metallic rods to extract and conduct lightning into the earth, with safety to the buildings to which they are affixed, is now generally known" (Maryland State Archives). Thank you, Ben Franklin. For decades there was controversy over ideal rod

34
Chestnut shape lightning rod ball, c. 1890. Ribbed aqua glass, 4" high

35
D & S ten-sided lightning rod ball, c. 1900. Robin's egg blue glass, 5" high

36
Reyburn, Hunter & Foy lightning rod ball, 1875. Amethyst glass with caps, on copper rod; ball 5½" diameter; rod 36" high

34

35

36

length and whether pointed rod tips were more effective than blunt tips. But, by the late 1840s, traveling, competing lightning rod salesmen were commodifying these safety devices, replacing home-grown, self-installed devices with high-class factory-made systems and a variety of models that sported weather vanes and a profusion of blown molded-glass lightning rod balls. Emphasis on safety, house pride, and confidence in a scientific outlook were the selling points.

The diameter of glass lightning rod balls averages out at a bit over five inches, about twice the diameter of target balls. They have distinctive rough blown-molded edges on their top and bottom collared apertures, through which the lightning rod slipped. Companies that were already manufacturing home-canning jars and glass insulators for telegraph companies made the original lightning rod balls. Lightning rod ball designs are audaciously colored

and distinctively patterned with deep bold embossing; often the manufacturer's name is part of the mold design. Milk glass, Vaseline glass, ruby glass, ambers, olives, cobalts, oranges, pastels, and purples were molded in opaque, transparent, and translucent quilted patterns, globes, crescent moons, and stars; ribbed, grape, and melon designs; and faceted styles that departed from the strictness of the sphere.

Lightning rod balls were architectural jewels on the roof of one's home, except when a massive electrical charge hit the vertical rod that was belted by a decorative glass orb. The emission of sparks and the descent of lightning often exploded the ball. That was what informed you that lightning had struck while you were out. And that is why later models were made of glazed, high-fired molded ceramic materials, why an orange Diddie Blitzen ball sells for more than three thousand dollars, and why there are reproductions on the market.

37

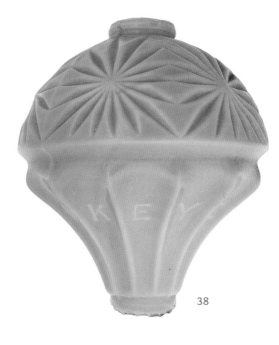

38

39

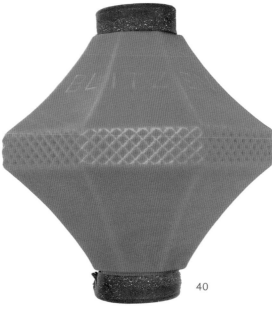

40

37
Reyburn, Hunter & Foy lightning rod ball, 1875. Amethyst glass with caps, 5½" high

38
Hawkeye lightning rod ball, 1898. Blue milk glass, 5" high

39
Goshen lightning rod ball with moon and star pattern, c. 1900. Milk glass, 5" high

40
Diddie Blitzen lightning rod ball, c. 1900. Opaque orange glass with caps, 4" high

41

ALL NEW DESIGNS **TATTOOS**

SLIGHTLY MOISTEN THE SKIN, THEN PRESS ON

42

FIRE AND WATER are the means of destruction, respectively, of the last two categories of unintended survivors: cockamamies and figural fireworks. The etymology of the word *cockamamies* is from *decalcomania*. Since the 1930s, decals have adorned homely, inanimate surfaces; and cockamamies—sham tattoos—have been transferred to skin. Mostly applied by children, cockamamies satisfied their innate need to decorate themselves. They could be purchased as novelties, typically four or five transfers on a penny sheet with instructions to cut the tattoos, not to tear them apart. They also came as prizes packaged by savvy manufacturers with candy and bubble gum. Cockamamies with lettering or labels were printed backward on the paper sheet for readability on the skin.

Two methods of application prevailed. Cockamamies that were one-color, line-image transfers from tissue paper instructed the user to *slightly moisten the skin, then press on.* An expeditious tongue swipe would do the job. Too much water caused the ink to run, an irremediable problem, the first "less is more" lesson for many kids. Multicolored cockamamies instructed the user to *dip the transfer in warm water for 15 seconds to loosen the design, then slide the decal into the desired position; that's all, have fun.* If you leave the decal soaking for more than fifteen seconds, the transient water-soluble glue runs away. The school of hard knocks rules in cockamamieland. These transparently inauthentic tattoos birthed a linguistic twist yielding up the adjective *cockamamie,* meaning absurd, hare-brained, silly, ridiculous, or without value. *Harmless colors, washes off with soap and water* was mostly true. Used cockamamies went down the drain in sudsy bubbles. Any that remain were never used.

FLYING FORTRESS U.S.A.   AMERICAN SOLDIER

U.S. SAILOR   CAPITOL DOME

43

44

45

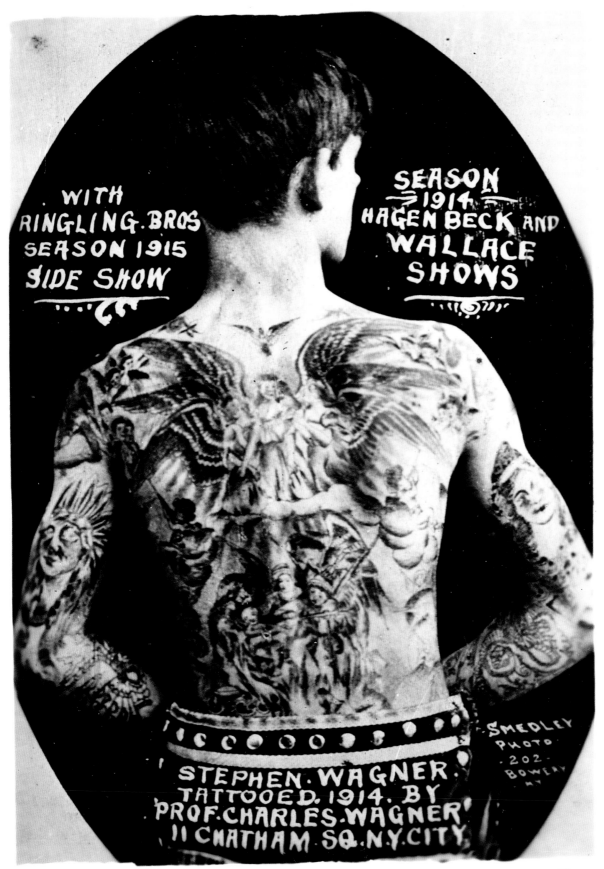

WITH RINGLING. BROS SEASON 1915 SIDE SHOW

SEASON 1914 HAGENBECK AND WALLACE SHOWS

STEPHEN. WAGNER. TATTOOED. 1914. BY PROF. CHARLES. WAGNER. 11 CHATHAM. SQ. N.Y. CITY.

SMEDLEY PHOTO 202. BOWERY NY

41
Cockamamie ad, 1940.
1¾" high. Johnson Smith & Company catalog, Detroit, Michigan, page 391

42
Display card with cockamamies, 1942.
Printed paper and card stock, 10" high. USA

43
Leaf of cockamamies, a two-cent candy store purchase from a display card, 1946. Printed paper, 3" high. USA

44
Fierce Indian Cockamamie applied, 1968. Printed transfer, ¾" high. USA

45
U.S. Navy cockamamie applied, 1942. Ink, 1¾" high. USA

46
Photograph of Stephen Wagner tattooed by Professor Charles Wagner, 1915. 7" high

46

FIREWORKS CAN be momentarily figural when their gunpowder-propelled sparks are aloft in precisely staged and colorful profusion, taking shape as fountains, portraits, flowers, hearts, stars, torches, bow ties, flags, flares, and cascading waterfalls. Pyrotechnic extravaganzas are brief and immaterial. Assembled with precision and generations of formulae, prior to ignition the fireworks that produce ephemeral, breathtaking, and awesome beauty often look like bandaged homemade bombs.

The fireworks that I admire are figural when unspent. They start out as small paper sculptures of chickens or pagodas or aircraft carriers or airplanes or any object artfully rendered. Igniting the wick is meant to prompt the hen to lay multiple colorful combustible eggs or to send the plane screaming through space while firing turret and wing guns. The wick of the aircraft carrier sends showers of sparks forward and upward from the guns, a lift charge sends the glowing aircraft hurtling skyward to explode loudly, and the carrier itself is impelled forward to extinction by an internal burst charge.

Most of these fine figural fireworks were made in China, the country that discovered gunpowder in the tenth century A.D. Hunan alchemist Sun Si Maio is credited with extracting minerals from ore to make firecrackers and their subsequent variations. His tools and workbench are the property of the state. Many inventions, including printing ink, the compass, and gunpowder, hence fireworks, were a by-product of the Chinese alchemical pursuit of wealth by the transformation of base minerals into gold. Chinese beliefs that sparks were an omen of good luck, that smoke purged the atmosphere, and that loud sounds frightened evil spirits led to their use as celebratory necessities, along with the rapid development of the chemistry and technology of fireworks in China. The export of fireworks to Europe and Asia in the mid-1800s was big business, and Chinese immigrants to America brought their enthusiasm as well as their customs of celebration. Records tell of

47

fireworks accompanying the signing of the Declaration of Independence and the inauguration of George Washington.

I can be as astonished as the next guy during a pyrotechnic display, but I am awestruck at the fineness of design of schematically correct paper tanks and aircraft carriers that were made to destroy themselves, fragmenting to smithereens. Consider the printed caution on the bottom of the aircraft carrier: *Emits Showers of sparks. Use only under close adult supervision. For outdoor use only. Light fuse, put it on water and get away. Made in China.*

Hopefully, the body of water is larger than a bathtub and the user is wearing running shoes and knows which way to run. Currently there are five fireworks production facilities in China. They are in Liuyan (Hunan), Beihai (Guangxi), Jianghu (Jiangsu), Donguan (Guangdong), and Pingxiang (Jiangxi). Their press kit notes that "safety standards have become increasingly important," and that factories exporting fireworks to the United States are involved in a fireworks improvement program. The goals of the program are to "improve the safety of fireworks distributed in the United States." Anyone want to tour a factory? What of the quality of product shipped elsewhere? Should we cleave to Grucci or Sousa fireworks now that they've had their explosions? Collecting excellent latent incendiaries and never reducing them to ash is probably the best idea.

Unexpected survivors are objects that never fulfilled their obliterating destinies. They live on in the protective custody of shadowy corners, caches, hidey-holes, stashes, and in my collection.

48

49

Thus there is in the life of a collector a dialectical tension between the poles of disorder and order. Naturally, his existence is tied to many other things as well: to relationship to ownership ... to a relationship to objects which does not emphasize their functional, utilitarian value—that is, their usefulness—but studies and loves them as the scene, the stage, of their fate.

Walter Benjamin, *Illuminations* (New York: Schocken Books, 1985), 60.

49
Tank fireworks,1973. Printed paper, gunpowder, and mineral compound, 3" long. China

50
Battleship fireworks (top and side), 1999. Printed paper, gunpowder, and mineral compound, 7" long. China

50

Lists, Mental Collections, and Deaccessioning

chapter 20

WHEN TRAVELING in countries in which I have passing familiarity with restaurant parlance, I easily dismiss menu translations into English. In countries in which the language is utterly unfamiliar, I am grateful for a clue. No matter how lame their translation into English, my Bulgarian, Urdu, Amharic, or Kazakh is worse. I have impulsively ordered food from untranslated menus by the way the word or phrase echoed against my incomprehension, allowing destiny to play its part. This resulted in my introduction to head cheese (*sultze*) in Karlsruhe, Germany, in 1960; rhubarb soup (*barbarossa*) in Krakow, Poland, in 1965; bits of roasted burro (*carne asada*) en route to Palenque, Mexico, in 1974; and blood pudding (*sanguinaccioni*) in Tarragona, Spain, in 1980.

There are those menus that are translated into sixteen languages but only one dish is available anyway, and others in which the dish is unfamiliar and translates as the same phrase in sixteen languages, for example, *hoppel poppel*. I never found out what that dish was because I didn't order it, although it was on menus throughout Czechoslovakia, Romania, Hungary, and Poland.

Diligent and sincere attempts to translate dishes into English sometimes wax poetic, but they can also be innocently hilarious in beguiling and imaginative ways that evade even an English-speaking comedian.

Seated at a tourist restaurant for a snack with my husband and our two young children in Rome in 1981, I perused the menu that had been poorly translated into the four most common tourist tongues. It was then and there that I started my list of really funny mistranslations that evoke images heretofore unimagined. Falling off the seat laughing was no longer enough for me. The restaurant in Rome had banana splints and scrumbelled eggs listed along with many minor misspellings. My list has grown to include synchronized enchiladas, life oysters, beaars, chicken soup with pee, hot spicy egg pant, freg legs, filet on a wire, potatoes jumped in butter, divorced fried eggs, fried cow chunk oaf meat, thinly sliced friend in butter, fried eggs mounted on tortillas, four small bears on ice, and many more.

> Well, 'slithy' means 'lithe and slimy' ... You see it's like a portmanteau—there are two meanings packed up into one word.
> Lewis Carroll, *Through The Looking Glass*, 1872.

Clustered in Bay Ridge, Bensonhurst, and Borough Park (parts of Brooklyn) there are more shop names ending in "Plus" than in any other part of the world. "Plus what?" you might ask. Locksmith and Keys Plus (key chains?), Sari's Wigs Plus (false eyelashes?), Moe's Appetizing Plus (pets?), Chrystina's Shoes and Boots Plus (sandals?), Bagels Plus (lox?), Glenda's Purses and Bags Plus (knapsacks?, luggage?, gloves?, hang gliders?), Nail Plus (tooth? earring? screw?), Francine's Department Store Plus (yet another department?), et cetera.

No Bed, Bath and Beyond, these mom 'n' pop shops generally fit within the surmise of the square footage of small neighborhood stores. What is the meaning of the "Plus" convention in this part of the world? Do they think that eager and curious shoppers will come in to find plus what? This is the beginning of my next list. I will be in the good company of a list of drive-ins and delis with 'n' in the middle like Eat 'n' Run, Chew 'n' Sip, Git 'n' Go, Pop 'n' Taco, Browse 'n' Bite, Strips 'n' Chips, Chat 'n' Chew, and Peel 'n' Eat.

I admire Joanne A., a British rare-book dealer, who for many years has kept a list of acronyms. In November 1980, Joseph N. started his list of inventive first names in documented use, in a standard address book. He filled it, then successive books, with 2,800 names over a 25-year period. Joseph N. has an ear for music and offbeat names; beside each name is a parenthetical indication of sex. He does not search for these names as much as they find him. He wins

the prize for "stick with it" among list makers. After reading the list carefully, I think there is more going on here than inventive spelling. These names are not simply exotic ethnic variations; they burst with creative purpose. The imagery brought to mind by my associations with salient syllables couldn't possibly be the inspiration for naming a child, for example, *Chevelva* (Chevrolet and Velveeta?). I am prepared to leave the origins and inspirations of these crescendo names a mystery, content that Joseph N. is their chronicler; the task of refining the list is a sufficient a challenge as the whole is worthy of publication. Here is a sampling: AntJuan (M), Bexham (M), Bruklin (F), Cauleen (F), Chaniquqwa (F), Claudyjah (F), Cloyde (M), Dabreeda (F), Dandyas (M), Diamondque (F), Doequick (M), Dysick (M), Ellagance and Signifigance (sisters), Female (rhymes with tamale) (F), Glammorgucci (F), Jarvious (M), Jazzmen (F), Jreamasia (F), Kamealeoun (M), Kanard (M), Kashka (M), Lataschia (F), Neumonia (F), Phanta-Z (F), Starletta (F), Syphilus (F), Turkoise (F), Urethera (F), Urina (F), VaGina (F), Vonteego (M), Yanketta (F), Yvondne (M), Yizziyya (F), and the possible cousins (F): Marquashia, Star-quasia, Tykakeecha, and Yackesha.

Professionally rendered store signs with garbled or misleading messages also get my immediate and complete attention. A sign inviting entrance to a camera store in lower Manhattan, immaculately rendered in **Helvetica Bold** font, reads *Se habla Espanol*; *parlez-vous Francais*? We speak Spanish; do you speak French? In that case, how can we communicate? Do you have a translator? What was the brain behind the message thinking? Was the sign maker just taking dictation? Was the sign maker ignorant of Spanish, French, and English, just rendering abstract symbols? In Brooklyn, I recently passed a sign that read *Phones for the Corebian*.

1
Phones for the Corebian (before closing) misspelled sign on Church Avenue in Brooklyn, New York, 2000, 40" high

2
Phones for the Corebian (after closing) misspelled sign on Church Avenue in Brooklyn, New York, 2004, 40" high

2

In 1965, driving across the country, I started a list of soft ice cream stands with names like Dari Curl, Kreamy Korner, Cup 'n' Cone, Dari Tweet, Kris-O-Crème, and Sani White, and supermarkets with names like Pack & Pay, Pick & Pack, Pick & Pay, Pic & Wheel, Shop & Go, Shop & Bag, Stop & Shop, Stop & Stuff, Stop & Stare, and In & Out. These lists are works in progress. In Las Vegas, there are signs describing displacements in time and place, pseudo-locations that have to be noted. In the Venetian, the Grand Canal is on the second floor, imagine that. At the Excalibur, you can take the *Escalator To Medieval Village*, and then you can take a *Bridge To The Sahara*. Displacements is my current favorite list. Over 'n' Out.

I've been toying for years with the idea of writing a list of collided and elided words that have been said to me in casual conversation. In describing his agitated and thwarted state of mind upon returning from the Motor Vehicle Bureau, a friend said *flusterated*. *See you tomorning* was my son Jesse's way of saying goodnight. A waiter described the preparation of a mushroom appetizer as *saulteed*. A student told me that her encounter with the university bureaucracy was *oblitherating*. This list is a latent collection owing to my not having a pen and paper with me every time I hear a choice elision. I make a mental note of it, later forgetting; hence I have to make a decision to be peaceful about momentary in situ amusement or to inscribe with vigilant purpose. This goal applies as well to a list of indelible smells that are irremediably and irredeemably connected to memory, for example, the aroma of oil of clove and the dentist's office.

The most primitive purpose of a list is memory prompting. Lists are a handy form of acquisition when you find personal satisfaction in a category of objects that you keep picking up on, yet you can't or don't want to take the objects home. Where photographic representation is possible, it just doesn't encapsulate the concept; in fact, it misrepresents it. Lists satisfy the collecting urge and are free. Lists themselves are material, though barely so. Literary insights about collecting are another kind of list. The entries are a bit longer but there aren't many, since few writers have a clue. There are other less material collections than lists, which don't cost money or require any space.

3
Soft Ice Cream stand, 1977, Weedsport, New York

4
Sign in the Venetian casino, 2005. Cast bronze, and printed plastic, 2005. 18" high. Las Vegas, Nevada

5
Sign in Excalibur casino, 1992. Printed plastic, 22" high. Las Vegas, Nevada

6
Group of leaf impressions in cement, 1987–2004. New York City

3

4

5

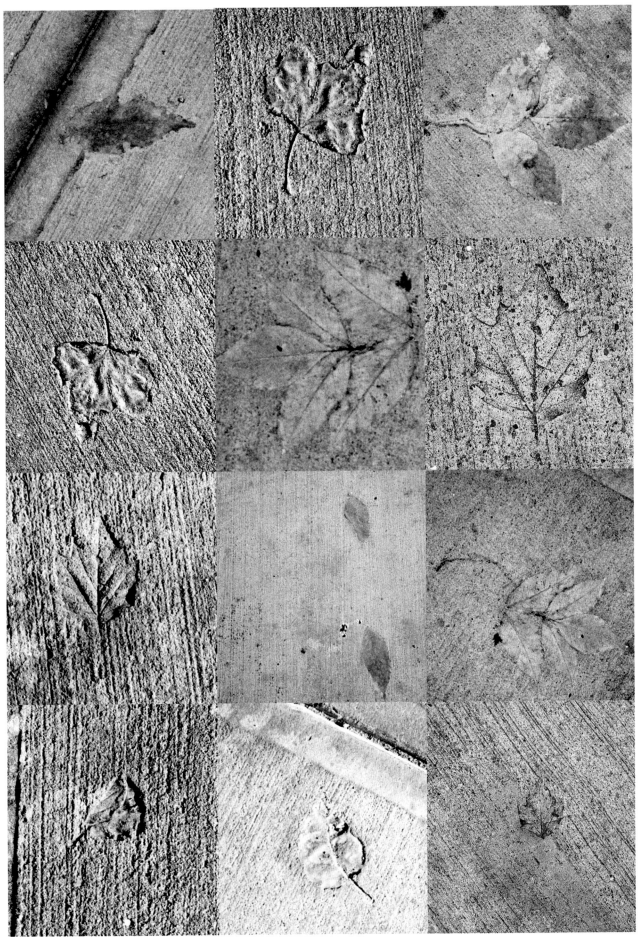

MENTAL COLLECTIONS are collections of those things that become yours because you remember them categorically. Cognitive possession, with conscious self-acknowledgment of collecting a visual stratum or subject matter is sufficient. An example would be New York City fossils. I am a walker in my city and look at everything, hoping for visual enthrallment. There are rare sections of sidewalk upon which the impressions of settled leaves remain from the moment they were newly paved, while the cement was still wet. On the southeast corner of West Houston Street and Sixth Avenue there are intaglio imprints of gingko and maple leaves, perfectly preserved vestiges from New York's Devonian period. At the intersection of Stuyvesant and Ninth streets there is a flawless tracery of pigeon tracks meandering across the city's Cenozoic era. On Fourteenth Street between Sixth and Seventh Avenues there are intricate outlines of serrated leaves nearly obliterated by Pleistocene chewing-gum wads.

A related MENTAL collection is of asphalt embedments that also happen by accident, but are more common than fossils in cement. Particularly at busy city intersections, such as Houston Street and Broadway or Thirty-fourth Street and Avenue of the Americas, pieces of hardware that are not essential to the forward motion of vehicles fall off and are subsequently run over by other vehicles. Asphalt has some volatility even in winter, and metal objects, including bottle caps, keys, and bricks, merge with the road surface, creating memorable echoes of Pompeiian relics. During the warm summer months you can watch it happen. Through the seasons you can observe familiar vestiges submerge as newer chunks of truck linkage top them off in a kind of slower LaBrea Tar Pit subsumption or glaciology.

7

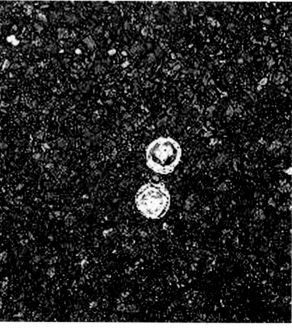

8

9

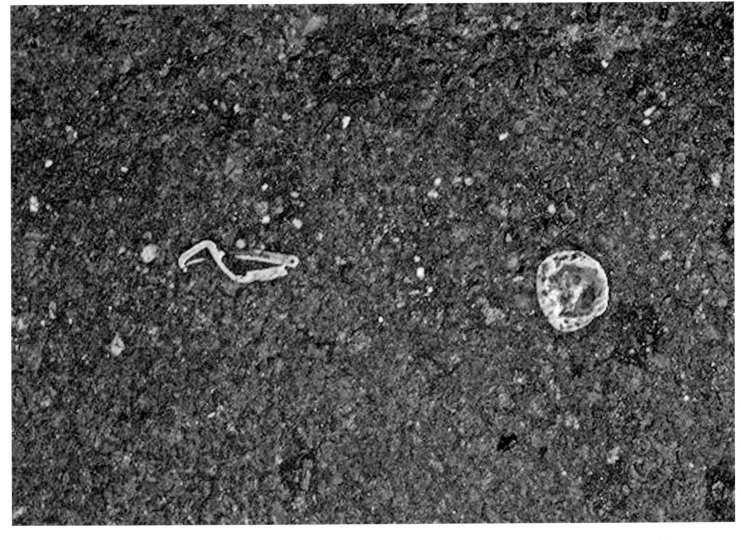

10

Signatures in cement don't happen by accident, but they can be a mental collecting source. Sidewalk sgraffiti, unlike graffiti, requires a patch of freshly poured cement. In the old days, before the USA was a twinkle in George Washington's eye, someone carved an *X* in the colonial Spanish stone pavement of Morelia, Mexico. There are incised messages in Roman pavements. There seems to be an irrevocable attraction of narcissists and lovers, lacking stone carving tools or skills, toward wet cement and the irresistible bid for immortality. Being a gambling woman, I would wager that the inscriptions outlast most relationships.

Another kind of mental collecting is of those material things that you want to keep in your memory because they are surprising in their varying forms but don't require the memorization needed for Renaissance art history. An example might be homemade birdhouses. My friend Dorothy G. and I share several MENTAL collections of objects that we have seen at antique shows and flea markets that are too physically cumbersome to actually collect (lithographed tin dollhouses) or are notably labor intensive in their making while being so astonishingly ugly that we would not want to own them (post-1950 sequined and beaded fruit). We add to these collections by pointing out examples of possible additions and discussing their qualities.

> But you leave traces of yourself with every decision you make, every fence you build, every tree you fell or plant, every quarter-acre you choose to irrigate or leave dry. In twenty-years' time, a self-portrait emerges, and it exposes all the subtleties of your character, whether you like it or not. The land and the shape of the buildings show precisely how much disorder you can tolerate, how many corners you tend to cut, how much you think you can hide from yourself. Neatness may reflect nothing more than a passion for neatness, or it may be a sign of small ambitions.
>
> Verlyn Klinkenborg, *The Rural Life* (New York: Little, Brown & Co., 2002), 91.

11
Group of cement inscriptions with footprints and tire track on cement sidewalks, 1999–2003. New York City

12
X markings on pavement. Incised marking in stone, c. 1550. Morelia, Mexico; spray paint on asphalt and incised cement, 2003. New York City

12

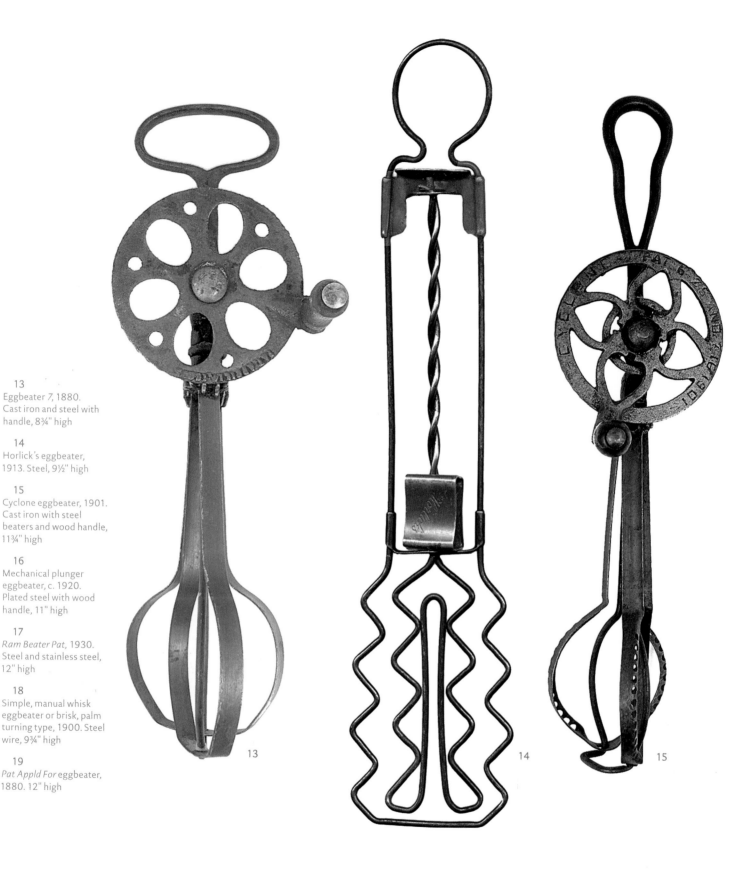

13
Eggbeater 7, 1880.
Cast iron and steel with
handle, 8¾" high

14
Horlick's eggbeater,
1913. Steel, 9½" high

15
Cyclone eggbeater, 1901.
Cast iron with steel
beaters and wood handle,
11¾" high

16
Mechanical plunger
eggbeater, c. 1920.
Plated steel with wood
handle, 11" high

17
Ram Beater Pat, 1930.
Steel and stainless steel,
12" high

18
Simple, manual whisk
eggbeater or brisk, palm
turning type, 1900. Steel
wire, 9¾" high

19
Pat Appld For eggbeater,
1880. 12" high

13   14   15

MY SHOULDA, COULDA, WOULDA collections are mental notes laminated with palpable regret that I hadn't acted on my earlier impulse to acquire certain objects. For instance, had I started in the 1970s, when eggbeaters of the past were affordable, I might have had the mightiest and most brilliantly sculptural collection of eggbeater models. I believe that mechanical eggbeaters have even more varieties of form than the better mousetrap. There are hand-operated egg macerators, whippers, aerators, agitators, blenders, combs, churners, emulsifiers, homogenizers, serraters, and mixers. These have single and paired paddles, blades, oars, arms, and wands with up-and-down, rotary, or undulating action; or reciprocal or alternating motion that can be spiral or looping or wavy or you name it. Instead, I have seven

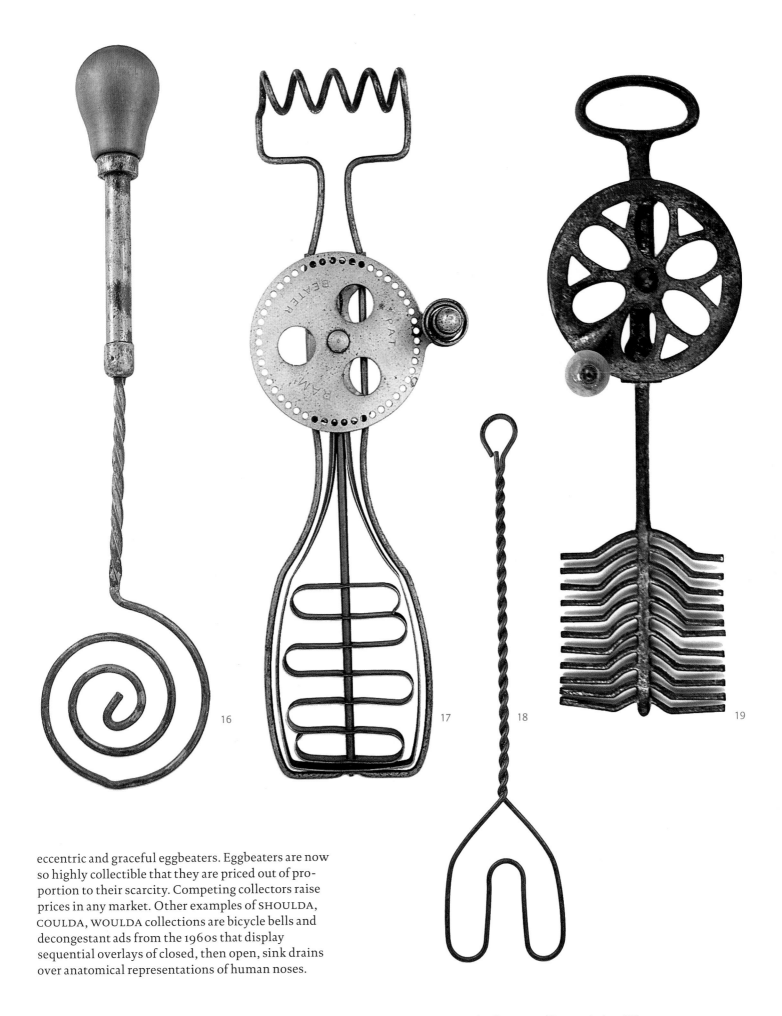

16   17   18   19

eccentric and graceful eggbeaters. Eggbeaters are now
so highly collectible that they are priced out of proportion to their scarcity. Competing collectors raise
prices in any market. Other examples of SHOULDA,
COULDA, WOULDA collections are bicycle bells and
decongestant ads from the 1960s that display
sequential overlays of closed, then open, sink drains
over anatomical representations of human noses.

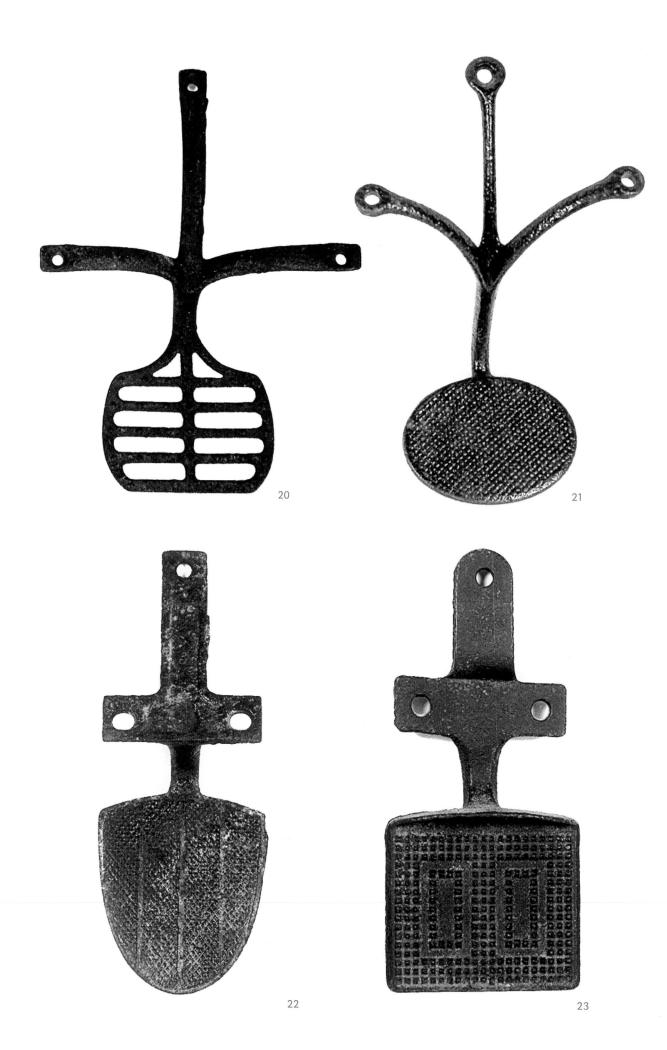

20

21

22

23

24

25

ANOTHER CATEGORY of mental collection is the SHOULDNA DEACCESSIONED group. I have sold m duplicate Coca-Cola trays and *Horrors of War* card without a sense of loss. My husband and I have giv extensive collections to several worthy museums because we believed that the objects and artworks belonged in the public domain where they could b seen and enjoyed by multitudes. However, I often think wistfully of my former collection of cast-iron carriage, buggy, and wagon steps. They have become a mental collection with visiting privileges. They were donated to the New York State Historical Association where I still believe they rightfully belong, but I miss them.

20
Rounded rectangular buggy step with oval cutouts, 19th century. Cast iron, 4" high. USA. NYSHA #0058.2001b

21
Oval buggy step with raised crisscross design, 19th century. Painted cast iron, 9" high. USA. NYSHA #F0056.2001B

22
Spade-shaped wagon step with raised crisscross design, 19th century. Painted cast iron, 2½" high. USA. NYSHA #F0061.2001

23
Square wagon step with raised dot design, 19th century. Painted cast iron, 3½" high. USA. NYSHA #F00602001

24
Squared carriage step with *V* cutouts and closed center, 19h century. Cast iron, 8" high. USA. NYSHA #F0051.2001a

25
Rectangular buggy step with cutouts, 19th century. Cast iron, 3½" high. USA

For Better or For Worse

27
Tank candy container
(bottom), 1944. Glass,
candy pellets, and waxed
card stock, 1¼" high
label. Victory Glass
Company, Jeanette,
Pennsylvania

28
Roz Chast cartoon, *The
New Yorker.* 10¾" high.
© The New Yorker
Collection 2003 Roz
Chast from cartoonbank.
com. All Rights Reserved

I SOLD MY collection of AUTOMOBILE HOOD ORNA-MENTS to prove to myself that I could sell a collection that wasn't comprised of duplicate and redundant examples. The sale was a result of upgrading. It was not a triumphal experience; cascading riches did not offset the vacancy. Collectors go through stages of enthrallment with their objects; some relationships are profound lifetime love affairs, others are infatuations, some are flirtations, and every possessive permutation in between. Relationships to objects evolve over time, and spheres of control are mutable relative to changes in our lives. The particular flavors of our charms against chaos may mutate. So, deaccessioning objects that are no longer pertinent to the collector is the other side of the collecting coin and one way in which what goes around, comes around.

THE SALE OF my vintage GLASS VEHICLE CANDY CONTAINER collection is an example of premature deaccessioning. I wasn't sufficiently distanced from the collection; I was just testing myself. Moved by the décor of Maxwell's Plum and by Werner Leroy's passionate attention to what I had lovingly amassed, I underestimated my connection to it. Nevertheless, the tale had a happy ending because my brother Bill then gifted me with his more extensive collection that had been kept in storage. He had truly outgrown it. I was the appreciative recipient and my collection has been upgraded. The epilogue is that I recently found a Victory Glass Company toy tank complete with World War II candy pellets and the intact waxed-paper-label seal on the bottom. The seal was exactly as I had remembered it from sixty years ago.

THE PRAXIS OF COLLECTING
Enthusiasts collect objects of ardent fascination that are compelling beyond possible physical flaws. Imperfections may not even be noticed at the smitten stage. Seasoned collectors accept that there may be a more perfect example of any prized possession out there. In the quest for collateral bounty, a more complete or excellent sample of something one already owns may reveal itself, at the right price. Acquisition of the specimen just referenced is called *upgrading*. Deaccessioning of the less perfect piece may come next.

Every time I saw Andy Warhol, who was a world-class collector, he would ask, "So Marilynn, what are you collecting now?" Andy never deaccessioned anything, that is, until the ten-day auction of his estate at Sotheby's, New York, in 1988. Andy went for quantity. Duplication wasn't an issue; more was better, more and more cookie jars, Native American jewelry, wristwatches, glass refrigerator containers, Art Deco figures, basketry, carpets, Folk Art, contemporary art, tribal art, carpets, and much more. April 23 through 30 and May 1 and 2, 1988, spotlighted the range and breadth of Andy's collections. He would have been gratified to see it all laid out. Sotheby's six *Andy Warhol Collection* catalogues are themselves a collection. The 30 million dollars realized from the auction sales of his collections funded the Warhol Foundation and the Andy Warhol Museum. Unlike Andy, most collectors upgrade and deaccession during their lifetimes, enjoying the action and purification of refining and honing beside the invigoration of acquisition.

The broad spectrum of the Warhol cornucopia was, for the most part, distinguished by Andy's fine eye, as evidenced by the quality of the individual pieces. Each piece of the reclusive Collyer brothers' Harlem fortress was garnered as an integral piece of ballast to stabilize Homer and Langley Collyers' bizarre lives. Their compaction of newspapers, discarded baby carriages, and miscellaneous detritus of New York, as material insulation from the outside world, is an extreme case history ending posthumously with 360,000 pounds of pack-rat junk delivered to the New York City dump. The Collyer collective embodied the bricks-and-mortar of seclusion, and theirs became the cautionary tale of mothers like mine. In singular ways, the Collyer brothers and Warhol were out-of-the-box thinkers. The destinies of the Warhol and Collyer hoards demonstrate that society prizes some objects over others, and that those who orga-

MINIATURE WARTANK
· MADE IN GLASS ·
FILLED WITH CANDY PELLETS
INGREDIENTS: SUGAR, STARCH, CORN SYRUP,
CERTIFIED COLORS. CONTENTS ¼ OUNCE OR MORE
MANUFACTURED AND PACKED BY
VICTORY GLASS CO.
TOY DIVISION   JEANNETTE, PA.

HOME ECONOMICS

You guys never throw anything out! You're starting to live like the COLLYER BROTHERS.

What IS this? It's a drawerful of TWIST TIES!!

And this—it's a museum of BAND-AID BOXES!!!

But they're made out of metal.

Old grocery receipts, dried-out rubber bands, jar lids, a box of yellowing Christmas cards without envelopes, coupons that expired in 1979, keys to nothing, packets of soy sauce from God knows when, deposit slips from vanished banks, MORE twist ties ...

You can't save all this stuff...

It's PATHO-LOGICAL!!!

WAIT!!!

DON'T THROW THAT PURSE AWAY!

But it's ripped! It has gum and a bobby pin stuck to the bottom!! It's DISGUSTING!!!

I'll take it to the shoemaker. Maybe he can repair it.

That's BATS. He'll charge you fifty bucks. For that, you can get a brand-new purse at Macy's!

But I LIKE that one.

And, besides, why should I give Macy's my business? They don't know me or your father.

28

nize their accumulations in ways that others perceive to be coherent have a chance at informing future generations. Selectivity and organization impart the key differences between random piles of stuff and collections.

When the inner connoisseur is ready to deaccession belongings, if close family members concur, I believe that prized objects should be given to the public domain, if that is practical. If a museum curator or director grasps the finer points of one's amassed bounty, the public-at-large should be afforded that brush with material culture. Museums, we hope, will preserve and serve up these objects to future audiences who will see them with the perspective and clarity that distance affords.

If personal predilection is not at ease with a museum destination or one's finances preclude donation, antique dealers have been known to trade or give credit on desirable items, although most would rather buy your collection dirt-cheap from your heirs and thus make a posthumous fortune on your visual wisdom. Interested collectors are sometimes inclined to trade or to buy outright at fair value. They have reciprocal concerns about their own personal museums, and perhaps a conscience to deal with. Circumstances depend upon who you know and your innate-charm factor. The trick is to avoid all buyers who, like J. Wellington Wimpy of Popeye cartoon fame, would "gladly pay you Tuesday for a hamburger today." Antique and art values are unequivocally and conclusively established at auction where no one has a special advantage and collectors, dealers, museums, and galleries, and those seeking gifts for others are all bidding against each other for the same object. If what you are attempting to deaccession for the best price is not of Christie's or Sotheby's caliber, eBay is an excellent alternative. The broadest possible target audience is out there, looking specifically for your possession by category search. Basic prerequisites for access to this market are a computer and credit viability. The range of bidders is limited only by computer literacy and interest in what you are offering up.

A means of deaccessioning, in a way that makes one comfortable, is essential to most collectors as the reverse of the accumulating coin. "Pack-ratism" becomes a cumbersome and tedious life of disarray after awhile, unless unlimited space is available or you're a Collyer brother. Exchanging downgraded pieces and specimens that no longer fascinate is part of the diaspora of trophies that is the flux of the collecting world. The dense profusion of objects laden with potential at an antique show could not happen unless bounty was deaccessioned. Flea markets, those concentrated moorings of possibilities, wouldn't exist without the turnover of stuff. The visual procession that is an auction completes a temporal orbit of ownership. Detachment by the collec-

tor from an object of former fascination is part of the assembly of choices that one has when one is an accumulator. It comes with the territory. I think of the willing placement of objects on the market as a relief, an aria, as so many phoenixes rising from the flames. It is only a sundering and irremediable dissociation if the collector is not ready for the separation, as when a well-intentioned mother cleans out cabinets or an unsympathetic spouse severs the zealot's grip. The relection can be likened to receding water creating permanent dry land.

> One has only to watch a collector handle the objects in his glass case. As he holds them in his hands, he seems to be seeing through them into their distant past as though inspired.
> Walter Benjamin, *Illuminations* (New York: Schocken Books, 1985), 61.

If you've read this far, chances are that you are either a collector or trying to understand one. Collecting is analogous to gastronomy; it's about savoring, ingesting, assimilating. What is collected is accretion; it becomes part of you, enhances your being. Collectors of books feel that they own the knowledge between the covers; it is theirs by ownership and osmosis. No matter what is collected, the collector is imbued with the arcane qualities and unique graces of his oddments. That sublime state is evidenced in a nimbus of inner peace and knowing rather than a proprietary stance. The acquisition of a desired article conveys this state. Collecting exists on the border of memory and commerce, the spline of the private universe and the public world from which the object derives. It is about emotional investment lubricated by rarity, narrowing down the voluminous possibilities of remembrance and reality. Without pride, collectors move from the general to the particular and back again; they co-opt without self-consciousness. They may have epicurean predilections but can be intoxicated or humbled or unnerved by the most improbable leavings to the uninformed eye. Collecting is not a team sport, but, in the aggregate, all collectors are complicitous in history's service.

The armature of a collection is the collector. Looking hard at the praxis of collecting, it is about self-authorizing action in the service of aggressive sensitivity backed up by one's own Talmudic rules. It is about binary vision. It is about exigency, strategy, and valor; it is not an allegory. Caught *in flagrante collecto*, a devotee can be observed unblinkingly separating the essential from the incidental while asking eloquently nuanced questions that could not necessarily be formulated about any other aspect of his or her life.

29
Combination spitoon and footstool (lid closed and open), c. 1870. Burled maple intricately inlaid, velvet upholstered top and ivory melon ball legs, enclosing a Bennington spitoon, 9" high

29

chapter 21

So What's Left?

IN 1974, at OK Harris Works of Art, I had just finished installing the title lettering on the wall for an exhibition of twenty-five exemplary nineteenth-century quilts. I was standing near the top of a twelve-foot ladder erasing the lettering guidelines when a group of culture seekers arrived, shepherded by an imperturbable leader who asked how long it took me to make the quilts.

Most Americans have functional sense about the material support systems of their lives. Kitchen appliances, circuit breakers, computers, VCRs, DVD players, iPods, and cell phones that connect them to the world, so they know the functional subtleties as required by use. What has immediacy in their lives has value. Many of those who make token museum or gallery visits for a dose of culture expect to be mystified and don't make use of basic comprehension of cues, clues, and labels to interpret the works that they see. They abdicate common sense. Recognition of nineteenth-century styles notwithstanding, reading the five-inch black lettering on a white wall would have been a tip-off that I didn't make the quilts. Yet many people who lack sensitivity to material objects have a trophy painting over a sofa and a collection of something, or know a close family member who amasses goods. Collecting isn't necessarily about aesthetic judgment. It's about defining personal domains, choosing one's own precincts of concentration, embracing, organizing, and refining, strategic reconnaissance, and giving safe haven.

SUBSCRIBER NAME

Marilynnn Karp

Ms. Marilynnn Karp

Marilynn G. Kerr

Marolyn Karp

MR. & MRS. MARILYNN KARP

DR. MARILYNNN KARP

Marilyn Karf

MARILANN KARP

M. KARP!

Dr Marilynnn Karp

Dr. Marilynnn Karp

To : MARILANN KARP

Dr. Marilynnn Karp

Dr. & Mrs. Ivan Karp

Pay to the order of: Maril Ynn

Dr. Marilynnn Karp

Mr. and Mrs. Marilynn Karp

Dir: M. Kaup

IVAN + MARILAND KARP

Mr. Ivan Karp
Drive Marilynn Karp

Ivan & Maryland Karp

MARILYNN KART

MARILYNN KARPAKA

Prof. Marilyn Darp

Mrs. Marilynn Karp Aka
Mrs. Marilynn Pereira Gelman

Ivan & Maryland Karp

MR MARYLNN KARP

Professor Mary Karp

Mrs Mari Lynn Karp

1

SINCE CHILDHOOD I have collected misspellings of my name (understandable since the spelling of my name is infrequent, but still, not my name). Taken from envelopes received in the mail—Marylnn, Mary, Marland Marailan, Mari Lynn, Maryland, Mary-lin, Mariland, and Marilynnn. My favorite in this category is *Marilynnn Karp has just been declared a $1,666,665.00 winner.* I know of one other Marilynn, married to a catalogue-sales telephone order taker who was astonished to finally have taken an order from a Marilynn with two nns. He explained the origin of the spelling of his wife's name and mine, having researched it. My parents took my name out of a 1939 name book that proffered the atypical spelling. Then, I married Ivan Karp and began collecting misspellings of his shorter and simpler names. Fewer letter variables, contrary to logic, offer greater opportunity for misspelling. A sampling of the yield is Bivan, Ivah, Invr, Iva, Ivar, Igor, Fran, Ivik, Ivang, Stan, Irva, Irving, Ivor, Siva, Nan, and Irvang. In the Karp category we have Kaup, Carp, Caart, Kart, Kang, Darp, Prak, Kalp, Zarp, Kilp, Karpaka, Karrp, Kapp, and Kapaga. There is a Dr. and Mr. Marilynn Karp, an Ivan Karp a.k.a. Marilynn, and a Mr. Ivan Karp and Driver Marilynn Karp. Clearly the sender knows who wears the pants in this family.

The need to collect is about fulfillment of one's own sense of personal acuteness, attainment, and achievement, not about any outside measurement, including aesthetics. Rare and formidable are the collections amassed by a collector with immaculate perception. The very best collections have a visual-conceptual balance that is unassailable.

The satisfactions of collecting are deep and urgent. Every object has a story to tell and every hoard is a biography. Collectors are goal-oriented, wily, and deliberate, and have imaginative reach. At the helm of a collection there may be a blandly conventional person or an idiosyncratic character or one apparently in a fugue state; be assured that there is singleness of purpose behind each façade. Collectors are heedless, undaunted, imperturbable, and self-reliant seekers with one eye on their mark. They literally and simultaneously embrace material culture and are enfolded by their collections. There is optimistic probity and a paucity of self-consciousness in a collector's first speculative inquiry to a dealer about detected loot. Anticipation is seismographically perceptible; there is something of the gleeful pirate running fingers through swag in connecting with one's objective.

Hi M,
You have been on my mind this last week. We have changed the windows and I have been the dutch cleanser girl chasing dirt and rearranging everything. Of course this affords deep communion with beloved treasures and thinking of new ways to reconfigure them; always the most fun. I took on the pens and pencils of daily life, cups everywhere in the house, in various project boxes etc. and rearranged the working tools. I put new categories in picnic tins, consolidated plants, redistributed the watering cans, etc etc. It is awesome. I spent all weekend here . . . could not leave it for Fire Island.
D.
D. G. to M. G. K. in e-mail, July 2003.

2

3

LATENT COLLECTIONS are laden with potential but have not been fully actualized. Most of them are comprised of common objects, at least familiar, but unnoticed unless regarded from an unconventional angle. Allied by a concept and a community of their kind, they reveal something about culture and about the nature of collecting. My LEAPS OF FAITH collection is an example of a collection that ripened from latent to actual during the course of writing this book. Examples of the many faces of leaps of faith found in material objects now reveal themselves regularly. The collection is no longer dominated by concept; the concept is a unifier.

A latent collection has a concept that is clear, but the population of qualifying objects needed to flesh it out it hasn't yet been located. My BEFORE AND AFTER postcards are a latent collection in the process of transmuting into an actual collection—caught in the act of becoming. They're really hard to find. Mount Rushmore has been captured on a horizontally divided, textured vellum postcard by the Black Hills Novelty & Mfg. Co. In one glance, the viewer may observe the undistinguished face of the raw mountain in the upper section of the card, and in the lower portion its transformation by Gutzon Borglum, from 1927 to 1941 when he died, into gargantuan likenesses of George Washington, Thomas Jefferson, Abraham Lincoln, and Theodore Roosevelt. The sculptor's son Lincoln finished the work after Gutzon's death. The portraits are in the Black Hills of southwest South Dakota and are visible for sixty miles.

An example of a vertically divided before and after postcard is a glossy Victorian humor card from the Vaudeville Comic Co., Anglo Series, c. 1890. A straw-hatted suitor standing on a rain barrel in her yard embraces the maiden through her window on the left panel of the card. In the right panel, his platform gives way; the suitor plunges into the rain barrel, and the maiden throws her hands up in shock and despair. The title of the card is *Goodbye Little Girl.*

Another before and after postcard incarnation is sequential. A picture of a monument or landmark taken during the day may be reissued depicting the same view illuminated at night. Serial vellum-finish postcards of Natural Bridge, Virginia, were issued by Tichnor Bros., Inc., of Boston, Massachusetts, calling it *one of the seven natural wonders of the world,* claiming also that it is *fifty-five-feet higher than Niagara Falls,* and advertising hotel as well as cottage accomodation *open all year.*

126:—BEFORE AND AFTER, MOUNT RUSHMORE MEMORIAL, BLACK HILLS, S. DAK.

4

GOODBYE LITTLE GIRL.

756

Natural Bridge, Va.

Night Illumination. "The 4th Day". Natural Bridge, Virginia 15

6

7

8
Youth with mechanical
wings by Richard Thuss,
c. 1900. Copper, 13½"
high. Poland

9
Bleriot monoplane
cufflink commemorating
the first airplane crossing
of the English Channel
(July 25, 1909), 1909.
Coin silver, 1" diameter.
France

10
Youth surfing on Bleriot
monoplane by Carlien,
1909. Bronze, 25¾" high.
France

11
Bleriot monoplane
lighter commemorating
the first airplane crossing
of the English Channel,
1909. Brass, 2½" high.
France

12
Medallion comme-
morating aviation,
depicting Bleriot's
monoplane, 1909.
Bronze, 2¾" diameter.
F. Montagny, France

13
Medallion
commemorating
Admiral Richard E. Byrd's
conquests of the North
and South Poles (1926–
29), 1929. Stamped
Whitehead-HOA,
bronze, 3¼" diameter

In Poland in 1966 I bought a bronze sculpture from a *Desa* shop, a secondhand store. The objects therein had been vetted by the authorities and deemed saleable to tourists for export. This particular sculpture portrays a youth on a rocky prom-ontory, poised for take-off on one foot, with sturdy bronze triple-strut wings strapped to his arms and shoulders. No Icarus with wax-and-feather wings, he is confident and placid in his belted loincloth and bare feet. This became the mate-rial center of the latent HISTORY OF FLIGHT collection that my husband and I have discussed over intervening years. Since our middle European acquisition, we have spied a large bronze of a man fighting off threatening beastly birds, which we have dubbed No. 1 in the HISTORY OF FLIGHT collection, as well as a melodra-matic bronze of a huge bird and a man in heated battle, which we have claimed as No. 2 in the collection. This remains a latent collection because the sculptures weren't masterfully executed, and therefore we declined ownership. We did acquire an elegant bronze Art Nouveau sculpture of a graceful male figure surfing clouds astride the wings of a Bleriot monoplane. The whole shebang is kept aloft by three puffing cherubic winds. It is a bona fide work of art and has been revered for thirty-six years on our coffee table as No. 8 in the hypothetical and ongoing narrative history of flight.

The other pieces that comprise the material portion of this latent collec-tion are two commemorative medallions. One celebrates aviation, depicting an airplane gliding over bridges, cities, and fields. Above is a female nude laconically swimming through space—the spirit of flight? Above her, a large bird, looking like a cross between a duck and an eagle, soars masterfully. The other medallion commemorates the 1926–29 conquests of the North and South Poles by Rear Ad-miral Richard E. Byrd by depicting his plane, coming in for a landing between icy crags with a large eagle hitching a ride on top of the fuselage. Qualified examples of this narrative may take more than my lifetime to fill out, so the latent HISTORY OF FLIGHT collection may become an intergenerational latent collection. We're holding out for works of art here, not illustrations of a concept. Some collections are more latent than others.

THE IRREPRESSIBLE CALL OF THE OBJECT

There is a genus of slot machines in Las Vegas, made by Integrated Gaming Technologies that, when unplayed, standing at attention amid a battalion of other flashing slot machines, distinguishes itself by means of an audio track that murmurs "YoooHooo" into the passing crowd against the backdrop cacophony of actively jingling, tune-emitting slot machines. This attempt at snaring a susceptible slot player is ingenious as a gambling tool and the closest illustration I can offer someone who has never experienced the tug at a distance of what a collector feels when an object of interest reveals itself, often simply in vague outline or as a blur. The call of the object is irrepressible and happily, not universal.

Dorothy G. is drawn to objects made of the wrong materials. One part of her collection is comprised of picnic baskets and lunch boxes that are made of metal lithographed to look like wicker or raffia. Tradition carries through in the most unlikely ways. In fifty years, will anyone remember that, until the 1940s, wicker picnic baskets were an item? Will anyone picnic? Will the word *picnic* be obsolete? Another part of this rare collection is comprised of rocks made of glazed ceramic, wax, soap, cast metal, Styrofoam, cast polyethylene, plaster, papier mâché, sponge, carved and painted wood, and polyurethane. Three of her "rocks" are impressed with the date *1620*. Those of us tuned into American history trivia recognize 1620 as the date that the Pilgrims landed

14
Glass "ice" candleholders,1958. 2½" high

15
Lithographed tin "raffia" basket, 1928. 6" high

16
Lithographed tin "wicker" basket, 1932. 3½" high

17
Wax candle rock, 1989. 2" high

18
Styrofoam rock, 1977. 1¾" high

19
Plastic rock, 1984. 2¾" high

20
Painted plaster rock, 1981. 3½" high

at Plymouth Rock. I can accept these pieces as lame souvenirs of an American place; but her other rocks offer no clues to guide the curious. Most are not heavy enough to be paperweights. The eye may be fooled but touch belies the illusion; there is visual irony afoot. All of these ersatz rocks must be purchased, whereas genuine rocks are free. It is the witty ambiguity of their non-rockishness that is tantalizing.

One of Dorothy's subdivisions in the rocks subcategory is Rosetta Stones. These are made of various plastics, including a foam Rosetta Stone mouse pad. The Rosetta Stone was an ancient basalt slab found by Napoleon's troops in 1799 in Egypt. Bearing parallel inscriptions in Greek, demotic characters, and Egyptian Hieroglyphics, it enabled the decipherment of the latter, a monumental breakthrough in comprehending the culture of ancient Egypt. Now it is a computer accessory.

Dorothy G. also collects glazed ceramic ashtrays that represent motors, irrigation pumps, and other industrial equipment. These were produced by General Electric and other manufacturers as giveaways for their distributors. They were handy items endorsing brand recognition for use on office desks and in lunchrooms. Eventually they reached secondary markets and Dorothy's collection.

There is no accounting for why a category of objects has a singular resonance for the collector. Amie K. has saved and compiled every movie-ticket stub from every movie she has attended since April 11, 1996, when she saw *Grosse Point Blank* and realized that retaining the stub from each movie she saw made a tangible and gratifying connection. She had collected three hundred movie stubs by her twenty-third birthday.

I collect wait-your-turn tickets with numbers that indicate when one may approach a counter and make a request. Mostly bakery, butcher, and deli counter tickets, with an occasional Motor Vehicle Bureau wait-your-turn coupon, these numerical crowd routers keep those who wait calm. They maintain the illusion of an orderly queue and respect for fellow shoppers whether they deserve it or not.

Another field of ephemera to which I respond involves those menus, crossing all ethnic cuisines, provided by coffee shops that are open twenty-four hours a day, seven days a week. 24/7 menus vigorously flaunt an astounding array of offerings in New York City. The variety of foods available at any time reflects the aggregate composition of nationalities in this city and stands in polar opposition to the Big Mac.

21

22

23

24

25

26 27

25
Saved movie-ticket stubs, 1996–2005. 1½–2" high

26
Wait-your-turn ticket, No. 74, 2002. 2" high. Globe Ticket Company, USA

27
Wait-your-turn coupon, No. F060, Department of Motor Vehicles, 2003. 2½" high

28
24/7 Restaurant menu, 2003. Printed paper, four folds (side one), 11" high

28

The most profound enchantment for the collector is the locking of individual items within a magic circle in which they are fixed as the final thrill, the thrill of acquisition, passes over them. Everything remembered and thought, everything conscious, becomes the pedestal, the frame, the base, the lock of this property. The period, the region, the craftsmanship, the former ownership—for a true collector the whole background of an item adds up to a magic encyclopedia whose quintessence is the fate of his object.

Walter Benjamin, *Illuminations* (New York: Schocken Books, 1985), 60.

ROUTES TO THE PRIZE

Sometimes it's personally important and meaningful to compose a collection to which you are able to add consistently. It is not necessary to wait for a specific event, such as a flea market or antique show, to open. If movie-ticket stubs and coffee-shop menus are too lowbrow for you, take heart; life is a vast opportunity for collection gratification if you have priorities clearly in mind. Breakfast at a diner followed by a trip to the car wash or dining out with wine are fraught with effervescent possibility.

Diner place mats come in a wide variety of printed designs. Eve E., a therapist, uses the unprinted sides to type long, single-spaced, meaningful and funny letters to her friends. Used place mats are more personal than stationary. She collects them for redistribution and redirection to an alternative useful life, recycling destiny. The possibilities for categorical acquisition of place mats imprinted with maps or with children's puzzles and activities provide examples of another way of collecting paper place mats. Diners are a gold mine of possibilities,

without even considering perishables, the dishes, utensils, or anything that you could be arrested for pocketing. Charlotte G. collects imprinted napkins. Sugar packets are ever present.

Beside each diner cash register, business cards are usually stacked or posted on a nearby bulletin board for the taking, having been left by local tradespersons and businesses (likely diner regulars) for anyone in need of a house painter or carpentry, insurance, photography, automotive repairs, and real estate listings. Melia M. has collected these worldwide since she was a young child. She does not specialize. She has simply collected one of every business card that she has ever seen. Most of the enterprises that her cards represent are no longer viable, but she never intended to use them anyway. Unlike Melia M., I only resonate to portrait business cards, not limited to *hot, kinky coed* cards. Real estate brokers' cards, with a photograph of the sales associate meeting you eye-to-eye beside the usual text information, give me a special thrill. They are halfway to a personal introduction whether or not you want one. They really put themselves out there just short of a handshake, and you could be Jack the Ripper. Close, but no cigar, are the business cards showing corrections by hand and handwritten web-address additions, although each is unique in a handmade way. There are many things left to collect that have no competing collectors . . . yet.

A trip to a car wash can be an astounding revelation regarding the variety of automobile air fresheners on the market. The car-wash establishment in Brooklyn that I frequent early on Sunday mornings displays, by visual count of hanger pegs, multiples of 620 varieties of card air fresheners. This number does not include air-freshener liquids, solids, or beads; only cards meant to dangle from the driver's rear-view mirror. My own preference is the actual smell of my car interior to Strawberry-Kiwi or Vanilla Blossom, Pinot Sauvage, Sierra Winds, or Blueberry.

29
Portrait business cards, 2005. 2–2¾" high

30

31

32

33

34

35

30
Automobile air freshener, 2004. Hula Hula scent die-cut printed plastic, 7½" high

31
Automobile air fresheners, 2004. Leather and Eternity scents in printed die-cut card stock, 3½ and 4" high

32
Automobile air freshener, 2004. Orange Pinecone in *Peach Wild Forest Cone* packaging, 7½" high

33
Automobile air freshener, 2004. "Great" scent hunk in *Baywatch* packaging, 7½" high

34
Automobile air freshener, 2004. Native American chief's head in *Money House Gold* rendition of *Opium* packaging, 7½" high

35
Automobile air freshener, 2004. Airborne angel and child *Angel's Blessing* packaging, 7½" high

36
Automobile air freshener,
2004. Passion fruit scent
La Virgen de Guadalupe
in *I Love Jesus* packaging,
7½" high

37
Group of automobile
air fresheners in various
scents including a
mango-scented rainbow
in printed die-cut card
stock, 2004. 2¼–4" high

I must be in the minority as, in this emporium alone, three hundred square feet of real estate are devoted to carded air fresheners. There are other car accessories such as baseball door-latch cap replacements, golf-ball stick-shift replacement knobs, cassette-sized Kleenex boxes, maps, and window decals, but they are isolated in a relatively small display area. The insistent fragrances of Rose, Super Cherry, Extra Strength Coconut, Sunny Citrus, Ice Cream Cone and Fresh Fruit can be imagined. But, what do Rainbow, Bird of Paradise, Money House Blessing, Flying Carpet, Ultra Norsk, Camouflage, Target, Cloudy Skies, Cuba, Smiley Face, Baywatch, Proud to be an American, or I Love Jesus Spice Especial smell like? What do Angel's Blessing or Virgin of Guadalupe air freshener convey besides the unfathomable? Considering the raucous cacophony of fragrances that cannot be contained by the individual packaging, I believe that I'll settle for a mental collection and leave the actual collecting to someone else. The point is that one encounters potential collections everyday during life's ordinary course that are there for the taking. Hallelujahs and hosannas to other collectors. They will preserve where I won't tread.

36

37

Those of us who regularly dine with wine (not the screw-top variety) will have witnessed a recent revolution in the cork world. Cork that is used for the core of baseballs as well as for wine-bottle stoppers is the bark sheathing or *periderm* of *Quercus suber*, the cork oak tree, a native of Mediterranean countries and cultivated particularly in Spain, Portugal, India, and parts of the United States. It takes eight to twelve years for bark to regenerate after the first bark stripping when the tree is twenty years old. Successive bark restrippings clearly make cork a renewable resource, but the length of time required for regrowth is at odds with present-day wine consumption. Waiting for corks to develop is like watching sedimentary layers settle. Consequently, composite corks made of compressed cork fragments, and then plastic corks have recently appeared as wine-bottle stoppers to which traditional corkscrews may be applied. At first, new corks masqueraded as *Quercus suber*, but they have recently come out of the closet. Charlotte G. has an excellent selection illustrating cork evolution. Particularly liberated are the corks of New World wine cultures that are imprinted with fetching or quizzical text messages and images that parody earlier European wine corks.

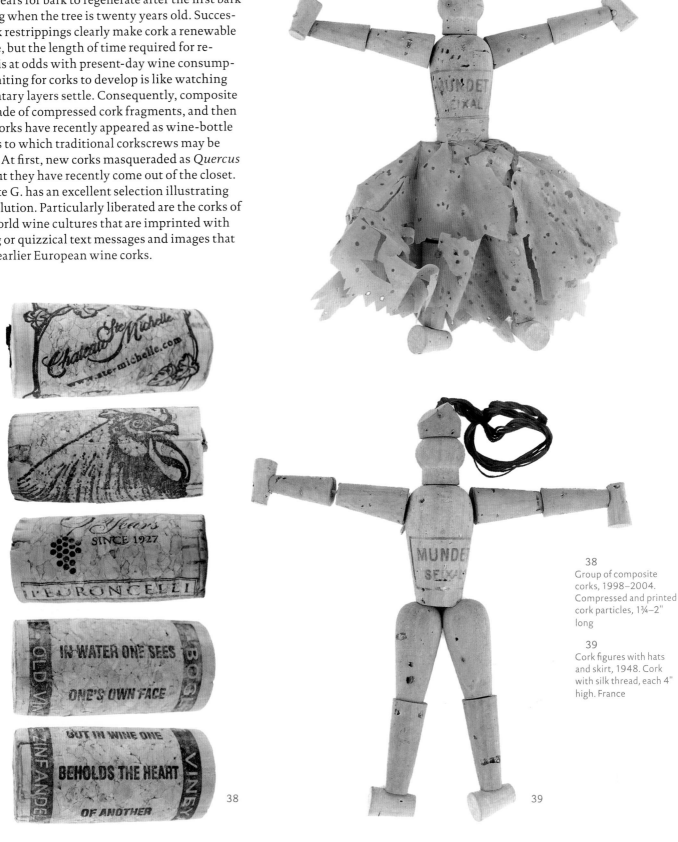

38

39

38
Group of composite corks, 1998–2004. Compressed and printed cork particles, 1¾–2" long

39
Cork figures with hats and skirt, 1948. Cork with silk thread, each 4" high. France

40
Group of wine bottle
corks, 1982–2002.
Printed whole cork, 2"
high

41
Group of wine bottle
corks, 2002–5. Printed
plastic, 1½–2" high

40

41

WHERE DOES IT ALL END UP?

In the mid-1970s, a group of John Augustus Roebling's drawings for the construction of the Brooklyn Bridge were discovered in one of the locked, vaulted chambers beneath the bridge. They became the property of the Municipal Archives, which was housed at the time in a large, open loft, above a Burger King on Park Row (formerly Newspaper Row) between Beekman and Ann Streets around the corner from Mendoza's bookstore, which specialized in rare history books. The space was filled with high steel shelving that democratically, if not archivally, supported the objects that tangibly testified to all of New York City's history in quasi-alphabetical order. No object was given more honorable treatment than any other. Everything from Peter Stuyvesant's peg leg to John A. Roebling's drawings had its warehoused place on an industrial steel shelf. If the Mayflower had landed in New York City, you could have found the equivalent of Plymouth Rock somewhere near *P*. When Roebling's drawings turned up, everything post *R* was shoved toward *Z* to make room for the scrolls. The Municipal Archives was the quintessential collection of collections.

Ivan, who has profound knowledge of historical architecture and is one of very few qualified appraisers of architectural fragments and drawings, was selected to appraise these drawings for the City for insurance purposes. I went along as his record keeper and as the necessary someone to hold one end of each twenty-five-foot scroll while he held the other. We were shown into the Municipal Archives premises at 9:00 A.M. on a Monday morning and were told that someone would return at noon to check on our progress or lock up if we were finished. By 9:02 we realized that we were the only people in the virtual football field of treasures. How could they know we wouldn't take anything? Talk about letting the fox into the hen house. We finished measuring and evaluating the drawings by 11:00 and meandered between mayoral trophies and trial records in epiphanies and revelations of cosmic proportions. The two high points for me were a folio of Audubon's original watercolors and Abe Reles's suitcase and clothing from his protected-witness stay before his "fall" from the Half Moon Hotel window in Coney Island, which sat under *K*, perhaps for Kid Twist, his Murder Inc., moniker. Shortly after noon, a laconic city employee with a key asked if we were finished and subsequently battened the hatches.

This public collection, with its succession of amassers, is the most memorable collection of collections that I have touched and that has touched me. It was a holy place. It was a disarrayed Smithsonian Institution, a *grande dame* taken unawares by unexpected visitors. What conjugated the multifarious contents of the steel shelves was the connection of each object to the history of New York City.

Now the Municipal Archives lives at 31 Chambers Street in an orderly and secure setting that may be more accurately described as museum or library-like. Museums are collections of collections overseen by successive collection-keepers called curators. Like private collections, museums are about defining areas of concentration; embracing, organizing, and refining; strategic reconnaissance; and giving safe haven. The main difference is that there isn't one impassioned collector with a sense of personal domain at the helm. Many museums began as private collections that entered the public realm out of collector pride and obsession (Pitt Rivers Museum, Mercer Museum); generosity, beneficence and charity (Cooper Hewitt Museum, Morgan Library); chance circumstance (Smithsonian Institution); or bequest (Frick Collection, Ashmolean Museum). Some museums originated as complicated permutations of the above.

chapter 22

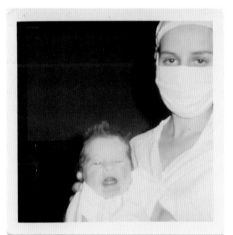

Just in Time

IN AUGUST 2002, I went to a Wal-Mart for the first time to buy birdseed to refill my outdoor bird feeders. When I questioned the greeter about its whereabouts in the field-sized superstore, she pointed southeast and advised looking for Pet Supplies. My husband said, "Just follow the birds." I looked up. Flocks of birds live in this Wal-Mart, among the steel superstructure struts near the high ceiling. We spent a few minutes observing different bird species in flight, spotted a few nests, and strained to listen for chirps. The pet-supply aisles were in a low traffic area of the store and were a virtual stage for the observation of ornithological feeding, frenzied pecking at sacks of species-appropriate seed. I didn't see any jays, orioles, cardinals, or hummingbirds (liquid food), but I did see grosbeaks, finches, and sparrows who paused in their repast when I got very close. Needless to say it took a minute for me to identify an unperforated (non-leaking) sack of seed.

1

I feel enlivened and gratified to have unexpectedly witnessed the ongoing adaptability of nature in the face of relentless human incursion and perhaps the origins of *Fringillidae Walmarticus* or *Fincho superstorius*. Corporate headquarters is probably unaware of the steady drain on their birdseed stores or bird droppings on their upper shelves. I searched the Internet for *birds* and *Walmart* to see if anyone had noted the phenomenon. I was rewarded with pages of Wal-Mart entries on bird-related products for sale, including seventeen different bird calendars for 2004, books, targets, bird-watching guides, statuettes, candleholders, birdbaths, clocks, garden décor, cages, CDs, DVDs, videotapes, audiotapes of bird calls, picture frames, toys, greeting cards, and birdseed. No reference to live birds in residence. Perhaps the bird pair who built the strip of audiotape into their woodland nest moved into Wal-Mart as the logical next step toward a more civilized life. I wished that I had a camera in hand, although I knew that there was no way to photographically capture the unexpected bird presence in situ. Perhaps a Disney animated musical re-creation, but not a still, photographic record.

A photograph isolates and decontextualizes a moment and freezes it as a memory cue. The subject is mnemonic and triggers unique responses to a recorded incident among witnesses who have a relationship to the moment. Others who view the photo are unencumbered by the event that it portrays and may have singular responses based solely on the prompt of the image. Thereby it becomes a photographic artifact. Photographers are collectors of moments frozen in time and place. Collectors of photographs are not necessarily photographers. Photographs that others have taken may be husbanded around a subject matter or assembled around an attitude.

Jay K., a painter by profession, collects 3½-by-3½-inch color snapshots taken from the 1950s through the early 1970s. These standard format, mostly Kodacolor photographs display a uniform compositional blandness and a quality of odd color saturation. Regardless of subject, each photo is amateur, mysteriously undramatic, and astoundingly dull. Jay is clear about his fascination with decoding the who, why, and wherefore (he knows the when and how) of the snapshot and its consistently innocent lack of compositional vitality. His current interest is in gathering every variable of the genre. They blandly indicate what not to do when taking a picture. There is no reason for them to surface now, even at low-end flea markets. Why would a dealer think anyone would want them? His collection is the finest example of the articulation of an atmosphere spanning two decades.

1
Kodacolor prints, 1965–72. Each 3½" high

2
Kodacolor prints, 1965–69. Each 3½" high

Leonard D., also a painter by profession, found in a secondhand shop a carton of tintypes, posed studio photographs and Peter Pan prints taken between 1885 and 1950, amassed over the lifetime of one woman. He was captivated by the voyeuristic intimacy of her parents' wedding photograph, the infant, the aged, doting mother, devoted father, the surrounding middle-class hopefulness of her childhood, the energy of her school years, her attendant parents, and the home in which she spent her life. The Keuka College flapper, her early adulthood, the Grand Tour (Eiffel Tower behind), childless middle years, aging parents, her friends, the weathering of the family residence and changes in window treatments, her aging and death at forty-three—all were confirmed by the photograph. The permafrost of photography attests to her shy, frolicsome, and withdrawn moods. The woman is long gone, and these photographs were locked outside a family circle in which they might have had significance. Leonard laid out the images in chronological order, deduced that Herkimer, New York, was the geographic location of the photographs, and drove there to find the house. He searched likely residential neighborhoods, and eureka! he found it. Earlier he had fantasized about knocking on the door of the house and returning the photos to their place of origin. Confronting the residence, he thought that the people who lived there

were likely the people who sold the house contents. He drove to Herkimer cemetery, found the headstones of father, mother, and daughter, paid respects, and drove home. He put closure on the lamination of her life to his by burning the collection. "She had an unremarkable life except that I noticed her," he dispassionately declared. Sometimes extreme actions must be taken so as not to have one's life subsumed by stuff. Limits imposed by the collector separate the gatherer from the Collyer brothers.

I have found summary versions of the life of a person, now deceased, in a box or folder at flea markets. Each is a complete story told from the point of view of hindsight, usually comprised of photographs, membership cards spanning a lifetime, report cards, a newspaper clipping or two, military records, permits, a Social Security card, driver's license, and sometimes a plane-ticket stub or a grade-school report of which someone was proud. If these lives are in a small box, I take them home so that they are no longer souls wandering in limbo. Each box is a collection with only one subject matter. As a group of collections, they have been assembled around an attitude. Lives in boxes are proof that you can't take it with you. Collecting is an individual source of peace in the midst of the dramatic jeopardies of life.

"HERE TODAY and gone tomorrow" describes another photographic collecting posture—photographs of subjects in flux. Handmade misspelled signs (corrections impending) and rural mailboxes that meet federal standards but are jerry-rigged and face imminent change exemplify temporary situations that may be read into the record of history by photographic means if a collector is so inclined. This would be an example of photographs collected around specific subject matter rather than an attitude. The occasional off-register or blurred photographic postcard represents a subject matter that one spies in racked multiples; it is a printing-alignment error that got away. Ray J., a collagist, found the prismatic effect of these images interesting and collected many of them.

3
Misspelled contractor sign photograph, 1998. 3" high. Summit, New York

4

5

4
Cards, photographs, and papers that outline the life of Cresson Pugh, 1919–34

5
Cards, photographs, and papers that outline the life of Isadore M. Mackler, 1918–58

6
Cards, photographs, and papers that outline the life of Burton E. Young, 1902–62

6

7

Photographs of groups of people validating or commemorating an event are examples of a familiar use of photography, from our earliest class photos to the professional meetings that certify adulthood to family unions and reunions that may have been recorded. Industry changes resulting from new technologies, such as the advent of digital photography, make for sweeping changes. When 45 rpm records were offered as an alternative to 78 rpm records, I opted for the 78s when there was a choice. I didn't believe that such a sweeping change could be effected successfully. When Elvis Presley and Harry Belafonte recordings came out on 33 rpms, I took a chance since 33s offered multiple songs per record, but I was doubtful of the success of that changeover. I was reserved about expressing audiocassette skepticism and quickly warmed to CD technology. The United States has a short history filled with a succession of inventive technologies, which causes an accordion-like illusion, artifactually elongating our two hundred odd years and lending a flavor of instant nostalgia to images rendered by means of preceding technologies. Try to find a sound system that will play 78 rpm records now.

The change cups offered by casinos to help slot players lug their coinage around are specimens of the blank canvas for changing designs. The shape and size of the cups aren't mutable. From casino to casino they nest as if extruded from the same disks, but the range and variety of imprinted casino logos define a timeline to the cognoscenti. James D. has collected them for twenty-five years.

7
Misspelled sign on building, 2004. 37" high. Nashville, Tennessee

8
Casino change cups, 1985–2004. Each 6" high

9
Misspelled sign in restaurant lavatory, 2004. 7" high. Nashville, Tennessee

10
Rural mailboxes meeting federal guidelines, 1967–2005

8

9

10

Group photographs are replete with the trimmings of material culture, as contained within a specific and limited circumstance. The Oneonta Star Fife and Drum Corps 1892 Thanksgiving Day performance at the Armory has been memorialized in black and white. Eight swim poseurs at Atlantic City in 1900 convey much more than swimsuit styles of the year: background stores, the Bath House, people passing, hairstyles, positions, and expressions complete the information halo. As with sheet music covers, the totality of the image is far greater than the sum of its parts. Group photographs are about people preserved in their contemporaneous material contexts, inevitably of the past. These pictures define the extreme borders of the palpable past in the present. It is likely group photographs will be regarded with greater objectivity and other insights in many future presents. The subject sitters were not thinking of this when the photographs were snapped. Smile, you're on candid camera for eternity.

11

12

11
Group photograph of nine dancers in Russian costumes, 1925. Black-and-white print on paper, 8" high. NYSHA #0005.2002(11)

12
Group photograph of Atlantic City beach posers, house and shops in background, 1900. Silver gelatin print on paper, 6" high. NYSHA #N0005.2002(0)

13
Group photograph of *Happy Coon Minstrel Band* members holding instruments, with Brown & Burpee storefront in background, c. 1880. Sepia tone print on paper, 9 high. NYSHA #N0005.2002(2)

14
Group photograph of band members holding instruments, American flags in background, c. 1915. Silver gelatin print on paper, 10" high. NYSHA #N005.2002(1)

13

14

15

16

17

15
Group photograph of
Scottish fraternal order,
1906. Sepia tone print
on paper, 7¼" high

16
Group photograph
of *Oneonta Star* Fife
and Drum Corps on
Thanksgiving Day, signed
by each member, 1892.
Black-and-white print on
paper, 7¾" high. NYSHA
#N0023.2001(0)

17
Group photograph of
Cub Scout troop, 1938.
Sepia tone print on
paper, 6" high

18
Nix-Mao champion Ping-Pong set, 1972. Wood and printed rubber, 10½ and 2" high. Made in Hong Kong

19
Gorbachev birthmark cockamamie (front and back), 1989. *Lick 'n' Stick Tattoo* printed paper, 5" high. Made in USA

20
Growing Up Skipper figure (box back), 1974. Barbie's younger sister grows from a girl to a teenager in seconds by turning her left arm counterclockwise: *See her grow tall and curvy. Turn her arm clockwise and she's young and cute again.* 10" high. Mattel, Inc.

SOME COLLECTORS nimbly recognize the aura of an object that is quintessentially representative of and bound to a place and time at the moment that it is offered to the public. There are events, situations, temporary circumstances, fads, fluid styles, accidents, and technological changes that occur as a flash in the pan. If one is sufficiently alert to nab their artifactual representations, a collector may possess an object that unpredictably and irrefutably defines an era.

During the early 1970s, President Nixon reached out to Mao Tse-tung to open diplomatic relations with the People's Republic of China. This was the second most significant event of his presidency and was commemorated by a series of Ping-Pong matches between American and Chinese players. Second only to Watergate as defining Nixon's presidency,

the peculiar qualities of this period live on in Nixon and Mao Ping-Pong paddle sets with a caricature of Nixon's face on a blue field and Mao's on a red (what else?) background. The images of two world leaders intended for use in aggressively and percussively slamming little white balls in a table-tennis game made this an era-defining artifact for me in the same elevated collectible class as the *JFK Coloring Book*, the Growing Up Skipper doll (rotate her arm clockwise and she becomes taller and sprouts breasts), and Johnstown Flood dishes. The Spiro Agnew watch, Gorbachev Birthmark cockamamies, Saddam Hussein dart boards, and Twin Tower salt-and-pepper shakers are failed runners-up, topical possibilities that didn't pan out.

Manufactured tokens of situations or events can lock that moment into place, preserving the flavor of a time, or can be shabby souvenirs that corrupt the view. Some events cannot be captured at all. The quintessential accident of a timely novelty that materializes an event is poetry beside which the wannabes are drivel. Aesthetic impact isn't the only determining factor. There's a mysterious calibration that skirts some ephemeral objects into arenas of the sleazy and others glide toward cultural perpetuity.

18

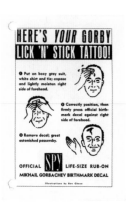

19

20

SITUATIONS AND places that are memorialized by products are tokens of experience, souvenirs. What do we call products that ironically come to represent a situation that occurs later? *Mayor's Own Marinara Sauce* was for sale in grocery stores throughout Rhode Island, to benefit Providence schoolchildren through the Vincent A. (Buddy) Cianci, Jr., Scholarship Fund. This mayor's smiling, mentoring face beams forth from the four-color label with self-confidence in his goodness and leadership. Just heat and eat, and your family can share the generations-old recipe that made the Ciancis great. In not his first brush with the law, on June 27, 2002, Cianci was found guilty of conspiracy and racketeering, having solicited bribes for municipal contracts, political favors, tax breaks, and city employment. The FBI's Operation Plunder Dome revealed a history of payoffs, shakedowns, extortion, and kickbacks during Cianci's mayoral terms, which ran consecutively from 1974 to 1998. In 1983, he had assaulted Raymond DeLeo, a contractor dating his ex-wife, Sheila. Evidence presented by the prosecution revealed that Cianci threatened to have him shot, threw liquor on him, burned him with a cigarette, whacked him with a fireplace log, threw an ashtray at him, and threatened to sue him unless he paid the mayor five hundred thousand dollars. In court, Mayor Cianci pleaded no contest, received a probationary sentence, and returned to office after winning a Rhode Island Supreme Court ruling.

The Mayor's Own Marinara Sauce is the event horizon of improvidence and of chutzpah, and as soon as I heard of it, I asked my friend Ann A., a travel agent and resident of Rhode Island, for a trophy jar of the stuff. She had one on her kitchen shelf that she kindly sent to me with a note saying that they were taken off the market as soon as he was convicted. Does the Son of Sam law cover profiting from spaghetti sauce, or were the citizens of Providence finally embarrassed by their six-term mayor? Will the innocent sauce return to the grocery stores of Providence with a new label? *Pro bono publico*, for the public good, is a collection of by-products of indiscretion. The jar of marinara sauce stands beside Al Capone cigars. This is a collection in the act of becoming; I feel confident that political hubris and addiction to power is uncontainable. Are cigars and marinara sauce intellectual properties? I'm hoping to see a James Traficant (Dem. representative, Ohio) hair management system; a Marion S. Barry Jr., (Dem. mayor, Washington, D.C.) twelve-step recovery program DVD with a voice-over of his juicy malapropisms, Dapper Don & Son designer shirts and a Philip Giordano (Rep. mayor, Waterbury, Connecticut) line of mother-and-daughter action figures.

21

22

23

21
Mayor Vincent A. "Buddy" Cianci's Own Marinara Sauce, benefiting Providence schoolchildren, 2002. 7" high. Providence, Rhode Island

22
Al Capone mug shot, c. 1927. 3¼" high

23
Display of Al Capone cognac-dipped cigars, 2005. 9" high

LOST
AFRICAN GREY
PARROT
(name Rexy)

- Grey body and head, yellow iris (eyes) with bright red tail feathers
- Lost August 25, 2004 9 am around Watts and Thompson Street.
- Rexy has a ankle band and he is our children's loving bird.
- If found please call Sabie or John at 646-555-6615 or 6616 (cell #'s)

Missing
Big Black
Quarter
Horse
"Shadow"
Call
Cathy Feller
888-8408

Missing Since Thursday-Friday June 16, 2005 Answers to the name "Dax" Last seen wearing a silver choke collar, In the Riverview/New Hamburg area. If you have any information PLEASE call 497-9401 ASAP!

24
Lost Pet posters with and without identifying photographs, 2000–2005. Ink and photocopy on paper, 4–11" high

25
Group of FBI Wanted posters, 1977–2001. Printed paper, 13–17" high

24

LOST PET POSTERS are ephemeral examples of temporary circumstances or accidents that are laden with content and define an exigent moment in someone's life (and probably the animal's as well). The photograph of the pet, emotional tone of the description, circumstances of the disappearance, color of the photocopy paper, location and means of attachment, instructions on how to contact the owner, and the amount and specific qualifications for reward payment make for a collection of materialized, polyvalent moments. In contrast, Missing Persons notices are too laden with content to consider collecting; call me finicky.

ON THE OTHER hand, FBI Most Wanted posters that hang in U.S. post offices make me an eager voyeur. They present dated, clearly formatted information that is more easily grasped and complete than Lost Pet poster layouts, and drama equal to Missing Person notices, but without the tragedy because these are the perpetrators, not the victims. Exposing the details of their lives to the scrutiny of John Q. Public is informative and somehow just. Photographs, sometimes successive, if the person has eluded capture for many years, with accompanying

text are the stuff of fiction: fodder for the imagination. Imagine the shock if recognition was yours. Would you be frozen in your spot thinking of Arnold Schuster, shot for fingering Willie Sutton, or are you a risk-taking heroic type? Each FBI Wanted poster is the ready-made outline for a book. Wanted posters of Patty Hearst and Osama bin Laden are prizes for those who had the foresight and acted within the window of opportunity. It's a free collection if you're around when your postmaster replaces the previous batch with the latest.

ON THE SUBJECT of identifiying the Most Wanted from printed media, shortly after the United States invaded Iraq, in April 2003, a set of playing cards showing the Most Wanted Iraqis was developed by the Defense Intelligence Agency for our troops. U.S. armed forces have a history of card playing during down time. The ubiquity of Saddamesque mustaches and multisyllabic Arabic tribal and family names made potential identification difficult. Creating a sense of familiarity by means of these playing cards seemed to be an effective way of significantly raising the odds of identification should contact occur.

I was in rapture upon introduction to the deck by

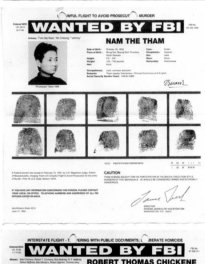

25

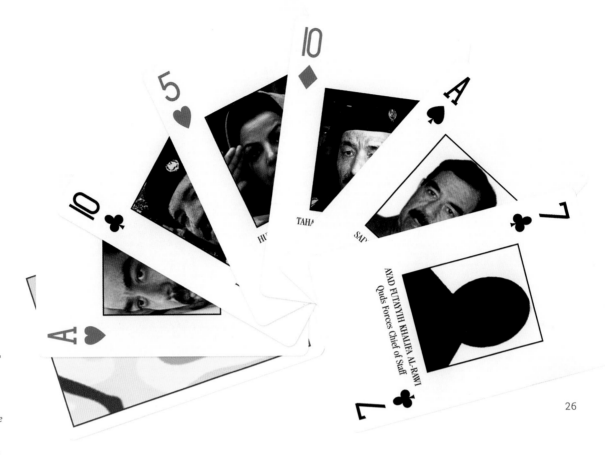

26

the 11:00 P.M. nightly news, and I mused on getting my hands on a marker deck for these extreme times. The official United States list of most wanted Iraqis numbered fifty-five participants in the deposed regime; each deck of playing cards has fifty-two cards and two Jokers, one listing tribal titles and name sequences, the other listing Iraqi military ranks. How did our side decide which three Iraqis were not really so wanted? Who made the decision?

The cards were printed by none other than the U.S. Playing Card Company, which has a history of printing cards for our armed forces. During World War II they printed spotter cards for the Civil Defense home front and troops abroad, showing the silhouettes of enemy planes, ships, and tanks. The company also printed gift decks for prisoners of war held in German camps. When moistened, these cards delaminated, disclosing segmented escape-route maps. During the Vietnam War, decks of aces of spades were supplied to our troops to wear in their helmets, as the death card was a fear-inspiring symbol for the North Vietnamese and the Viet Cong. The Pentagon did not copyright the Iraqi Most Wanted cards and anyone may produce them, which has apparently been the case. Many more than the two hundred decks sent to the combat zone have been for sale on the Internet since May 2003. The imprimatur of authenticity is the U.S. Playing Card Company Joker logo.

This deck belongs in a future museum of touchstones of self-righteousness. It is an extreme and valuable bit of material culture and has spawned copies and response decks. The first was the activist Yes Men's fifty-five-card deck of the Most Unwanted American Politicians and CEOs involved in the war on Iraq. They were also known as Regime-Change Playing Cards and sold through Greenpeace. Corporate America's Most Wanted, Republican Chickenhawks (Republicans for the war as long as they don't have to serve), Uggabugga's GOP Cards, W Deck (George W. Bush in variety drag), War Profiteers, and Iraqi Most Wanted Playing Cards of Looted Museum Art, U.S. Military Heroes, and the Capitol Shopping Mall's American Patriotic Playing Cards are some of the card decks that I have seen. They are fluidly changing mementos of a fad, either political parodies of the Defense Intelligence Agency's deck, straightforward acclamations of patriotism or activist obsessions, with the exception of the Iraqi Most Wanted Playing Cards of Looted Museum Art deck. It takes no political stance and might actually make the antiquities illustrated on each card too hot to be sold on the international antiquities market. The other spin-off decks smack of another moment in tunnel vision and, I venture, will have the same longevity as a good issue of *Mad* magazine.

The articulate clarity of outline of a meaningful object benefits from hindsight. It has always

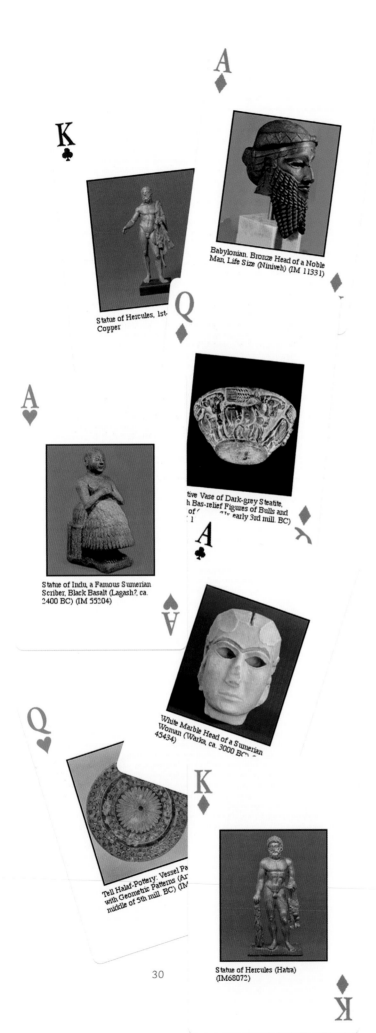

Statue of Hercules, 1st.
Copper

Babylonian. Bronze Head of a Noble
Man, Life Size (Niniveh) (IM 11331)

tive Vase of Dark-grey Steatite,
h Bas-relief Figures of Bulls and
of ʼ ʼ early 3rd mill. BC)

Statue of Indu, a Famous Sumerian
Scriber, Black Basalt (Lagash?, ca.
2400 BC) (IM 55204)

White Marble Head of a Sumerian
Woman (Warka, ca. 3000 BC) 45434)

Tell Halaf-Pottery: Vessel Pa
with Geometric Patterns (Ar
middle of 5th mill. BC) (IM

Statue of Hercules (Hatra)
(IM68072)

been difficult to identify and evaluate the almighty significance of things in one's own lifetime. Seers, messiahs, and great visionaries do just that, and they are the rarest of rare birds. It's sufficiently challenging for most of us to steer a safe course, accumulating the things that we prefer to have around us, from childhood to old age.

SOME OF US who scan the past—looking at a much diminished range of objects than existed when they were new—try to prevent the irreversible elimination of what we feel are significant and resounding things. Along the way we are intoxicated by the improbable, unnerved by the prodigious richness of the world, and inebriated by the potency of the spectrum. This is not a bad fate. When we find a treasure, it's just in the nick of time because artifacts made in the past have the insuperable handicap of not improving in condition or becoming more plentiful over time.

A good flea market or antique show is not an allegory. It's a testament to durability. It is the unconditional venue of seeking and possessing, acceptance and rejection, scanning and cleaving, virtue and imperfection, compromised expectations and fulfilled invitations. It's the vortex of the whirlpool, theater, a parade, and a carnival. It is centuries conflated into one mown field or arena. It is an exquisite aria and it has no equivalent in richness or riches.

Each object has a story to tell, somewhat fleshing out a time. In the marketplace, each object is displaced, dissonant, in limbo, and may be weathered, touching, ravishing, undervalued, ancestral, poised, majestic, humble, radiant, bland, refined, abject, magnificent, graceful, humble, obscure, radiant, simple, and/or puzzling. Each is a material incident in which time and place coalesce in a pungent way.

Everyone at the marketplace shares a connection, is a partner in commensalism; everyone either benefits or is unaffected. Enthusiasts of unloved things—items without a significant or established collectorship—share the potent belief that most of the world is blind to their singular perception. It doesn't matter. They may be correct and, in the end, their collections may redeem them from their socially flawed posture. We live and yearn.

> For inside him there are spirits, or at least little genii, which have seen to it that for a collector — and I mean a real collector, a collector as he ought to be—ownership is the most intimate relationship that one can have to objects. Not that they come alive in him; it is he who lives in them. So I have erected one of his dwellings... and now he is going to disappear inside, as is only fitting.
>
> Walter Benjamin, *Illuminations* (New York: Schocken Books, 1985), 67.

There is no need for me to keep a skull on my desk,
to stand with one foot up on the ruins of Rome,
or wear a locket with the sliver of a saint's bone.

It is enough to realize that every common object
in this sunny little room will outlive me—
the carpet, radio, bookstand and rocker.

Not one of these things will attend my burial,
not even this dented goosenecked lamp
with its steady benediction of light,

though I could put worse things in my mind
than the image of it waddling across the cemetery
like an old servant, dragging the tail of its cord
the small circle of mourners parting to make room.

      Billy Collins, "Questions About Angels" from
Memento Mori (Pittsburgh: University of Pittsburgh
Press, 1999), 50.

30
Group of *Iraqi Most
Wanted* playing cards
(looted museum art
from the Iraqi National
Museum), 2003. 3½"
high. Jim Baldwin and
Denis Belton, USA

31
Youth surfing on Bleriot
monoplane (back) by
Carlien, 1909. Bronze,
25¾" high. France

31

THANKS TO:

IVAN C. KARP, my platform and forum, whose rapt support keeps me aloft and whose sense of humor keeps me enchanted; AMIE ODESSA KARP, last child, alert always to the wondrous ironies of life, born with a wry side-wise view that keeps me current; JESSE NEVADA KARP, first child, inspired writer who feels the electric presence that significant objects possess; ZOE ANNABELLE KARP, bright baby in whom resides infinite possibility and perhaps a third sequential collecting generation; WILLIAM GELFMAN, my generous, funny brother who wrestled with me but fought the battles of childhood at my side; RUTH NEWMAN, who (with inestimable and patient support) hand-carried me over the threshold of the text age into the immaterial realm of the computer era; CARL WILLIAMSON, prodigious and gifted young man who coaxed, conjured, and digitally captured the essential character of beloved objects; JEREMY FRANKLIN BROOKE who, with forbearance, fastidiousness, and finesse, fine-tuned regiments of paper treasure into clarion self-representation; MAREN BERTHELSEN, gracious, caring, helpful, and persevering locator of quoted poets for permissions and for guiding me in how to ask for them; DOROTHY TWINING GLOBUS, soul mate, sounding board, and junking buddy nonpareil; JOHN BAEDER, for forty years of snapshots of sign follies tendering inadvertent puns and misspellings and of license plate absurdities; EVE ELIOT, for thrift shop companionship and wisdom dispensed while rooting around dodgy places; CANDY ADRIANCE, life-saving manager and indefatigable shopper in third world marketplaces; ELISABETH SEARLES, for years of fearless driving, generous insights, and good humor while slogging through hot, wet, and muddy outdoor antique shows; BOB GINDER, whose fine eye inevitably alights upon the greatness in small and humble things; HOWARD BERK, wise, patient, enduring, and essential friend; MARCIA SCOTT STILLMAN, model of kindness residing in the details; CARA WOOD, friend for all seasons, and chief cheerleader for this book; ANDREW JEREMY SCHULMAN, who said, "You have to write a cookbook," and to KEN GOLDGLIT, who said, "It's time to write your book"; HARRY ABRAMS, who bought the largest sculpture out of my first exhibition and whose legacy closed a circle with the publication of my first book; MICHAEL JACOBS and ERIC HIMMEL at Harry N. Abrams, Inc., who wanted to make this book an *extraordinary object*, and especially to DEBORAH AARONSON, who saw what I saw and made it happen, but resides in the book, independent of me, in the serial comma; WILL LIPPINCOTT, for championing IFC and for his witty support and articulate guidance through a new world, and to MICHAEL BLAINE and SALLY WOFFORD-GIRARD, whose mutual generosity was the roadmap to Will; JOHN KOEGEL, for guidance in the murky land of permissions, and for making clear the distinction between editorial and commercial use in copyright; KATHY STOCKING, for efficient and timely cooperation in sending NYSHA's documentation and photographs of works that we had previously donated; BILL MEIER, insulator magician and internet friend who kindly revealed the majesty of insulators in tif.land; KATHRYN & CARLO LAMAGNA, collectors of the fine, the esoteric, and the celebratory; RICHARD FRIEDBERG, lawn sprinkler fount of wisdom, who also makes a great gin and tonic; JAMES DELGROSSO, world-class craps player and avid student of material casino culture; JACQUELINE MARX ATKINS, textile researcher into uncharted territories; ALICE ZIMMERMAN, LENNY SCHNEIR, PAUL & KAREN RENNIE, BARBARA MILLSTEIN, LILY MAISON, ROBERT LERCH, ALAN HERMAN, JAY KELLY, JOE NEWMAN, and the others who shared their collections, and to WARNER LORD and DON MALCARNE, who offered their arcane knowledge about a special crutch; JULIO, RONNIE, DAN & BERT NORMAN, for the timely arrival of Texas *monitos* and Mexican King's Cakes and to JUDITH BRUNSON for Louisiana *fèves*; HEIDI TRACHTENBERG, whose expert palate and unflagging good nature sweetened my time-outs with dark chocolate and fine pastry; ROBERT ROHM, compassionate fellow traveler and hovering caretaker in a dire time; NOREEN LEWANDOWSKI AND TOBY ZUCKER SHORE lifetime friends; ANN MARCUS, W. GABRIEL CARRAS, and those NYU colleagues who, over thirty-nine years, have encouraged and supported out-of-the-box thinking in the context of a great university; JORGE LUIS BORGES, BILLY COLLINS, EMILY DICKINSON, DONALD HALL, PHILIP LEVINE, PAUL MULDOON, PETER STILLMAN, and WALLACE STEVENS, dear poet companions who have informed, empowered, and kept me company; and to my favorite antique dealers who share the vision and know it: RICHARD AXTELL, KATHY BROWN, ANDRE BURGOS, DAVID COHN, POLLY DUFRESNE, ELAINE FRIEDMAN, PATRICIA FUNT, JOEL GOODMAN, JOLIE KELTER, MICHAEL MALCÉ, JOEL MATHIESSEN, KEN SCHULZ, JANET WEST, and WILLIAM WOODY.

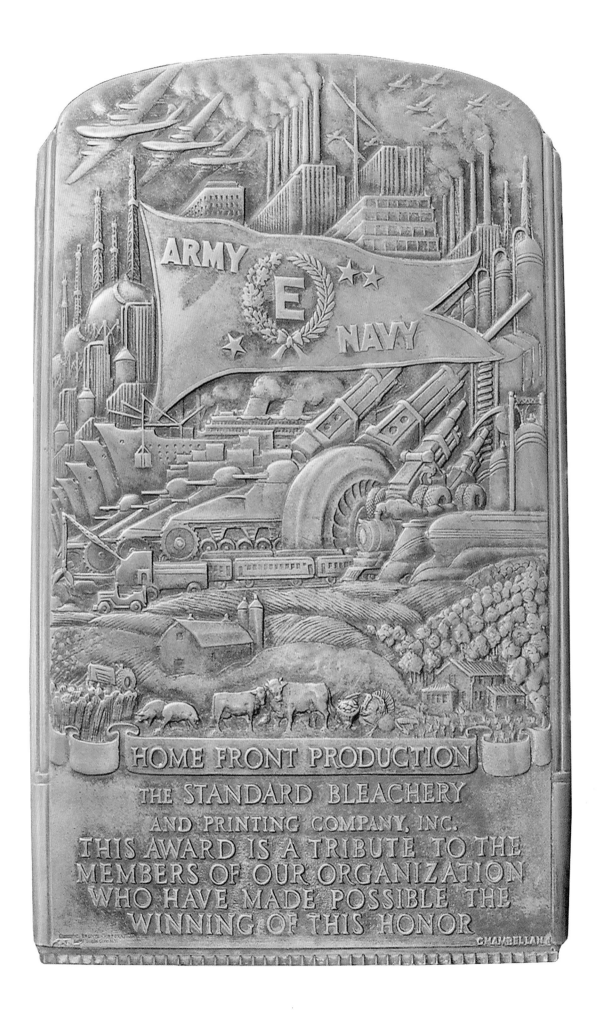

Commemorative World War II *Home Front Production* plaque, stamped Chambellan, 1943. Bronze, 15" high. General Bronze Corporation, Long Island City, New York

CREDITS

Numbers in parentheses refer to caption numbers.

Editor: Deborah Aaronson
Designer: Helene Silverman
Production Manager: Maria Pia Gramaglia

Library of Congress Cataloging-in-Publication Data

Karp, Marilynn Gelfman.
In flagrante collecto : caught in the act of collecting / Marilynn Gelfman Karp.
p. cm.
ISBN 0-8109-5540-7
1. Collectors and collecting. 2. Collectors and collecting–Social aspects. I. Title: Caught in the act of collecting. II. Title.

AM231.K37 2006
790.1'32–dc22

2005029625

Published in 2006 by Abrams, an imprint of Harry N. Abrams, Inc.

Printed and bound in China
10 9 8 7 6 5 4 3 2 1

HNA
harry n. abrams, inc.
a subsidiary of La Martinière Groupe

115 West 18th Street
New York, NY 10011
www.hnabooks.com

CASE: *Sanitized For Your Protection* toilet-seat band, 1999. Printed paper, 2" high

ENDPAPERS: Group of six-inch wooden rulers with imprinted advertising on front and back, 1900-34. Wood with embedded metal strip, 6" long